# The BODY

# The BODY

## CHARLES COLSON
### WITH ELLEN SANTILLI VAUGHN

WORD PUBLISHING
Dallas·London·Vancouver·Melbourne

THE BODY: BEING LIGHT IN THE DARKNESS

Unless otherwise indicated, Scripture references are from The New American Standard Bible (NASB), © The Lockman Foundation 1960, 1962, 1963, 1968, 1971, 1972, 1973, 1975, 1977.

Other Scripture quotations are from the following sources:

The King James Version (KJV).

The Holy Bible, New International Version (NIV). Copyright © 1973, 1978, 1984 International Bible Society. Used by permission of Zondervan Bible Publishers.

The New King James Version (NKJV). Copyright © 1979, 1980, 1982, Thomas Nelson, Inc., Publisher.

*The Good News Bible,* Today's English Version (TEV)—Old Testament: Copyright © American Bible Society 1976; New Testament: Copyright © American Bible Society 1966, 1971, 1976.

Irina Ratushinskaya's poem, "Believe Me," appears on page 81 from Irina Ratushinskaya, *Pencil Letter* (New York: Random House, 1989). Used by permission.

**Library of Congress Cataloging-in-Publication Data**

Colson, Charles W.
       The body : being light in the darkness / Charles W. Colson with Ellen Santilli Vaughn.
              p.   cm.
       Includes bibliographical references and index.
       ISBN 0–8499–0866–3
       1. Mission of the church.   2. Church.   3. Christianity—20th century.   4. Christianity—United States.   5. United States—Church history—20th century.   6. Christian life—1960–   I. Vaughn, Ellen Santilli. II. Title.
       BV601.8.C64   1992
       262'.7—dc20                                                                92–30721
                                                                                            CIP

23459   MP   987654321

*Printed in the United States of America*

*Soli Deo Gloria*

# Contents

# *Part 1*

## *What Is the Church?*

One of our great allies at present is the Church itself. Do not misunderstand me. I do not mean the Church as we see her spread out through all time and space and rooted in eternity, terrible as an army with banners. That, I confess, is a spectacle which makes our boldest tempters uneasy. But fortunately it is quite invisible to these humans.

> *Screwtape, a senior devil, instructing a junior devil on how to tempt and trap humans. C. S. Lewis,* The Screwtape Letters

# 1

## The Story of a Church: Riverton

*R*IVERTON SITS AT A BROAD BEND OF THE South River, and life there has always been as leisurely as the wide, slow-moving water.

One hundred seventy years ago a young businessman named Curtis Clark Perry built the town's first cotton mill. The river carried Perry's bales to ports throughout the South, and over the years both the Perrys and Riverton prospered.

The town's founding family reproduced, weaving an unbroken line of Perrys who shipped cotton and developed a thriving textile business.

The town grew as well. Because of its gentle southern lifestyle, temperate climate, and twelve golf courses, Riverton eventually became a haven for upper-scale retirees. And when Xerox built a huge corporate center just outside of town, its employees and their young families brought new vigor to the community.

Along the river, the original homes of Riverton, with ivy-twined porches and long green lawns, still shelter descendants of the town's founding families. Fanning out from the historic homes are substantial, tree-lined neighborhoods with names like River Park and Steeplechase. Beyond them spread the newer suburban communities, dotted with shopping malls and swim clubs.

Southeast of the river is the heart of town, where Riverton takes pride in its historic re-bricked sidewalks and graceful pots of begonias hanging from old-fashioned, wrought-iron street lamps. Clusters of antique shops, gift boutiques, and picturesque cafes offer nostalgic browsing, topped off with the hand-mixed cherry Cokes you can still buy at the soda bar at the Riverton General Store.

Riverton would not be Riverton, though, without its churches. The oldest structure on Main Street is the First Methodist Church, a towering red brick edifice built by Curtis Perry, Jr. and maintained by the ample endowment left after his death. Today, Dr. E. M. Lee presides over the church's flock of a thousand members. The recent departure of some to the newer churches in the suburbs has done nothing to dim First Methodist's perception of itself as the preeminent church in town.

Four blocks east on Main stands Riverton Community Church, formed sixty years ago when a group led by Curtis Perry's great-grandson split away from First Methodist. Today an outsider would be hard-pressed to find any difference between the two churches, although Riverton Community has grown larger than its Methodist rival, primarily because of the strategic planning of Dr. George Killian.

Dr. Killian, a short, precise man whose sixty-something life is neatly scheduled by his frequently consulted Day-Timer, has pastored Riverton Community Church for twelve years. During that time, mainly through the outreach of his cassette tape ministry, he has developed a growing reputation as a Christian conference speaker.

It was Dr. Killian who led Riverton Community through its first building program. If the church was to grow, he maintained, it needed space; so he developed a ten-year plan. About eight years ago, as part of that plan, the church bought the empty lot directly behind it and the former auto dealership on its right. Thus, unlike First Methodist, which was hemmed in by an antique store on one side, the Riverton Library on the other, and backed by generations of deceased parishioners in its sprawling graveyard, Riverton Community had room to expand.

Edmund Perry, descendant of the original Perrys and a partner in the family business, chaired Riverton Community's building committee and brought the same high standards to the church project that he exacted in his company. Ed and his wife, Patricia, are pillars of Riverton Community, as were their parents before them.

At the building committee's direction, the original sanctuary became a chapel for special services and small, intimate weddings. Its mahogany pews were stripped and refinished to a gleaming rich, deep honey, warmed by the sunlight streaming through the intricate stained-glass windows. Little brass nameplates studded the pews as well as the wooden frames beneath the windows, citing the benefactors who had provided them. This restoration meant a great deal to members like Ed and Patricia, who had been married in the old sanctuary.

Though it had cost hundreds of thousands of extra dollars, the congregation felt it important to match the pre-World War I brick of the old building, and the architects had designed the new structure so it emerged from the old like a fresh, new branch from a stately old tree. This preservation and transformation of Riverton Community Church was lauded by the state historical society.

Inside, the new sanctuary could seat a thousand, and the building committee had voted to stay with pews rather than the theater-style seating so many churches were installing. Filled with air and light, this new facility seemed to send the right message to the upscale worshipers flocking to Riverton.

Every time George Killian pulled into his personal parking space in front of the glass-and-brick entry, he took great satisfaction in the tasteful way old and new merged so flawlessly. The tradition of generations past, the men and women who had built this church nearly a century earlier, was represented by the graceful old steeple rising from the original structure, while a soaring new steeple, an exact replica but nearly twice as tall, rose from the addition.

Riverton Community also boasted an immense new parking lot, which dwarfed First Methodist's. Every Sunday a phalanx of ushers, wearing fresh carnations in their lapels and armed with walkie-talkies, directed the gathering flock of luxury cars. Their owners would glide into the same parking spots every week, just as they would slide into the same pews Sunday after Sunday.

The only problem with George Killian's growth strategy was that he had not counted on the exodus of some of the very people his ten-year plan was designed to cultivate.

It all began when a group of church members started meeting in one another's homes for weekly Bible study—several young couples, a few elderly widows, and some singles from the Focus class. Dr. Killian applauded their efforts to study the Scripture on their own, though he had heard that their exegesis often lacked the precision of his Sunday sermons. But by all reports, the group spent a tremendous amount of time in prayer. (Perhaps that was why this group began lobbying for the congregation to spend more time in prayer, worship, and singing during the Sunday morning service.)

Dr. Killian was enthusiastic about their enthusiasm—until it began to interrupt the orderly flow of his services. Most of the congregation came from the corporate world, and he prided himself on providing the same standards of punctuality and efficiency they expected in business meetings. His parishioners could set their watches by the call to worship, opening prayer, welcome, opening hymn (all four stanzas), a missions moment or some other special announcement, offertory hymn, offering, choir anthem, sermon, closing hymn (first and last stanzas only). In at 9:30, out at 10:30; in at 11:00, out at 12:00. And by Monday morning, copies of Dr. Killian's meticulous twenty-two-minute sermons had been reproduced on cassette and were being sent out to his growing list of disciples. Some said privately that it all worked just like Jiffy Lube.

But this Bible study group's desire for expressive worship had threatened all that. In the end, the matter escalated to an unfortunate climax, with several dozen members leaving the church.

Some of the "worship" group elected to stay, however, and the pastor had to admit that they were among the most active members in his congregation. They volunteered for nursery duty, taught Sunday school, and chaperoned youth retreats; when he preached, they had their Bibles open and their eyes intent on his. Actually, this concentrated attention unnerved him a bit at times—unlike other parishioners who fixed him with a genial, wide-eyed Nancy Reagan stare, their minds more on brunch or that long drive on the ninth fairway than on his explication of Scripture. But he tried not to think about that.

Meanwhile, those who left Riverton Community had gone down the street and around the corner to the town's most unconventional house of worship, St. Giles Episcopal.

St. Giles had no building of its own. For the last year or so the relatively new congregation had met at Riverton High School, under the ministry of Father John Conway, a tall, bearded man with a loud laugh and a tender heart.

John Conway was a religious mongrel—and an outsider. Originally from Chicago, he had grown up in a Christian and Missionary Alliance home; his parents had been missionaries to Ghana. As a child, John had "given his heart to Jesus." In his teens, he had recommitted himself through the ministry of Young Life. Then, during his freshman year at the University of Michigan, he shifted his faith into neutral. The next few terms were a blur of frat parties, kegs of beer, and a string of good-time girls with names like Muffie and Suzie.

John studied abroad his junior year. In the summer, before returning home, he backpacked through Europe and ended up at L'Abri, Dr. Francis Schaeffer's Switzerland retreat which seemed to attract young people with questions about Christianity. In that discursive atmosphere he had realized that the truth about Christ demanded an all-or-nothing commitment of his life and energies—and he made that commitment. During his senior year of college John joined the InterVarsity chapter on the U of M campus and was discipled by the director and several members.

After graduation he worked for a couple of years with a small, parachurch outreach to inner-city kids in Washington, D.C., which eventually led him to Trinity Seminary in Pittsburgh to study for the Episcopal priesthood.

While at Trinity, John met Emily Perry, a medical intern doing her residency at Allegheny General Hospital Center. He had run into her—literally—at an ice skating rink during an outing sponsored by St. Stephen's Episcopal Church. Emily was a petite bundle of energy with long, dark bangs and a habit of talking with her hands. She certainly didn't fit John's image of a Southern debutante.

When they exchanged the usual get-acquainted details about family backgrounds during one of their first dates, he learned about her privileged childhood as a daughter of Edmund and Patricia Perry of the founding family of Riverton.

"I'll always be thankful for the way my folks brought me up," Emily had said. "I felt so secure. It wasn't the money—I took that for granted. But I always knew my parents loved me. They were committed to family, to their church, to their community. They were thrilled when I did well in college and went on to medical school. That fit the mold."

As they sat on the floor of John's studio apartment near the seminary sharing a pepperoni pizza and a liter of Diet Coke, Emily described her own spiritual journey and her parents' reaction.

"But when I came home and started talking about Jesus, it made them nervous. Religion was great. Faith had its place. Being a Christian was like being a Republican. We just were. But when I talked about Jesus and what He meant to every aspect of my life and my plans for the future, that kind of freaked them out for a while. They were worried about my joining a cult."

The unlikely match sparked, and John and Emily were married the summer before John's last year of seminary. Then, as he finished seminary and Emily completed her residency, they both sensed a growing pull toward Riverton. Though the attraction was somewhat reluctant on their part, in the end they knew God was calling them to Emily's hometown. In an unusual step, John received permission from his presiding bishop to start a new church, and with Emily's income to keep them afloat, the Conways moved to Riverton.

It had been a joyous homecoming. Once Ed and Patricia Perry realized that their daughter wasn't going to make the typical Riverton choice and marry an attorney or a banker, they had welcomed John into the family. Besides, Emily and John were settling in Riverton. Patricia harbored thoughts of grandchildren, while Ed felt a thrill of pride every time he thought of his daughter setting up her own medical practice. He was sorry Emily and John wouldn't be a part of their church, but John was so enthusiastic about his new congregation—and, as Patricia had pointed out, it was wonderful that John was reaching out to the new people in town who wouldn't feel comfortable at First Methodist or Riverton Community.

So Emily Perry Conway practiced internal medicine at Riverton Medical Center, while her husband, Father John Conway, practiced it at St. Giles Episcopal Church.

Once the young couple got settled, it was as if John Conway had been created by God for the express purpose of starting a church in Riverton. He and Emily began with a prayer group in their home. The group quickly grew into a core of twenty families.

They rented the high school auditorium for their Sunday services, and once there they continued to grow. The congregation swelled to several hundred. Each week they moved in like an army, setting up a temporary nursery and children's Sunday school in the classrooms, arranging the cafeteria for adult classes, and hanging bright "Jesus Is Lord" banners in front of the Riverton High School Tigers' colors on either side of the stage in the auditorium—their sanctuary.

Then, to the accompaniment of strumming guitars, a tambourine, and a friend of Emily's who played the flute like an angel, the services would begin. They were festive celebrations, but they were also sobering. During the time of personal confession, members often wept, acknowledging their sin as they sought the Lord's cleansing.

As Patricia Perry had predicted, newcomers who felt their wardrobes or autos or professions wouldn't quite fit at Riverton Community or First Methodist were quite at home at St. Giles. Among them were workers from the cotton mills, orderlies and technicians from the hospital, and several teachers from the area schools. Then came the group that had left Riverton Community.

John felt badly about the latter. He didn't want anyone to think he was recruiting from other churches, nor did he want to create any hard feelings with Emily's parents. But after talking at length with these former Riverton members, he could see why they had come.

John and Emily prayed for the congregation and the pastor at Riverton Community. They even prayed that something would come along to shake up the comfortable, complacent congregations in town and bring all the churches together in a common cause.

The answer came in an unlikely way.

The whole thing started in early April when the fire department announced that it was abandoning its obsolete main station next door to Riverton Community Church to move into a new facility closer to the golf club communities at the north end of town. The church members were happy with the department's decision. Idle firemen had sometimes eaten lunch on the church lawn and left wrappers and soda cans behind. And there had been those rare but disturbing occasions when the fire alarms went off during a service.

Relief gave way to consternation, however, when Father John Conway announced that he had gotten the city's permission to lease the old station and use it as a shelter for the growing number of homeless on the streets of Riverton. Every night these displaced people could be seen bedding down on the benches near the bus terminal and rummaging through the garbage bins at the strip malls. Several of the suburban churches had started van runs, bringing food to those who lived like shadows in Riverton's alleys and parks.

This growing problem troubled Riverton's city council. Real estate values had been skyrocketing as more and more Northerners sampled the town's sweeping golf greens and idyllic lifestyle. Per capita income—and tax revenues—were now the highest in the state. Zoning was strictly enforced. And the community had recently been written up in a national journal as "the most tranquil community in America."

That tranquility disappeared the moment Father John Conway's announcement about the shelter appeared on the front page of the *Riverton Daily News*. Downtown merchants quickly organized a neighborhood association, and the Chamber of Commerce and the Real Estate Board expressed alarm. The Riverton City Council announced that it would hold public hearings to discuss the matter at its next scheduled meeting.

But Father John was already mobilizing for action, rallying concerned individuals from various churches. And one Saturday morning a group of fifty—volunteers from St. Giles, a suburban Baptist church, the nearby Catholic parish, and a Presbyterian congregation—swarmed over the firehouse with hammers, brooms, and paintbrushes.

Soon the old station, smelling of fresh white paint, had neat rows of eighteen cots made up with crisp, clean sheets and warm blankets. Eighteen personal care kits had been assembled: toothbrushes and toothpaste, razors and shaving cream, soap and combs. Though the facility could sleep only eighteen, each evening the consortium of churches supplied food for far more. In the first week of operation the old firehouse had sheltered its eighteen and fed more than a hundred men, women, and children who seemed to appear from nowhere.

Father John had trained some of the members of his church for small-group evangelism and discipleship. Rob Groves, a weatherman from the local television station, was one of these, and he started a Bible study for any homeless men who were interested. They began by reading the Gospel of John together. Rob's wife, Barb, started a similar group for the homeless women.

Once they felt comfortable, the men's responses to Rob's comments and questions about Scripture sparked some of the liveliest discussions of faith, life, and what it means to be part of the body of Christ that he had ever heard. After Father John sat in on some of the meetings, he told Emily he wished he could tape the sessions and send them out to Dr. George Killian's mailing list. They would certainly shake up that complacent fan club.

Meanwhile, the controversy over the shelter continued to build. The *Riverton Daily News* ran lead editorials on two successive days, the first arguing that the town had a duty to care for the homeless, the second decrying the use of such an "inappropriate location."

During his announcement slot in the order of service the following Sunday morning, Dr. Killian announced that the "shelter matter" would be discussed at the next church board meeting, scheduled for later that month.

Down the street, the First Methodist board met in Dr. E. M. Lee's study after Wednesday evening prayer meeting. Dr. Lee's reference to the apostle Paul's words, "When one suffers, we all suffer," was met with silence. The thought of vagrants littering Riverton Community's parking lot brought a certain perverse but unspoken delight to some of the older men, who could remember their parents' accounts of the split in their church.

After some discussion the Methodists decided that strict neutrality was the wisest policy. They would send observers to the city hearings, but would say nothing. After all, this wasn't really their problem.

As far as Riverton Community's congregation was concerned, Father Conway's shelter plan could not have come at a less propitious moment. They were already struggling with an issue that left them little energy to deal with the homeless.

About six weeks earlier certain members had persuaded Dr. Killian to move the early Sunday service from 9:30 to 10:00, thus allowing a full hour for adult Sunday school, which had been running only a half-hour, from 9:00 to 9:30. Dr. Killian didn't like changes, particularly since it meant imposing a corresponding delay on the 11:00 service. But he did want to accommodate the group, which included a number of those who had stayed when their friends moved over to St. Giles. They were pouring so much of themselves into the church he felt that he owed them something.

So he had carefully described the new arrangement during his Sunday announcement period, noting that it would allow everyone to take advantage of the tremendous training Sunday school provided. Nothing would change in the order of service, he stressed; worship would still last exactly one hour.

Though he knew he was walking on the eggshell sensibilities of some of the congregation, Dr. Killian had not anticipated the ferocious response his announcement generated.

It turned out that a sizable percentage of the 9:30 regulars had observed the long-standing custom of leaving the church lot by 10:35 and proceeding directly to the nearby Riverton Country Club for brunch. The brunch, a sumptuous and popular affair, began at 10:30. By 11:00, all of the desirable tables were taken and the wait became lengthy. The change in service times posed a grave threat to their Eggs Benedict, and the 9:30 faithful responded accordingly.

Early Monday morning, Harold Kendall, retired CEO of PPG Industries, stormed into George Killian's office. During the twelve years he had been on the board of Riverton Community, Harold had kept careful watch over its accounts and practices. His resistance to any change in church policy or procedure made the structured Dr. Killian look permissive.

Laura Hall, the pastor's secretary, later reported that the two men were closeted for forty-five minutes. Though their voices were occasionally so loud that she could hear them through the closed door, she could not quite make out what was being said.

When Harold finally emerged from Dr. Killian's office, she did hear him say, "George, you'd better think about this. You can't endanger the finances. Over the past ten years the 9:30 congregation has been responsible for more than half of your weekly budget. You don't want to jeopardize that when we still have this huge mortgage hanging over us." He pointed up at the ceiling, as though the massive steeple shooting up into the Riverton sky was about to descend upon them.

Dr. Killian put his hand on Kendall's shoulder. "I hear what you're saying, Harold," he said. "But a half-hour time difference isn't going to affect us all that much. After all, the preaching, the music, and the format are all going to stay exactly the same."

But Harold Kendall was no minor prophet. The very next week when the early service began at 10:00, attendance was down sharply. It was the same for the next four weeks. Dr. Killian received a number of courteous but pointed letters, and an informal petition was circulated. When he saw the petition, Jack Graham, chairman of the board, scheduled a meeting of the entire administrative board for mid-July.

Meanwhile, hot and bothered as the church members were about the change in service times, the matter of the homeless shelter next door was hotter still.

Dr. Killian wished the problem would just go away. He had had a very uncomfortable meeting with Michael Smithson, an 11:00 pillar of the church and one of the few in the congregation he considered a friend, although George Killian wasn't really close to anyone.

"You need to be careful with this homeless problem, George," Michael said. "Think how this will affect people who visit Riverton Community! So many are drawn here because of your tape ministry and your church growth seminars. Aren't they going to wonder if your own church begins to shrink because of a bunch of unshaven losers bunking up next door?

"I hate to sound so cold—I know the recession has really hurt a lot of people. But I think most of these street people are victims of their own laziness. After all, doesn't the Bible say that God helps those who help themselves?"

Killian ran his hand through his thick white hair and looked out of his office window for a moment, then back at Smithson.

"I've been thinking about this a lot," he said. "In fact, it has really cut into my sermon preparation time. And as much as I would like to help the homeless, I can't do everything. I'm called to lead our people here at Riverton Community. People have expectations when they come here, and we need to be a place where those needs are met.

"Our congregation is primarily upper middle-class business-men and their families. Most of them have worked hard to succeed. They have plenty of stress in their lives, and they want their church to be a sanctuary. A place where they can come and be fed and strengthened for the week to come. That's why I plan the service and my messages so carefully. No surprises. Order. A peaceful, affirm-ing environment."

"I know, George," Smithson agreed. "And that's been a big fac-tor in our growth."

Dr. Killian nodded his appreciation of this recognition, then continued his assessment of the situation. "Those homeless people need help. But right now I can't let that situation interfere with my first calling to the people of Riverton Community Church. I'm not going to get involved with the shelter controversy. It would send the wrong message."

The City Council meeting was scheduled for the first Thursday in July. The Sunday before there was a noticeable tension among members at both services at Riverton Community. It didn't help that this week's missions moment came in the form of a letter from Jillian Walker, the youngest daughter of the Walker family, long-time members. Jillian was in Peru for the summer on a short-term mis-sion program supported by the church.

A friend of Jillian's from the college and career group read the letter to the congregation:

Dear Riverton family,

Thank you so much for your generous support. I had seen pictures of the orphans and the devastation that the civil unrest here has created. But the people's suffering didn't really touch me until I saw it firsthand.

Riverton Community's financial support has made a big difference here. We have used the fund to set up a feeding station for refugees left homeless by the guerrilla fighting in the mountains. They have nowhere to go, no one to help them, and we feel God has placed us right here right now so we can make a difference and they can know that church people really do care about them. We feed them and try to help them find housing. We have had several decide to become Christians. They have told us, "We know Jesus is real because we have seen His love in you."

Thank you again for sending your support to this needy place so far away from home. I will look forward to seeing you all and telling you more when I get back.

Ed Perry looked at his wife. She was smiling. As the organ began the prelude to "Use Me Today, Lord," Patricia turned toward him and whispered, "What a sweet letter! Emmett and Molly must be so proud of Jillian helping those poor people in Peru!"

Ed smiled and nodded. But as he did, he was thinking not of the Peruvians, but of the people at the fire station next door.

The Riverton City Council meeting began precisely at 7:30 P.M. on the following Thursday, and the chairman was quick to let his own sympathies be known.

"Seems to me," he interjected after the Chamber of Commerce president and a long string of witnesses had presented their case, "that the problem here is not homelessness but shiftlessness. We cannot afford to jeopardize the peace and safety of a community that all of us have worked so hard to protect."

There was a loud burst of applause.

The outcome appeared so certain that Harold Kendall and Jack Graham simply smiled and kept quiet. Technically they couldn't say anything anyway because their own administrative board had not yet met. However, that would not have deterred them had the course of events looked less promising.

But then the city attorney, Walter Grant, who worshiped at the West End Golf Club every Sunday morning and thus was above suspicion in any intramural church maneuvering, noted that under zoning code C-1, the fire house "as a matter of right" could be used as an "inn, motel, or other place of public accommodation."

At that, Father John Conway and a group of shelter supporters offered the only smiles the attorney could see as he peered over his reading glasses and announced that the statutory language was unambiguous. A chorus of groans swept the room.

The Civic Association representative was on his feet waving his hand, but before he could be recognized, Grant continued. "But there is the matter of parking."

The room fell silent.

"Three spaces are required beyond the two the station already has," said the city attorney. "There must be five spaces in total for the eighteen beds at the station."

There were murmurs of approval.

"Of course," Grant explained, "the code allows that these three spaces could be borrowed from an adjacent neighbor. The most likely candidate would be Riverton Community Church, which possesses a 450-car parking lot right next door."

He looked directly at the two Riverton Community members, who shifted in their seats and said nothing. The chairman again received applause when he said he would entertain a motion to ban the shelter project altogether.

But Grant objected, citing ordinance 362-79: "The petitioner is entitled to thirty days in which to perfect his application." He could do this, the city attorney noted, by "borrowing" three spaces from a neighboring property owner. Grant said this very deliberately, again looking at Harold Kendall and Jack Graham.

Father John Conway promised the council he would return with his application in full conformity within the stated time, and the meeting ended. They would convene again on August 14.

Five days later the scheduled meeting of the Riverton Community Church board was called to order. Now there were two contentious items to consider: the change in the schedule of the first service and the sudden turn of events involving the shelter.

All thirty-eight members of the governing board were on hand for the meeting, along with several dozen church members who had been warned that they could participate in the discussion but could not vote. Normally the administrative board met in the church library, but because of the numbers they had to move to the chapel in the old part of the building.

The meeting was called to order by Jack Graham. One of Riverton's most respected attorneys, Jack was a regular patron of the annual horse show. His demeanor and style—after all, he was a third-generation lawyer—quieted the tension-filled group.

"Ladies and gentlemen," he intoned, "we gather tonight for a most serious deliberation. We need to consider both the proposed homeless shelter and the matter of the scheduling of our services. I suggest that we discuss the shelter issue first—after Dr. Killian invokes divine blessing on these proceedings."

Dr. Killian's rich voice filled the room. After he finished, everyone felt better for a second or two.

Then the floor was opened for discussion, inviting a furious babble of voices.

"I'm not insensitive to the needs of the homeless," shouted the Sunday school superintendent, her voice shaking with anger, "but they pose a serious threat to our community. We've all seen the accounts on the news. Most of them are drunks. Some have serious mental problems. We simply aren't equipped to handle them right here in the heart of Riverton."

From the back someone mentioned the recent incident of a strange man exposing himself at the elementary school playground, most likely one of the people they would be sheltering. A few individuals applauded, even as someone else angrily objected that the police had not identified the man who had committed the crime. Why assume it was one of the homeless?

Jack Graham had to rap sharply on the Communion table several times before he could regain order. Then he pointed at Jim Warren.

"Jim, you've had your hand up. What would you like to say?"

Warren, an electronics instructor at the local junior college and one of the "worship" group, stood up.

"As I see it," he said, "no, let me correct that, as the Bible sees it, we have no choice. We may not want to do it, but we need to reach out to these folks and help them. Matthew 25 says—"

Before he could finish his sentence, it seemed that everyone in the room was speaking at once. Jack pounded the table again. When the din subsided, Jim was still standing, Bible in hand, but it was Harold Kendall who seized the moment.

Harold was a medium-sized man with liver spots on his bald head. While not physically imposing, he usually managed to take charge.

"Perhaps it will help put this present problem in perspective if we think about our past," he said deliberately. "We must remember that this building is not just ours. It is a holy place entrusted to us by our forebears, and we will pass it to our children. It has stood here for sixty years, a monument to the faith of those who built it.

"It is here that many of us were confirmed and married, and from here we have buried our loved ones. I don't think it's a coincidence that we are holding this meeting in our old sanctuary, with these noble pews and beautiful stained-glass windows named in memory of our loved ones who have gone before and which remind us of God's great blessings to us. We are the stewards of this holy place.

"We can't forget all this when we consider the shelter next door. The homeless are not a problem for the church; the government should be handling them. The church should be a place set apart. And even though this shelter has only just begun, we've already seen what its continued presence will mean for Riverton Community Church.

"I'm sorry to say it, but I need to be clear, lest we all get swept away by the bleeding hearts among us. Several of us have seen some of the men from the shelter urinating on our property. Television news crews have trailed camera cables through our flower beds. The homeless people take shortcuts across our lawn; they don't stay on the brick paths. If you've encountered any of them up close, you know they don't smell good. They scare away church visitors."

Kendall then went on to profile what that would mean to budget projections. If the shelter remained, membership—and revenues—would decline by at least 20 percent. The change in the early service, from 9:30 to 10:00, had already cost the church more than it could afford. The two together were more than the church could possibly manage. Their mortgage was not something to take lightly.

Kendall's speech so frightened some and so angered others that the lines seemed clearly drawn. After another hour of discussion, which really did nothing except separate and entrench the viewpoints even further, the matter came to a vote. Someone suggested that the vote be taken by ballot.

As the clerk passed slips of paper to the board members, Ed Perry was thankful he could vote secretly.

"Just write 'yes' if you want to give the shelter the parking spaces and 'no' if you don't think that would be wise at this time," Jack Graham instructed.

Ed stared at the small white slip in his hand. For some reason it reminded him of the wafers passed during Communion. *This is My body, broken for you,* he thought involuntarily. Well, this wasn't about the body of Christ. This vote was about their church. It was about parking spaces and building codes, for goodness' sake. He couldn't let Emily and John's crazy ideas get to him. If they wanted to get their church all wound up in helping the homeless, then they had a right to do that. But they didn't have a right to dictate to Riverton Community.

He pulled out his heavy gold pen, steadied the slip of paper on the Bible from the pew rack, and wrote NO in firm, decisive strokes. He folded the slip once and dropped it in the offering plate.

The vote against the shelter passed by a large majority, as did the vote to return the first service to its 9:30 time slot.

And so it was that Riverton Community Church led the opposition to the shelter at the city council meeting in August. Jack Graham argued that the city had a duty to take care of the homeless. Public funds ought to be made available, and Riverton Community would certainly support the council's resolution to provide those funds. Furthermore, he argued, the shelter as presently constituted was inadequate. It was inappropriate to care for only eighteen while there were perhaps a hundred in need. "After all," he said in his most authoritative tone, "Jesus fed not five but five thousand."

Most of the council members nodded, as did the representatives from First Methodist, who otherwise sat unmoved throughout the proceedings.

"Unfortunate though it is," Graham concluded, "the conduct of the clients at the shelter simply is not compatible with the dignity expected in what we all would recognize to be a sacred place. We have had well-documented instances of inappropriate behavior."

He then called upon Harold Kendall, who, ignoring occasional snickers in the crowd, methodically listed every recorded instance of what he described as "church desecration." His litany was thorough: "8:30 A.M., June 14th, human excrement found at the base of the basement stairwell; 4:20 P.M., June 15th, two beer cans collected at the southwest corner of the parking lot; 2:30 P.M., June 17th . . ." and so it went.

The representatives from the shelter group waited patiently through all this. Then Father John stepped forward, his head bent slightly over a sheet of paper in his hand.

"I'm sorry that for some of our local churches this opportunity to serve those in need has been perceived as a nuisance," he said quietly.

"I wish that the lovely building complex of Riverton Community Church did not happen to reside next door to the homeless shelter. But it does. And we of this coalition have to follow our consciences—and the mandates of Scripture—rather than capitulate and make life easy for our brothers and sisters who would just rather not be bothered.

"I have in my hand a letter from Calhoon County, which owns the small square of land at the rear of the fire station where they have a shed for storing outdoor maintenance equipment. The county is willing to store its equipment elsewhere. If we provide the funds to raze the shed, the county will permit us to create the three additional parking spaces needed for the shelter to continue to operate. We have already raised those funds.

"Therefore," he concluded, "the only matter we now bring to this council is a petition for permission to rename the Riverton fire station." Father Conway paused and smiled broadly. "We'd like to call it the Light House."

Twenty minutes later, Ed Perry left the council meeting with mixed emotions. He had spoken briefly to John and Emily, who were now over in the far corner of the room laughing with city attorney Grant and toasting the council members with Styrofoam cups of coffee. He had seen Kendall and Graham leave together immediately after the meeting ended. Harold's face had been red with anger. Ed himself wasn't really angry. Disappointed perhaps. Even a bit ambivalent.

He got into his gray Mercedes and drove through the center of town, studying it as though he had never seen it before. The neat brick sidewalks, the annual summer sale at the Antique House, a group of young people laughing as they piled out of Pepper's Grill.

He slowed down when he got to Main Street and idled the car near the curb in front of the church. Beyond the parking lot, the big doors of the old firehouse were open, throwing warm squares of light out into the summer evening. Inside, he could see a small group of men sitting in a circle, heads bowed over the books in their laps. It looked like they were having some kind of study group.

Then he looked at his church next door and felt, as always, a
surge of pride at the sight of the neatly mulched flower beds, the
lush, crewcut lawns, the beautiful texture of the old brick walls.

There were no lights on in the dark building. Just the big spot-
lights on the new steeple rising into the evening sky.

# 2

## *Identity Crisis*

I am my own church.
*Respondent to Gallup poll on the church*

$U$NFORTUNATELY, EXCEPT FOR NAMES and places and certain disguised details, the story of Riverton Community Church is true. It took place in a town like Riverton in 1989.

Admittedly examples like this lend themselves to generalizations. And we are well aware that across America and around the world, thousands of congregations maintain a biblically faithful, exemplary witness. Still, for many of us, parts of the story strike uncomfortably close to home.

For the good people of Riverton Community, church was as much a part of the rhythm of their existence as their work or home life. Sunday morning worship, followed by brunch or an agreeable social hour, was for many the pinnacle of the weekend. Most were also active in church functions during the week, from suppers in the fellowship hall to the annual couples' weekend at a retreat center in the mountains. They worked hard on church committees or served on the board from time to time.

And the church was important to them psychologically. While the world around was changing rapidly, Riverton Community remained a stable institution—solid, respectable, something people could cling to even as old values slipped away around them. It provided a sense of continuity in the town as well. The grand edifice was a reminder that while everything else might crumble, the church stood strong and tall.

So it was not surprising that the folks of Riverton Community fought valiantly to protect not only the orderly pattern of their lives, but also their property. In protecting their property, they believed they were protecting their church. They were one and the same.

Riverton Community is not unique. No perception is more firmly rooted in our culture than that the church is a building—a view held by both churched and unchurched.

Who does not say, "I'm going to church"? We call the place where we worship, *the* church. And when we say we are "building a church," we mean we are constructing a facility, not that we are building men and women in spiritual maturity. In a thousand common expressions we refer to the church as a place.

This is no harmless colloquialism. It both presupposes and conditions our view of the church, creating what some have aptly called the "edifice complex," wherein the importance and success of the church is directly measured by the size and grandeur of the structure itself.

But this perception of the church as a building is only a symptom of a much broader problem—a genuine identity crisis. Not only do we see the church as bricks and mortar; we also misunderstand its character and its biblical purpose and mission.

We have trouble even defining what the church is. Is it a local congregation or a denomination? Is it all Christians worldwide or just those who are on membership rolls? What about those who watch services on television, those who are baptized as infants, those who have never been baptized?

And what is the church supposed to do? Worship? Evangelize? Grow? Feed the hungry, elect politicians, fight pornography? The list goes on and on. Just engage anyone, Christian or not, in a conversation about the church and you'll hear a variety of opinions—good, bad, indifferent.

It's no surprise that nonbelievers don't really know much about the church's identity or mission. But when Christians themselves are undergoing a widespread identity crisis, then we are in big trouble. For this confusion strips the church of its authority. If the church, like Riverton Community, is perceived as a building, a place one goes for weddings, funerals, or to drop in as it suits our fancy, then it is no surprise that 81 percent of the American people say they can arrive at their own religious views without regard to a body of believers.[1]

This loss of authority also affects behavior. George Gallup has found that while almost half the country attends church services, only 6 to 10 percent of all Americans are what he terms "highly spiritually committed."[2]

Gallup compared the behavior of churched and unchurched in a variety of categories—people who called in sick when they weren't, people who puffed their résumés, people who cheated on tax deductions—and found "little difference in the ethical views and behavior of the churched and the unchurched."[3]

Astonishingly, another survey found a deterioration in behavior among those who professed to be born again.[4]

Gallup also found little difference in charitable habits. Only 25 percent of evangelicals tithe. While 40 percent say faith in God is the most important thing in their lives, those who make between $50,000 and $75,000 a year give only an average of 1.5 percent to charity, religious or otherwise.[5] This same group spent 12 percent of their income on leisure pursuits.[6]

So while the church may seem to be experiencing a season of growth and prosperity, it is failing to move people to commitment and sacrifice. The hard truth is that we have substituted an institutionalized religion for the life-changing dynamic of a living faith. For most of us the church is the building where we assemble to worship; its ministries are the programs that we get involved in; its mission is to meet the needs of its parishioners; and its servants are the professional clergy we hire to shepherd us. Church growth has come to refer more to such things as location, marketing, architecture, programs, and head counts than to the maturity of the body of Christ.

When compared with previous generations of believers, we seem among the most thoroughly at peace with our culture, the least adept at transforming society, and the most desperate for a meaningful faith. Our raison d'être is confused, our mission obscured, and our existence as a people in jeopardy. Worst of all, our leaders know it—but seem unable or unwilling to do anything about it.*

In light of this, it should not surprise us that while plenty of people are still walking through the doors of churches, secularism

---

*Recently when researchers asked pastors how they believed Christ would rate their church if He were to return today, less than half of 1 percent queried said that He would rate them as highly effective; 43 percent believed He would find them respectable, if not wholly successful; while 53 percent said Christ would rate the church as having little positive impact on souls and society (George Barna study cited in EP News Service, 7 February 1991).

reigns as the dominant world-view of American culture. It is hard to imagine, therefore, a more urgent or critical task than the recovery and restoration of the biblical view of the church. And as ambitious and daunting as it seems, this is the task we have humbly and prayerfully undertaken in the following pages.

The first stirring for this work goes back many years. Along with many others, I have long been bewildered by the paradox Gallup describes as "religion up, morality down." At first I believed it was simply a lack of understanding of personal discipleship and the pursuit of holiness. These were issues addressed in *Loving God,* published in 1983.

The hungry response to that book has been more intense than to anything else I've written, including *Born Again.* Serious Christians know they need discipleship; they want to be faithful and to make a difference.

But the fact is, even Christians who understand their personal identity as followers of Christ will not make a widespread difference in the decline and decay around us—unless we have a high view of our corporate identity as the body of Christ.

Many Christians have been infected with the most virulent virus of modern American life, what sociologist Robert Bellah calls "radical individualism." They concentrate on personal obedience to Christ as if all that matters is "Jesus and me," but in so doing miss the point altogether. For Christianity is not a solitary belief system. Any genuine resurgence of Christianity, as history demonstrates, depends on a reawakening and renewal of that which is the essence of the faith—that is, the people of God, the new society, the body of Christ, which is made manifest in the world—the church. As we will argue in these pages, there is no such thing as Christianity apart from the church.

The church is not incidental to the great cosmic struggle for the hearts and souls of modern men and women. It is the instrument God has chosen for that battle—a battle we are called to by virtue of being members of His body. To bring hope and truth to a needy world, *the church must be the church.*

Seeing all this, under heartfelt conviction, in the fall of 1988 I began collecting material and studying contemporary theologians such as Francis Schaeffer, Christopher Dawson, Carl F. H. Henry, Richard Neuhaus, and Helmut Thielicke as well as the classics, both Protestant and Catholic. From the beginning this work also involved

Ellen Vaughn, who has been my colleague since 1980, working with me on five previous books and other writing projects. The two of us consulted theologians, church leaders, pastors, and laypeople of all confessions.

As we were immersed in our work for this book, the world suddenly turned upside down. The Berlin Wall came down! Eastern Europe was free! Seventy years of Communist repression ended! Incredible.

Then, out of the turmoil, came astonishing reports of the church's role in fueling the revolution. So in the fall of 1990 Ellen traveled to Romania, Hungary, and Poland where she interviewed church leaders and ordinary Christians, stayed in their homes, worshiped with them, and visited the memorable scenes of the revolution. That same year I traveled to the Soviet Union and later to Czechoslovakia and Hungary, getting a taste of the exciting spiritual forces at work and meeting some of the most extraordinary Christians I've ever known.

Here at home, Ellen and I visited scores of local congregations, from one of the country's fastest growing megachurches to a tiny band of believers on death row. And from that research, our study of Scripture, and our own sense of what God is doing and wants to do in His body comes this book.

In the pages that follow we'll look at the church as it is commonly perceived, from the outside and inside. We'll address the biblical definition of the church and its characteristics, both the universal and the local confessing congregation.

Understanding the nature and character of the church is absolutely vital. Too often Christians want to rush off and organize anti-pornography or anti-abortion campaigns, work for criminal justice reform, clean up inner-city neighborhoods, and defend religious liberty. All noble and worthy good works, but all doomed to failure unless they proceed out of who we are as God's people.

We cannot give what we do not have. We cannot impart values we do not hold. We cannot do until we are. To be the church—our highest calling—depends on understanding the very character of the body of Christ on earth. Only then can we understand what it means to live as the people of God, serving God in today's world.

If the church is the body of Christ, what exactly does that mean? And what exactly is the church? In part 1 we'll deal with that question, looking at some contemporary examples. In part 2 we'll examine the great tension: the church versus the world. In the battle for truth—which is the great issue of our times—how can the church be the custodian of the truth, guardian of Holy Scripture, when it does not stand independent of culture? In part 3 we'll examine how the church operates in the world. What are the people of God to be and how are they equipped to become that?

But before we begin, a few caveats are in order.

First, this is not a book about churches. It is a book about *the church.*

Some readers may wonder why great churches (like the ones they belong to) are not discussed in detail; others will be looking for specifics on how to improve evangelistic efforts or expand prayer groups. They will be disappointed. Many great how-to books are already available on these subjects (see the recommended reading list in the appendix). Our purpose here is to expound the great doctrine of the church, inspire the grand vision of the church, and restore a high view of the church.

Pastor Robert Patterson laments the lack of both scholarly and popular work in this regard, at least among evangelicals. Only once in thirty-four years of publication has the Evangelical Theological Society addressed the doctrine of the church, Patterson says. And most popular books deal with church growth, evangelism, or pastoral leadership.

Patterson cites this as evidence of the low view envangelicals have of the church. Evangelicals disregard baptism, the structure of ministry, and accountability, he says, putting emphasis chiefly on the individual's personal relationship to Christ. This is in part due to the entrepreneurial nature of the parachurch movement and the fierce independence of many evangelical churches.[7]

In the course of our research we have discovered at least one of the reasons for this: You cannot deal with the doctrine of the church without walking through doctrinal and denominational mine fields—and setting some off in the process.

Which brings us to the second warning. While we have attempted to address this subject from the most inclusive perspective possible, believing passionately that the church consists of God's people from every race and nation and confession, we are nonetheless aware that our own views will invariably color how we perceive the church. I am a Baptist with a thoroughly Reformed theology; Ellen is a Presbyterian; we both have a catholic—small "c"—universal view of the church; and the reader will have to take this into account. However, we have made every effort to write as inclusively as possible about those matters which orthodox believers and confessions have held in common down through the ages when we pledge our loyalty to "one, holy, apostolic, catholic church."

But—and here is the third caveat—some readers may find this inclusiveness difficult to accept. They cannot surrender the old prejudices that not only make them feel comfortable, but affirm that they are really right. Others genuinely believe that the fundamental differences within the church are irreconcilable. We understand that belief. But if it is true, we have a bigger problem than this book—because Jesus Himself called us to be *one*.

Of course there are doctrinal differences between sacerdotal and nonsacerdotal churches, between Arminians and Calvinists, between premillennialists and postmillennialists, and we should not attempt to gloss over these as some twentieth-century ecumenists have done. The differences do matter, and doctrinal disputes exist. And, as will be argued later, some may even serve a healthy purpose.

Despite these differences, however, we need to come together around the great truths all believers have shared regarding Christ's teaching about His body. It is a difficult line to walk, but walk it we must if the power of the church is to be felt in today's world.

As a fourth caveat, we would note that there are issues other than confessional differences that may offend some readers. For in the course of our work we found ourselves questioning practices with which modern evangelicals have been comfortable. Like hit-and-run evangelism. Or the notion that evangelism is the first call of the church. Or the tried-and-true methodology that is obsolete in the post-Christian culture in which we live. Or the idea that unless certain words are said, certain prayers repeated, one may not make it into the kingdom. We call that the sin of presumption.

We didn't set out to be controversial, but better that than simply being comfortable. At any rate, we have consulted with some of the best theological minds, whose help we later more fully acknowledge and for which we are profoundly grateful, and we can only trust that if this book stirs debate, it will invigorate—rather than further divide—the church.

We realize this is far from a definitive work, nor does it claim to be. But we pray that the themes will rekindle the grand vision of the church for many believers today.

Finally, we want to point out that we've drawn many examples from prisons and from the oppressed church in the East. It is natural that we use the former since, through Prison Fellowship, we spend a great deal of time with the church behind prison walls. And we chose the latter because the persecuted people of God in the East have contributed to the greatest story of the twentieth century: the collapse of Communism. Besides, the truth is, some of the greatest challenges for the comfortable church in the West come from our brothers and sisters around the world.

By now some of you may be asking, why is Chuck Colson writing on the church? What are his credentials? After all, he is a layman who never attended seminary (which happens to be one of my great personal regrets) and never pastored a local congregation (for which, I'm quick to confess, I would lack the patience).

It is a fair question, although in defense I might add that I've been part of the universal church for more than nineteen years, and as leader of Prison Fellowship for seventeen of those years, I have worked with and gathered insights from pastors and laypeople in some of the most vital congregations in the United States and around the world. I may be an "outsider" to the pastorate, but then again, that may not always be a disadvantage. As Os Guinness has said, "If you want to know about water, the last one to ask is a fish."

During the Reformation, *Coram Deo* became a rallying cry for the Reformers. It meant "in the presence of" or "before the eyes of God," and, as R. C. Sproul has written, nothing marked the Reformation more than an awe of the holy, majestic God who had called men and women to Himself. It drove the Reformers to their knees in fear and reverence.

This was the same awe and reverence found in the very earliest accounts of the church, where we read that "great fear seized the whole church"—the fear of the Lord. In fact, the early church "was strengthened; and encouraged by the Holy Spirit, it grew in numbers, living in the *fear* of the Lord."[8]

How desperately the church today needs to take hold of that awe! To understand that we live day by day in the presence of God; that, in truth, we live each minute, each instant, not knowing whether in the next we will meet Him face to face.

*Coram Deo.* Filled with this holy fear and reverence, the early church changed the world and the Reformers transformed the church and the culture. And fearing God rather than man, the persecuted church in Eastern Europe and the former Soviet Union revolutionized the world.

What the church needs most desperately is holy fear. The passion to please God more than the culture and community in which we spend these few, short years. And it is to that end we write.

Before we can begin to understand what the church is to be and to do, however, we need to fully understand its present identity crisis. It was on a trip to the Orient some years ago that I first began to see this clearly.

# 3

## Gimme That Hot Tub Religion!

I didn't go to religion to make me happy. I always knew a bottle
of Port would do that. If you want a religion to make you feel
really comfortable, I certainly don't recommend Christianity.

C. S. Lewis

**W**HEN MY WIFE, PATTY, AND I WERE IN Japan a few years ago, our hosts
suggested we take a free afternoon to visit what was then the fastest
growing church in the world. So three Japanese pastors crowded
themselves, Patty, and me into a small Toyota and headed for a hilly
area just outside downtown Tokyo.

After winding through crowded streets, we turned onto a beautiful tree-lined drive leading to imposing black gates marking the
entrance to the headquarters of the PL Kyodan (the Perfect Liberty
Church). Since only members of this Buddhist sect could be admitted, we had to content ourselves with peering through the gates.

Rich green lawns stretched as far as the eye could see, blending
into a distant, sprawling golf course. From the front gates the drive
meandered toward an elegant white mansion surrounded by artis-
tically sculptured Japanese gardens. Except for the pagoda roof, it
might have been mistaken for Jefferson's Monticello or Washington's
Mount Vernon.

Within the gates, we learned, was a "town" of three thousand
residents. Perfect Liberty Church boasted the most complete recre-
ational facilities in all of Japan, along with such landscape delights
as artificial lakes, cherry trees, and waterfalls.

While we gazed at the grandeur of the complex, called "paradise"
by its founders, our host explained the simple theology of the Perfect
Liberty Church: We are all children of God who find The Way to eternal peace and welfare by freely exercising our individuality. Since "all

of life is art," one can find free creative expression in prayer, golf, or group sex. The important thing is total freedom for individual expression, which results in complete joy and fulfillment. Perfect Liberty also offers a utopian vision of the future. In time, it promises, as the movement spreads, all evil will disappear and humanity will live in perfect liberty and harmony. No wonder it is the fastest growing religion in Japan, winning almost a million followers in its first decade of existence.

It is also the richest religion, for the Perfect Liberty Church teaches that giving is a prerequisite to salvation. Worshipers bring "treasure bags" to the altar, and they are always overflowing. When you can buy happiness, why be stingy?

During our flight back to the States, I read some literature I'd picked up on the Perfect Liberty Church. Periodically I would nudge Patty with a "Look at this!" and pass her a booklet containing some outrageous statement.

"What nonsense," I said at one point. "Imagine this! They're saying that you can do whatever you want as long as it makes you happy. And they call that church!"

Hours later, while settling into our Los Angeles hotel room for the night, we flipped on the television and scanned the channels, waiting for something to catch our eye. It did.

A man and a woman were seated on an overstuffed sofa in the middle of a grand, gaudy set. A huge stained-glass window shimmered in the light next to a portrait of Jesus on black velvet. Large, steroidal palms spilled out of every corner. The white-and-gold baby grand was a showstopper, but it was really the two on the sofa who fascinated us.

His salt-and-pepper hair, combed back in neat waves, looked like it might be held in place by epoxy cement. His dark eyes and mustache would have made him seem as sinister as a Wild West villain if it weren't for the charming foil provided by his mate. She was a Southern belle done by Frederick's of Hollywood, with a fuchsia ruffled dress and huge silvery-blonde hair. She sat primly, holding her Bible, alternating adoring glances at her husband with arched-eyebrow nods to the studio audience, apparently coaxing them to adore him too. Her smile remained as fixed as his hair during the twenty minutes we watched. Perhaps relaxing it would have cracked her makeup.

But it wasn't just the absurd scenery and costumes that captivated us. It was the message of this Christian—yes, Christian—

program: You can have perfect peace and joy and happiness and prosperity, the host said. God wants no one to suffer or be deprived. Just ask. Ask and you will receive in abundance. Yes, abundance, abundance, abundance.

It was a virtuoso performance, the man's gestures and voice modulation expertly timed. One moment he excitedly invoked rapture, the next an oozing, comforting, syrupy mode. The woman nodding and adoring. The audience undulating back and forth.

Patty and I found ourselves nudging one another as we had on the airplane. "What nonsense. . . . Imagine it. And they call this the church—"

Suddenly my voice trailed off. Patty and I stared at each other. I think we realized at precisely the same moment that what we were watching on that set was no different than what we had seen and heard about the Perfect Liberty Church in Japan. This was simply Christianized Buddhism.

But the parallels do not end with this televised travesty. For when we peered through those gates at that ludicrous Buddhist sect, what we really saw was a reflection of the identity crisis in the church.

The roots of the church's identity crisis are found in the consumer mentality so pervasive in our culture. Aside from those hierarchical denominations that assign members to the parish in which they live, most Americans are free to choose which church they will join or attend. And choose they do.

Ask people what they look for in a church and the number one response is "fellowship." Other answers range from "good sermons" to "the music program" to "youth activities for the kids" to "it makes me feel good." People flit about in search of what suits their taste at the moment.

It's what some have called the "McChurch" mentality. Today it might be McDonald's for a Big Mac; tomorrow it's Wendy's salad bar; or perhaps the wonderful chicken sandwiches at Chick-Fil-A. Thus, the church becomes just another retail outlet, faith just another commodity. People change congregations and preachers and even denominations as readily as they change banks or grocery stores.

Polls tell us what these consumers are seeking. According to a *USA Today* survey, of the 56 percent of Americans who attend church, 45 percent do so because "it's good for you"; 26 percent cited "peace of mind and spiritual well-being." Specific doctrines did not seem important, the pollster reported. Most appeared to be "looking for that inner and more subjective kind of payoff" from religion.

This survey, one sociologist observed, was but a reflection of the "culture of narcissism."[1] But the church seemed blissfully unaware of the fact. A leading evangelical journal even hailed the survey, gushing, "Seventy-one percent of those who attend religious services were positive and enthusiastic about their involvement."[2]

Other indicators point in the same direction. According to a recent survey, the books selling in Christian bookstores are the "touchy-feely" ones that focus on self-esteem, self-fulfillment, and self-analysis while "devotionals and missionary biographies gather dust on the shelves. So do books encouraging self-sacrifice."[3]

We've encountered this mind-set over and over again, as in the case of two friends to whom Patty and I have witnessed for years. One Sunday when we were in their city, they agreed to accompany us to church. On the way, the woman said, "Oh, I hope the pastor will cheer me up today. I'm so depressed. I found a dead bird at the back door this morning."

Another longtime acquaintance told me he was now attending a Unity church.

"Why?" I asked. "You are a Christian, and that is a cult."

"Really?" The man looked surprised.

"Of course it is, " I said. "They don't believe in the Resurrection or even one true God."

"But my wife and I love it," he said. "We always come away feeling better."

Even secular observers have noted how this demand for "feel better" religion is affecting church life and practice. A 1990 *Newsweek* cover story heralded the dramatic religious resurgence among the nation's baby boomers, reporting that more than 80 percent consider themselves "religious and believe in life after death." But "unlike earlier religious revivals, the aim this time (apart from born-again traditionalists of all faiths) is support, not salvation, help rather than holiness, a circle of spiritual equals rather than an authoritative church or guide. A group affirmation of self is at the top of the agenda *which is why some of the least demanding churches are now in the greatest demand.*"[4]

What many are looking for is a spiritual social club, an institution that offers convivial relationships but certainly does not influence how people live or what they believe. Whenever the church does assert a historically orthodox position, one that might in some way restrict an individual's doing whatever he or she chooses, the church is accused of being "out of touch"—as if its beliefs are to be determined by majority vote or market surveys.

Spiritual consumers are interested not in what the church stands for but in the fulfillment it can deliver.* Thus the under-forty-five generation, 60 percent of whom define themselves as independent spiritual seekers, reject the notion that one should be limited to a single faith. The result is "an age of mix 'em, match 'em, salad bar spirituality."[5] And it really doesn't matter whether it is orthodox or New Age; a majority of Christians believe all religions worship the same God.[6]

This consumer mentality, in turn, pressures churches to respond in kind. When the findings of a major foundation study revealed the sharp decline of several Protestant denominations, the chief researcher acknowledged with disarming candor: "The challenge, I tell ministers, is that they must ask themselves why people are in front of them on Sunday mornings instead of somewhere else. The church is in a competitive situation for people's leisure time."[7] We are competing with cable television, Nintendo games, theme parks, and health clubs.

If people are looking at religion as a product, then the church reckons it has to furnish a competitive product. It's not a conscious process. Few church boards sit down and decide to replace their orthodox doctrines with warm, soothing nostrums. But pastors feel the pressure to make the message as inviting as possible to draw people in. So the process is gradual: a little rationalizing here . . . a little rounding off there . . .

The spiritual odyssey of one evangelical church reveals how the process works and where it can lead.

Realizing that the median age in the church was rising—a grave danger sign, according to church growth experts—the pastor of this long-established Baptist congregation commissioned a market survey of upscale families in his area. The first discovery was that most of the potential market was put off by the term "Baptist."

---

*According to George Barna, astute observer and critic of the church, this consumer demand will intensify and shape the church of the future. Increasingly people will demand personalized religious systems that will meet their need for a religious perspective without requiring the sacrifices and commitment that traditional Christianity demands.

"People don't like denominational tags anymore," the pastor told a *Newsweek* reporter. "All they want to know is what's in it for me."

The obvious solution? Rename the church.

Then, examining the next point on the market study—accessibility—the church picked a location right off a freeway and built a new building. Nothing that would scare anyone off, of course. The six-million-dollar building with beamed ceilings and huge stone fireplaces (for barbecues) has no crosses or religious symbols; it looks like a dude ranch.

Some would argue that this congregation was simply striving to be "user friendly," a computer term that has spilled over onto everything, including church planning. Unfortunately they didn't stop with names and architecture. They also decided to abandon standard theological terms.

"If we use the words redemption or conversion," the pastor explained, "they think we are talking about bonds." So he has banished all "hellfire and damnation" preaching and proudly displays a version of the Bible he personally produced, which is just right for the McChurch generation. All essential passages are in boldface and it can be read in thirty half-hour sittings.

Wonderful! All of God's knowledge, the mystery of the ages, consumed in just fifteen hours!

Not surprisingly, the congregation couldn't be more enthusiastic.

"There's a spirit of putting people over doctrine. The attitude is that they are for life, love, and liberty," one member enthused.

"The church totally accepts people as they are without any sort of don'ts and dos," says another. "When relatives visit, they wish they had a church like ours," she brags. Why not? What's not to like?

Churches across the country are responding to the McChurch consumer by disguising their identity. Even a conservative bastion like Denver's Full Gospel Chapel has changed its name to the Happy Church. "It draws people," says the pastor.[8] Apparently so. The church has just taken over a $7.8 million shopping mall.

Hard to argue with success. Except that capitulating to consumerism has profound consequences for the church.

*First, it dilutes the message.* Some clergy have simply "airbrushed sin out of their language. Having substituted therapy for spiritual discernment, they appeal to a nurturing God who helps His (or *Her*) people cope. Heaven by this creed is never having to say no to yourself, and God is never having to say you're sorry.'"[9]

Sociologist Robert Bellah makes the same point, decrying the tendency in evangelical ranks to "thin the biblical language of sin and redemption to an idea of Jesus as the friend who helps us find happiness and self-fulfillment."

*Second, responding to the market means more than "airbrushing" a word here or there; it changes the very character of the church.* The body is transformed from a worshiping community into a comforting haven from life's pressures. The meaning of church fellowship, as reported by one of those in Bellah's study, is to find "how I can love them [other church members], how I can help those beautiful and special people to experience how wonderful they are."[10] This is not a search for truth. It is the "warm fuzzies" of the mutual support movement as they splash around together in their suburban hot tubs.*

What J. I. Packer calls "hot tub religion" embraces anything that makes us feel better about ourselves. Which is why Tai Collins, the former Miss Virginia who allegedly was involved in a tryst with a U.S. senator and then posed nude for *Playboy,* can enthuse over the Presbyterian church she has recently joined. Her volunteer work there, she says, is "very fulfilling." When asked if it would affect her nude modeling, she replied, "I don't think so. I mean there's a lot of people in my church that have been in *Playboy.*"[11]

*Third, responding to the market can pervert the gospel.* Certainly the church should provide comfort for the grieving, the suffering, and the needy. But ministering to the afflicted is entirely different from the self-realization therapy that teaches us to look within ourselves to discover and heal our wounded psyche. As we will discuss later, self-realization and God-realization are diametrically opposed.

The gospel teaches that our hope is not in finding our true self but in losing our true self. That which defiles us is what is in us, Christ said. When we honestly look inside at our sin-scarred lives, we ought to be repulsed by our "true" selves. We then repent and die to ourselves so that Christ's atoning grace might cleanse us.

---

*Interestingly enough, attitudes are the same among Protestants and Catholics. The two things most Catholics want are "personal and accessible priests" and "warmer, more personal parishes" (Bellah, *Habits of the Heart*). Whether from formal or informal traditions, people want their emotional needs fulfilled, with little interest in doctrine or acknowledgment of authority.

Adjusting to ourselves is precisely what we mustn't do, says Robert Coles, renowned Harvard psychologist and Christian layman. "Adjustment and adaptation is so often an acquiescence to the most banal and crude, if not blasphemous, in a given society."[12]*

This is why the feel-good, restore-your-self-worth, therapeutic gospel is so dangerous. It is but a short step from therapy to the health-and-wealth, name-it-and-claim-it heresy, forms of which are propagated in conservative churches as well as by unscrupulous televangelists. Pay your money for God's blessings, proclaim Robert Tilton and others.

Therapy and the promise of material reward may lure people into our churches, but so might free reefers handed out in the sanctuary—and it's debatable which would do more harm.

**Fourth, succumbing to consumerism strips the church of its authority.** The feel-good gospel opens the door to the most dangerous movement of our day. Seeking to provide inner peace instead of pointing individuals to an ethical ideal of which they now fall short, it perilously parallels and makes credible the New Age movement.

Perhaps this is why, while 80 percent of Americans profess to be Christian, about half of all Americans believe in ESP, more than a third in mental telepathy, one-quarter in reincarnation, and one out of five say they have been in touch with the dead![13]

More than fifteen million Americans find "born-again Christianity too tacky, Protestantism and Judaism too suburban and Catholicism too papal."[14] So instead of flocking to churches, they flee to mountaintop highs, touchy-feely retreats, and healing spas where they discover the mystical power of crystals.

By responding to market pressures, the church forfeits its authority to proclaim truth and loses its ability to call its members to account. In other words, it can no longer disciple and discipline. But as alien and archaic as the idea may seem, the task of the church is not to make men and women happy; it is to make them holy.

---

*Richard Neuhaus is equally blunt. "The Christian proposition is that the discontents, the feeling of alienation, the inability to be 'at home' with existent reality, are all signs of health to be celebrated. The fatal disease is the premature 'resolution' of that which cannot be and must not be resolved except by resolution of all things in the consummated Lordship of the Christ" (Neuhaus, *Freedom for Ministry*, 71–72).

No wonder the church has an identity crisis. We speak glibly about going to church (even though the church is not a place) to feel good (absolutely the wrong reason). Then we compound the error by measuring the church against the wrong standard.

Over the years, I've conducted my own pastoral poll. "How are things going in your church?" I'll ask. With few exceptions, the answers are quantitative: "Membership up 20 percent . . . a hundred baptisms last year . . . starting a new building . . . going to three services . . ."

Cultural values have so captured the church that we equate success with size. It's a reflex reaction. If a church isn't growing, someone is doing something wrong. Maybe the pastor and the board haven't analyzed the market well enough or invested in the right programs. This is why church growth has become the hottest business in the religious world today. If "the customer is king," then the church has to react as any organization does to consumer demand, which means finding the right marketing strategy. According to one Church Growth Movement (CGM) leader, a minister's performance is measured not by faithfulness to the gospel but by whether "the people keep coming and giving."[15] With the right strategy, there's no limit to growth; it's simply a matter of finding the right formula. To this end, many professional organizations furnish churches the same services commercial marketers or political campaign strategists subscribe to: polls, market studies, message analysis, image making, advertising, and product labeling.

Church growth has not only become big business; it also emulates big business. Church growth literature often speaks of products and services and investments: $x$ amount of time and money invested in a particular project will yield $y$ results. Believing that successful business principles can produce similar results for the church, one megachurch sent groups to study firms like IBM, Xerox, and Disney World.[16]

There is nothing wrong with growth itself, of course. Nor is there anything inherently wrong with marketing strategies.

Some church bodies, for example, aggressively seek to evangelize unchurched people. One example of this is Willow Creek, one of the nation's fastest growing megachurches, which targeted a large Chicago suburb. As we will discuss later, Willow Creek has proven the value of intelligent technique: surveying neighborhoods, finding out what people want in a church, and carefully constructing appealing programs that draw people to attend services.

The trouble comes when we confuse technique with truth and when the mission or message is compromised. Many churches, like Willow Creek, have found the right balance; behind all the music and skits and fanfare stands a solidly orthodox message that deepens the spiritual life of their members.

Indeed, growth may be a sign of God's blessing. It surely was when Peter preached after Pentecost. People were convicted, repented, and were baptized—three thousand on the first day—and the Lord was "adding to their number day by day," with five thousand in one day alone.[17] That's the kind of growth that would be the envy of even the slickest professionals in the CGM. But it was the Lord adding to the numbers, not marketing experts.

That is the key. What matters is not whether a church uses skits or contemporary music or squash courts. What matters is biblical fidelity. If a thoroughly orthodox church challenges people to live holy lives and is growing, it is being blessed by God.

But if a church disguises its identity and preaches a message intended to keep everyone in a state of perpetual bliss, then its growth is man-made. "Growth for growth's sake, man-made growth can be spiritually deadening, " says Richard Neuhaus. "Institutional growth is the last refuge of ministries that are spiritually sterile."[18]

The real pressure elders and church boards should be putting on their pastors is for growth all right—but spiritual growth, not numbers.

And while growth is not the sure measure of success, neither should lack of growth be a sign of failure. Take the case of Brian, a young pastor of a small Baptist church in Southern California. I first met Brian when he drove me to the airport after a speaking engagement. As we were cruising along the freeway, I asked my standard question, "How are things going in your church?"

He hesitated for a moment, then said, "We've kind of been through it." There was a pause. "In fact, we've cut our membership a bit," he said, glancing at me quickly as if expecting me to be disappointed. "To be precise, we've cut our congregation in half."

"What happened?" I asked.

"Well, we had 220 members, but nothing was happening. I mean the place was dead, and no matter what I preached, nothing changed. So one day the deacons and I prayed. We said, 'Lord, bring only Your people here. We want those who are ready to repent and really give themselves wholly to You. Only bring those folks here.'

We even stood at the door of the church silently praying this as people filed in."

Brian glanced at me several times to see if I was questioning his sanity. Who in this age of church growth, in California of all places, would pray for people to stay away from their church?

"An amazing thing happened," he explained. "God answered the prayer. People began dropping out, one by one. We went from 220 to about 100. Then the place began to change. We almost went broke, but people got serious with God, they got involved—and now membership is creeping back up."

And then he grinned and added, "I think we may be going to have revival."

Brian just might be right. Often before revival there is a drop in church attendance. When the Holy Spirit convicts, there is anguish and pain; people confess their sins and repent. Those who are hardened of heart usually flee. Separating the chaff from the wheat signals that the church is becoming pure and holy, becoming the people of God's own choosing. For holiness and biblical faithfulness are the true measures of the church.

The church—the body of God's people—has little to do with slick marketing or fancy facilities. It has everything to do with the people and the Spirit of God in their midst. What matters is the *character* of the community of faith.

This has been pointedly portrayed in Eastern Europe, where the people of God clung to their faith in circumstances we can scarcely imagine. They weren't worrying about church growth or feeling good. Folks generally don't when they're staring down the barrels of AK-47s.

# 4

## The Story of the Church: Timisoara

*T*IMISOARA SITS NEXT TO THE BEGA RIVER, and for decades life there has been as drab as its gray waters.

Founded in medieval times, Timisoara was part of the kingdom of Hungary. After World War I, along with the rest of Transylvania, it was annexed by Romania. After World War II, Romania was seized by the Soviet Union. Since then, the university town of Timisoara had grown more and more dreary, until its shops were full of nothing and its faces were full of fear.

In the center of downtown lies a long, rectangular paved mall studded with statues, plots of grass, and beds of flowers. In one of the grassy areas stands a wooden cross surrounded by candles, flowers, and black-and-white photos. It is a shrine to the martyrs of Timisoara, the men and women who died here in December 1989.

The brown, turreted Orthodox cathedral stands at one end of the rectangle. At the other end rises the white, balconied opera house. Buildings with apartments on their upper levels and shops on their first floors line the long sides of the rectangle.

A few blocks from this central square, on a corner across from a tram stop, sits a massive, ugly building. An optician occupies the ground floor on one side of the building; the other side is occupied by the Hungarian Reformed Church. On its gray stone wall two simple wreaths hang next to small plaques proclaiming in four languages: "Here began the revolution that felled a dictator."

Visit Timisoara today and you will notice all this, for Timisoara is no ordinary town. This is where the Romanian revolution began . . . with just a few candles in the darkness. . . .

When the Soviets overran Romania in August 1944, there were only 750 Communists in the entire country. One of them, a short, fleshy-lipped former shoemaker named Nicolae Ceausescu, had just been released from prison, where he had spent much of World War II. He was rewarded for his foresight by being named secretary general of the Union of Communist Youth.

Under young leaders like Ceausescu, Romania's nightmare began. Multiplying like cockroaches, the Communists eliminated the light of opposition any way they could. Students and peasants, pastors and priests—over the years, millions were thrown into prison. Many died there.

Meanwhile, Ceausescu climbed through the party ranks, dreaming of the day Romania would be his. By the early 1970s his dream had come true. He was president of Romania, with the party and the army firmly behind him.

Ceausescu's leadership was marked by his manipulation of Western leaders.[1] To capitalize on the West's Cold War attitudes toward Moscow, he distanced himself from the Soviet Union. But Ceausescu was no moderate Communist leader. Ruling from a kitschy Versailles-style palace in Bucharest, he brutally plundered Romania and reshaped it in his own sick image.

Romania's soil has been called the most fertile in Eastern Europe, yet the Ceausescu government managed to starve its people. While citizens shivered in long lines to buy bread laced with sawdust, the government shipped most of Romania's food abroad. Meat, butter, sugar, oil, and flour were strictly rationed. Vegetables were scarce, citrus fruits nonexistent.

While their people competed for bony chickens and occasional pork knuckles, the Ceausescus and top party officials had difficulty keeping their cholesterol levels in check. A menu from a birthday dinner for Elena Ceausescu made Marie Antoinette seem frugal: three kinds of caviar, pâté de foie gras, filet mignon, roast beef, baby pork, pork chops and pork loin, venison, roast turkey, cornish game hens, pheasant, lobster, frogs' legs, smoked salmon, and three kinds of trout.[2]

When he wasn't choosing which type of caviar to consume, Ceausescu was promoting his pet program of "systematization," which razed thousands of rural villages and transferred their citizens to apartment blocks in designated urban-industrial centers. Raw concrete and exposed joints pockmarked these mid-rise flats that were a warren of dark, tiny rooms and flimsy walls, smelling of sewage and old garbage. Heated by a central system controlled by some sadistic state functionary, the blocks were maintained at about fifty degrees during the winter. Many families had hot water only once a week, and electricity was rationed as well. Forty-watt bulbs were the highest wattage allowed in homes that had current only certain hours a day, and bulbs were removed from the streetlights. At night the roads were utterly black, flanked by worthless steel stalks.

Seeking to fortify his labor force, Ceausescu demanded that all good Romanian families produce five children. "The fetus is the property of the entire society," he decreed. "Anyone who avoids having children is a deserter who abandons the laws of national continuity."[3]

Birthrates increased with his regime, as did infant mortality. Unable to feed their babies, many parents were forced to abandon them. Eventually more than two hundred state-run orphanages dotted Romania, miserable monuments to Ceausescu's most helpless citizens.

Meanwhile the Securitate, a spidery network of secret police that webbed the country, enforced the wretched status quo. An estimated one in four citizens informed for the secret police, who harassed and imprisoned anyone who didn't salute the regime.

But Ceausescu's greatest repressive fervor was reserved for Christians.

He began by gaining control of many in the Romanian Orthodox Church. Deciding that compromise was a reasonable price to pay for existence, many priests and bishops entered the Communist fold. These church officials cleared all activities with the Department of Religious Affairs and reported the names of all who attended services. Priests were required to relate the confidences of their parishioners. Church publications sang the praises of the regime and reprinted words of wisdom from its leaders. Prayers were said for the health and prosperity of the Communist government. The apostle Paul's admonition to the Romans—"be in subjection to the government authorities"—was a favorite verse cited by those in charge.[4]

Over the years, Catholics were suppressed and their churches coopted by the Orthodox majority. Baptists, Adventists, Pentecostals, and other Protestant groups formed a tiny minority among Romania's twenty-three million people; yet the authorities sought to seduce Protestant church leaders as well, assuming that if they could manipulate the shepherd, they could gain control of the flock. Some pastors compromised with the state; others did not. One who did not was a young Reformed pastor named Laszlo Tokes.

Laszlo Tokes, a large, handsome man with a deep, compelling voice, had become pastor of the Hungarian Reformed Church in the center of Timisoara in 1987. His predecessor, Leo Peuker, had pastored the congregation for years and was well known as a government collaborator. Peuker had even worn the red star of Communism on his clerical vestments.

Under Peuker's unsavory blend of church and state, the membership had shrunk to fewer than fifty parishioners. Services had been reduced to ritual. With no catechism, no confirmation class, and no Bible studies, the only time people gathered together was for Sunday morning services or for funeral rites when one of their dwindling number died.

Then early in 1987, while conducting one of those funerals, Peuker himself had a fatal heart attack, and Tokes became "probationary" pastor of the Hungarian Reformed Church. He quickly gained immense popularity, not only with the elderly in his congregation but also with students from the university.

While the Communists weren't particularly concerned about the old people, they did care about the students. Religion should have been irrelevant to this generation coming of age in the last decade of the century of Lenin.

Tokes's superior didn't care for him either. For years Bishop Laszlo Papp had compromised with the authorities, and he didn't appreciate the threat of this young pastor's nonconformity. So Bishop Papp kept a wary eye on Tokes. In spite of this surveillance, however, the young minister would not allow the travesty of a church in name only to continue.

Tokes mourned for his town and his country. The secularism of the atheistic regime had bitten deep into the hearts of the people. Still, he knew the church could help set those hearts on fire. His Reformed faith had given Tokes eyes to see what could happen when the church understood its identity, when the people stopped thinking of their faith as just a Sunday morning ritual and understood that the church was the community of the people of God that could infiltrate the world.[5]

"Now we can start a new phase," Tokes announced to his small congregation. "To do that we need the help of every member of the presbytery and every parishioner. It is not a matter of my being in charge. I am not the only pastor here; we must all be pastors to each other."[6]

Tokes reorganized the church and requested more hymnbooks, more Bibles. Young people were prepared for confirmation. Catechisms were restored. Revitalized worship services celebrated the great festivals of the church calendar.

The authorities were scandalized by his initiatives, but Tokes was actually within the bounds of the Romanian constitution, which officially guaranteed freedom of religion. In practice, of course, the authorities violated that freedom all the time.

In Peuker's old files Tokes found dusty baptismal records of families who had once been part of the church but had dropped away because of the collaborator's empty rites. Tokes invited them back. New converts were baptized. New tithes came in. The celebration of Communion took on new meaning as parishioners remembered the body and blood of Christ and realized that, indeed, the risen Christ was among them.

Within two years, the membership rolls of the Timisoara Hungarian Reformed Church had swelled to five thousand. But the growth was more than numbers; people were being discipled.

As the church body grew, Tokes began to attend to the building itself. The dark old sanctuary echoed with the sounds of hammers and saws as carpenters constructed a new balcony. Growing crowds of worshipers soon tested its strength. People arrived by the tramload, their voices ringing in joyous celebration, singing the great hymns of the faith.

Listening from near and far, both the Securitate and the ecclesiastical superiors knew they could not allow the church to continue like this. Tokes's booming voice proclaiming the Word of God from the pulpit echoed in their minds like a bad dream. There was no place for this passionate Christian faith in Ceausescu's Romania.

Tokes further complicated his case by granting an interview in August 1989 to a Hungarian television station. During the interview he criticized Ceausescu's "systematization" plan. Some fifty thousand citizens of Hungarian descent would be affected, Tokes charged, and this was just another chapter in the Romanian government's repression of Hungarians.

Tokes's statements were broadcast on a Hungarian program called "Panorama," which made its way to Radio Free Europe, the BBC, and other Western radio stations. They, in turn, transmitted the clandestine interview back into Romania. Ceausescu's government was not pleased.

Earlier that year Bishop Papp had accused Tokes of "violating the laws of both church and state" and officially suspended him from ministry. Yet Tokes kept preaching the truth and exposing the lies of the Ceausescu government—and his stubborn congregation kept growing. Worst of all, this sanctimonious upstart was breaking down the walls between churches that the Communists had so carefully erected for their own purposes.

In a spirit of unity, Tokes told his elders, "I want to invite each church to visit us. Not just its priests or clergy, but the whole congregation as well. We will have a Communion festival together. I will preach and so will the visiting priest. There will be hymn singing from both traditions, and we will invite the believers to take part with songs and poems."[7]

For their first such festival, the Hungarian Reformed Church invited the members of the local Catholic parish. Tokes figured that since the Reformed Church had emerged from the Catholic Church, it was only natural that they hold this festival on October 31, the day Martin Luther had launched his Reformation. Both sides of that centuries-old divide would extend their hands to one another.

Immediately after that celebration of unity, the authorities increased their pressure. The secret police had encountered types like Tokes before. Intimidation and repression would take care of the problem.

The methods of the Securitate were anything but subtle. They threatened members of Tokes's church, and parishioners had to run a gauntlet of secret police just to enter the building each Sunday. Once the service began, agents would stand in front of the church cradling machine guns in their arms or dangling handcuffs in front of them. Merely attending church services became a silent act of protest.

Meanwhile, Tokes was denied his ration book; without it he was unable to buy bread, fuel, or meat. Parishioners, who by now had learned the real meaning of fellowship, shared from their own slim resources, smuggling firewood and food to the pastor and his family.

Tokes was also barred from meeting with friends or relatives. Friends used children or old women to carry their messages to Tokes; others were searched by the secret police. His phone was shut off, except for incoming abusive and threatening phone calls for which the secret police then charged him long-distance rates. Afraid for their four-year-old son, Mate, Tokes and his wife, Edith, sent the child to live with relatives.[8]

Their fears were well founded. The Securitate contacted one of Tokes's friends, an architect who had worked on the church balcony construction project, and ordered him to comply with their campaign against the pastor. The architect refused. A few days later his body was found in a Timisoara park. The police termed his death a suicide.

Then Tokes himself was attacked. Four men, their faces concealed behind ski masks, burst into the pastor's small apartment in the church building. Laszlo and Edith happened to have visitors that evening, who helped them fight off the attackers with chairs. The assailants ran away, leaving Tokes bleeding from a knife wound in the face.

Soon after that the secret police must have concluded that killing Tokes would simply make him a martyr. Instead, they would render him ineffective by exiling him to a small, remote village outside of Timisoara. A court ordered his eviction from his home and church, setting the date for December 15, 1989.

On Sunday, December 10, Laszlo Tokes looked out over the upturned faces of his congregation. These Christians had paid a high price to worship, each of them braving the gauntlet of secret police in order to enter the church building, their names noted on the Securitate's endless lists, and their physical lives made more and more miserable by their stand even as their souls grew more and more prosperous.

"Dear brothers and sisters in Christ," Tokes announced, "I have been issued a summons of eviction. I will not accept it, so I will be taken from you by force next Friday. They want to do this in secret because they have no right to do it. Please, come next Friday and be witnesses of what will happen. Come, be peaceful, but be witnesses."[9]

Tokes could see the pain on the faces of the faithful and the smooth, inscrutable looks of the informers sprinkled throughout the congregation.

Five days later, on December 15, 1989, the secret police came to take Laszlo and Edith. They brought a moving van for the Tokeses' belongings, but they never got to load the truck. For massed protectively around the entrance to the church building stood a human shield. Heeding their pastor's call, members of the congregation had come to protest his removal.

Residents of Romania were used to friends and loved ones disappearing in the night, hauled off to prison or interrogation at the whim of the secret police. But on this day a flame of hope sprang up within the crowd. Perhaps they really could prevent their pastor's departure. Perhaps they could make a difference this time.

The brick-and-concrete home of the Hungarian Reformed Church sat directly across from a tram stop. Each time the crowded cars unloaded, passengers could see the people gathered outside the church building.

"What is going on?" they asked. When they learned what was happening, many joined the group. Some were from other churches; some were just curious or supportive onlookers.

Meanwhile, Lajos Varga, a friend of Tokes, began making telephone calls, rallying believers from all over Timisoara—Baptists, Adventists, Pentecostals, Orthodox, and Catholics. And later that day when Tokes opened the window of his flat to talk with the people, he experienced what he called "the turning point in my life."

"These were not only my parishioners, with a few Baptists and Adventists, but Orthodox priests and some of their Romanian flocks. I was very moved," he said, "and it changed what I now see as my old prejudices—that we cannot make common cause, cannot fight side by side. Now that I have seen Romanians, Germans, Catholics, and Orthodox defending me, I know that I have to work for reconciliation between the nationalities and creeds in this country."[10]

He called out in Hungarian and then in Romanian: "We are one in Christ. We speak different languages, but we have the same Bible and the same God. We are one."[11]

Below, the people looked at one another, struck by the truth of his statement. Though hungry and cold, they continued to stand shoulder to shoulder in a semicircle around the church entrance.

Darkness fell, and Timisoara's Communist mayor, Peter Mot, visited Tokes. He could stay on at the church, the mayor said, if the crowd dispersed.

When Tokes shouted this news to the people, someone shouted back, "We don't trust them, Father!"[12]

Then Mayor Mot appeared at the window. "You Romanians, go home," he said, attempting to play on ethnic divisions. "Let the Hungarians be rebellious and stay here!"[13] But his divide-and-conquer strategy did not work.

Adina Jinaru, a Romanian Orthodox believer who lived nearby, looked around her at the great diversity of people joined together to support the Hungarian pastor. The crowd was infiltrated by Securitate agents as well; she could tell by looking into their eyes.

A burly, hearty Baptist pastor named Peter Dugulescu was also part of the crowd, as was Daniel Gavra, a student from Dugulescu's congregation. Gavra made his way through the people toward Dugulescu.

"Look, Pastor," he said, opening his jacket surreptitiously because of the Securitate agents.

The way things were escalating, Dugulescu half-expected to see some sort of weapon. But the lump in Gavra's jacket was a paper packet filled with dozens of candle stubs.

It was past one o'clock in the morning when Tokes opened the window of his apartment a final time before he went to bed. He couldn't believe his eyes. Light from hundreds of candles pierced the darkness. Hands, cupped close to the people's hearts, sheltered the flickering flames, and the flames lighted their faces with a warm glow.

*I do not know where I will be tomorrow or the next day*, Tokes thought. *I know only this moment. And I know that the Spirit of God Himself is with us.*

The extraordinary demonstration continued throughout that night and into the following day. Then, late in the afternoon, the people took the protest a step further than a show of solidarity for Laszlo Tokes. For the first time in their lives, Romanians shouted their secret dreams aloud: "Liberty! Freedom!"[14]

Students began singing a patriotic song that the Communists had banned years before: "Awake, Romania!" And much later, as night fell on December 16, someone began shouting: "Down with Ceausescu! Down with Communism!" Part of the crowd headed downtown to the city square, while the remainder kept guard at Tokes's church.[15]

Before dawn on December 17 the secret police finally made their move and broke through the people. As they did so, Laszlo and Edith took refuge in the church sanctuary near the Communion table. Tokes wrapped himself in his heavy clerical robe and picked up a Bible, holding it like a weapon.

The bolted church door gave way with a splintering crash, and the police swarmed into the building. They beat Tokes until his face was bloody. Then they took him and Edith away into the night.

With their pastor gone, the crowds moved from the Hungarian Reformed Church to the central square of Timisoara. By now armed troops, shields, dogs, and tanks filled the streets. But even with the army in place, the people did not retreat. For this had become a full-scale protest against the intrusion of the state. There was no turning back. The people of Timisoara massed in the city square, shouting and singing. Daniel Gavra and many others distributed candles. And when darkness fell, the people lighted their flames against the night.

The Communists responded with the brute force they had always employed when threatened by freedom seekers. They ordered their troops to open fire on the protesters.

Hundreds were shot. Among them was Gavra. He and a number of other believers marched into the square carrying the new flag of the revolution: Romania's tricolor with its Communist emblem scissored out of the middle. As they marched, Gavra linked arms with a young Pentecostal girl.

The soldiers opened fire, and the girl slipped from his arm. She was dead by the time she hit the pavement. Daniel barely had time to comprehend what had happened when there was another explosion and he fell, his left leg blown away by a barrage of bullets.

In the confusion of the crowds and the darkness, the savage gunfire claimed victim after victim, but the people of Timisoara stood strong. Though shocked at the cost of their stand, they knew there was no middle ground. They had decided to stand for truth against lies, and stand they would.

By Christmas 1989, the world reeled with the results of that stand: Romania was free and Ceausescu was gone. The people of Timisoara rejoiced. Churches filled with worshipers praising God.

A few days after Christmas, Pastor Peter Dugulescu opened the door of the hospital ward where Daniel Gavra had been taken after he was shot. The boy was still recuperating, his wounds bandaged and a stump where his left leg had been. But Daniel's spirit had not been shattered.

"Pastor," he said, "I don't mind so much the loss of my leg. After all, it was I who lit the first candle."[16]

# 5

## *On This Rock*

He cannot have God for his father who does not have the church for his mother.

*Augustine*

$L$ASZLO TOKES LIVED THROUGH THE VIOLENT DAYS that followed his exile and arrest. After the revolution he returned to Timisoara. Bishop Papp fled the country after Ceausescu's fall, and Tokes was appointed to fill his place as bishop of Oradea.

"Without speculating or organizing the whole movement, it was really a miracle," Tokes told us, reflecting on those December days when the people of God came together in unity. "The people moved together and sang together and prayed together and acted together. The Spirit of God was there above our wills and our resistance. We did what was dictated for us by our faith through our conscience."[1]

When the church is the church, as the believers of Timisoara show us, the people of God moved by the Spirit of God do the work of God, and evil cannot stand against them. That is the mandate Jesus put before His followers centuries ago in a beautiful town in the lush area at the foot of Mount Hermon, source of the springs that feed the river Jordan . . .

Many believe it to be the pivotal moment in the great drama recorded in the New Testament—that day the young Nazarene and His disciples arrived in Caesarea Philippi. Strange rumors had swirled about this Jesus ever since the wild-eyed prophet called John the Baptist had thundered the fearsome words: "Repent, for the kingdom of heaven is near."[2] Some even said He might be a king.

This carpenter's son taught the crowds in mysterious parables and bewildering statements like, "Blessed are the poor in spirit." He healed the sick and fed thousands from meager rations. He annoyed and troubled the increasingly restive religious authorities.

Who was this man who was arousing such passions and such controversy in Palestine?

That was the very question Jesus put to His followers that day in Caesarea Philippi: "Who do people say that I am?"

"Some say you are John the Baptist," the disciples replied. "Others say Elijah, and still others believe you are Jeremiah or one of the other prophets."

Then Jesus looked straight into the eyes of these men who had turned from their trades, even their families, to follow Him: "But what about you?" He asked. "Who do you say I am?"

To which the irrepressible Peter replied, "You are the Christ, the Son of the living God."

One can almost imagine a hush in heaven at that moment. The words had been spoken. Soon the whole world would know that the long-awaited day was here. The Messiah had come.

Such faith, Jesus said, could only come from God. "Blessed are you, Simon son of Jonah, for this was not revealed to you by man, but by my Father in heaven."

Jesus' next words, however, are critical for understanding the nature of the Christian faith. For in direct response to Peter's confession, Christ announced: "On this rock I will build my church."

And to that church He promised a vast grant of authority, which He called "the keys of the kingdom of heaven."

"Whatever you bind on earth will be bound in heaven," Jesus said, "and whatever you loose on earth will be loosed in heaven."[3] The church was to be His instrument on earth, and whatever was done in His will would have eternal significance and consequence.

Whether Jesus meant He would build His church upon Peter himself or upon Peter's confession of faith is a point about which Christian traditions disagree. But the critical historical fact remains: Jesus' response to Peter's confession was to announce that He would build His church. And from this declaration we learn four crucial lessons about the church.

***First, the church is not a building. The church is people.*** Just looking at the original Greek text of this passage shatters one of the most widespread misconceptions about the church. *Ekklesia,* the Greek word translated "church" in the New Testament, never refers to a building or a structure. An *ekklesia* was a gathering of people.

Jesus' word choice was well understood by the people of Palestine. For the culture at large, *ekklesia* meant a public assembly of citizens. It was used when they were "called out" of the city to vote. But its Hebrew counterpart also meant the congregation of Israel constituted at Sinai and assembled before the Lord. It meant those whom He brought together and called by His name. The people of God.

Nowhere in the New Testament does anyone say, "Let's go to church," nor is the church referred to as a building, except as a metaphor.[4] All references to the church, including the metaphorical "body" and "holy nation," refer to God's people. As the hymn writer put it:

> The church is not a building,
>   The church is not a steeple,
> The church is not a resting place,
>   The church is a people.[5]

**But it is more than simply a collection of people; it is a new community.** Modern Christians, especially evangelicals, see the Christian faith primarily, if not exclusively, as the gospel of "Jesus and me." Christianity is simply a personal relationship with Jesus. Accept Christ into your life and you will be saved.

This is true as far as it goes, but it falls woefully short. Although we are justified through our faith, Christianity is much more than just a private transaction with Jesus.

When Peter made his confession, Jesus did not say, "Good, Peter. You are now saved and will have an abundant life. Be at peace." Instead, He announced the church and established a divinely ordained pattern. When we confess Christ, God's response is to bring us into His church; we become part of His called-out people. When we become followers of Christ, we become members of His church— and our commitment to the church is indistinguishable from our commitment to Him.

Radical words. For we know many Christians who say they are believers but are not members of a church. By that, some mean that they are not members of a local congregation. But many mean that they do not need the church in any sense.

Yet according to the Scripture, Christianity is corporate. This is why we speak of the body with its different parts, the community of the redeemed, the holy nation and royal priesthood—or, as Carl Henry calls it, "the new society of God's people, the new society of the twice-born."[6]

The church is no civic center, no social club or encounter group, no Sunday morning meeting place. It is a new society, created for the salvation of a lost world, pointing to the kingdom to come.

And if we properly understand the exchange between Peter and Jesus and the rest of Scripture, we come face to face with a truly staggering truth about the nature of this new society: It is so dear to our Lord that He purchased it with His own blood.[7]

If the good people of Riverton Community Church had realized this awesome, terrifying fact, they would have abandoned their petty, self-centered ways and dropped to their knees.

For we are part of the body for which Christ died![8]

***Therefore, the church belongs to God.*** How often have you heard a pastor or a board of elders or deacons say "my church" or "our church"?

Unfortunately, they often mean it. And most congregational squabbles arise over precisely this point: Who owns the church? Who has the authority? Whose church is it anyway?

Early in my Christian life I was invited to give the message, consisting of my testimony, at two Sunday services of a well-known church. The practice was to videotape both services, then choose the better and release it for broadcast the following week.

During the first service something happened that could only be explained as an anointing of the Holy Spirit. I lost all track of time, yet finished exactly as the cue card saying "stop" was raised in front of the camera. I wasn't sure what I had said, but as I closed in prayer, people, without an invitation, knelt in place, tears streaming down their faces. A holy hush came over the congregation.

Afterward, as we waited for the second service to begin, the pastor's assistant began coaching him. When I prayed at the conclusion in the next service, he urged, the pastor should move up beside me, put his arm around my shoulder, look at the camera, and beckon people forward.

The second service was nothing like the first. Aware of the carefully laid plans and the need to repeat "the performance," I was self-conscious, watching the clock. Then as I began my closing prayer, the pastor moved up next to me, slipped his arm around my shoulder, and made a great dramatic gesture toward the congregation . . . and the grinding camera. Nothing happened.

After the service I asked the pastor's assistant to use the first service tape for the television broadcast that week. "No, no," he said, shaking his head. "The second was much better."

I pressed the point, but he kept shaking his head. Finally he put his hand up, palm outward like a cop holding back the traffic. "You don't seem to understand, Mr. Colson," he said. "This is Dr. Showforth's church!"*

How easily we are impressed with ourselves and our own inflated importance. How foolishly we seek our identity in office or position in the church. Where were we when God created His church? We live and breathe and serve at His pleasure. And if it were our church or our ministry, we'd fall miserably short. The instrument for making disciples, for making men and women holy, for the redemption of mankind in human hands? How absurd.

"I will build My church," said Jesus. Those unequivocal words should be posted over the entrance of every church building in the land.

*And the church will triumph.* "The gates of hell will not prevail against it," Jesus promised, giving the assurance of a sovereign God that ultimately His new community of called-out people will triumph over the forces of sin and evil.

But this also has to be taken as a commission. We can't sit back and wait for the final victory; this is a call for the people of God to be a holy people, to stand against evil, and to fulfill their Sovereign's demand for justice and righteousness in the present.

When the people of God understand this commission, then the church becomes the church.

These lessons are clear enough, but they still leave many questions. How do we define this church? To most of us, the church means our own denomination or the congregation where we worship on a Sunday. So how does that relate to what we have just been talking about—this new called-out community of God's people? What's the relationship between the worldwide church and the particular place where we worship? And is everyone sitting in the pews on Sunday morning part of the church?

The word *ekklesia* does not help us with these distinctions because in some places in the New Testament it refers to all of God's people worldwide, in others it designates a local congregation

---

*The pastor's name has been changed.

meeting in a private home, and in some cases it means a collection of representatives of local churches meeting to conduct common business.[9] No distinction is made in Scripture because, unlike modern Christians, the New Testament writers believed that to be part of the church in one aspect was to be part of the church in all aspects.

It is the loss of this New Testament understanding of the comprehensive character of the church in both its spiritual essence and visible manifestations that is at the heart of modern-day confusion. We need to see this character clearly and appreciate its interrelationship if we hope to recapture God's vision for His people.

### The Church Universal

In its essence the church is a spiritual entity, for it is created by God Himself as He works the reality of salvation in those whom He wills. Only God knows who is in this vast invisible cloud of witnesses passing across the ages. And it is universal since He calls men and women from all races, colors, backgrounds, and corners of the globe.

For this reason, Christians, from the earliest creeds onward, have confessed to being part of "one, holy, catholic, apostolic church." This is the body of Christ in the world.

But only by belonging to a visible community of faith can individuals truly make visible the reality of the church.

From the beginning it was clearly God's plan that the Body would be made manifest to the world by gathering into confessing communities to fulfill His mission—that is, to administer the sacraments, preach the Word, and make disciples. Thus, immediately after Pentecost, He established the pattern: Individual believers were to gather into particular communities.

### The Church Particular

When those moved by Peter's powerful sermon asked what they should do, the apostle replied, "Repent and be baptized."[10] Then they would receive the gift of the Holy Spirit, he told them, and would be among those whom the Lord called to Himself—that is, the church. So "those who accepted his message were baptized," not only as a sign of the forgiveness of their sins but also of their entry into the visible church, and then they gathered together for the apostles' teaching, fellowship, breaking of bread, and prayer.[11] This is the normative, biblical pattern by which those redeemed by the saving power of Christ become part of the visible, or how those in the universal become part of the particular.

When Christians in the early centuries gathered together, they became known as the *communio sanctorum,* meaning "the communion of saints."* And they were indeed that, bound together as only men and women could be who were surrounded by an angry, hostile society ready to feed them to the lions. But by manifesting the church, they made visible the mystery of God's salvation, and this witness changed the world.

This is the process by which the visible church has fulfilled its mission and witness to the world through the centuries. It's not unlike an army, where men and women of all sizes and shapes sign up to serve. At the beginning these recruits are one big disorganized mass of humanity, and only the Pentagon knows who they are. Until it is trained and organized, this army is useless. So men and women are assigned to training units to learn the skills and disciplines of soldiers. Then they are stationed into divisions and headquarters and honor guards and counterintelligence, all working together so the army can do its job. Only when it is fully uniformed and deployed can the world see the army at work.

So it is with the church. Its recruitment is universal, but it has to be broken down into visible fighting units. It may have command structures, such as denominations or episcopal government. And it may have special training forces to equip its fighting units: parachurch movements such as Prison Fellowship and Evangelism Explosion and others. These are visible structures we create to enable God's army—the Body—to do the job it is called to do.

### Where Do We Fit?

There is today a widespread belief that one can be a Christian or develop one's own faith system apart from the church. The proposition is ludicrous. For everyone regenerated by God is by definition a part of the universal church. It's not a matter of choice or membership.

---

*As Calvin argued so powerfully, it is this—the communion of the saints—which is the true expression of our invisible essence, not the mere ritual or routine participation in external forms (see Calvin's *Institutes,* 4.1.9–12).

And following the pattern made normative in the Book of Acts, each believer is to make his or her confession, be baptized, and become part of a local congregation with all of the accountability that implies.[12] So membership in a church particular is no more optional than membership in the church universal.

Unfortunately it is not uncommon for Christians to drift from congregation to congregation, usually where their friends lead them or where the pastor happens to give the most satisfying message. Many have no sense of roots or responsibility, and some never even join a local church.

As we noted earlier, commitment to the church is at an all-time low, particularly among evangelicals, who frequently are more concerned with an individual's personal experience or Christian jargon or even political views than with his or her church commitment. The latter would, in fact, be the last thing most would use as a spiritual yardstick.

Yet membership in a confessing body is fundamental to the faithful Christian life. Failure to do so defies the explicit warning not to forsake "our assembling together."[13] His understanding of this prompted Martin Luther to say, "Apart from the church, salvation is impossible."[14] Not that the church provides salvation; God does. But because the "saved" one can't fulfill what it means to be a Christian apart from the church, membership becomes the indispensable mark of salvation.

"So highly does the Lord esteem the communion of His church," Calvin wrote, "that He considers everyone a traitor and apostate from religion who perversely withdraws himself from any Christian society which preserves the true ministry of the word and sacraments."[15]

Those are strong words. But if, as we will later argue, it is impossible to fulfill the Great Commission apart from the church particular, if apart from the church particular one cannot participate in the ordinances or sacraments, then one cannot claim to be a Christian and at the same time claim to be outside the church. To do so is at the least hypocrisy—at the worst, blasphemy. And if the purpose of the church is to herald and point to the coming kingdom of God, as both Protestant scholars and Vatican Council II agree it is, then the Christian life must be rooted in community; for the kingdom to which it points is itself the ultimate community.

Which is why writer Warren Wiersbe says he does not attend church to hear a sermon or to have fellowship, though he enjoys both, but "to bear witness that Jesus Christ is alive and worship Him."[16]

There is, as Neuhaus puts it, "no Christianity apart from the historical community that bears its truth."[17] Therefore, our understanding of this community shapes our view of ministry, accountability, and Christian duty. Failure to understand this is the root cause of much of the identity crisis we spoke of earlier—and one good reason why less than 10 percent of those who say they are Christians are living what they say they believe.

To deal with this identity crisis, Christians must also understand the need for the universal and the particular to support each other.

When someone is converted and thereby comes into the church universal, *the first step of discipleship* is membership in the church particular. It is the duty of those who are involved with new converts to guide them not just into a Bible study or fellowship group but into a local church where the Word is taught and sacraments administered.

But the other side of the coin is equally important: The church particular must in every sense feel and behave as a part of the church universal. Often evangelicals—Pentecostals and Baptists in particular—fail to understand this reciprocal duty. Just look at the number of congregations that include "independent" in their name. Although they are signaling their independence from any denomination or ecclesiastical structure, the name often suggests that they are independent from the rest of the Body. And some actually come to see themselves that way as they jealously guard their own views on doctrine or practice.

Of course, as we will discuss later, believers and congregations should stand for what they believe to be biblical truth and defend their view of liturgy or sacraments or eschatology or other matters upon which Christians honestly differ. And there may even be occasions when believers, to remain faithful to their confession, must separate themselves from those who renounce the truth or are clearly apostate.

The overarching fact, however, is that one cannot be part of a body God has created and at the same time declare that one is "independent" of that body. It is to deny what God Himself has ordained.

All Christians are in one body—the church universal. These believers then become the visible church as they become part of local congregations—the church particular—which may be structurally independent or part of an episcopal government or denominational fellowship. The whole equals the sum of the parts. All neat and tidy. All clear and uncomplicated? Right?

Unfortunately, no. In practice it just doesn't work that way. Look out over any congregation on any Sunday morning and you will find lukewarm believers, cultural Christians (those who were born in America and, believing it to be a Christian country, go to church occasionally and thus call themselves Christian), and even a sprinkling of New Agers (maybe more than a sprinkling these days). There will be some seekers, some reprobates, and those who with all their heart confess Christ—all mixed together. And we call it the church. No wonder we face confusion confounded!

### The Church of Faith and the Church of Fact

This is the great tension. On the one hand, there is the church God has created and intends for ultimate consummation. The bride of Christ. Spotless, pure, and holy. Bathed in a radiant glow and waiting at the altar for the Bridegroom.[18]

Then there is the present reality. Little congregations and vast denominations meeting in white wooden chapels and grand glass cathedrals. Street-corner preachers, Salvation Army bell-ringers, and television orators who promise miracles for dollars. And most of them spend much of the time either bickering or ignoring each other. This church, the one the world sees, resembles nothing so much as a gigantic flea market with the vendors competing against one another, hawking their wares in a huge, discordant din.

It is the distinction between the theological and the sociological, the Spirit and the institution; what some have called the church of faith versus the church of fact.[19] What fallen man has created.*

Messy, ambiguous, imperfect? Sure it is. There is no perfect or model church. But we should not despair—for at least two reasons.

First, tensions allow for a variety of expressions which, often confounding human wisdom, reach people who might not otherwise be reached.

---

*From the beginning Christians have recognized that the true church could not be measured by its externals. Augustine made this point, observing that it was well known that many unbelievers shared with members of Christ's body in the sacrament (see Augustine's *City of God* 1.35).

There is richness in our diversity that strengthens the overall witness of the church. Different confessions, because of their own emphasis, make differing aspects of the spiritual reality visible. Historically, for example, Protestants have done a better job of making visible the spiritual reality of the Word in preaching, while Catholics have better made visible the spiritual reality of worship.

But there's a second and even more important reason. The great scholar John Courtney Murray, who believed "religious pluralism is against the will of God," was forced to acknowledge that it is "the human condition; it is written into the script of history." The institutional church, like all other institutions, comes under the influence of the Fall. But as Murray and many others have recognized, this dynamic may well save us all from the one fate worse than chaos: triumphalism.[20] That is, the very real temptation to believe that we have all of the truth, thus confusing ourselves with the kingdom of God.

As has been said, the church is like Noah's ark: The stench inside would be unbearable if it weren't for the storm outside. This is the church we have. And as imperfect and even repugnant as we find it at times, we need to acknowledge that it is through this church of fact that truth is being proclaimed and portrayed.

Not always clearly; not always unequivocally. I cringe when a church leader does some dumb or dreadful thing. I want to scream that the National Council of Churches isn't speaking for me (and it isn't). But somehow through all of the muddle, the message is kept alive. People often come to church for all the wrong reasons, but God touches them, and nearly apostate churches are resurrected. God does it, using us just as we are.

The church of fact is always struggling to conform to the church of faith, and the Christian must live in the midst of this tension—a faithful part of the universal and the particular, of the visible and invisible, of the faith and the fact.

Admittedly, the pettiness and failures, the division and discord, can be disheartening at times. What a sorry mess we mortals often make of things in the name of the church! But our comfort comes from God's promise that He will build His church—sometimes in extraordinary ways, as the story of a young Russian girl so gloriously illustrates.

# 6

## *I Will Build My Church*

$\mathcal{S}$HE WAS TEN YEARS OLD, A STURDY CHILD with tendrils of thick, brown hair escaping from a tightly woven braid. At the moment her dark eyes were focused beyond the dirty windows of her classroom. Outside, the steely sky swirled with tiny snowflakes, a rarity in the seaside city of Odessa.

Rocking back and forth at her wooden desk, wrapping one leg around the other, Irina Ratushinskaya could not keep her eyes on the teacher. Snow in Odessa! It was more precious than bread. If you waited in line long enough, you could always get a stale loaf or two. But snow was different. The stalls of the market merchants and the shelves of the miserable stores would always be bare of such magic, no matter how long you waited.

Snowballs! Forts! Scoops of snow licked from a worn woolen mitten! As she watched the flakes fall, Irina's chest tightened. Soon it would all be gone, the mysterious white lace melting away, leaving only the everyday brown of Odessa. All because she and her classmates were stuck in a boring drift of lectures.

This was atheist instruction time, and attendance was compulsory; for in Nikita Krushchev's Soviet Union, young minds represented the best hope for the future. Two years earlier, the 1961 Cuban missile crisis had nearly brought the world to nuclear confrontation, establishing the huge stakes of the superpower standoff. Krushchev saw education as the tool that would forge the eventual ideological triumph of the Soviet Union. Instructors who wanted to be part of that glorious future had to vigilantly stamp out the tiresome myths that, in spite of forty-six years of Communist indoctrination, refused to melt away.

Already Irina and her classmates had been told about a Baptist woman who had roasted her child in an oven. It seemed implausible to Irina. After all, "Auntie" Vera, the janitor at her grandparents' flat, was a Baptist, and her children were alive and well. Then the seventh graders had performed a play depicting priests as oafs and fools.

Everyone seemed to be against God: the Young Pioneers, the teachers, the headmaster, the speakers on the radio—the whole country. It didn't seem fair. Even in schoolyard games they were not allowed to gang up on one person. Also, it seemed odd that they all pitched such a furious battle against someone they said didn't exist anyway.

Today Irina was wondering, as she often had, why the teacher even bothered with the truckloads of words she was dumping from the front of the room. "God doesn't exist," the instructor said again. "Only silly, ignorant old women believe in Him."

*Can't they tell they are giving themselves away?* thought Irina. *Adults tell you there are no gremlins or ghosts. They tell you once or twice, and that's it. But with God, they tell you over and over again. So He must exist—and He must be very powerful for them to fear Him so greatly.*

With that logic firmly in mind, she returned to what was foremost in her mind at the moment. The snow.

*Okay, God, if You did not exist, we wouldn't have to listen to this lecture. So it's Your fault we're sitting here missing the snow. If You're so powerful, make it keep snowing![1]*

That was Irina Ratushinskaya's first prayer. And white flakes fell like manna for three days from Odessa's gray skies, the city's largest snowfall in sixty years. School was canceled, and Irina and her friends galloped down the wide avenues, throwing snowballs and relishing the fresh crystals that fell so softly on their faces. As she felt the gentle, melting kisses from heaven, Irina thought about this God her teachers denied, the One who could make snow fall from official Communist airspace.

She began to talk to Him secretly, late at night, asking endless questions. Not politely, but with passion and fervor. Was He kind?

*If He is not kind, I don't want to have anything to do with Him, even if He is all-powerful.* But if He was kind, but not all-powerful, then she didn't want to depend on Him either. What good was a God who was not powerful?

And though she conversed with Him, Irina felt it improper to ask God for anything.

*What have I ever done for Him that I should expect any favors? Why should He intercede in our earthly life if we have decided that we can manage without Him? After all, here I am living in an atheistic country and doing nothing about it, so how can I start demanding that God do this or that?*

*In fact, if I do have a complaint, it's that I don't know what He wants from me. This is through no fault of mine, when all is said and done; I had no choice about where to be born. . . .*

Yet the moment she thought this, an answer seemed to echo from within: *Don't worry, you will find out what you need to know when the time comes.*[2]

Irina's reasoning served her well for the next few years, and when she was fourteen, a pivotal, though seemingly insignificant, event occurred—an epiphany reminiscent of Augustine's famous agony over his youthful prank of stealing pears from a neighbor's tree.

At the end of a long, dreary history lesson, when the teacher left the students alone for a few minutes, one of Irina's classmates heaved a chestnut across the room. The large nut crashed into an inkwell, which smashed on the floor, which splashed a huge splatter of black ink on a nearby wall.

Hearing the commotion, the teacher came running back into the room.

"Who broke the inkwell?" she shrieked.

Silence.

The interrogation continued, with each student being questioned, one by one, by a senior teacher. When Irina's turn came, she put on her most agreeable, obedient face and began to lie with gusto, throwing in the detail that she had been searching for something in her satchel on the floor and hadn't seen anything.

After hearing Irina's testimony, the grand inquisitor moved on to the next student, Seryozha, who looked the teacher straight in the eye and said bluntly, "I'm not going to tell you."

His example pierced Irina's conscience, and much later that evening as she made her way home in the dark, she thought, *I am becoming what THEY want me to be—a cowardly, spineless creature, with no concept of honor, but ever obedient. . . . One who considers a glib lie to be an act of heroism. . . . Can it be that for me, the means now justifies the end? . . .*

*I shall never, ever lower myself like that again before anybody,* she vowed. *If I must disobey in order to preserve my self-respect, then I shall do so openly. . . . I'll learn how to behave decently from books, and also I'll think a lot and talk to God more. Then my soul will remain my own: Nobody will be able to manipulate me to suit themselves.*[3]

From that point on, instinctively knowing that she would become a servant to one master or another, Irina chose her side, with a code of behavior far different than the communist masters desired. As she explored the great Russian books lining her parents' bookshelves—for her mother was a teacher of literature—she found an enormous variety of situations and epochs, but a striking similarity among the characters' inner conditions and the situations in which life placed them.

In the writings of Dostoevsky, Pushkin, Turgenev, and Tolstoy she found a reflection of the God whom she knew was kind and all-powerful. The values of good and evil did not change, but seemed somehow to be written on the souls of men and women, regardless of their culture or training.[4]

As Irina contemplated the reflections of God and His invisible laws of human nature that she had found both in her own conscience and in the literature she loved, she wondered how she would respond to future tests. Would she compromise the straight for the crooked or trade truth for a lie? *What kind of times will I live in when I grow up?* she mused. *What kind of orders will be issued to me?*[5]

Adolescence brought its inevitable assaults of hormones and doubt. Bewildered to find herself transformed from a confident child into a gangling, spotty-faced gargoyle, Irina's childlike faith in God became more complicated. Suddenly her beloved books offered no solace, and she had no way to get a Bible.

Pushkin told her the truth lay in Russian Orthodoxy; Tolstoy's theories confused her. *Maybe I'm not a Christian at all,* she thought. *After all, I know so little about Christ. Just a few quotes here and there, picked up from various books, not enough to form a complete picture of Him. There's nobody trustworthy to ask, either.*

One night as she agonized over her faith, she was gripped by a familiar urge—the fury of a poem coming on. She crept quietly from her narrow bed to the cold communal kitchen her family shared with others and scribbled out the essence of her pursuit of God:

How the road to Him to find?
With what the hope and pain to measure?
People seek a God who's kind.
God grant they find, and trust, and treasure.

Later, as an adult, she would see both the amateur nature of the poem's construction as well as the sophistication of its search. But even at that point it was not a quest without comfort, for as she traced the words with her stubby pencil, she felt a benevolent eye looking over her shoulder: *I shivered despite a delicious warmth, for I knew whose glance it was. He had not abandoned me. He was with me. And He didn't mind that I couldn't pray properly.*[6]

When Irina was twenty-three years old she obtained her first Bible. A Jewish friend emigrating to the United States gave her an eighteenth-century volume of the Scriptures printed in Old Church Slavonic. Eagerly she spent a month and a half learning the ancient, intricate alphabet printed on the delicate, thin pages. Then, finally, she was able to read the Old and New Testaments.

> All the revelations I had either guessed or read about else-where fell into place, like the pieces of a jigsaw puzzle. I realized that yes, I am a Christian, and my loving God confirms that it is so, and not otherwise! Russian literature, which had earlier saved my young soul from rejection and pride, confirms the same. But I did not experience the typical zeal of a neophyte: there is one God for all, for all faiths except paganism. Is it for us, humans, to try to carve Him up amongst ourselves? He will show the way, He will instruct: for we are all His children.[7]

In time Irina matured from these first unformed reflections on her newly discovered faith. Meanwhile, in the world outside her mind and heart, the comparative thaw of the Krushchev years had brought about a counterreaction. By 1965 an iron yoke again choked the nation; by 1967, when Leonid Brezhnev came to power, there was a sustained, systematic persecution of those flocking to underground dissident groups. By 1983 Yuri Andropov, the former chief of the KGB who had so cruelly orchestrated the crushing of Hungary in 1956, reigned over the structures of the Soviet Union.

Human rights activists, religious dissidents, and other free-thinking citizens met in cells deep beneath that outward structure, and by this time Irina's poetry was well-known to those whose re-solve it steeled. It was known as well to the KGB, and the secret police targeted her work as "anti-Soviet" since it celebrated Christian faith and human rights rather than the Communist regime. She was arrested.

Irina, now twenty-eight, was sentenced to seven years hard labor and seven years internal exile and sent to the Barashevo labor camp in Mordovia, part of the Soviet Union's notorious Gulag.

The Communist authorities had not changed, and the lessons Irina had learned as a schoolgirl served her well. Fortified by her Christian convictions, she refused to compromise with those who would have her exhibit a servile obedience by ratting on fellow prisoners, making a false confession, or praising the regime.

Despite their cruel attempt to kill her with cold and starvation, Irina survived, thin and frozen. But her soul, nourished by the peace of God and love for her fellow inmates, suffered no deprivation.

Her poetry flourished as well. She wrote verses in her head during KGB interrogations, and woke in the night with her heart ablaze to commit new lines to memory. Much like one of her heroes, Aleksandr Solzhenitsyn, she recorded her writing on tiny bits of paper that would one day emerge from the Gulag to tell her story.

Human rights groups and Christians in the West eventually raised an outcry over Irina's case, and in 1986, two days before Mikhail Gorbachev's Reykjavik summit with Ronald Reagan, she was released. But the KGB still monitored her every move, as well as her husband's, until they managed to make their way to the West and freedom.

Irina's first book, *Grey Is the Color of Hope,* detailed her life in the camps; her second, *In the Beginning,* traced her early life and influences, telling how a girl in an officially atheistic country, deprived of Bible or Christian training, found Christ and became part of the Orthodox Church. Her own story, she said, was the tale of an entire generation: young Soviets who saw through the lies of their elders and, much to their leaders' dismay, turned to God and the church.

Irina Ratushinskaya spent much of her prison term in solitary confinement, and it was there she first recorded an astounding sensation—something she felt not just once, but many times. After her release she compared notes with other Christian prisoners and found that they had experienced the same phenomenon. It came much as the presence of God had manifested itself to her as a child: the benevolent eye looking over her shoulder, the sense of delicious warmth in a freezing land. It was the comfort of God's presence with her, sharing her suffering, assuring her of His love.

After her release, Irina discovered that thousands of Christians—parts of the body of Christ all over the world—had been praying for her, standing before God's throne in solidarity with her, petitioning Him for her. She related the effects of those prayers in her book, *Pencil Letter:*

> Believe me, it was often thus:
> In solitary cells, on winter nights
> A sudden sense of joy and warmth
> And a resounding note of love.
> And then, unsleeping, I would know
> A-huddle by an icy wall:
> Someone is thinking of me now,
> Petitioning the Lord for me.
> My dear ones, thank you all
> Who did not falter, who believed in us!
> In the most fearful prison hour
> We probably would not have passed
> Through everything—from end to end,
> Our heads held high, unbowed—
> Without your valiant hearts
> To light our path.

# 7

## *The Sin of Presumption*

Win Over 10 Percent of Your City's Total Population to Jesus on
ONE DAY!!

*Advertisement in* Religious Broadcasting

*H*OW DOES GOD BUILD HIS CHURCH? Does He orchestrate snowfalls for brown-eyed girls in atheistic countries? Does He bury Himself in the pages of books the Communists forgot to ban? Is He inevitably and irrefutably evident in the frantic denials of those who fear His rule? Does creation itself reveal "the road to Him to find"?

New life in the Spirit is conceived in the secret place of the soul, hidden from human eyes. This is the wonder and mystery of God's regeneration of men and women. And never in this life will we quite know how God calls His people to Himself.

What we do know is that the wind of the Spirit blows where He wills. We hear the sound, we see the evidences, but we know not how this mysterious breath of God touches human hearts. God builds His church in the most unlikely ways and places, stirring the convictions of the heart, bringing men and women to the knowledge of sin, to repentance, to the Savior Himself—and knitting them together in His body.

In spite of all this, Irina's inspiring story can be troubling to some. After all, she did not learn about Christ in an evangelistic crusade and "make a decision"; she did not read a tract that opened her eyes of faith; she never went to Sunday school or youth fellowship; she did not grow up in a Christian home where she learned the Bible in family devotions; she never heard the gospel preached, never had a friend give her the "Four Spiritual Laws." For many years she did not even have a Bible.

Many, particularly in evangelical ranks, believe that a person must have an experience that fits a certain pattern: The individual must know the precise moment he or she prayed "the sinner's prayer" and be able to recount that dramatic experience of "accepting Christ"—words that are almost liturgical to some.

For me, that expectation proves no problem. God intervened in my life powerfully, in a moment I will never forget. Witnessed to by faithful friends and humbled by the Spirit, in a flood of tears I surrendered my life to Jesus Christ in words that fit the pattern. For others, it's not that way.

After my much-publicized conversion, Christian brothers and sisters used to swarm around Patty whenever she accompanied me to public events. "And when were you born again, Mrs. Colson?" they would ask, eager for another gripping conversion story.

At first this drove Patty to tears, causing her at times to avoid such occasions. To this day it sometimes sets her teeth on edge.

"I don't know," she would reply. "All I know is I believe deeply."

Her pursuers would shrink away, and more than once were heard to say, "Poor Mr. Colson. His wife isn't born again."

But Patty, like Ruth Graham and millions of others, cannot pinpoint a precise moment or sudden awakening. She grew up in a Christian home, always attended worship services, can never remember a moment when she didn't believe, and in recent years she has experienced an ever-deepening relationship with Christ.

For some the salvation formula has almost become a procedure whereby one makes a simple choice, as simple as walking through the right door. A few years ago I attended a service where a young evangelist displayed this attitude.

When it was time for the altar call, he strode across the platform to the congregation's left and drew an imaginary circle with a great sweep of his arms.

"In here," he explained, "is self on a chair. Go ahead. Draw it out in your own mind." Heads were nodding all around me.

Then he moved to the center of the platform and, with a grand dramatic gesture, created a second circle.

"And in this," he intoned, "is a chair, and above it is a cross. Man you see is reaching up to God, but He isn't there. Man is still on the throne himself." Now scattered "amens" erupted from the pews.

With deliberation he then walked to the right and drew yet another circle. By this time his words were flowing rhapsodically.

"And in here," he said, his voice breaking momentarily, "is the entrance to the kingdom of God."

Then with great emotion he called people to come forward to walk through the third circle to enter into the very presence of God Himself.

And come forward they did, as if in cadence with his words, "Come, come, all ye who are heavy laden, come into My kingdom. The third circle. Experience the forgiveness of your sins and the blessings of God." Dozens were at the altar by the time he finished a lengthy invitation that left even the choir exhausted.

It was a mesmerizing performance, and I said a quiet prayer of thanks that this young man was not Jim Jones, that he was faithful to Scripture, that he loved God and had a heart for the lost. Probably many who came forward that day were saved and the angels rejoiced. But no doubt many also left the service believing that becoming a Christian is as simple as walking through an imaginary circle and uttering a prayer—or, that walking through that circle is *the way*, perhaps the only way, into the kingdom of God.

Over the past twenty years I've been in countless crusades and have seen thousands of people raise their hands, signifying decisions for Christ. I've seen them come forward and heard them utter the correct words. I've called them to do so myself and have seen the numbers tallied. Unfortunately, often what we are witnessing is nothing more than a "human" conversion.

Days later only a handful of those "converts" show up for Bible studies. Or they behave as Christians for a time, but eventually fall back to their old ways. And we encourage this whenever we establish our method, any method, as *the way* into the kingdom, or lead people to believe that simply uttering certain words will assure their salvation. It is a dangerous delusion. For there is a great difference between a decision and a true conversion. Conversion is a process which begins with God's regenerating work—an instant when the Spirit gives life—and continues as we grow in faith through the process of sanctification.

So does this mean we should abandon all tracts and banish the sinner's prayer? Not at all. I have led many in the sinner's prayer and will continue to do so. In Prison Fellowship we frequently use the "Four Spiritual Laws" and recommend Evangelism Explosion and similar evangelistic programs. They are very useful techniques for presenting the Good News and explaining the gospel.

But they are precisely that—techniques. They are neither sacred steps to salvation nor reliable rubrics that assure God will work in some preprogrammed way. Nor are they the exclusive way into the kingdom.

Some knowledge of spiritual truth is in every human heart.[1] There is no such thing as an atheist. Those we call atheists are actually people fleeing from the truth--usually rebelling, not on intellectual grounds, but on moral grounds. Refusing to submit themselves, they exchange the truth for a lie and are dead in their sins.

But God works as He wills to overcome our rebellion. Like the wind that blows through the trees, He can neither be seen nor directed. He touches the heart. He breathes through snowflakes. The point is, *He* does it. *He* calls people to Himself, conceiving the new life in the Spirit in the secret place of the soul. He does so through one mediator between God and man, Jesus Christ.

The belief that there is but one method or formula by which we enter the kingdom is what we call the sin of presumption: presuming to know the mind of God and to program by human means who is or is not secure in the faith and hence in the church.

This mind-set is not only presumptuous, it's patronizing. Once when I was scheduled to address an evangelistic outreach gathering, the host gave me a single-spaced, typed sheet with the instructions that this was the precise script I was to use in the invitation.

I assured the man that I had given invitations hundreds of times and would feel most comfortable—and effective—using my own words to encourage people to commit their lives to Christ. But the man insisted that his script be followed.

Did he want me to just stop at the end of my message and read it? I asked. No reply.

But during our time of prayer together before the service, the host asked God to wipe my mind clear of anything I had prepared and replace it with His (the Lord's, I assumed) words.

I had worked on my talk for days, praying that God would give me the appropriate message. This man's prayer for God to expunge all that struck me as presumptuous at best. I bit my lip and prayed silently that God would not allow me to be sidetracked by this kind of manipulation.

In the end, I did not read his script. But people responded to the invitation to follow Christ, and I believe that many people met Him that day.

When we regard our own methodology as normative, we eventually question the faith of those who do not conform to it.

This presumption, so contrary to biblical teaching, is a major cause of the disunity that plagues and cripples the witness of the church.[2] And it is all the more dangerous because it often begins with the noblest of motives: the desire that others will experience what we have. Unfortunately it can soon become harshly judgmental and can even result in writing off entire denominations or traditions.

I can't tell you how many letters I've received over the years protesting my use of Mother Teresa as an example of holy living. Many even suggest that I visit her so I can give her the plan of salvation. To me this reaction is astounding. How could anyone deny this woman's faithful witness? Certainly no one who has been in India and seen the incredible impact she has had upon millions of Hindus. Because of Mother Teresa, they revere the word *Christian*, even though proselytizing is against the law in that country. Who knows how many souls have come into the kingdom through her witness and the worldwide fame she has earned but never sought? And while, to my regret, I haven't met Mother Teresa, friends of mine who have tell me of her total, single-minded devotion to Jesus as Lord and Savior.*

---

*For anyone questioning Mother Teresa's Christian commitment, I would recommend reading Malcolm Muggeridge's *Confessions of a Twentieth-Century Pilgrim* (New York: Harper & Row, 1988), esp. 138–39. Reprinted here for edification is one of Mother Teresa's letters to Malcolm Muggeridge:

> I think, dear friend . . . I understand you better now. I'm afraid I could not answer your deep suffering. I don't know why, but you are to me like Nicodemus (who came to Jesus under cover of night), and I'm sure the answer is the same. "Unless you become a little child."
>
> I'm sure you will understand beautifully everything—if you'd only become a little child in God's hands. Your longing for God is so deep and yet He keeps Himself away from you. He must be forcing Himself to do so because He loves you so much as to give Jesus to die for you and for me. Christ is longing to be your food. Surrounded with fullness of living Food, you allow yourself to starve.
>
> The personal love Christ has for you is infinite—the small difficulty you have regarding the church is finite. Overcome the finite with the infinite. Christ has created you because He wanted you. I know what you feel—terrible longing with dark emptiness—and yet He is the one in love with you. I do not know if you have seen these few lines before, but they fill and empty me:
>
>> My God, my God what is a heart
>> That Thou shouldst so eye and woo
>> Pouring upon it all Thy heart
>> As if Thou hadst nothing else to do.

Many who have written do not sound very Christian themselves. Often there is a tone of outrage, and many quote a Christian leader to whom in the course of an interview Mother Teresa supposedly expressed some universalist statements. "Thus," they write, "she cannot be saved." When I finally attempted to track down the facts, I learned that the leader referred to denies that the episode ever happened. But rumors never let facts stand in their way, so this one lives on, and the letters keep coming to my office.

Some are downright vitriolic: "How dare you hold up someone who does not speak our language"—that is, our evangelical jargon—"someone who does not proclaim the gospel." *Proclaim the gospel?* She not only proclaims the gospel often in public messages, she proclaims it with her life. In responding to these diatribes, I often add my favorite quote from Francis of Assisi: "Preach the gospel all the time; if necessary use words."

One correspondent reacted to my use of this statement, sending me a sixteen-page treatise on why Francis himself could not have been a Christian. I confess that in exasperation I suggested that the man might make better use of his time building the kingdom rather than questioning the salvation of someone who died almost eight hundred years ago.

The sin of presumption is consuming. It's amazing how much time people spend judging those whose views or church traditions might differ from their own. This quickly leads to arrogance and lovelessness and inevitably divides the Body, grieving the heart of God.

This is not to suggest that the believer should not be discerning or challenge others when necessary. There are clear biblical warrants for doing this.[3]

Certainly there are those who claim to be Christian but clearly are not. Many New Agers, for example, call themselves Christians because they claim to believe in Jesus, though for them He is but one of the many manifestations of a pantheistic god. And there are those who live in egregious error, embracing a false faith and ignoring the truth. Others who claim to be Christians live in stubborn, unrepentant sin and need to be called to account. (More about that accountability later.) Indeed there is widespread apostasy within the church, within whole denominations in fact, which any Christian should challenge.

This may sound confusing, perhaps even contradictory. On the one hand, we seem to be arguing, as Calvin did, that we can't know for certain who God has called as His people. So maybe we are supposed to accept everyone? On the other hand, there is a biblical mandate to be discerning, to flee apostasy and lovingly confront those in our midst who are not professing or living the truth.

The answer is neither universalism nor judgmentalism. And admittedly it means walking the razor's edge.

The means by which men and women are saved and come into the church cannot be reduced to human formulas that put God into our own little box. As Carl Henry said recently, "Not even evangelicals can straitjacket the Holy Spirit." But Jesus did teach His disciples that they would be known by the fruit of their lives.[4] So the evidence of one's faith is a good measure of whether he or she is indeed part of the church of faith, and it is our duty to be discerning about that.

Another distinction that may be helpful is between the church universal and the church particular. The universal body, as we've noted, is solely the work of God. Who are we to question, let alone know, whom He calls? He has the people of His own choosing in every nation of every color and political persuasion and from every confessing tradition.

But on the particular level there is a human element. Individuals commit to one another to form a local, visible, confessing congregation in order to fulfill the purpose of the church. It is within that community that we worship and study and participate in the ordinances and sacraments. There we can, as we will discuss later, insist upon doctrinal agreement, including many of the methods and practices we follow. Within that body which we help to create we have a clear biblical warrant to hold each other accountable for faithfulness in confession and living.

Ultimately, of course, the sin of presumption hardens hearts and destroys the unity of the body. It sets Christian against Christian, denomination against denomination until we forget whose church this really is.

And nothing is more destructive of our communion, regardless of its cause, than disunity. In fact, it can even be downright dangerous, as some folks in a peaceful Boston suburb discovered.

# 8

## *Extending the Right Fist of Fellowship*

*I*T WAS THE RIGHT HOOK THAT GOT HIM. Pastor Waite might have stood in front of the Communion table trading punches with head deacon Ray Bryson all morning had not Ray's fist caught him on the chin two minutes and fifteen seconds into the fight. Waite went down for the count at the altar where most members of Emmanuel Baptist had first declared their commitment to Christ.

Donald Waite's navy blue, three-piece worsted was almost impossible to wrinkle, but two of his front teeth were so loose that he would have trouble with corn on the cob for the next three summers. Ray Bryson's hand was broken in two places. Some of the townspeople dubbed him Sugar Ray after that Sunday, but never to his face.

Nothing in the history of this rather typical New England community on the outskirts of Boston could have prepared them for the Sunday morning donnybrook. After all, the days of the Boston Tea Party were far behind them.

Many at Emmanuel Baptist traced their ancestry back to a Christian group known simply as "those who follow the Holy Way." Protective of their own and unyielding on questions of either their pilgrim ancestry or the inerrancy of Scripture, those in the Holy Way had built the town of Newton from a farming village into a thriving suburb by the end of the Second World War. Guarding the Christian faith from the forces of compromise and worldliness was their generational watchword.

But none of the town's founders could have anticipated the massive ethnic and religious reshaping of Newton in the second half of the twentieth century. The Jewish population grew dramatically, and the Baptist population began to shrink. Emmanuel tried to stem the tide with a bus ministry. Eventually four bright blue buses toured the area each Sunday displaying the church slogan, "God Is with US at Emmanuel Baptist Church."

Attendance rose for a few years. But gradually more and more banquet space in town was reserved for bar mitzvahs, and the plan to build a larger sanctuary at Emmanuel was put on hold. Temple Beth Shalom even began beating Emmanuel regularly in the church softball league.

No one anticipated the retirement of Pastor George Linheart either. He had pastored Emmanuel Baptist for twenty-five years, guiding the faithful through change and challenge, preaching with conviction on temperance, television, and the Trinity.

The pulpit committee searched the Northeast for five months before deciding to call Donald Waite as their new pastor. Waite was a fourth-generation New Englander, with ancestors who had been Baptists before the Great Awakening. He was fresh out of a Navy chaplaincy and wore his dress whites to the interview. His spit-shined shoes were reflective black pools, and each button on his coat glimmered like real gold. Donald's wife, Flora, owned an impressive collection of hats, some displaying large ornamental flowers. She spoke only when spoken to and carried a purse large enough to bail water. In a town that thrived on the salty air of Boston harbor, the Navy uniform inspired confidence and the hats were a source of fascination and some amusement.

The Waites settled into the parsonage just before Christmas, and the new pastor started his pulpit ministry with a series of sermons on "Submitting to Pastoral Care and Leadership." He also began a visitation program, calling on the church members in their homes. Appreciating his eagerness to get acquainted, the members hospitably scheduled their pastor for a luncheon, a dinner, or an afternoon tea.

Every host or hostess asked the same question: "Pastor, is there anything you need?" And each time Pastor Waite made the same request.

"Since I'm new to the flock," he would say, leaning back in his chair, "anything that you could tell me about the people in the church would be of enormous help. I just don't know enough about everyone."

The people of Emmanuel Baptist did not disappoint him. Within a few months, Donald Waite was privy to most of Newton's well-kept secrets. Mrs. Campbell's drinking problem, Frank Fowler's secret divorce, the Clemens family battle with mental illness, and Brian Maguire's time in prison were among the offerings.

Many church members praised Waite's ability to listen. He was so patient. So understanding. Some even arranged additional meetings to relate stories they had forgotten to share at first. Waite carried an appointment book and made notes, capturing each rich detail. By early March he had bought a larger appointment book and was starting to exert unusual control over the congregation.

When Frank Fowler demanded an agenda change during a church business meeting, Pastor Waite suggested a ten-minute break.

"You're being pretty tough on the rest of us, Frank," Waite said as the two men stepped outside and strolled around the parking lot. "I would think that a man who has made mistakes—especially marital ones—would be more compassionate."

Ordinarily Frank, who had one bad eye from a Vacation Bible School accident, would have squinted in the harsh lights of the parking lot, but he was looking at his shoes.

"I think I can keep the secrets I know about you, Frank," Waite went on, "especially if you could find a way to be more cooperative when it comes to church business." Frank may have been looking at the ground, but he saw the pastor's meaning clearly.

Waite's talent for getting his own way was as large as his appointment book. One of his pastoral conferences could reduce the most disagreeable church member to sulking silence. And by April most of the folks at Emmanuel had decided they couldn't trust any of their friends from the church.

Late that month when the deacons and their wives gathered for their annual potluck supper, Ray Bryson voiced what many of them were thinking. "If things continue this way, I don't think Donald Waite should be our pastor."

Frank Fowler squinted his agreement, Brian Maguire nodded nervously, and the deacons decided to call a meeting of the whole church to discuss the issue. The bylaws required such a meeting before a pastor could be dismissed.

Before the dinner was over, however, Pastor Waite had received a call from one of the wives, detailing the entire conversation. His sermons on pastoral leadership had paid off.

Very quickly the church divided into two hostile camps. Those who felt the pastor should be removed began sitting on the left side of the church. On the right sat members who wanted to give him more time. The choir was split and given to vacillation, the organist sided with the pastor, and the church secretary didn't want to get involved.

Flora Waite resigned from her position as assistant director of the Dorcas Society after one of the ladies commented that blackmail was far worse than gossip. Offertory envelopes contained more than tithes. Routinely they were dropped in the collection plate imprinted with particular dogma. "Waite No Longer" read some. Others declared, "Support the Pastor." And there was always one proclaiming, "The organ is too loud."

The deacons began to sit as a group on the left side of the church, pressing together in the front pew. In the past, one of the deacons had always made the morning announcements. But ever since the weekend of the potluck, Pastor Waite had read the announcements himself, each time omitting the board's call to special assembly. For four weeks he simply kept the meeting from being announced.

On the third Sunday in May he was apparently going to do the same thing. Connecting the lapel mike to his suit, Waite solemnly stepped down in front of the wooden Communion table with its ornately carved command: "This Do in Remembrance of Me."

"If anyone is visiting today," he began, "please raise your hand and our ushers will come by and give you some information about Emmanuel Baptist Church."

At that point, Frank Fowler got up from the front pew and strode up the stairs of the platform to the pulpit. Bending toward the microphone, he smoothed out a piece of paper and started to read: "This is to announce a special congregational assembly for this afternoon to discuss Pastor Donald Wa—"

Suddenly he could not be heard. Flora Waite, at the piano, had begun pounding out "Have Thine Own Way" and was immediately joined by Sharon Carlson at the organ, drowning out the rest of Frank's message. Pastor Waite began singing loudly into his lapel microphone, and some on the right joined him.

Before they could begin the second verse, Frank pulled the organ power cord from the wall, and Brian Maguire shut the piano lid. Flora Waite beat on his arms for a minute and even lost her hat in the scuffle, but Brian held on.

There was an awkward pause. Deacons still in their seats coughed nervously and crossed their legs. Most of the choir was leaning forward, and one of the tenors was taking notes.

Then Ray Bryson got up and walked over to the pastor in the slow deliberate way that one approaches an injured animal. The veins in Ray's neck were showing as the two men hissed under their breath at each other.

After a minute, Ray appeared satisfied. He turned to go to his seat, but his feet were tangled in the microphone cord and he fell down. There was an audible gasp from the congregation. Pastor Waite delayed for one brief moment before reaching to help him up. It was long enough to convince those close to the front that their pastor had indeed pushed Ray Bryson.

Ray must have thought so too, because he bounced to his feet and hit the pastor square in the nose with his fist. The lapel mike registered the impact.

Flora Waite screamed and ran to help her husband, but she never got close to him. Within an instant a majority of the congregation converged on the Communion table, punching or shoving. Many came down the center aisle to help break up the combatants, but remained to fight after their side began to fall behind in the skirmish. The melee soon spilled over to an open space beside the organ.

Two tenors and a baritone jumped over the wooden railing of the choir loft and began exchanging punches with members from both sides of the aisle. Mary Dahl, the director of the Dorcas Society, threw a hymnal at one of the tenors, but the missile sailed high and wide and splashed down in the baptistry behind the choir. Sharon Carlson had given up on the organ and moved to the piano, where she tried to restore order by playing "Blest Be the Tie That Binds." Anne Fowler, Frank's wife, told her to return to her seat.

When Ray Bryson's right hook finally took the pastor down, someone grabbed the spring flower arrangement from the altar and threw it high in the air in Ray's direction. Water sprinkled everyone in the first two rows on the right side, and a visiting Presbyterian experienced complete immersion when the vase shattered against the wall next to his seat.

The fight ended when the police arrived on the scene. They restored order, took down names for the report they would file, and recommended that some of the men seek medical attention. Ray Bryson's hand was broken, and Mary Dahl's knitting needles were confiscated.

The following Wednesday each of the deacons received a notice to appear at the Newton Courthouse for a hearing.

Pastor Donald Waite had also been summoned. On the day of the hearing, both he and Flora appeared at the courthouse. They sat on one side of the aisle in the hearing room, and the deacons drifted toward the other.

When the court officer entered, breaking the uncomfortable silence, Brian Maguire recognized him immediately as David Goldstein, one of the stars on Temple Beth Shalom's softball team. For several minutes Goldstein looked over the police description in front of him. The one time he looked up, he seemed to focus on the tape on Waite's nose and the cast on Ray's hand.

"I know some of you from the softball league," he finally said, removing his glasses to rub the bridge of his nose. "We may have had our differences on the ball diamond, but the cause of religion in our city is at stake here. There must be some way you can settle your dispute among yourselves." No one could look at him.

"I have been a pastor in the service for many years," said Donald Waite, standing up. "And I have never met a more stubborn-necked people than those in this church." At that, the deacons raised their heads, and Frank squinted in the light. But Waite was just warming to his theme. "Now I have been in the Way for a long tim—"

"In the way of what?" asked Goldstein, and then decided not to wait for an answer. "I'm dismissing this case," he said, rapping his gavel with sudden force on the desk.

Waite sat down awkwardly as Goldstein continued. "No charges will be pressed at this point, but I urge you to work this out within your own church. Your Jesus Christ may allow this sort of thing in His followers, but the Commonwealth of Massachusetts will not permit fistfights as a regular order of church service."

The leadership of Emmanuel Baptist Church filed quietly out to their cars and drove off in different directions. On the back of each car was a bumper sticker declaring, "God Is with US at Emmanuel Baptist Church."[1]

# 9

## One Lord, One Faith, One Baptism

It's about time for Christians who recite the creed and mean it to come together for fellowship and witness regardless of denominational identity.

*J. I. Packer*

On the sunday following the fistfight at Emmanuel, Pastor Donald Waite issued a formal call for allegiance at the morning service. The church split pretty much down the middle, with less than half supporting him.

During the next few months, while the deacons attempted to force him to resign, Waite held meetings with the dwindling faithful in the parsonage. Finally, he resigned.

Emmanuel, thereafter renamed Newton Baptist Church, declined steadily over the following two decades, largely due to its dreadful image in the community. Ultimately, disunity spelled death for this particular body.

A bizarre example, but a real one. Mercifully not a typical one. We don't often swing at each other, at least not physically. Then again, perhaps Emmanuel is not so bizarre—at least not as the outside world sees us.

Take my own denomination, the Southern Baptists. Over a decade ago conservatives mounted a needed effort to restore orthodox balance to the denomination, but this quickly deteriorated into angry rhetoric and name calling. Throughout the 1980s, Southern Baptists made headlines. Not for their outstanding mission work or the wonderful pastoral care provided to millions, but for the knock-down-drag-out battle for denominational power.

Strangely, the combatants seemed to savor the publicity. I was with one friend, a conservative, when he picked up a headline and proudly pointed to a hatchet job on a liberal—believe me, I recognize the technique—and boasted, "That will show them."

Attitudes on the other side were no different. I attended a luncheon with a group of moderate leaders, one of whom, a good man, had recently given an angry sermon against the conservatives in which he threatened to withdraw his church from the denomination. His threat had been well publicized, and these men were passing around the articles, seemingly pleased at having gotten so much press.

Doctrinal issues have been disputed in the church since the beginning, and such argument can be healthy. When we do this unlovingly, however, we unleash our own base instincts. We become more strident to mask our own insecurity, and we use doctrinal disputes as an excuse to grab power.

Over an eighteen-month period, ending in early 1989, more than twenty-one hundred Southern Baptist pastors were forced out of churches.[1] For doctrinal reasons in the church debate? No. According to one survey, 58 percent cited personality differences (that's spelled *split in the church*), 46 percent, failure to live up to expectations (*not enough growth*), and 42 percent, leadership style too autocratic (*power-hungry pastor*). All that church strife in one year in just one denomination.

But Southern Baptists aren't alone, and the consequences of this for the church are tragic.

The Methodists, who through Charles Wesley gave the church some of its most stirring hymns, periodically battle bitterly over whether to dispense with "Rise Up, Oh Men of God" as too sexist or whether to dispatch "Onward Christian Soldiers" as too militaristic.

Francis Schaeffer pointedly acknowledged that fifty years ago Presbyterians failed to show love for one another in their doctrinal disputes, "and we have been paying a price for it ever since."[2] The Presbyterians continue splitting every few years, creating a whole menu of newer, purer forms and leaving behind the less orthodox.

At least four or five groups within the Episcopal communion are fighting to resurrect some semblance of its orthodox heritage. And pro-choice nuns and radical theologians wage guerrilla warfare within the most hierarchical confession of all, the Catholic Church.

Nor is the struggle confined to the generals at denominational headquarters; the privates and sergeants fight in the trenches as well. Pick any community at random and odds are at least one local church is in the midst of a bloodletting. As I write, one evangelical bastion I'm familiar with has been ravaged. The pastor was charged with administrative lapses, although many believe the problem arose because he was too conservative. Open, mean-spirited sessions ensued, thoroughly covered by the press. Many left when the pastor was removed, but the denominational governing body wrote letters to other churches in the denomination ordering them not to take in the errant members. Meanwhile, the local congregation is withering.

Sometimes our disagreements become even more sordid. The incredible spectacle of one televangelist suing another provided a bonanza for the tabloids: "Swaggart Charges Gorman with Adultery" . . . "Gorman Exposes Swaggart's Sin." Gorman argued that the rivalry and lawsuits were really over the fact that he was invading Swaggart's "territory." Both were seeking to recover millions of dollars for their television empires to support their jet planes, baronial estates, and coteries of aides and camp followers. Ordinary citizens watched the spectacle with disgust, while the church writhed in pain.

Interdenominational strife is not as prevalent as it once was, but it still occurs—and often in a way that mars the witness of the Body. A few years ago an international group of evangelical leaders met to prepare for a large conference in a country which happened to be predominantly Catholic. Since the conference was on a universal subject—evangelism—I urged that Catholic evangelicals be invited.

"Never," one of the participants shouted, slamming his fist on the table. "We fought that battle four hundred years ago, and we're not going to surrender now." Apparently he wanted to continue the Reformation warfare. A cease-fire would spoil his fun.

He prevailed, and as a result the political leaders in the country snubbed the conference; the local Catholic bishop, himself an evangelical in the renewal movement, on the closing day of the conference led a separate evangelistic rally. All of this, of course, was widely reported by the press.

In view of all this, it is not difficult to understand the two most frequent reasons people give for avoiding church: "All Christians are hypocrites," and "Christians are always fighting with each other."

To the first I invariably reply, "Sure, probably so. Come on and join us. You'll feel right at home." But I haven't come up with a very good answer to the second.

Holding the church to its historic faith, both in its practices and institutions, is a necessary corrective. But shouldn't it be done in love and with understanding, showing grace instead of rancor?

Rancor not only destroys witness, it also exposes weakness of conviction. The less secure people are in their beliefs, the more strident they become. Conversely, the more confident people are of the truth, the more grace they exhibit to those who don't agree. "Tolerance is the natural endowment of true convictions," wrote Paul Tournier.[3]

Remember, Jesus said, referring to His disciples: "By this all men will know that you are My disciples, if you have love for one another."[4]

## Why Unity Is So Important

So what are we to do, subject as we are to human weaknesses? The church of fact does fall short. And we do have honest differences that need to be debated and discussed. And we are called to be pure and to challenge error. Yet Scripture also commands: "Make every effort to keep the unity of the Spirit through the bond of peace. There is one body and one Spirit—just as you were called to one hope when you were called—one Lord, one faith, one baptism; one God and Father of all, who is over all and through all and in all."[5]

Can there really be "one body and one spirit . . . one Lord, one faith, one baptism" and at the same time be divisions or separations between Christians? The Scripture is clear on this; unity is a matter of obedience.

We must strive for unity because it is the essence of the church. As one prominent German theologian writes: "Since He is Lord of all who confess His name, communion among all Christians and their churches is a mandate integral to faithfulness."[6]

The church is, by definition, one. "God is one, and all who are God's are one. The church is a communal articulation of that truth," writes Richard Neuhaus,[7] a point the Reformers emphasized.*

---

*"The reformers argued that the body (referring to the invisible church) was controlled by one head, Jesus Christ, animated by one Spirit, the spirit of Christ. This unity meant that all those who belong to the church share in the same faith, are cemented together by the common bond of love and have the same glorious outlook upon the future" (Louis Berkhof, *Systematic Theology*, 572).

A second reason for unity is one dear to the hearts of evangelicals: without unity, evangelism is frustrated.

Jesus made His most moving plea to the Father on behalf of His disciples—that is, His church: "That all of them may be one, Father, just as you are in me and I am in you. May they also be in us *so that the world may believe that you have sent me.*"[8]

The message is clear. The world isn't looking at our tracts and rallies and telecasts and study manuals. It is looking at us and how we behave. When it fails to see the unity of Jesus' followers—the church—it fails to see the validation that Christ is indeed the Son of the living God.

Which brings us to the third critical reason for unity: the world. Aggressive secularists don't care whether we are Eastern Orthodox or Baptist or charismatic; they can't distinguish between post- and premillennialism, nor would they care if they could. They want only to discredit the church because its views are hostile to their own world view. So when we are divided, quarreling among ourselves, we play right into their hands, diminishing our own already weakened influence.

While we may never achieve perfect doctrinal agreement on all points, shouldn't we at least make common cause in defense of our common orthodox faith in Christ and belief in absolute truth?*

Through the centuries many have echoed this fervent plea. Even in the midst of the contentious Reformation era, John Calvin wrote that when it came to standing against the Great Deep—atheism—he regarded Rome as his ally. And a century ago Abraham Kuyper, perhaps the greatest Reformed Protestant intellect of modern times, argued powerfully for an alliance between Rome and those in the Reformation tradition: "A so-called orthodox Protestant [should] perceive immediately that what we have in common with Rome concerns precisely those fundamentals of our Christian creed now most fiercely assaulted by the modern spirit."[9] While our contemporary, Aleksandr Solzhenitsyn, reminds us: "In recent years the major Christian churches have taken steps towards reconciliation, but these measures are far too slow; the world is perishing a hundred times

---

*As Francis Schaeffer pleaded: "Let us raise a testimony that may still turn both the churches and society around—for the salvation of souls, the building of God's people, and at least the slowing down of the slide toward a totally humanistic society and an authoritarian suppressive state" (Schaeffer, *Great Evangelical Disaster*, 91).

more quickly. No one expects the churches to merge or to revise all their doctrines, but only to present a common front against atheism."[10]

The mandate for unity is clear, but putting it into practice is another matter. How do we deal with differences that have existed for two thousand years? Should we ignore doctrinal convictions? Do we fellowship with anyone who claims to be Christian? Is unity achieved at the price of orthodoxy?

### What Is Unity?

These are not simple questions, and to answer them we need to examine exactly what we mean by unity in the church universal and the church particular.

First of all, in the church universal it is not the kind of ecumenism that the World Council of Churches has advocated in recent years. Solzhenitsyn, in fact, was quick to point this out immediately following his statement above. He said that the WCC has done more to spawn Third World revolutionary movements than to defend the true church. Because of this, ecumenism has unfortunately come to mean "reducing all elements of faith to the lowest common denominator." The only unity this achieves is the belief in nothing, save perhaps the fatherhood of God and the brotherhood of man, terms which World Council circles today would shun as sexist.

True unity is not sought by pretending that there are no differences, as modern ecumenists have done, but by recognizing and respecting those differences, while focusing on the great orthodox truths all Christians share. This was Kuyper's point as well as Calvin's. While they unrelentingly pursued and defended their doctrinal differences with Rome, they nonetheless sought out that common ground of orthodoxy on which they could stand together.

C. S. Lewis called this common ground "mere Christianity," likening it to "the great level viaduct which stands solidly over the dips and valleys of heresy and apostasy through the years."[11] Through that viaduct the mainstream of Christian belief flows from people to people, country to country, century to century. Articulated in the classic confessions and creeds, it embraces such fundamentals as the Virgin Birth, the deity of Christ, the Atonement, the Resurrection, the authority of Scripture, and the Second Coming.

While mere Christianity is a good formula for the church universal, something more is required for the church particular where believers come together for discipleship and worship. Here doctrinal agreement is essential if believers are to be of one mind and one spirit in submission to one another under the authority of their agreed-upon form of government or governing structure. Any division in the church particular destroys the ability to worship—we are commanded not to take the Lord's Supper in disunity—or to be equipped for service, as explained later.

Actually, this is where our understanding of the orthodox fundamentals and doctrine provides the basis for working out the most difficult issues. For example, do we accept everyone who says he or she is a Christian? No. Those who deny the fundamentals, such as the bodily resurrection of Christ, cannot be part of the confessing body. When we encounter this kind of disbelief, the church must correct, discipline, or disfellowship. Or, as some traditions call it, "excommunicate." The distinction is critical: uniformity within the church particular, but unity with diversity in the Body or church universal.

### Unity with Diversity

Thus, within the orthodox tenets, room remains for our honest, doctrinal disagreement in the church universal. Not for a moment do we expect that Christian bodies will resolve issues like the sacraments, baptism, and ecclesiology on which there has been disagreement for nearly two thousand years. If Calvinists and Arminians haven't been able to settle the question of free will and predestination in four hundred years, there's no particular reason to expect that they will . . . until that day when the Lord makes it all clear.

Meanwhile, we have a healthy freedom to pursue these differences openly and lovingly. In fact, this kind of tolerance spares us, as we wrote in chapter 7, from what might otherwise result at the hands of fallen and arrogant humans. Remember the Crusades? The Inquisition? The Catholic and Protestant martyrs of the Reformation?

Respect for differing views also provides some defense against the natural desire to incessantly probe the mystery of the gospel. (There are those who would consider it the ultimate intellectual achievement to unravel the hidden counsel of God.) But the pursuit of doctrine for the sake of doctrine can be idolatrous. The gospel will not be demystified.* God will not be mocked by the pretensions of those who believe that they might fully and certainly know His mind. Was that, after all, not the sin of the Garden?

Diversity within the Body, while it may chafe and bind and even pain, provides a healthy corrective. The Holiness movement challenged what some saw as the cerebral, doctrinal rigidity of certain Reformers. Regardless of who was right, no one could deny that the movement breathed life into the church and brought millions to a new awareness of righteous living. Likewise, today's charismatic movement, despite some excesses, has refreshed moribund churches with the vitality of the Holy Spirit.

The fact is, we can learn from one another. Personally, while I've formed strong doctrinal convictions, I've been enriched deeply by my fellowship with those who hold different, but equally strong doctrinal convictions—particularly my Catholic, Anglican, Orthodox, and Lutheran brothers and sisters. Doing so has also helped me not to trivialize the ordinances or sacraments and other acts of worship.

The sign of the cross is a good example. After praying with an Orthodox sister one day, I said my "Amen" and then watched her make the sign of the cross with such depth of feeling that I had a powerful urge to make the sign myself. I resisted—for fear someone might consider it a betrayal of my Baptist tradition. How foolish I felt when I later discovered that believers since the very beginning and through the centuries have made the sign of the cross, signifying that they had been crucified with Christ.

Abraham Kuyper wrote that he was "not ashamed to confess that on many points my views have been clarified through my study of the Romish theologians."[12] Respecting and appreciating different

---

*Theologian R. C. Sproul says that the Christian puts himself in grave danger when he attempts to probe the hidden counsel of God. And Catholic theologian Father Tom Weinandy makes an interesting distinction: "There is a difference between striving for doctrinal purity and rationalistically probing the mysteries of the gospel. The true theologian or church body wishes to know ever more clearly the mysteries of the faith so that. . . . we know better what the mystery is, not that we comprehend the mystery and so deprive it of its mystery. The Trinity is three persons in one God. Jesus is the one person of the Son existing as God and man. This is doctrinal purity, but the mystery survives, and actually with the clarity comes more mystery—more awe and reverence. Now the rationalistic approach does not want to clarify the mysteries of our faith but to solve them, making them completely understandable to the human mind. This can never be done" (letter from Father Weinandy to Charles Colson, 18 June 1992).

traditions not only teaches us more about our faith, but encourages a measure of theological humility.

This attitude helps us avoid the kind of rigid conformity that says everyone must look, act, talk, and think just alike. And this also helps us make the gospel accessible to all people.

A Ugandan pastor provides a powerful illustration of this point.

Kefa Sempangi came to the United States for training at Westminster Seminary, where he was not only well educated with orthodox theology but also with conservative, Western evangelical culture. When Sempangi returned to his own country after several years, he was horrified to see Ugandan Christians dancing in the streets, hands upraised, chanting in unknown tongues. At Westminster, at that time, the young pastor had learned that worship was solemn and reverent. Charismatic expression was distrusted.

As he sat in his room one night watching his exuberant countrymen dancing in the streets, it suddenly struck him: *These people could never identify with what I learned at Westminster. There's nothing unorthodox here. This is simply their natural means of expression, and they can use it to worship God just as I do.*[13]

Cultures may differ and individual expressions may vary, but the intent of the heart is the same. Ecuadorians may present in drama or dance the same biblical truth that conservative Scottish preachers exposit from the pulpit.

I have beloved friends who, whenever they attend my church, feel uncomfortable over the hand-clapping informality. That's fine; they love the Lord no less because they choose a more somber mode of worship. Some individuals are drawn to liturgical services, others to those which emphasize teaching, still others to music. Pluralism about the form of worship, as distinguished from who we worship, is healthy; it broadens the outreach of the church.

Neuhaus puts it with his customary eloquence when he says that one should engage in "the most vigorous advocacy of what one believes to be right," but at the same time make "a mutual pledge of allegiance to reverence one with another within the mystery of our being a people led by God toward that time in which we shall 'know even as we are known'."[14]

Calvin, who saw that the Devil's chief device was disunity and division and who preached that there should be friendly fellowship for all ministers of Christ, made a similar point in a letter to a trusted colleague: "Among Christians there ought to be so great a dislike of schism, as that they may always avoid it so far as lies in their power. That there ought to prevail among them such a reverence for the ministry of the word and the sacraments that wherever they perceive these things to be, there they must consider the church to exist . . . nor need it be of any hinderance that some points of doctrine are not quite so pure, seeing that there is scarcely any church which has not retained some remnants of former ignorance."[15]

### The Real Basis of Unity

The great German pastor, Helmut Thielicke, had a good suggestion: Rather than fighting each other, he argued, "God demands of both sister churches (Protestant and Catholic) that they relentlessly question *themselves* and grow more mature in the process."[16]

From the very beginning of the church there were doctrinal differences. In fact, such difficulties occasioned many of the epistles now in the New Testament. Yet those believers, who had to endure not just mockery or scorn but the threat of death, were united over one baptismal confession: "Jesus is Lord"—a profession which comes only under the power of the Holy Spirit.

Over the first centuries more differences rose between the brethren, such as the Montanists, the Novitianists, and the Origenists. Yet the church achieved such a remarkable witness and visible demonstration of love for one another that they overcame persecution and won much of the then-known world to Christ.

What was the secret?

First, the church feared the Lord, about which more will be said later. And second, believers shared a core set of beliefs which they held to be far more important than any points upon which they might differ. These have been called *the rule of faith:*

- God the creator exists in three persons, Father, Son, and Holy Spirit.

- Born of the virgin, He suffered, died, rose again, and was exalted at the right hand of the Father from whence He will come again.

- The Holy Spirit brings the benefits of Christ's saving work to people who believe in Him.

- Christians are expected to unite with a local church, submit to the authority of bishops and elders, live a holy life conducive to the spread of the gospel.

- God will judge the world and receive His own at the end of history.[17]

Because of the assault of modernism in this century, we might add something the first-century church took for granted: belief in the authority of God's inerrant Word.

### The Road to Unity in the Church Universal

"By this will all men know you . . . that you love one another." One Lord, one faith, one baptism. Unity with diversity. How can we achieve what the first-century church did? Mere Christianity. The kind that elicits the Tertullian response, "See how these Christians love one another."

*First of all, we can repent of the sin of presumption and of our ill-informed prejudices.* Just think about what we are really saying when we imply that someone can't be a Christian because he or she hasn't prayed the sinner's prayer, or gone through the "Four Spiritual Laws," or responded to an altar call, or any of the prescribed formulas. We are actually saying that there is some kind of celestial formula which God does not have the power to change.

Probably two of the most stubbornly held beliefs today are: among evangelicals, that one can't be a Christian if he or she is Catholic, and among Catholics, that one cannot be saved apart from the work of the Catholic Church, despite Vatican Council II's clear words to the contrary.[18] Still, there are some encouraging signs of change.[19]

At the worldwide charismatic gathering in London in 1991, the chaplain to Pope John Paul II, Raneiro Cantalamessa, publicly asked forgiveness from the assembled thousands for his "sin against the unity of the body of Christ." The crowd sat in stunned silence as the cleric repented for once believing that Protestants could not be part of the church.[20]

Repentance of the sin of presumption can heal cultural as well as ecclesiastical differences. One hundred twenty years ago in Evanston, Illinois, racial discrimination forced black members to leave First Baptist Church. They founded Second Baptist, and for a century the two churches were separated. Then in 1991 First Baptist, with three hundred members, presented a resolution to Second Baptist, which now had three thousand members, asking forgiveness. Soon thereafter the two churches planned several joint services and the two churches are now working together.[21]

*Second, we can actively reach out and build bridges to those of different traditions.* John Wesley, a giant in church history, said to those with whom he was embroiled in a serious theological dispute: "If thy heart be as my heart, give me thy hand." Reaching out to each other can sometimes break down formidable barriers. John Aker, head of the Slavic Gospel Mission, offers a remarkable example.

When this able young minister was pastoring the Evangelical Free Church in Montvale, New Jersey, he developed a close bond in Christ with a priest from a nearby parish, Ken Herbster. Together they came up with a bold scheme: Aker would preach at the mid-morning Mass in Father Ken's church, and the priest would preach for the Sunday evening service at Aker's church.

To "cut their losses," they later quipped, they chose Super Bowl Sunday when attendance might be somewhat diminished. But neither man was prepared for what happened.

Following John's message at the mid-morning Mass, the Catholic congregation spontaneously stood and applauded. That evening, without prompting, the same thing happened when Father Ken preached at the Evangelical Free Church.

Later that year the two pastors led a joint Easter sunrise service on a hill just outside of town.[22]

Now, there have been many ecumenical pulpit exchanges in recent years. Protestants preach about self-esteem or human dignity in a Catholic church, and a priest may deliver a message about aid to Central America in a Protestant service. What made John Aker's experience so remarkable was that both he and Father Ken preached powerful gospel messages of salvation through Jesus Christ. And it was all the more remarkable because John Aker, of all people, should have been most unwelcome in a Catholic parish. For he had once been a Passionist monk, was released from his vows, converted to Protestantism, and graduated from Trinity Evangelical Seminary.

If any man knows the differences that divide, John Aker does. But he also knows that what binds us together is stronger than that which divides us.

Some Christians have spanned denominational barriers to build communities. One which grew out of the charismatic renewal is a community in Ann Arbor, Michigan, known as the Word of God. It consists of fifteen hundred people, two-thirds Roman Catholic, one-third Protestant. They make no attempt to minimize their differences; each group maintains its own worship service. But in other respects they have developed a common life. The Word of God community, which has spun off other communities in Latin America and the British Isles, also sponsors serious discussions among Protestant, Orthodox, and Roman Catholic leaders through the Center for Faith and Renewal.[23]

When historians examine and record this era in church history, they will doubtless note the singular contribution of the charismatic movement toward unity in the Body. In Northern Ireland, for example, renewal movements have sprung from the rock-hard soil of old-line Presbyterianism and traditional Roman Catholicism. We've been in prisons there and seen Catholic and Protestant ex-terrorists, arms wrapped around one another, worship and rejoice as one.

And there are signs of progress here at home.

A great friend of mine, a conservative, Reformed scholar, for many years expressed concern over my association with Roman Catholics. So recently I was elated to read an article in which he wrote: "Fresh winds are blowing everywhere among Catholics and Protestants . . . because everybody who belongs to Jesus belongs to everybody who belongs to Jesus, I've decided to turn my polemical guns on the enemy--not so much on my family."[24]

Many are discovering, as my friend has, that when it comes to unity, biblical orthodoxy is more relevant than denominational identity. In many ways, for example, conservative Catholics have more in common with conservative Baptists than they have with liberal Catholics.

Old walls are indeed breaking down. While Protestants have historically emphasized the personal relationship with Jesus, one recent survey found that more Catholics claimed that personal identity than Protestants. And majorities of all groups, Catholics and Protestants, say they believe Jesus is the Son of God, also fully human, that He was resurrected and will come again. Church bureaucracies may be drifting away from the historic creeds, but a substantial number of churchgoers seem to be joining hands in their common orthodox beliefs.[25]

"It is a true sign of the church when true Christians love one another," said Francis Schaeffer. "The church is to be a loving church in a dying culture."[26]

*This has enormous implications, for it means we can cooperate for common witness.* It would be refreshing if, instead of squabbling with one another, churches were to join hands in meeting community or social needs. For this very reason Prison Fellowship makes a conscious effort to involve volunteers from every denomination. I remember all too well how inmates reacted to individual church proselytizing when I was a prisoner. So we go to prison not in the name of one denomination, but in the name of Jesus Christ.

And we make a concerted effort to work with other prison ministries as well. It isn't always easy. The entrepreneurial bent in evangelical ranks is as intense as anything I remember from my experiences practicing law. But it is important to make the effort. I have personally raised money for other prison ministries simply to demonstrate that we are one in Christ and can work together.

Wherever people of good will cooperate for the cause of the gospel, the witness is powerful.

Mike Timmis, a Roman Catholic, is a ruddy-faced, ebullient lawyer and businessman in Detroit. In the early 1980s, Mike and his wife, Nancy, attended an executive dinner party (evangelistic outreach targeted toward business leaders) at which they responded to an invitation to make a total commitment to follow Christ. Mike and Nancy have been eagerly involved ever since. They have built hospitals in Africa, managed relief efforts in Latin America, and supported a host of evangelistic campaigns, particularly within the Catholic Church. But one of their most important areas of witness has been in their own city.

A few years ago the archbishop of Detroit asked Mike to help fund a nondenominational, Christ-centered school in the inner city. A gifted entrepreneur, Mike met with Lutheran, Presbyterian, Episcopalian, Baptist, and Catholic lay leaders. They formed a steering committee, rolled up their sleeves, and in faith began serious planning. They found a site in a needy area of the city and began fund raising in earnest.

With private funds from various denominations, three new elementary schools--called Cornerstone schools—were opened in August 1991. The mission statement describes them as "Christ-centered" ecumenical schools that stress excellence and sound moral teaching. Already students are showing vastly improved achievements, and in the process the church is making a profound statement to the Detroit community. Not only is the church showing its concern for the inner city, but also their love for one another.

A group of young people at Shively Christian Church in Louisville, Kentucky, understand this kind of unity too.

The young people at Shively Christian Church, led at the time by Youth Pastor Dave Stone, were fiercely competitive with their neighbor, Shively Baptist, in all things, especially softball. They were also serious about their Christianity, faithfully attending the summer Bible camp led by the youth pastor.

One week the Bible lesson was about Jesus washing His disciples' feet, from John 13. To make the servanthood lesson stick, Pastor Stone divided the kids into groups and told them to go out and find a practical way to be servants.

"I want you to be Jesus in the city for the next two hours," he said. "If Jesus were here, what would He do? Figure out how He would help people."

Two hours later the kids reconvened in Pastor Stone's living room to report what they had done.

One group had done two hours of yard work for an elderly man. Another group bought ice cream treats and delivered them to several widows in the church. A third group visited a church member in the hospital and gave him a card. Another group went to a nursing home and sang Christmas carols—yes, Christmas carols in the middle of August. One elderly resident remarked that it was the warmest Christmas she could remember.

But when the fifth group stood up and reported what they had done, everyone groaned. This group had made its way to none other than their archrival, Shively Baptist, where they had asked the pastor if he knew someone who needed help. The pastor sent them to the home of an elderly woman who needed yard work done. There, for two hours, they mowed grass, raked the yard, and trimmed hedges.

When they were getting ready to leave, the woman called the group together and thanked them for their hard work. "I don't know how I could get along without you," she told them. "You kids at Shively Baptist are always coming to my rescue."

"Shively *Baptist!*" interrupted Pastor Stone. "I sure hope you set her straight and told her you were from Shively *Christian* Church."

"Why, no, we didn't," the kids said. "We really didn't think it mattered."

And, of course, it didn't.

***Finally, Christians must make common cause in the battle against secularism.*** And here we can really learn from our brethren in the East, where, facing a leviathan bent on destroying them, the Christians stood together.

Remember Laszlo Tokes's discovery when he looked out the window of his besieged parish? Christians of every denomination standing together between the church building and the tanks.

When I was in Czechoslovakia I met Father Vaclav Maly, one of the real heroes of that country's revolution. He told me that even now, after the fall of Communism, he still meets weekly with Protestant brothers. I must have looked surprised, for he quickly added, "They [the Communists] tried for forty-five years to divide the Body. We must bring it together."

In the West, every area of life is being undermined by the dominant secularist world-view. Myriad moral issues confront our society—the dignity of life, medical ethics, religious liberty, justice—and God's people belong out there in the trenches together. This was the appeal of Solzhenitsyn and Schaeffer and Kuyper. Nothing less will enable the church to stand against the surging forces from the "Great Deep," as Calvin called it.

What does this mean? It means attorney William Ball, a leading Roman Catholic layman and skilled defender of religious freedom, defending the religious liberties of the Amish; it means Baptists defending Cardinal John J. O'Connor when the *New York Times* attacks him for daring to criticize pro-abortion legislators.

When Catholic priests and Protestant laypeople stand together, peacefully praying, in front of abortion clinics, it is a powerful witness. Many have been arrested, but I doubt that they've sat around in those bleak jail cells debating the Council of Trent.

Harmony and oneness in spirit can be achieved only when Christians put aside their personal agendas and submit themselves to the authority of the Holy Spirit. For the Holy Spirit, which empowers the church, can never lead believers into disunity.

I experienced a dramatic demonstration of this in 1978 when Michael Alison, senior member of the British Parliament, invited me to England to explore the possible formation of Prison Fellowship there.

Michael and his wife, Sylvia Mary, had convened more than three hundred Christians from all over the British Isles in London's historic Church House. The group included Protestants and Catholics from Northern Ireland, where open warfare was being waged in the streets; chaplains of various denominational stripes who were understandably protective of their flocks; and a number of people already working in prison ministry, who were less than excited at the idea of some upstart group sponsored, of all things, by Americans.

The meetings began on Friday night with a series of speeches, including mine, setting forth the vision of Prison Fellowship. Spirits seemed high.

The next day as we assembled in the majestic Grand Hall, it all changed. One by one the critics raised all of the objections I had anticipated, and then some. The Anglican chaplain general and his Roman Catholic counterpart might not have agreed with one another very often, but they did that day. "There is no need for any new group to be organized," they said. Some equally passionate advocates spoke up at that point. And so it went, with the debate seesawing, back and forth, throughout the day.

Still feeling the effects of jet lag, I was relieved when Michael Alison announced late in the day that after one more speech there would be a vote by a show of hands. Seated just to Michael's right, I watched the faces of the group as the final speaker concluded with a stirring appeal. Some seemed to tighten, and the chaplain general looked particularly grim. Others nodded and exchanged glances. And then all eyes riveted on Michael.

"All those in favor," Michael said, and hands went up everywhere. The result was obvious from the dissenters' moans. Then about a dozen hands were raised in opposition.

I breathed a sigh of relief. I could return home satisfied. Prison Fellowship England would be under way—and I knew that eventually the chaplains would come around. People started getting out of their seats.

Suddenly Michael banged the gavel and announced, "In view of the fact that the decision is not unanimous, we will delay any action until we can meet again."

I couldn't believe it. *What's wrong with him?* I thought. *He's just thrown the whole thing away.*

"If this be of the Holy Spirit," Michael explained, "He will say the same thing to all of us. And if it is not God's doing, we want no part of it."

I left discouraged, feeling the trip had been wasted.

Six months later the group assembled again. This time the vote was unanimous, and Prison Fellowship England has been one of the strongest ministries of the fifty now operating around the world.

For me, the lesson couldn't have been plainer, just as it is in the Book of Acts. There we read that the believers assembled in the Upper Room in obedience to the Lord's command, waited in continuous prayer, and were of one mind. Then the Spirit came and gave life to the church, which thereafter transformed the world.

Unity is the attitude from which the church's actions flow. It is the prerequisite for effective witness.

Disunity in the church would be understandable if Christianity were simply a relationship. Jesus and me. In that case, of course, everyone's experience would be different. Disunity would be understandable if Christianity were nothing more than a set of creeds and confessions. But Christianity is more than these. It is centered in the One who professes to be ultimate reality, the personal God who gives us life and meaning and who calls us to be His body at work in the world. If we really understand this, disunity becomes impossible.

The early church, led by apostles who had lived with Christ Himself, understood their Teacher's call to unity. It undergirded all that they did. The Book of Acts tells us the early church members were devoted to prayer, held their possessions in common, were "of one mind," and broke bread together. Linked by a common "fear of the Lord," they also knew God's power and presence among them. And they knew they were responsible to proclaim the truth. One truth.[27]

In the next two chapters we'll look more at these characteristics of the church, with the intent of seeing one thing clearly: When the people of God, united in His name, proclaim the Word of God, they can turn their world upside down. That happened in first-century Jerusalem. It also happened in a little church in Connecticut in the eighteenth century.

# 10

## The Flaming Word

As God can send a nation or people no greater blessing than to give them faithful, sincere, and upright ministers, so the greatest curse that God can possibly send upon a people in this world is to give them over to blind, unregenerate, carnal, lukewarm and unskilled guides. And yet in all ages we find that there have been many wolves in sheep's clothing . . . that prophesied smoother things than God did allow.

*Jerry Falwell*

*T*HE FARMING VILLAGE OF ENFIELD, Connecticut, had been largely untouched by the extraordinary events taking place throughout New England. A surge of revival was sweeping the populace. Cold, dry churches were suddenly transformed, and whole communities had been changed. It was happening all over the colonies.

Just a day's ride to the south, in Middletown, thousands had recently flocked on foot, on horseback, even by ferry down the Connecticut River to hear fiery English evangelist, George Whitefield. For miles around folks were still talking about that amazing day. After Whitefield's eloquent, moving "evangelical message of man's irremediable sinfulness and Christ's effective salvation," people wept in contrition over their sins. In response to his, "My brethren, I beseech you," they fell prostrate on the ground, crying out to God.[1]

Yet Enfield remained, some thought, the most wicked community in all of the colonies. Its smug, self-satisfied townsfolk wanted no part of the exuberant demonstrations occurring around them. Christians in neighboring areas had been praying that Enfield not remain isolated "while the divine showers were falling around them." Then on July 8, 1741, their prayers were answered.

A meeting had been called for late that summer afternoon in the Enfield meetinghouse, a white clapboard building at the town's center. The planned speaker had to cancel, but local officials had prevailed upon Jonathan Edwards, a well-known pastor from Northampton, Massachusetts, to come and preach. Since the thirty-seven-year-old Edwards was then recovering from a debilitating illness, he was somewhat frail. Some wondered if the long ride on horseback would unduly drain his strength.

The bare wooden pews of the Enfield meetinghouse were full that afternoon, although there was an air of levity as the service began. Staring at the faces of the congregation, Edwards thought, *How thoughtless, loose, and vain these people seem.* They stared back at him as if to say, "We aren't going to be carried away with all this foolish emotionalism we've heard about."

Edwards strode into the pulpit, took out his sermon manuscript, and began to read in calm, measured tones, "My text this evening is found in Deuteronomy, chapter 32, verse 35: 'Their foot shall slide in due time.'" Then, as he began profiling the wrath of the mighty Lord of heaven and earth, the listeners lost their smug looks. And the long sermon that followed shook not only the town of Enfield, but all of New England.

*"There is nothing that keeps wicked men at any one moment out of hell, but the mere pleasure of God,"* Edwards proclaimed. *"God holds the righteous and the wicked for His purpose. Perched perilously on the slippery slope, the wicked stand under condemnation. . . .*

*"The God that holds you over the pit of hell, much as one holds a spider, or some loathsome insect, over the fire . . . His wrath towards you burns like fire . . . He is of purer eyes than to bear to have you in His sight. . . . You have offended him infinitely more than ever a stubborn rebel did his prince. . . ."*

As Edwards continued, the men, women, and children crowding the narrow pews before him began to shake with moans, tears, and shrieks. Several times he had to pause and ask the people to quiet down so he might continue. He did so relentlessly.

*"Moreover, God is exceedingly angry with some yet living. His wrath is burning, the pit is prepared, the fire is hot. Yet, many of these do not realize their fate. They flatter themselves; they are unaware that God's wrath is like waters being dammed up before exploding. . . .*

*"Yet it is nothing but His hand that holds you from falling into the fire every moment. It is to be ascribed to nothing else, that you did not go to*

*hell the last night; that you were suffered to awake again in this world, after you closed your eye to sleep."*

Men and women were out of their pews now. Some fell to the floor.

*"O sinner!"* he proclaimed. *"Consider the fearful danger you are in: It is a great furnace of wrath, a wide and bottomless pit. . . . You hang by a slender thread, with the flames of divine wrath flashing about it . . . you have no interest in any Mediator, and nothing to lay hold of to save yourself, nothing to keep off the flames of wrath, nothing of your own, nothing that you have ever done, nothing that you can do, to induce God to spare you one moment."*

Men and women were clinging to the pillars of the place as if to keep their feet from sliding out from underneath them, and their cries continued even after Edwards finished. Another pastor, Eleazer Wheelock, stepped into the pulpit and offered a prayer which quieted the congregation. Then he and Edwards mixed with the people.

As the people filed out of the meetinghouse, however—as an eyewitness later wrote in his diary—their countenances were cheerful. And thereafter Enfield was swept up in the wave of righteousness surging across the American colonies. It was the Great Awakening, out of which a new nation was born.[2]

Jonathan Edwards's sermon, "Sinners in the Hands of an Angry God," is most frequently thought of as a classic example of "hellfire and brimstone" preaching. Most imagine Edwards as a passionate orator, playing upon the emotions of frontier farmers, adept at producing the kind of remarkable outpouring which occurred that day in Enfield. Picturing him in the mode of today's revivalists, they see him gesturing wildly, shouting words of wrath and shame at the quaking congregation. But that is far from the truth.

Standing solemnly at the pulpit, hunched over the tiny writing on the pages of his thick manuscript, Edwards *read* his sermon. As was his custom, he delivered the incendiary words in a monotone, looking up now and then to stare without expression at the back wall of the meetinghouse.

Edwards was a quiet scholar who graduated from Yale at age seventeen and who just before his death at age fifty-four was inaugurated as the second president of Princeton. Considered to be one of the greatest intellects of the Western hemisphere, he is also widely regarded as the greatest theologian America has produced.

But the reaction to his preaching in Enfield that day was not a demonstration of theological brilliance, dramatic oratory, or emotional preaching. It was the power of God's Word, convicting of sin and then offering the infinite grace of Christ's outstretched, nail-scarred hands.

*The power of the Word.* It is the very foundation on which the church rests and the very essence of its unity. It lies at the heart of the church's mission. "Go and make disciples of all nations," Jesus commanded in the Great Commission, "baptizing them in the name of the Father and of the Son and of the Holy Spirit, and *teaching them* to obey everything I have commanded you."[3]

This is why Luke, in describing the early church, lists teaching as the first task of the apostles as they gathered the new believers together. The Reformers emphasized this characteristic, and clear biblical preaching became central for the Reformed churches. But all traditions have recognized its priority. In our day, Pope John Paul II has described the proclamation of Christ as the church's "supreme duty. The church's service to the kingdom is seen especially in her preaching which is a call to conversion."[4]

The ministry of the Word takes two forms: preaching, which is largely the task of the pastor and is one of the pastoral offices assigned in Scripture, and teaching, which is to be continuously carried on at every level within the church.[5]

## Preaching the Word

Numerous books have been written on the subject of preaching—many of them classics—but no work on the church would be complete without some discussion of the office of the one who must carry out this duty. Church pulpit committees or boards must periodically search for pastors; bishops assign and reassign them to local congregations. In doing this they usually apply human yardsticks: education, eloquence, charisma, pastoral heart, administrative ability (and the often unspoken requirements: Is he a money-raiser and a church-builder?). But alongside one essential criterion, all these others pale into insignificance: Is the individual in question learned in the Word, wholly committed to preach and teach the truth, and is he anointed by the Holy Spirit for this call?[6]

For the pastor is not only the one who petitions God on the congregation's behalf; he is God's voice to the congregation—that is, charged with preaching *the* truth. So while pastors are human and need to be held to account, which is the task of the church officers, the congregation must realize that the pastor does not just work for the church.[7] This consideration is a frequent source of confusion and even division within the church. And because the pastor and the congregation's governing body need to be clear in their understanding, some churches have actually spelled it out in covenant agreements.[8]

Conversely, the pastor must understand his primary duty. While every pastor wants to please church authorities, keeping the church happy may be a sign of spiritual infidelity, as one outstanding Christian preacher discovered.

Theodore Epp, founder of Back to the Bible radio ministry, realized something was wrong when he stopped receiving critical mail. Convicted that he was not challenging the flock enough, he changed his preaching. "I'm afraid that when I'm pleasing everybody, I'm not pleasing the Lord," he later said, "and pleasing the Lord is what counts."[9]

This is not to suggest that a pastor is only successful when he is upsetting people! But he must be certain that he is first and foremost faithful to the One he serves. He is fulfilling a divine commission when he preaches. Just as an ambassador is entrusted not with his own message but with his superior's message, so the minister is entrusted with the Word of God. Before it is delivered, therefore, every message should be laid at the foot of His throne with one question: "Is this faithful to You, my Lord?" Or as one German pastor would always pray in the pulpit, "Cause my mind to fear whether my heart means what I say."[10]

The call to preach should never be undertaken lightly. It is the most awesome trust.

When I was a Marine lieutenant, I was conscious that I had fifty lives in my hands. I didn't dare show it, but I was frightened. A 747 pilot knows that he is responsible for three hundred or more lives. But can there be anything more terrifying than to know that you are actually speaking for God—the holy, majestic "I Am"? Can there be any greater responsibility than to shepherd the church of God which Jesus purchased with His own blood?[11] Even with the anointing of the Holy Spirit, the charge is terrifying, considering our own frailty.

This sense of holy awe must have been in Paul's mind when he wrote that he preached with fear and trembling.[12] Moses, Isaiah, Solomon—along with most of the major figures called by God to lead His people—at some point shrank in fear, groping for excuses: I can't speak well enough . . . I am too young . . . I have unclean lips . . .

Martin Luther felt the same way. Here was a man who put his life on the line, standing alone against the combined might of church and empire. Yet when he preached, he said, his knees knocked. Luther understood that it is less dangerous to risk your life than to betray God's trust.

The great preacher Charles Haddon Spurgeon wrote, "We tremble lest we should mistake or misinterpret the word." Thousands would flock to hear this man's sermons, which were then reprinted and circulated around the globe. His intellect was extraordinary: he was reported to have read twelve thousand books in his life; he could go to his bookshelves and from memory find material on any subject. Here was a man who had every reason to be supremely confident; today he'd be heralded as an evangelical superstar. Yet Spurgeon used to counsel young men to avoid the ministry--unless they felt irresistibly compelled, certain of God's call. "To preach the whole truth is an awful charge," he said.[13]

Another great intellect and preacher, Helmut Thielicke, wrote: "The men of God were never bold, brash pushers, for they were not like the false prophets motivated by their will or their urge to power," but were aware of the "thick darkness" which covers the earth and which they are called to penetrate. In referring to our natural inability to perform this holy task apart from supernatural empowerment, Thielicke said: "He who is frightened in this sense is experiencing a creative terror; he is close to the core of the matter."[14]

Even when we read the reassuring words of Matthew 10:19–20, we often miss a crucial distinction. "Do not worry about what to say or how to say it," Jesus told His disciples. "At that time you will be given what to say, for it will not be you speaking, but the Spirit of your Father speaking through you" (NIV).

However, this empowerment is not, as I for one have so often prayed, that God should give *us* the words to speak; that is a "presumptuous assumption that the right thoughts will occur . . . at the right moment." Rather, the promise is that His Spirit will speak through us, using often, as Thielicke says, our own feeble words.

Think of it: "God's own Spirit will enter into you and He Himself will confront men through your own poor words."[15]

So if we understand Jesus' words, we see that the preacher's state of mind is critical. We should not pump ourselves up with boldness and "the courage to preach"; some already have too much boldness and not enough substance to go with it. Instead, we should be "frightened by the overwhelming power of the promise but nevertheless [relying] on the power of that promise, open our mouths to speak."[16]

Compare that to the demeanor of today's self-important spiritual superstars who strut across the stage, so proud and confident— far from the attitude described by Paul or Luther or Edwards or Spurgeon or Thielicke.

Instead, the preacher should stand shaking and trembling, knees knocking in holy awe. For at that moment the only source of his power is God's promise, and his only objective is to speak the whole truth, the transforming message of God's judgment and God's grace.

But note carefully: The charge is to preach the *whole* truth.

"Away with this milk and water preaching of the love of Christ that has no holiness or moral discrimination," proclaimed Charles Finney, one of the great preachers of the last century. "Away with preaching a love of God that is not angry with sinners every day. Away with preaching a Christ not crucified for sin."[17]

Martin Luther believed so strongly that conviction of sin must precede conversion that he would not minister comfort to "any person except those who have become contrite and are sorrowing because of their sin—those who have despaired of self-help."[18]

This is why the therapeutic gospel we discussed earlier is such a dreadful heresy. It works from the outside in to restore self-esteem by enabling us to adjust to our circumstances; carried far enough, it can lead us to feel good about being bad. The gospel, on the other hand, is designed to transform our lives and circumstances; it works from the inside out. Therapy is concerned with changing behavior; the gospel, with changing character. Therapy gives us what we think we need; the gospel gives us what we really need.

Now don't misunderstand. Psychology or psychiatry can play an important role in helping. But behavior science cannot be blended into the gospel, either in counseling or, least of all, in the message preached.

All of us share responsibility to see that this does not happen. Pastors should not be misled: there is no synthesis here; we are dealing with antithetical propositions. Nor should laypeople pressure their pastors into situations where they feel they have to respond to the "feel good" marketplace. And elders and deacons must guard the ramparts to keep this false gospel out of the church.

The charge from God is to preach the whole, unadulterated truth. And when that is done with integrity—as the people of Enfield, Connecticut, learned that summer day in 1741—God does His mightiest work.

### Teaching the Truth

At the height of her fame as the other woman in the Ivana and Donald Trump breakup, Marla Maples spoke of her religious roots. She believed in the Bible, she told interviewers, then added the disclaimer, "but you can't always take [it] literally and be happy."[19]

We may point self-righteous fingers at Ms. Maples, but don't many of us really operate on this same principle? We do not take the truth seriously. And often we do not take it seriously because we are not hearing it taught with authority.

The task of teaching involves all church leadership, not just the pastor. Nor is it limited to the inquirers' class or Sunday school. Teaching is a continuous activity that permeates every level of the church—from Bible studies, youth fellowship groups, and special video presentations to Christian life courses and book discussion groups. And, as will be discussed later, a host of resources are available to aid in this: discipleship classes in print and video, doctrinal study plans, even seminary extension courses.

The church must do everything it can to equip believers with an understanding of Scripture, of doctrine, and of the application of Christian truth to all of life, as we discuss in some depth later. And it must be teaching that affects how we live.

Make no mistake. Failure to teach is a betrayal of the Great Commission. And it is dangerous.

I'm continually haunted by theologian R. C. Sproul's chilling sermons based on the warnings of the prophet Hosea: "My people are destroyed for lack of knowledge."[20]

You may be wondering: Why such emphasis on the marks of the church? After all, unity and preaching of the Word are characteristics of every church, aren't they?

Well, no, they aren't. As we saw in the case of Emmanuel Baptist, unity isn't always present. And we all know of churches where the Word is not preached. Which leads to several other questions: How do we know when a particular church has fallen away from its biblical roots? How do we steer a new convert away from an apostate church and toward a faithful one? What tests can we apply to discern the fidelity of our own church? These are critical, practical questions, and they have been asked since the very beginnings of the Christian faith.

Scripture itself sets the criteria, and the early church creeds built upon that foundation. The Nicene Creed, for example, speaks of "one holy catholic apostolic church." The church is to be one—living in unity. It is to be holy—its members living righteous lives. It is catholic—that is, universal in its compass. It is apostolic—rooted in and proclaiming the apostles' teaching.

And whenever an early creed was promulgated, it came with long lists of canons: explanations in great detail of how the creed was to be implemented. So believers could not only know what it was appropriate to believe, but how to put those beliefs into practice.

The understanding was clear: When the church was true to biblical faith and faithfully being the church, it would be identifiable by the preaching and teaching of the Word, the ministry of the sacraments, and the loving exercise of discipline and accountability. These would result in a healthy, maturing body and the fruits of that maturity. Unity. Intimacy with Christ. Works of ministry and public witness to God's truth by all the members. The living dynamic of self-giving fellowship and mutual concern.

These are not abstract, textbook notions. These are the marks of the church. And this is why we discuss them here. For could there be any more important question, for our own protection as well as that of new Christians, than whether the particular congregation of which we are a part is faithful to its biblical character?

After all, that congregation—yours and mine—is the community that is to show the world what the kingdom of God is like. It is an awesome charge.

# 11

## Communio Sanctorum

The communion of Saints

The world drinks to forget; the Christian drinks to remember.
*Steve Brown*

*W*HAT DOES IT MEAN WHEN YOU PRAY the Lord's Prayer on a Sunday morning? *"Thy kingdom come. Thy will be done, on earth as it is in heaven . . ."*? You are asking the kingdom of God to come—and one day, in its fullness, it will. You are asking that God's perfect will, obeyed immediately in heaven, will also be done through you and the confessing community around you. So whether you are in a great cathedral or a rented hall, you are asking that your congregation will reflect, here and now, the kingdom in its eternal power and glory.

As we discussed in chapter 5, the church is a new community that God has chosen to signal or point to the coming kingdom. The church is not the kingdom of God. Historically, whenever the two have been confused, the church has brought grief upon itself and the world. The kingdom will not be brought in by our efforts; it comes when God brings it in.

But, as Carl Henry so lucidly argues, the church bears present witness to what that future kingdom will look like, or, as another great scholar put it, the Body will bear the image of Christ Himself.[1] We are, therefore, a testimonial community, a holy nation, a royal priesthood, called out of the darkness into His marvelous light. We are the community that shows the world what heaven will be like!

The apostle Paul gives a wonderful snapshot of what the world should see in our community as a precursor of what is to come. "For the kingdom of God is not eating and drinking, but righteousness and peace and joy in the Holy Spirit."[2]

What are the marks of this new community that reflects the kingdom to come? The first is unity, as we discussed in chapter 9. Then we saw in chapter 10 the primacy of the Word: We are people of the Truth. And now we look at the other characteristics of this new community:

- This new community called by God is *a fellowship;* its members bear one another's burdens and allow for real accountability and discipline. This fellowship is the true intimacy—and peace—available only to those united in Jesus Christ.

- The *administration of the ordinances or sacraments* is the visible means by which this new community celebrates the mysterious, glorious work of Christ and His righteousness.

- *Prayer and worship* mark the new community as it lives in communion with a holy God.

- And finally, this is a community *supernaturally endowed under the seal and in the joy of the Holy Spirit.*

### Fellowship or Koinonia

Surveys show that the number one thing people look for in a church is fellowship. But what most modern Westerners seek is a far cry from what the Bible describes and what the early church practiced. No term in the Christian lexicon is more abused than fellowship.

To some it means what we discussed in chapter 3: the warm, affirming, "hot tub" religion that soothes our frayed nerves and provides relief from the battering of everyday life. Often with the best of intentions Christians have turned this social notion of fellowship into an end in itself. For these folks the object of the Christian life is fulfilled when brothers and sisters are "together" or "spending time"—and that can be at an encounter group weekend retreat or on the beach at Waikiki.

For many others, fellowship means no more than coming together for church events. Instead of happy hours at the club, they have theirs in the fellowship hall (a name which, by the way, contributes to the wrong impression).

At the other extreme there is the well-intentioned but misguided discipleship movement. One shepherd imposes his spiritual strait-jacket on his followers with unyielding discipline. (This is the way cults are made.)

But the word for fellowship in the New Testament Greek, *koinonia,* means none of these; it is something much richer. Literally it means a communion, a participation of people together in God's grace. It describes a new community in which individuals willingly covenant to share in common, to be in submission to each other, to support one another and "bear one another's burdens," as Paul wrote to the Galatians, and to build each other up in relationship with the Lord.

In Scripture, this koinonia embraces both the vertical and the horizontal. "What we have seen and heard we proclaim to you also, that you also may have fellowship with us and indeed our fellow-ship is with the Father, and with his Son Jesus Christ," wrote the apostle John to the early church.[3] It was a concept the early believ-ers understood because it paralleled the Old Testament concept of God's people sharing together in the covenant community in which He Himself chose to dwell. Biblical fellowship involves serious commitment and obligations. An example from the early church illustrates the point.

In the second century a pagan actor was converted to Christ. Since most drama of that day encouraged immorality, and since young boys were often seduced into homosexuality in order to play the parts of women, this new believer soon realized he would have to leave the theater.

All he knew was acting, however, so he decided to support him-self by teaching drama to non-Christians. Before he began, he went to his church elders and explained his predicament and his plan.

The elders immediately objected. "If it is wrong to be in the the-ater, then it is wrong to teach others to be in the theater," they said. The logic seemed clear, but since it was a unique situation and the young man had no other means of support, the elders decided to seek the wisdom of Cyprian, the respected bishop of the church in Carthage.

After some deliberation, Cyprian told the elders, "You are cor-rect. What is wrong to do is morally wrong to teach." The church's duty was to hold the young convert accountable to this.

"But," Cyprian added, "if the young man cannot find other em-ployment, it is also the church's duty to care for him. And if your church is financially unable to do this, he can move over to us in Carthage and we will provide whatever he needs for food and clothing."[4]

No wonder much of the known world came to Christ in the early centuries. They could see how believers loved one another in true fellowship.

This reminds me of the way I was so lovingly and unconditionally supported by Doug Coe, Senator Harold Hughes, Congressman Al Quie, and Graham Purcell when I first became a Christian. Within the community of Christ, the fellowship of believers, we are to support each other. In the case of the young actor, his fellow believers even gave him financial support. But for equally loving reasons, they did something else: They held him accountable for disciplined behavior in his Christian commitment.

Fellowship is more than unconditional love that wraps its arms around someone who is hurting. It is also tough love that holds one fast to the truth and the pursuit of righteousness. For most Christians, the support side of the equation comes more easily than accountability and the subsequent discipline involved. Which is one reason the behavior of Christians is often little different from the behavior of non-Christians. Maybe it's because we simply haven't taught accountability. Or maybe it's because, in today's fiercely individualistic culture, people resent being told what to do, and since we don't want to "scare them off," we succumb to cultural pressures.

Even pastors at times seem reluctant to demand accountability. As in the case of a young couple, unmarried and living together, who asked a well-known evangelical pastor to marry them. Years earlier the young woman had belonged to the church and sung in the choir. Without further inquiry and without counseling, the pastor agreed to perform the ceremony.

Another equally prominent evangelical had on his payroll a recent convert who was living with his girlfriend. The pastor's counsel? "Think about getting married soon." Extreme examples? I would hope so.

But too often we confuse love with permissiveness. It is not love to fail to dissuade another believer from sin any more than it is love to fail to take a drink away from an alcoholic or matches away from a baby. True fellowship out of love for one another demands *accountability*.

John Wesley was so concerned with building a righteous fellowship that he devised a series of questions for his followers to ask each other every week. Some found this rigorous system of inquiry too demanding and left. Today, the very idea of such a procedure would horrify many churchgoers. Yet some wisely follow just such a practice. Chuck Swindoll, for example, has seven questions that he and a group of fellow pastors challenge each other with periodically:

1. Have you been with a woman anywhere this past week that might be seen as compromising?
2. Have any of your financial dealings lacked integrity?
3. Have you exposed yourself to any sexually explicit material?
4. Have you spent adequate time in Bible study and prayer?
5. Have you given priority time to your family?
6. Have you fulfilled the mandates of your calling?
7. Have you just lied to me?

When John Aker pastored the Evangelical Free Church in Rockford, Illinois, he kept a covenant fellowship with five other men; they called each other before services every Sunday morning to inquire about any prayer needs and to check one another spiritually.

Bill Hybels, pastor of Willow Creek Church in Barrington, Illinois, understands the critical importance of accountability. He regularly submits his life to a small group of spiritual mentors.

I've done the same thing. One of the Prison Fellowship board members reviews not just my expense records, but all of my priorities. And I make no major decision unless the circle to which I am accountable agrees unanimously.

But accountability is a hollow concept unless it is enforced. There must be teeth in a church's demand for orthodoxy and righteous behavior; that is what we call *discipline*.* Yet examples of real discipline are all too few. Although evangelicals pride themselves on defending orthodoxy, I can recall only one instance in recent years when questions of theological integrity actually resulted in discipline.

It involved one of the movement's most ebullient and popular speakers, sociology professor Tony Campolo. Tony delights in using

---

*Some Reformers saw discipline as one of the three classic marks of the church (see Louis Berkhof, *Systematic Theology*, 576).

his glib and ready wit to shock audiences—and at times he goes too far. Students love him. Others sometimes think him outrageous.

A few years ago Tony published a book entitled *Reasonable Faith.* It had some very good apologetic material in the opening chapters; it also contained some dreadfully muddled theology.

Soon after the book's publication, Tony was unceremoniously dumped from the program of a large youth gathering. He and his friends were furious. Tony believed he had been unfairly judged; sponsors of the event believed his views to be heretical.

The evangelical movement in America has many strengths, but cohesiveness is not one of them. Much of it is a vast, sprawling, unconnected network of rugged individualists and entrepreneurs. No magisterium, no council of bishops to settle disputes.

In this case, however, at the request of both sides, I polled a group of leaders and asked them to serve on an ad hoc committee to judge. By general agreement, J. I. Packer, a wise and scholarly man, was asked to chair the group, making him the closest thing evangelicals had to a bishop.

Despite murmurings about inquisitions and jokes about burning heretics, the committee met in a lengthy, judicious deliberation. Campolo presented his case; so did his critics.

Their decision was that Campolo had erred: The book did contain heretical materials. Tony promised to mend his ways, including corrections in future printings of the book, and the sponsors of the event asked his forgiveness for their rough handling of the situation. It was a good example of the kind of accountability and discipline that should occur more often.

Though it has been mercilessly berated by the media for doing so, the Catholic Church, to its great credit, does call heretics to account. The public reprimand of Professor Curran at Catholic University, who taught that divorce and abortion were morally justified—as well as other positions anathema to Rome and historic Christian orthodoxy, was a noble moment for the church.

And it is demanding of laity as well. In late 1989, the bishop of San Diego refused the sacraments to a pro-choice political candidate who openly defied church teaching. The bishop was assaulted by the press and political leaders, and the candidate was elected. To this, the cleric responded calmly and correctly: "No popular vote or public opinion can change in any way the divine law that directs and guides human kind."[5]

When New York Cardinal O'Connor suggested such church discipline for Catholic pro-choice public officials, an implied rebuke of Governor Mario Cuomo, the press went into a frenzy, particularly the *New York Times* (the same paper, incidentally, that had praised Archbishop Joseph Francis Rummel of New Orleans for denying the sacraments to a segregationist legislator in 1962).

Nor is this a particularly new issue, raised only because of the Catholic Church's position on abortion. In the sixteenth century Pope Urban VIII declared that anyone in the New World who kept Indian slaves would be excommunicated. Good thing the *New York Times* wasn't around in those days to express horror at the church's "political activity"!

Many in the press have accused the church of interference in politics and repression, but the charge is absurd. The church is simply abiding by its own standards; it has never held itself to be democratic. The church is hierarchical and authoritarian and ultimately answerable only to God.

Even pragmatically, no one should expect to join a church (which, after all, involves a free decision) and then refuse to accept its authority (its rules, if you will). For failing to attend a few meetings, one can be thrown out of the Rotary Club. For failing to live up to a particular dress code, one can be dismissed from most private clubs. For failing to perform the required community service, one can be thrown out of the Junior League.

Yet when the church imposes discipline—denying the benefits of membership to those who flout its standards—it is charged with everything short of (and sometimes including) fascism. But shouldn't the church have at least the same right to set its standards as the Rotary Club? People who don't like it can and should go elsewhere.

We weaken the church when we fail to discipline. When heretics like Bishop John Shelby Spong, whose outrageous works are celebrated on national television, are allowed to run loose without so much as a whimper of protest from weak-kneed denominational leaders, the world laughs at us—and rightly so.

Discipline should be applied not only to enforce orthodoxy, but to maintain righteous behavior in the church. Sermons on holy living are empty exercises unless the church is willing to back them up with action.

One notable instance was when the Assemblies of God suspended Jimmy Swaggart and ordered him out of the pulpit for one year after he was caught with a prostitute. The decision was coura-geous, for it meant a loss of millions of dollars to the denomination. (Ironically—though not surprisingly—the press, which at the time was daily bannering the horrors of the Bakker and Swaggart scan-dals and bashing evangelicals in general, took little notice of the church's action.)

But Swaggart, with characteristic entrepreneurial spirit, refused the discipline and announced he'd keep right on preaching. And many, foolishly, continued to support him until he committed the same offense a second time, bringing added shame on the cause of Christ.

Some years ago a major church in the Southeast provided an-other good example of what must be done when the church is con-fronted with a clear challenge to its standard of righteousness. The wife of one of the church deacons suddenly announced to her hus-band that she wanted a divorce. It came as a complete shock to him and to the church.

The next Sunday the woman came to church as usual, but this time she was accompanied by a male companion, her boss. They sat on one side of the church while the deacon and the couple's three children sat on the other side. The church soon became aware of what had happened, as the woman made no effort to disguise her intimate relationship with her boss.

The elders of the church decided it was their duty to meet with the woman and insist that she repent of the relationship and return to her husband.

She adamantly refused. "It's over," she said. "I'm never going back to him."

The elders then told her that she could not continue coming to church with her lover because that would be flaunting her adultery. The woman responded that the church was more important to her now than ever; she believed if she could just bring her boyfriend, who happened to be Jewish, to church, he might be won to Christ. (No one in the church had ever heard of adultery being used as an evangelistic tool.)

Three elders spent many hours counseling with her. She would not repent, she would not break off the relationship, but she insisted on attending church.

So one morning they called her aside, in a private room, before the worship service. All of the elders were present, and they offered her a choice. Either she repent and work at her marriage or withdraw her membership from the church. If she refused to withdraw, she would be expelled.

In anger the woman wrote a letter of resignation which was read aloud to the church board.

In a similar case in Collinsville, Oklahoma, a disfellowshipped church member sued and, with the help of the ACLU, dragged the church through years of litigation. Although the church ultimately prevailed, it spent more than a million dollars in legal fees, and the elders were labeled in the press as the "goon squad" and "the Ayatollahs of Collinsville."[6]

Such cases do intimidate. But, "discipline guards the purity of the church, preserves the church by removing evil, and provides severe but loving correction for one who is in danger of falling into perdition."[7] Without effective discipline, there can be no accountability.

True fellowship was manifest in the early church when the congregation was of one heart, shared their possessions, cared for those in need, and with great power gave witness to the risen Christ. The believers enjoyed the deepest communion and truly were what they called themselves: *communio sanctorum*—or communion of saints.

As the church expanded out of Jerusalem, this concept of one fellowship—one with another and with God—bound them in unity and became the very essence of the church's character and power.*

Today, that kind of fellowship would produce what it did then—a mighty outpouring of God's grace.

### The Sacraments

If no word is more abused and misunderstood than *fellowship,* the word *sacrament* runs a close second. And it is misused most often to divide. There are sacramental churches and nonsacramental churches. Some revere the term; others abhor it.

Not for a moment are we suggesting that the differences between Christian traditions should be minimized. In some traditions, the sacraments are considered efficacious, in others expressive. In the Lord's Supper, for example, the elements are symbolic to one, the actual body to another, and invoke the actual presence to a third. These are important issues, honestly and fervently held, and they

---

*Acts 11:28–30 and throughout the Book of Acts; see particularly the resolution of disputes in Acts 15.

go back a long way—originating not, as most assume, with the Reformation but with the early church fathers who held three distinct views of the sacraments. But the passion with which different traditions defend their views can sometimes blind us to the deepest reality of our Lord's commands and why He ordered them; that is, the underlying reality of the acts themselves.

Literally, a sacrament means an oath or a pledge. It is an act by which we swear to our faith.

In one sense, then, believers offer themselves sacramentally, as Paul describes in Romans. Their obedient life is a witness, an affirmation or pledge, of their belief.[8]

Similarly, the church itself constitutes a living sign of loyalty to Christ. Just look at the biblical imagery: a holy body . . . the presence of the Lord through His people . . . the bride, pure and spotless, waiting at the altar to meet the Bridegroom for the consummation of God's grand unfolding plan for mankind. The church stands as a visible sign of faithfulness, an outward manifestation of the work of God's grace.

But these signs—whether our lives or our baptism or our worship or our participation in Communion—are meaningful only insofar as they declare and manifest the reality of God's action through Christ. They are an expression of our faith in what God has done in us; what Augustine called the visible form of invisible grace.[9]

This is why the sacraments can never be demystified, even in traditions that consider the elements to be entirely symbolic. While the Reformers were correct in insisting that the sacraments be understood in light of Scripture, God's regenerative work still contains a mystery. We can celebrate it; we can affirm His inner work with our outward acts. But we can never totally comprehend it.

So while traditions may differ on the meaning of the various acts and on which acts are specifically ordered as sacraments, all would agree that the sacraments are centered on Christ who took on flesh and died and was raised.* And almost all traditions agree that the administration of the sacraments is the way the community of faith expresses its very essence, and thus is an essential task and mark of the church particular. They further agree that the two

---

*For the Catholic Church the seven sacraments are baptism, confirmation, eucharist, matrimony, penance, anointing the sick, and holy orders; for the Reformers and a majority of Protestant traditions, the sacraments are baptism and communion.

we will discuss here are distinctly and unequivocally commanded by our Lord: baptism and the Lord's Supper.

## Baptism

Infant versus adult. Immersion versus sprinkling. The work of grace in the act or represented by the act. What the act signifies. When it comes to the sacrament of baptism, Christians hold widely divergent views. But one thing all believers should agree upon is the need for baptism.* Yet it's astonishing how many Christians profess faith and totally disregard the biblical mandate.

One Christian friend told me of a new "brother," an influential Muslim he had been discipling. I was overjoyed until my friend explained that this man was continuing to read the Koran and to worship in a mosque. When I protested, he defended his new "convert."

"But he loves Jesus," my friend said. "We pray together in the spirit of Christ. He is a follower of Jesus."

"What about baptism?" I asked.

My friend shook his head. "No, he couldn't do that—it's a cultural thing—but he loves Jesus."

I never was able to convince my friend regarding that crucial dividing line. Baptism is the external witness of the invisible reality. It is the Lord's own command in the Great Commission, and it is the first oath and sign of admission into the church. Peter's first words to the new believers were, "Repent and be baptized"—and thereby was the church particular formed.

Most Westerners take baptism for granted, but for many in the world the act requires immense courage. In countries like Nepal it once meant imprisonment. For Soviet or Chinese or Eastern bloc believers, it was like signing their own death warrant.

But sometimes, even in this country, baptism demands courage. Like the prison in Kentucky where, following a Prison Fellowship seminar, nine men expressed a desire for baptism. The instructor did what all are taught to do in the ministry: to involve clergy of the denomination of the individual's choosing.

---

*With full respect for other views, I write as a Baptist, one who believes in believer's baptism. But insofar as possible, I've kept the discussion here generally applicable. I do believe that the ultimate significance of the act is obedience to Christ's command and a sign of faith and entry into the church.

The problem was finding a place for the baptism. The prison had no baptistery in the chapel. The only possibility was a fenced-off exercise area inside the prison compound used by all the inmates. But there were two problems: one was that the other inmates could observe the service through the chain-link fence; the second was that these nine who wanted to be baptized were all from the sexual offenders' unit and were already subject to scorn and abuse from the rest of the prison populace.

But the new believers were determined. So an old galvanized horse trough was wheeled into the yard and placed beneath the guard tower. Then the men marched out, one by one, to the accompanying jeers and catcalls from the main prison yard. They went into the water and came out, as our instructor later wrote, "broken, weeping," but overflowing with God's grace.

A sacrament? Indeed it was. A bold one. And, as the instructor added, "Straight out of the New Testament."[10]

### The Lord's Supper

Equally clear is the command, "Do this in memory of me." The very thought that Jesus has asked us to do anything in memory of Him should fill us with awe and reverence. And think what He commands: "This is My body . . . this is My blood of the covenant, which is shed for many for the remission of sins."[11]

Again, various traditions attach different meanings to the elements. But however we view them, it is important to remember the underlying reality. And whether symbolic or actual, when we receive the elements or when we go to the Communion rail, we are making a physical gesture. When we take the cup and the bread, it is a physical bonding. Communion is the holiest moment, when we signify our oneness with Christ. Failing to celebrate that communion, or doing so infrequently, can drain the vitality from a church body.

And failing to treat the sacrament with holy reverence is a grave error. Whenever I participate in the Lord's Supper, I think of Nadab and Abihu, Aaron's two oldest sons. Nadab would have succeeded Aaron as high priest, but both he and his brother were consumed by the fire of the Lord after they "took their censers, put fire in them and added incense; and they offered unauthorized fire before the Lord."[12] Similarly, Uzzah unthinkingly touched the Ark of the Covenant—and died.[13] These offenses may seem trivial, the punishment harsh, but God has never lightly suffered the desecration of the holy.

For this reason, Scripture sets forth three conditions for Communion: *First, only believers can partake.* Jesus' invitation to "remember Me" was to His disciples. Paul's instructions for the sacrament were to the church. And the act is the supreme signal of the inner work of grace in an individual's life.

For a nonbeliever to take Communion is to taunt God. This is why many churches, understandably, warn partakers of the meaning and significance of the sacrament and tell non-Christians to abstain.

*Second, believers partaking must be at peace with one another.* This is evident from Paul's anger that the church was divided and therefore should not be meeting for the Lord's Supper.[14] Before participating in Holy Communion, every believer should examine his or her heart and take whatever steps are necessary to be reconciled with fellow believers.

*Third, believers dare not come to the table except with a repentant heart.* "Whoever eats this bread or drinks this cup of the Lord in an unworthy manner," as Paul puts it, "drinks judgment to himself."[15] That should be a sobering warning, especially when the apostle adds that because of this offense many have fallen ill or died. Any pastor who takes the Word of God seriously should never administer Communion without adequately warning partakers. Those who are unrepentant should flee the table rather than trivialize the sacred.

And God does not view this sacred act lightly. Pat Novak, pastor in a nonsacramental denomination, discovered this when he was serving as a hospital chaplain intern just outside of Boston several years ago.

Pat was making his rounds one summer morning when he was called to visit a patient admitted with an undiagnosed ailment. John, a man in his sixties, had not responded to any treatment; medical tests showed nothing; psychological tests were inconclusive. Yet he was wasting away; he had not even been able to swallow for two weeks. The nurses tried everything. Finally they called the chaplain's office.

When Pat walked into the room, John was sitting limply in his bed, strung with IV tubes, staring listlessly at the wall. He was a tall, grandfatherly man, balding a little, but his sallow skin hung loosely on his face, neck, and arms where the weight had dropped from his frame. His eyes were hollow.

Pat was terrified; he had no idea what to do. But John seemed to brighten a bit as soon as he saw Pat's chaplain badge and invited him to sit down.

As they talked, Pat sensed that God was urging him to do something specific: He *knew* he was to ask John if he wanted to take Communion. Chaplain interns were not encouraged to ask this type of thing in this public hospital, but Pat did.

At that John broke down. "I can't!" he cried. "I've sinned and can't be forgiven."

Pat paused a moment, knowing he was about to break policy again. Then he told John about 1 Corinthians 11 and Paul's admonition that whoever takes Communion in an unworthy manner eats and drinks judgment to himself. And he asked John if he wanted to confess his sin. John nodded gratefully.

To this day Pat can't remember the particular sin John confessed, nor would he say if he did, but he recalls that it did not strike him as particularly egregious. Yet it had been draining the life from this man. John wept as he confessed, and Pat laid hands on him, hugged him, and told John his sins were forgiven.

Then Pat got the second urging from the Holy Spirit: *Ask him if he wants to take Communion.* He did.

Pat gave John a Bible and told him he would be back later. Already John was sitting up straighter, with a flicker of light in his eyes.

Pat visited a few more patients and then ate some lunch in the hospital cafeteria. When he left he wrapped an extra piece of bread in a napkin and borrowed a coffee cup from the cafeteria. He ran out to a shop a few blocks away and bought a container of grape juice.

Then he returned to John's room with the elements and celebrated Communion with him, again reciting 1 Corinthians 11. John took the bread and chewed it slowly. It was the first time in weeks he had been able to take solid food in his mouth. He took the cup and swallowed. He had been set free.

Within three days John walked out of that hospital. The nurses were so amazed they called the newspaper, which later featured the story of John and Pat, appropriately, in its "LIFE" section.

Is not the substance of the act what is crucial? Despite the differences between various traditions, would not all Christians agree that the Lord's Supper should be a moment of deepest reverence and communion when we memorialize and know God's grace in this intimate physical expression?

Father Lawrence Jenco, who was held hostage in Lebanon by Shiite terrorists for nineteen months, tells movingly what Communion meant to him. While blindfolded and chained to a radiator in a room with three other hostages, Jenco assembled bits of bread and water. He then offered the body and blood to his companions, one of whom was Benjamin Weir, a Presbyterian minister. It was, as Jenco described later, their moment of deepest joy, sustaining them through an unimaginable ordeal.

Those who have been confined for long periods are often emotionally scarred for life, but Jenco is filled with love and forgiveness. For during that time he knew, in its most intimate sense, communion with Christ.

Later Father Jenco and Reverend Weir and the others could, I imagine, passionately discuss whether the elements were consecrated or symbolic. But none of them would dispute that together they experienced God's grace in that horrid place.

That which brings us together—the magnificent saving grace of our risen Savior—is infinitely greater and grander than any differences we might sincerely hold over the nature of our affirmations of that grace.

### Prayer and Worship

Since those called of God into the new order are a community created by and bearing witness to Jesus Christ, we are to be in constant prayer and adoration.

More has been written on prayer than on any other aspect of the Christian life. Some are classics, like the work of E. M. Bounds. Others promote cheap grace: Pray so God will give you whatever you want in life. Some books are marvelously entertaining but theologically dubious, suggesting that prayer is the essential prerequisite to energize the angels in spiritual warfare with demons.

Yet the wide coverage of this subject is understandable, for prayer has been one clearly distinguishing characteristic of the church from the very beginning. When the disciples gathered in the Upper Room as Christ had commanded, they stayed there for ten days continually devoting themselves to prayer.[16] After that, the Spirit came and the church was empowered for ministry.

When the believers first gathered after Pentecost, they did so to pray, feeling a sense of awe at the wonders and signs the risen Lord was performing through the apostles. Peter and John, after their first arrest, returned to the church for prayer that they might preach God's Word "with great boldness." When Peter was later imprisoned, prayer was offered fervently by the church. In prison, Paul and Silas worshiped, praying and singing hymns of praise.[17]

The apostles appointed seven others to serve the needy so that they could devote themselves to prayer and to the ministry of the Word. The church prayed and fasted before laying hands on Paul and Barnabas to send them on their first missionary journey, and Luke tells us they were thus sent by the Holy Spirit. Similarly, when Paul and Barnabas appointed elders, they prayed and fasted.[18]

Prayer is the act by which the community of faith surrenders itself, puts aside all other concerns, and comes before God Himself. It brings us, inevitably, as Archbishop William Temple once wrote, to "the nourishment of mind with his truth; the purifying of imagination by his beauty; the opening of the heart to his love; the surrender of will to his purpose—and all of this gathered up in adoration, the most selfless emotion of which our nature is capable and therefore the chief remedy for all that self-centeredness which is our original sin and the source of all actual sin."[19]

The nineteenth-century lawyer-turned-evangelist, Charles Finney, argued that the church could do nothing without what he called, "the enduement of the Spirit, the power to savingly impress," which was God's response to total God-centered prayer. Without this the church could not be the church.

God-centered is the key phrase. The impediment to the empowerment of the church, Finney argued, was when prayer was not wholehearted, when the petitioner did not trust God to answer, or when prayer was self-directed. As the psalmist warned: "If I had cherished sin in my heart, the Lord would not have listened."[20]

We as a church pray not because it is the key to something—healing the sick, church growth, or even revival—but because God is God and worthy of our total obedience and reverence.*

True worship, in the same way, is radically countercultural, being directed not toward self but toward God. Richard Neuhaus puts it in sobering terms: "The celebration we call worship has less to do with the satisfaction or the pursuit of happiness than with the abandonment of the pursuit of happiness."[21] We worship God because, in the words of the Hartford Declaration—the 1975 document de-

---

*Healing, growth, and renewal may, of course, result from fervent prayer. Revivals in particular clearly move on the wings of prayer.

signed to explode modern theologies that were emptying God of transcendence—"God is to be worshiped."

True prayer and worship also run counter to the prevailing ethos in the church, which equates God's blessings with growth and material success. Remember the earlier account of the pastor and leaders of the church in California who prayed God would bring only His people to worship? This kind of shaking out is often a sign of revival—the moving of God's Spirit.*

## Under the Seal of the Spirit

The key for the empowerment of the church—what Jack Hayford of the Church on the Way calls the "foundational lesson"— is the moving of the Holy Spirit in the midst of a worshiping, prayerful community of God's people. Only then can the church be the church.

The truest measure of the church, therefore, is supernatural; that is, whether it is under the seal of the Holy Spirit. It began that way at Pentecost, and it must function that way today.

His Spirit is "the life of the church," writes Edmund Clowney, "He appoints officers; He imbues the covenantal people with power; He discloses the lordship of Christ—since one cannot say 'Christ is Lord' except under the power of the Holy Spirit; He gives for service—and is thus essential for equipping the saints; and He mediates true fellowship—koinonia means a sharing among those who have drunk of the same spirit." And He "seals the liberty of Christ's people in His kingdom since He fulfills the law in love, thus breaking the bonds of legalism."[22]

It was this presence of the Spirit in the community of faith that marked the early church, and "after they prayed, the place where they were meeting was shaken."[23] Then when Ananias and Sapphira

---

*Initially, a moving of the Spirit brings weeping and convicting pain, not growth. Revival comes to "scorch before it heals," says one revival historian. "It comes to condemn ministers and people for their unfaithful witness, for their selfish living, for the neglect of the cross, and to call into daily renunciation to an evangelical poverty and to a deep and daily consecration. It brings humiliation, a bitter knowledge of unworthiness and an open, humiliating confession of sin. . . . It is not the easy and glorious thing many think it to be who imagine it filled the pews and reinstated the church in power and authority" (James Burns, *Revival: Their Laws and Leaders,* 1909, cited in Wink E. Pratney, *Revival* [Springfield, Pa.: Whitaker House, 1983]).

were struck dead, "great fear seized the whole church"—and from there the church grew.[24] Throughout Acts, Luke records the sense of awe, fear, and reverence of God that the early church experienced.

And wherever this unmistakable seal of the Holy Spirit is upon God's people, as it was first in the Upper Room, there is the church.

A close friend, Dois Rosser, was in India a few years ago to construct buildings for churches in remote areas. One day he was asked to accompany an Indian friend who was working on a building in a particularly remote area of Central India. They drove for two and a half hours out into the country over rutted roads. Although it was the winter season, the weather was scorching, and Dois's face was soon covered with sweat and grime from the dusty roads.

Finally they came to a small Hindu village and from there made their way along a winding dirt road up a large hill. At the end of the road they parked, and the man led Dois up a narrow path on a barren hillside strewn with huge rocks, some as high as fifteen or twenty feet. The few clumps of vegetation looked as though they would hardly sustain life. It was, Dois thought, one of the most desolate places he had ever been.

At the end of the path they came to a small community, where the people swarmed out of little grass huts to greet them.

Dois was unprepared for what he saw—for this was a colony of lepers. Men, women, and children with their fingers eaten away, some with stubs where feet had been, eyelids gone, faces horribly disfigured.

As the two men approached, the people began to sing.

"Come let us show you our church," one of the elders said proudly, and the group, still singing, led Dois and his friend to a cleared area and a half-completed building on the hillside. Somehow these people had persuaded a stone mason to come and chip granite blocks from the boulders; then one by one they had carried these blocks to the clearing and mortared them into place in a rectangle. The walls of granite were now about waist high, and the people were joyous. No matter how long it took, they would continue accumulating what they could from begging in the town; they would finish their church. (At that moment, Dois vowed to himself to return with the help to finish the church building, which he later did.)

Before Dois left, the lepers asked if they could pray together. Again he was unprepared for what happened. Gathered in a great circle around the two visitors, the lepers prostrated themselves on that scorched earth, offering deep and reverent prayers, thanking

God for His goodness and grace and mercy. In that place of terrible poverty and suffering, in a land where Christians are outcast, there, under the seal of the Holy Spirit, was the church.

Halfway around the globe and in a very different place, this same spirit was evident when the beloved and gifted British pastor, David Watson, died at the age of fifty.

People who had been moved by David's teaching and writing and holy life gathered in churches and cathedrals across England. One memorial gathering was in St. Paul's, that grand seventeenth-century edifice designed by Christopher Wren, considered one of the great architectural attractions of London. More than two thousand people, including the Archbishop of Canterbury, the presiding archbishop, most of the ecclesiastical establishment, and many notables filled every available seat; many stood. A servant had died, and God's people from all across London, from all stations in life, of all colors and races, had gathered.[25]

As the service began, the presiding pastor reminded the worshipers of Watson's favorite festal shout, "Our God reigns." Suddenly, almost as if started by a gentle breeze, the shout began in the back of the great cathedral, sweeping across rows of grandly carved mahogany pews in a rising crescendo: "Our God reigns. Our God reigns." Some thought for certain that all of London could hear the thundering chorus.

This was the church proclaiming the enduring truth of all truths—*Our God reigns.*

And so it will be until the great consummation of history. Wherever those whom God has called to Himself come together to worship and proclaim Him Lord under the seal of the Holy Spirit—be it a hillside in India, a room of blindfolded men in Lebanon, a prison yard in Kentucky, or a great cathedral in London—there will be the church. Standing firm amid the winds of change. Standing strong against the tides of power. Standing boldly against the world for one enduring truth.

# *Part 2*

---

# *The Church versus the World*

The church is against the world, for the world.
*Hartford Declaration, 1975*

# 12

# *What Is Truth?*

THEY SAY THE POOL IS IN THE ALPS, somewhere between Italy and Switzerland. Hidden by early mists in the morning, ringed by mountain peaks, inaccessible except by a narrow footpath that forges a slender passage into the high valley.

Those few who discover it find also a tall, gray-haired figure draped in a toga of imperial Rome. He kneels beside the ice-blue waters, but he will not look up. Bending low over the pool, dipping his hands into the liquid ice bubbling up from underground springs, he rubs one hand over the other.

"I am innocent," he mumbles over and over, dipping and cleansing and wringing as he has for centuries. "I am innocent of the blood of this just person."

Legend? Yes. But the reality began early one morning in first-century Jerusalem when the Roman governor was awakened by an aide.

"They're causing trouble again," the soldier told Pontius Pilate. Gathered outside the Praetorium, holding torches aloft in the pre-dawn darkness, the Jews were shouting, "We must see Pilate."

This time it was the Jewish leadership, elders and scribes of the synagogue, including the chief priest himself. They had a prisoner with them, reported the aide, and were babbling something about treason and blasphemy.

Pontius Pilate groaned. He hated Jerusalem, and he hated the Jews. Normally he governed Judea and Samaria from his palace in

Caesarea by the sea, cooled by the Mediterranean breezes. But his superiors required him to come to Jerusalem for Jewish feast days and any other occasions that might breed turmoil. While the Jews had been ruled by the Romans for decades, they were still a constant source of trouble.

In Jerusalem, Pilate and his entourage made their headquarters in the Praetorium, a palace built by Herod the Great which housed the official government quarters. Here, despite the magnificent surroundings, the air felt trapped and stale. Pilate often tossed in his elegant bed, and his wife complained of tortuous headaches and troubled dreams in the walled city.

The Praetorium also boasted a large courtyard, convenient for the crowds who came to the governor for judgment or speeches. Pilate was used to addressing the Jews from a distance and preferred it that way. He was an immensely practical man, and the mysteries of their ancient faith irritated him no end. Their contempt for things Roman didn't help, nor did their stubborn refusal to honor the image of Caesar, their strict observances of religious rules, their endless prayers and sacrifices and incense floating in clouds above their temple courtyard.

These Jews also asserted the presence of an unseen God, a God whose name they would not even pronounce. It made Pilate nervous. The Romans had a pantheon of gods, of course, one for every conceivable situation, but the gods had their foibles too. Jupiter cheating behind Juno's back, Cupid's erring aim, Proserpina doomed to live half of each year in the underworld. The gods were helpful, even entertaining. But this solemn theocracy, this business about a king of the universe who demanded absolute allegiance was not only unfathomable; it was offensive. The Roman gods might at times display petty, humanlike jealousies, but nothing like this.

A year or so earlier Pilate's disdain had slipped out of control when some of the Jews had protested his use of funds from their temple treasury to finance the construction of an aqueduct. Their accusations were an affront to Rome. After all, as procurator of Judea he controlled the temple and its funds, and the aqueduct brought water to the city in which they lived. But in their usual zealous fervor they had accused him of sacrilege. Thousands of Jews, trooping in from all over the province for one of their strange festivals, had demonstrated outside the palace. So he'd decided to teach them a lesson.

Following his orders, a detachment of city troops moved in to quell the rioters. Many Jews were killed in the process, including the Galileans who had led the revolt. His soldiers had even managed to dispatch some of those pilgrims filling the temple with their endless sacrifices; they had severed the jugular veins of a number of Jews who had just offered their lambs for sacrifice. Pilate had relished the grim justice of the bodies of men and lambs, heaped together, their blood mingling on the holy altar.

The little massacre became the talk of Judea. Pilate even heard about it from Sejanus, his old friend and mentor. "Good work," Sejanus said. "Those Jews need to know who is really in control."

Until recently, Pilate had envied Sejanus as much as he admired him. The tribune had risen through the ranks of Roman privilege and power like a meteor, and Pilate had clung to the tails of his toga. Last year when the Emperor Tiberius left Rome for a rest at his residences in Campania and Capri, he had placed most of the government affairs in the hands of Sejanus, naming him "a partner in the work." Life at the pinnacle of the empire's politics had exhausted the seventy-year-old emperor.

Sejanus, along with his supporters, including Pilate, had been inducted into an elite group known as "friends of Caesar." The semi-official title connoted power, privilege, and prestige, and Pilate thrilled every time someone called him Caesar's friend.

If this title linked Pilate and Sejanus, a stronger bond was forged in their common hatred for the Jews. And that, ironically enough, was what led to Sejanus's downfall.

Sejanus had actually declared it his goal to "exterminate the nation [of Jews]" and had expelled all Jews from Italy.[1] With loyal men like Pontius Pilate in place, he hoped to flush the race from the eastern provinces as well as Palestine. In the process he would consolidate his power among the military, which also had no great affection for the Jews. His overriding objective, however, was to push the elderly Tiberius aside and become emperor himself.

But all had not gone well for Sejanus. The Roman legion of Syria had refused to honor his leadership, and loyal forces alerted Tiberius. The elderly emperor returned to Rome, where Sejanus and his key supporters in the city were tried and executed by order of the tribunal.

When this news reached Palestine, Pilate spent many an hour pacing, as if each step might distance him from Sejanus. His link to the traitor was well known, so Pilate knew he would survive only if he followed the emperor's ensuing decrees to the letter. But one of the first of Tiberius's orders was the worst. All the governors of the empire had received it, sealed by the emperor's own hand.

The new directive dramatically shifted the official Roman policy regarding treatment of the Jews. Tolerance was the position of the day, and Tiberius would be watching for any infractions. He wanted no more unrest in the provinces.

In an attempt at amelioration, Pilate ordered his people to cease minting the official Roman coins that had angered the Jews ever since Roman occupation. Gone was the pagan image they had refused, saying it violated one of their commandments, replaced by a plain coin without much decoration. Pilate ground his teeth even as he gave the order.

But now the troublesome citizens were outside his palace again. Pilate cursed and took his time. He splashed his puffy face with cool water and called his barber to comb his short, curly hair. A slave helped him adjust the folds of his toga. After the attendant had draped the ungainly piece of woven wool around him, arranging it expertly and flinging the bulk of it over his shoulder and around his left arm, Pilate straightened the rings on his hands, drank a chalice of Judean wine, and went to meet the Jews.

He had to go outside to do so, since their detestable religion prohibited them from entering the home of a Gentile. They even used the term "defiled." As if he were a piece of carrion rather than a governor of noble Rome!

When he stepped onto the balcony overlooking the massive stone courtyard, he saw the Jews below, their faces illumined by the glare of torches, shouting, pushing, shoving. Even the priests, normally so restrained, were screaming with passion.

In their midst stood a muscular man, bound with ropes and covered with dirt and bruises. Pilate's soldiers were in the process of pushing back the crowd and bringing the prisoner up the steps to the inner hall of the Praetorium.

"What accusation do you bring against this man?" Pilate shouted down to them.

"If he were not an evildoer," yelled one man, "we would not have delivered him to you!"

Pilate flushed. *The insolence of these people!* "You take him," he shouted. "Judge him according to your law."

Another priest shouted. "It is not lawful for us to put anyone to death."

*At least they understand their limits,* thought Pilate. The Jews retained the power to condemn a man according to their strange laws, but they needed the sanction of Rome to execute a criminal.

"He's perverting the nation," another shouted. "He is forbidding people to pay taxes to Caesar! He says that he himself is a king!"

By now Pilate could hear the booted feet of his soldiers as they led the prisoner into the hall behind him. He turned away from the crowd and went back inside.

The prisoner was in bad shape. Deep circles underscored his eyes, and bruises covered his body. It was obvious he had been brutally beaten. His robe, stained with blood, was sandy and gray where dust had been flung on him.

Despite his physical appearance, however, the man met Pilate's gaze, eye to eye. Pilate was not used to such a countenance. Prisoners usually hung their heads and stared at the dirt from which they had come.

He sat down and motioned for his aide to pour him another goblet of wine. "Are you the king of the Jews?" he asked the prisoner cynically, raising an eyebrow.

"It is as you say," the man replied, his voice low but firm. "Are you speaking for yourself, or did others tell you this about me?"

*Insufferable insolence,* Pilate thought. "Am I a Jew?" he shouted, flinging his goblet at the wall. "Your own nation, your chief priests, have delivered you to me. What have you done?"

"My kingdom is not of this world," responded the prisoner, returning to Pilate's initial question. "If my kingdom were of this world, my servants would fight so that I would not be delivered to the Jews." He glanced toward the armed soldiers on either side of Pilate and then at the ornate room, reflecting the pomp and power of Rome. "But my kingdom is not of this world."

In spite of his anger, Pilate was fascinated. These were riddles, to be sure, but the man had such an odd manner about him, something the governor had never seen before, something he couldn't quite identify. So self-confident, yet at the same time utterly lacking in self-consciousness.

"Are you a king, then?" he asked.

"You say rightly that I am a king," the man responded. "For this cause I was born, and for this cause I have come into the world: that I should bear witness to the truth. Everyone who is of the truth hears my voice."

*Back to riddles again,* Pilate thought. He hadn't any idea what the prisoner was talking about.

*Truth,* he thought. *In Rome the truth doesn't have much to do with whether one is king or not. In fact, truth doesn't have much to do with anything. It's all upside down. Sejanus is dead because he killed Jews and wanted to be king. These Jews want this prisoner dead because he claims to be their king. What does any of it really matter? What is truth? Or justice? It's all a matter of who holds the scepter.*

Pilate looked up. *Well, I hold it now. The eagle of imperial Rome.*

The prisoner was looking at him steadily, composed in the midst of the guards, the spears, the shouts of the crazy Jews filtering up from the courtyard outside. The man even had a look of compassion in his eyes. Pilate couldn't stand it.

"Truth," he said tiredly, shrugging as he got up from his seat and arranged the folds of his toga. "What *is* truth?" And he went back out to the balcony to deal with the Jews.

As he looked down at them, he realized that for some reason he wanted to save the strange prisoner. The truth of the matter at hand seemed thoroughly irrelevant, but these stiff-necked, screaming Jews should be taught a lesson—if he could do so without creating a riot.

He stepped to the railing of the balcony. "I find no fault in this man," he said softly, so the people would have to shut up to hear him. When his words registered, they burst into shouts of anger and accusation.

Pilate threw up his hands in resignation. They had shouted that this man was from Galilee. Well, Galilee was in Herod's jurisdiction. Let him deal with it.

"Send him to Herod," he told his soldiers. "Let him decide this case."

But soon the prisoner was back in Pilate's court. Herod hadn't settled the matter, but obviously he and his men had made sport of the Galilean. The man was now wearing a crown of spiked thorns and a blood-soaked purple robe.

So it began all over again. Pilate alternated between questioning the prisoner, who now refused to speak for the most part, and confronting the Jews with alternatives. They refused to accept anything but execution.

Then came a pause in the proceedings. A lithe, dark-skinned messenger, a bodyguard and attendant to Pilate's wife, appeared. He raised his eyebrows to the soldiers standing guard on either side of the governor, and they moved aside to let him through. He slipped behind the judgment seat upon which Pilate was sitting and bent respectfully toward the governor's ear.

"A message from your wife," he whispered. "She has had another of her dreams. She told me to come to you as quickly as I could. It is about the Galilean."

Pilate looked out over the simmering crowd of Jews. His wife often had troubled night visions in Jerusalem: sleeping shadows of tumbling walls and overturned stones. What could she have dreamed about this strange prisoner?

The aide bent again. "She said to tell you this: 'Have nothing to do with that innocent man, for I have suffered a great deal today in a dream because of him.'"

*Innocent!* The thought made Pilate's stomach turn over.

He dismissed the messenger with a nod and turned back to the people.

"I have examined this man and have found no basis for your charges against him," he shouted. "He has done nothing to deserve death. Therefore, I will punish him and then release him."

Back came the cries from voices hoarse with hatred. "Away with this man! Crucify him! Crucify him!"

"What?" Pilate finally shouted back, infuriated by their fury. "Shall I crucify your king?"

Then it happened. Led by a priest who knew Rome's ways, they howled like dogs that had picked up the scent of the quarry, "We have no king but Caesar." The incredible words never before heard from the mouth of a Jew now issued from the lips of the chief priest himself. Pilate stepped back in shock.

"Whoever makes himself a king speaks against Caesar!" the chief priest continued. "And if you let this man go, *you are no friend of Caesar!*"

They had him. Pilate saw the jaws of the trap spring tight. Sejanus had been stripped of his title; he was no friend of Caesar, the tribunal had charged. Then they had executed him.

Pilate wanted to triumph over the Jews in this stupid mess. But Emperor Tiberius had made the choice clear in his purge of Roman ranks: Friends of Caesar need have no other friends. If Pilate's choice was between this man and Caesar, he would take Caesar. He wasn't about to lose his life over someone who spoke riddles about kingship and truth.

"Water," called Pilate hoarsely. "Water!"

When an aide appeared with a deep basin, Pilate ordered him to hold it up high so the crowd could see it.

Then Pilate dipped his hands in the water and wiped them with a linen towel. "I am innocent of the blood of this just person," he said loudly. "You see to it."

And they did.

# 13

## *I Am the Truth*

One word of truth shall outweigh the whole world.
*Aleksandr Solzhenitsyn*

**W**HAT IS TRUTH?" THE CYNICAL ROMAN governor asked the Messiah.

Scripture provides no intonation or inflection, so we do not know how Pilate asked the question. But the account does record that after asking the question, Pilate turned away and offered Jesus back to the Jews. He did not wait for the Galilean's reply. So it is fair to conclude that he wasn't looking for an answer.

One thing is certain: He either did not understand or did not accept what Jesus meant. If he had, he could not possibly have turned away.

During His ministry, Jesus made many remarkable claims. That He and His Father were one. That He could forgive sin. That through faith in Him one has life eternal. Christianity itself rests on the astonishing claim that Jesus rose bodily from the dead and ascended into heaven. But of all these claims, the most remarkable is His bold statement: *I am the truth.*

In the midst of so many dramatic events, this statement is often passed over too quickly. Of course Jesus is the truth, we say . . . and then move right on to the Crucifixion, without considering the full import of His declaration.

For one thing, we commonly think of Christ's words metaphorically, as when He called Himself "the way" . . . "the door" . . . "the vine." But this is no metaphor.

I've asked many believers what they think about Christ's claim to be the truth. Many confess that they've given it very little thought, but when pressed, they often respond that Jesus was claiming that He was who He said He was. He was confirming that He truly was the Son of God, the Messiah.

Well, that in itself is a staggering proposition. But Jesus was saying much more. He was telling us something that, if properly understood, radically affects our view of the essence and character of the Christian faith as well as the very nature of the world.

The dictionary defines truth not only as "genuineness or veracity," but also as "that which conforms to reality or fact—that which is in accordance with what is, what has been, or must be."

The first part of that definition is quickly understood. Truth is veracity. Which means something is true when we can vouch for it or prove it; when it is evident through physical examination or proven through physical phenomena. It is true, for example, that the words you are reading are printed in black ink. It is true that the sun will rise at a precise minute and hour tomorrow morning, which we can determine.

And some phenomena may be true even though they are beyond known physical laws. It is true, for example, that Jesus was resurrected bodily from the grave. Though skeptics have for nearly two millennia tried to explain away this reality, the historical evidence is overwhelming.

But Jesus' claim does not just assert veracity *about* Himself; He boldly claims that He is *the* truth.

That claim fits the second part of Webster's definition; that is, truth is that which conforms to reality or fact, what is, what has been, or must be. And Jesus does not claim to be just one truth or one reality among many, but to be *the ultimate reality*—the root of what is and what was, the point of origin and framework for all that we can see and know and understand. It is the assertion that in the beginning was God, that He is responsible for the universe, for our very existence, and that He has created the order and structure in which life exists. Everything we know—all meaning—flows from Him.

Interestingly, the recent NASA satellite discovery of radiation fluctuations in the atmosphere, which could account for the formation of earth and other planets and galaxies arising from a big bang, profoundly affects scientific understanding of ultimate reality. And it does so in a way that confirms the ancient biblical view.

Since the Enlightenment, astronomers have asserted, as did the pagan world, that the cosmos is eternal. The most illustrious contemporary advocate of that view is Carl Sagan, who says the cosmos is all there is or ever will be. Thus there is no need for God to have created the world.

But this NASA discovery undermines these premises. It postulates that there was a beginning point from which, by some extraordinary force of energy, the universe was created. One scientist says all matter started as a tiny ball and was exploded with such a spectacular force that it expanded across millions of light years; and the force continues today as the universe continues its expansion.

Incomprehensible? Indeed it is by any known law of physics. Matter cannot come out of nothing by itself, let alone with a force of such unimaginable magnitude. Yet while this might defy the laws of physics, in this one critical respect, it affirms the process described in Genesis.*

Ultimate reality embodied in God and Christ is the most consistent theme in Scripture. When God described Himself in His extraordinary encounter with a terrified shepherd named Moses, what did He say? "I am who I am." Nothing more need be said. As the creator, God is the ultimate source of authority and meaning, the very essence of what is. Thus the Jews made the phrase "I am," *Yahweh*, their way of identifying God throughout the Scriptures. *Yahweh* appears more than six thousand times in the Old Testament.

No wonder the unbelieving Jews wanted to stone Jesus when He told them, "Most assuredly, I say to you, before Abraham was, I AM."[1] He was not claiming to be like God or sent by God. He was claiming to be *Yahweh*—the "I am."

Note as well the New Testament writers' use of the Greek word *logos* to describe Christ. We translate that as "word" because there is no good corresponding term in English. But, in fact, *logos* embraces what we would call intelligence, reason, and truth—that which is embodied in the very plan of creation itself.[2] So from *Yahweh* to *Logos*, the biblical accounts present God and Christ as the ultimate reality.

Understanding this provides an objective basis for knowledge and the understanding of all reality. Under the influence of Enlightenment thinkers, the modern world has separated faith

---

*According to the big bang theory the universe is still in process, while in the Genesis account creation was completed and God rested. But on the critical point—whether the universe always was or was created—modern science affirms the Genesis view.

and reason. In the last two centuries the divide has become virtually unbridgeable. On the one side are those things that we believe
can be proven—scientifically observable phenomena; on the other
side are those things, like God, that modern man believes cannot
be empirically validated and can only be accepted on faith.

A chair is in the room, goes the proposition in philosophy class.
You see it. But when you leave the room, how do you know that the
chair is still there? You don't know for sure. Perhaps it was only an
illusion; perhaps it was only there when you were looking. At best
we can establish phenomena only by empirical observations—or so
we have been taught. This means that unless a phenomenon can be
proved, it has no objective standing. This modern view erodes not
only historic Christianity but the props of civilization itself, as discussed later.*

But understanding Christianity as the truth means more than
simply deducing reality through physical examination. The truth—
ultimate reality—is not limited to what we observe. Thus, the Christian believes that there is no gap between faith and reason; to believe
otherwise would implicitly deny, as one theologian argues, "that all
truth is the truth of the one God revealed in Jesus Christ."[3]

All meaning and understanding are rooted in the ultimate reality of the God who is. Apart from Him, nothing was created.
Apart from Him, we are unable to perceive or to deduce truth
about anything. No wonder Malcolm Muggeridge, the great writer
and inveterate iconoclast, asserted with supreme confidence that
he could be more certain of the reality of Jesus Christ than of his
own reality.

This concept, what Francis Schaeffer described as "true truth,"
or "the flaming truth," is so ultimate and absolute that it is difficult
to articulate, and even more difficult to grasp. But ponder it . . . do
not pass quickly over this point. For throughout all of history this

---

*Immanuel Kant (1724–1804) held that the only things one could know for sure
were the phenomenological. Everything else had to be accepted by faith. The well-
known chair example originated with George Berkeley, the eighteenth-century
Irish philosopher who postulated *esse est percippi* ("to be is to be perceived"). David
Hume (1711–76), one of the Enlightenment's most influential philosophers, denied
all that is supernatural and miraculous because it could not be scientifically—empirically—verified. Likewise the logical positivists (such as A. J. Ayer, in his *Language, Truth and Logic*) of this century. The result of all this was to perceive God as
only a personal, subjective experience, and to separate Him from all other verifi-
able disciplines of life.

has been mankind's greatest quest: *What is reality?* Is there meaning? How do we know it? Do we live in chaos or order? How did we get here?

### How Firm a Foundation

Through the centuries the answers have ranged from the biblical view to a host of different philosophies. Modern men and women, however, have despaired of the quest. Under the influence of Eastern mysticism and secularism, they seek meaning not in some ultimate point beyond themselves, but within themselves.

The result is the moral exhaustion of the modern world, which is why it is so crucial for Christians to understand that Christ is the truth. Jesus is the Alpha and Omega, the beginning and the end from which all else flows—the *Logos* from which all creation sprang, the past and the future and what will be. And thus it is in Christ that all things are held together.[4]

To understand the importance of this belief in an ultimate truth that provides order, one has only to look at the history of Western civilization.

From the beginning, civilized Western thought and civilization assumed the existence of objective truth: the prevailing intellectual consensus was rooted in the Judeo-Christian tradition and the Greco-Roman idealistic tradition which explained the universe, humanity, and the purpose of life. This consensus became the cornerstone upon which the great philosophical systems rested, giving a form, substance, and context in which science, art, music, and commerce could develop and creating an environment in which political and ethical discourse could be measured. Whether one believed in the God of the Bible or not, this consensus provided secure philosophical ground upon which civilization could flourish.

At the most basic level, men and women could relate their own existence to the supernatural, a connection that provided a sense of personal significance. Apart from a transcendentally meaningful universe, the ultimate questions are too awful to contemplate. Severed from this connection, we are lost in the cosmos. Or, as Charlie Chaplin remarked after he was told there was no life on Mars, "I feel lonely."[5]

Precisely right. If a personal God is not there, who is? And what are we connected to? Like Doctor Who or Captain Kirk and the Starship *Enterprise*, we are adrift in time and space.

Or consider science. It is a modern myth that Christianity and science are mortal enemies. In fact, most of the early scientists were Christians. Copernicus, Kepler, Galileo, Newton, Pascal. All believed the world had an orderly structure that could be scientifically studied because it was created by an orderly God.

Several science historians have recently published works documenting the historical relationship between science and Christianity. While many civilizations demonstrated great technical expertise—Egypt with its pyramids, Rome with its aqueducts—only one, they say, produced the experimental method we call science. That was a Christian culture: Europe at the end of the Middle Ages. The reason, says one historian, was the biblical teaching of a rational God: "Experimental science began its discoveries . . . in the faith . . . that it was dealing with a rational universe controlled by a Creator who did not act upon whim."[6] And the scientific method has always depended on the assumption that the universe is ordered.*

The same point can be made with respect to learning. Western scholarship was prodigious because it assumed a unity of knowledge and that truth was an objective to be pursued. Indeed, the liberal arts university was instituted in the Middle Ages as a Christian undertaking expressly for the pursuit of truth.[7] But if there is no truth, then intellectual pursuits and education become merely a process. Fads displace learning, the intellect withers, and we end up refining the analytical without knowing what is to be analyzed.

Similarly, Western art, music, literature, and politics flourished as they reflected the order and significance of a meaningful universe. (This was particularly evident in the Reformation, as we will see later.) Remove order and you are left without form, void. With no objective standard to point to what is true or real, music echoes discord; art reflects nothingness; literature stutters into chaos.

When it came to ethics and philosophy, the moral consensus based on biblical revelation provided a framework for moral behavior through most of Western civilization. At one time, Francis

---

*Another science historian states that the idea of "laws" in nature comes from the "Hebraic and Christian belief in a deity who was at once Creator and Lawgiver" (A. R. Hall, *The Scientific Revolution, 1500–1800* [Boston: Beacon Press, 1954], 171–72). And sociologist R. K. Merton, in his famous thesis, says that modern science owes its very existence to the Christian notion of moral obligation. Since God made the world, it is not to be despised; it is to be used for the benefit of mankind (R. K. Merton, "Puritanism, Pietism, and Science," *Sociological Review*, 28/1 [1936]: 37–68).

Schaeffer says, he shared a platform with former cabinet member and urban leader John Gardner, during which Gardner spoke on the need to restore values to our culture. After he finished, a Harvard student asked him: "On what do you build your values?" Gardner, usually articulate and erudite, paused, looked down, and said, "I do not know."[8]

I repeatedly encounter the same reaction. When I have contended before scholars and college audiences that in a secular, relativistic society there is no basis for ethics, no one has ever challenged me. In fact, in private they often agree.

But nowhere is the existence of an absolute standard more vital than in politics and government. In the West, nations built sound political structures on the belief that ultimately man's laws were to be but a reflection of God's immutable, moral laws. This undergirded the United States Constitution.

But if there is no truth—no objective standard of what is good or just and, therefore, no standard of what is unjust—then the social contract is always threatened by the whim of the moment. And tyranny, either from the unrestrained passions of the majority or from a ruthless dictator, inevitably follows.[9]

Throughout the history of the West, regardless of what area of human endeavor one examines, the pattern has been the same.

### People of the Truth

"What is truth?" Pilate asked.

If the implications of Jesus' answer are overwhelmingly significant for the world, they are no less profound for the church. For if we understand what Jesus meant by His extraordinary statement, "I am the truth," it utterly transforms our view of Christianity.

Christianity is not some religious structure or social institution. It is not merely a set of beliefs or creeds about the nature of reality. The Christian faith rests on *the* truth: ultimate reality. The Christian experience begins with a personal relationship with Jesus Christ made possible as men and women are declared righteous by their faith. These born-again individuals then constitute a new society that points to the coming kingdom, which is centered on the core of all meaning—the God who was, who is, and who is to come, and the God who has revealed Himself in human history.

The One who said, "I am the truth," also said that "[the Father's] word is truth."[10] Truth is propositional and revealed; God has spoken through Scripture, and thus we are given a comprehensive revelation of reality. Thus, the orthodox creeds, which flow from Scripture and which have historically been regarded as the fundamentals of the Christian faith, are rooted in absolute and ultimate truth.

In the middle of the darkest night of Pilate's life, Jesus told him, "Everyone who is of the truth hears My voice."[11] Pilate had ears, but he did not hear. And so he turned away, asking, "What is truth?" even as he stood before the truth Himself.

But Pilate is more than a tragic figure of Shakespearian proportions, condemned by history to wash his bloodstained hands forever. For he symbolizes the very mind of man, particularly modern man. You can see Pilate asking his disdainful question in living color any day. Simply turn on your television.

# 14

## Lost in the Cosmos

Modern man has both feet firmly planted in mid-air.
*Francis Schaeffer*

Modern man is betting his life that this is it, and that there is no judgment and that there is no eternity.
*R. C. Sproul*

$C$HUCK, COME DOWN HERE. YOU'VE GOT to see this!" Patty called. While she was in the kitchen chopping vegetables for our dinner salad, she had turned on the television. The late-afternoon talk shows were just hitting the airwaves, and when she flipped to one of them, she came dangerously close to slicing off her finger.

What she had tuned in on was a "Donahue" segment featuring a panel of mothers who had decided that since their teenage kids were going to have sex anyway, they would rather have them do it at home. A matronly woman was describing the neat little code system she and her daughter had arranged: a green tag on the bedroom door meant that Mom should STAY OUT, SEX IN PROGRESS.

The other panelists nodded approvingly. How clever! How tolerant! How loving! How nineties!

This is what the world today calls reality.

"Donahue," "Geraldo," "Oprah," and "Sally Jessy Raphael" have become America's new town hall, where the great issues of the day are debated . . . well, not quite.

Watch and you'll see just about everything else: transvestites marrying transvestites; lesbian and gay lovers coming together to inseminate one another; sex slaves; people who were fired from their jobs because they posed nude in skin magazines; the merits of augmentation, liposuction, and other cosmetic surgeries; men who

**165**

filmed their wives having sex with other men . . . the parade is endless, and anything goes. Provided it is tragic, erotic, depraved, melodramatic, and, above all, sensational.

In a rare burst of candor the producers of these shows recently confessed to the fierce competition they face as they search frantically for the most bizarre and erotic subjects and guests, particularly during the seasonal rating sweeps. "You can no longer just put prostitutes on," said "Donahue" producer Ed Glavin. "It has to be prostitutes who are sex addicts, or prostitutes whose fathers love what they do," added an associate.[1]

When anyone in the audience dares to voice disgust or concern, he or she is quickly dispensed with by Phil's arching eyebrows—his Oh-boy-are-you-out-of-it look—and a grand sweeping wave of his arm as he moves the microphone to someone else.

And there are always those in the audience who strike the popular chord when they say, "Well, if this is what you want, who are we to object?"

The audience always applauds. For that, you see, is the conventional wisdom of the Donahueites—the "do whatever is right for you, and you are being faithful to whatever is true for you" school of thought. What Donahueites believe is that you—and only you—should decide what you want. No one else has a right to tell you what to do.

While Donahue professes to be a neutral interviewer, he is hardly reluctant to articulate his views. As he told Barbara Walters, "I'm for gay rights; I'm pro-choice," and he thinks the senators who challenged Anita Hill "should be strung up by their ——. They had the audacity and stupidity to carry on like that."[2]

Nor is Donahue's programming neutral. The immorality he promotes is damaging to the millions of Americans whose values are increasingly shaped by television.

But that isn't even the worst of it. It's the very *banality* of it all that sucks every bit of meaning, truth, and purpose out of life. And that's the real definition of decadence.

"Decadence," says Richard Neuhaus, "is the decay that results from the hollowing out of meanings. When decadence is in full swing, meanings are not simply hollow but we exult in the gutting of them. This we call autonomy, liberation, freedom."[3]

In this televised theater of the absurd, people are presented as insecure animals—most often likable ones, to be sure—who drift through life seeking nothing more than the fulfillment of their biological urges or their insatiable need for self-esteem. And all topics carry equal weight, with no objective moral distinctions. On this stage, the transvestite husband and the teenage exotic dancer and the occasional politician or professional who somehow sneaks onto the program are all graded the same way. Their nobility or heroism is established not by what they do, but by whether they are seen as doing what they find meaningful, whether they are *doing what is right for them.* Utter that phrase on Donahue, and you are guaranteed approval.

This relentless drivel renders viewers incapable of distinguishing between what is important and what isn't. Watch hours of this every week, and one's moral senses can be permanently neutered.

And that is happening to millions of Americans every day. Nielsen estimates that national viewership of *each* of these talk shows ranges from 2.5 million to 8.6 million—and many people watch more than one.[4] So it is safe to say that each day tens of millions are watching Phil or Oprah or Geraldo or Sally or one of their clones in what passes as moral discourse in American life. While in earlier times the citizenry gathered in town halls, the purest form of democratic discussion, today they lean back in their La-Z-Boys to watch Phil and Oprah preside over the great debates.

Some have actually argued that modern network television is essential for national survival on the grounds that it is the one instrument today that provides national cohesion.[5] If this is so, then television programming could properly be labeled our modern American religion, since the word religion derives from the Latin *religiare,* meaning "to bind together." While Scripture provided the most cohesive force in culture forty years ago, it seems that the base of common understanding and communication today is the television networks.

Admittedly television does provide a useful cohesive function during times of national crisis. When the space shuttle *Challenger* exploded, Americans gathered around their televisions to mourn. When hostage Terry Anderson was finally released, millions cheered the satellite image as if they were there to greet him at the hospital in Wiesbaden. During the heights and depths of our common human drama, television can draw us together.

But day-in, day-out Donahueism celebrates no human drama. Instead, it trivializes the human experience and distracts from the great questions of life. No one in today's talk show audiences, let alone the hosts, stands up and asks: What is the meaning of all this? . . . How does this affect our lives? . . . Is it right? . . . Does this promote the greater good? . . . What is true? . . . What is the truth?

On one Donahue show exalting some particularly grotesque immorality, a young man stood up and said, "Jesus is the answer." Donahue rolled his eyes and whipped the mike to another person while the studio audience stared at the young man blankly. He might as well have descended from another planet.

Donahueites are so distracted by their fatal attraction to banal banter that they have, in effect, lost consciousness that there is such a thing as truth. Life is merely the individual's pursuit of whatever he or she wants. Pleasure most likely, unless you're into pain. Life has no higher purpose than individual gratification.

The Donahueite world-view is of a linear life. When a certain number of years have elapsed, it's over. Period. It's a pathetic picture, and one people seldom look at unless it is forced upon them— as it was with poignancy and wit in *City Slickers.* While this movie may not rank among the great morality plays of all time (and some would find parts of the film offensive), it certainly drives the point home, along with the cattle.

Comedian Billy Crystal plays the part of a bored baby boomer who sells radio advertising time. On the day he visits his son's school to tell about his work along with other fathers, he suddenly lets loose a deadpan monologue to the bewildered youngsters in the class:

> Value this time in your life, kids, because this is the time in your life when you still have your choices. It goes by so fast.
>
> When you're a teenager, you think you can do anything and you do. Your twenties are a blur.
>
> Thirties you raise your family, you make a little money, and you think to yourself, "What happened to my twenties?"
>
> Forties, you grow a little pot belly, you grow another chin. The music starts to get too loud, one of your old girlfriends from high school becomes a grandmother.
>
> Fifties, you have a minor surgery—you'll call it a procedure, but it's a surgery.
>
> Sixties, you'll have a major surgery, the music is still loud, but it doesn't matter because you can't hear it anyway.
>
> Seventies, you and the wife retire to Fort Lauderdale. You start eating dinner at 2:00 in the afternoon, you have lunch around 10:00, breakfast the night before, spend most of your time

wandering around malls looking for the ultimate soft yogurt and muttering, "How come the kids don't call? How come the kids don't call?"

The eighties, you'll have a major stroke, and you end up babbling with some Jamaican nurse who your wife can't stand, but who you call mama.

Any questions?

Any questions? No, the Donahueized culture is anesthetized. So mesmerized by the vapid, they are incapable of questions.

But the Donahueites, who trivialize into oblivion any deeper questions of life, represent only one of the groups influencing our culture. The other is more strident and deliberate. And it isn't oblivious to reality. In fact, it consciously seeks to erase the very concept of truth itself.

This second group is smaller in number, made up principally of cultural elites who have a well-formed world-view which they aggressively advance. We might name them after any one of many influential thinkers, but the namesake we have chosen is Ellen Goodman, an enchanting writer whose syndicated columns slickly attack what she sees as the grave peril of absolutism—the very notion that there could be such a thing as the truth. She and her cohorts are the shock troops in the vanguard of the forces of relativism.

A typical example would be a column she wrote during the ugly debate over Clarence Thomas's nomination to the Supreme Court. At the heart of this debate, although it was never plainly articulated, was the issue of natural law: whether society lives by some absolute standard of truth or by the subjective whims of those in influence.

When he stood beside President Bush on the lawn at Kennebunkport the day he was nominated, Thomas, visibly moved, expressed thanks to the Catholic nuns who had educated him. It took no more than this for Virginia Governor Douglas Wilder to publicly question whether Judge Thomas owed allegiance to the pope (notwithstanding that Thomas attends an Episcopal church).

Only thirty years earlier that same question, on the part of some imprudent Protestants about presidential candidate John Kennedy, set off howls of outrage and charges of bigotry. But there was scarcely a murmur when Wilder made his offensive statement. In fact, Ms. Goodman fell all over herself to rush to his defense: "It isn't liberals and it certainly isn't Douglas Wilder who have reopened the can of worms marked religion. It's the Catholic hierarchy."[6]

Then, while noting that there should be no religious test for office—a rather unremarkable concession since the Constitution is explicit on the point—she proceeded to excoriate the Catholic Church. Why?

Because Cardinal Joseph Bernardin had stated that "all Catholics are bound by the moral principles prohibiting abortion," she charged, while another of the clergy had the temerity to say that there was no way to justify a pro-choice vote.[7]

How arbitrary! How unprogressive! How dare the Catholic Church hold to an orthodox position that has not changed for two thousand years! How dare a Supreme Court nominee link himself in gratitude to nuns from that same church!

To Ellen Goodman, the church's historic stand is scandalous. She cites its failure to keep up with modern trends, claiming that only 7 to 18 percent of all Catholics agree with the church's stand.[8] In other words, in the Goodmanite school of logic, truth is determined by majority vote.

The media is filled with alumni of this school. Bill Moyers, although a Southern Baptist seminary graduate, is an accomplished Goodmanite. In an interview with Tom Wolfe, Moyers agreed with the writer when he said that our newfound freedom *from* religion has been a healthy development—Wolfe called it the fifth freedom. "Taking away religion's power to restrain others has been a fairly positive gain in the last hundred years," said Moyers.[9]

Every area of life is under similar assault from this disdain for truth. Only a few years ago Dr. Allan Bloom opened his book, *The Closing of the American Mind,* with the bald statement that "almost every student entering the university believes or says that he believes that truth is relative."[10] And people seemed surprised by his chilling conclusions about students and education today.

But relativism is firmly established as the reigning orthodoxy of American life. Speaking at the inauguration of Vartan Gregorian as president of Brown University, distinguished historian Arthur Schlesinger defended relativism as the enlightened course and decried the perils of absolutism: "It is this belief in absolutes . . . that is the great enemy today of the life of the mind." And then he added this heroic call: "The mystic prophets of the absolute cannot save us. Sustained by our history and traditions, we must save ourselves at whatever risk of heresy or blasphemy."[11]

It is difficult to find campuses in America where Schlesinger's views do not reign.[12] "There is no knowledge, no standard, no choice that is objective," says Barbara Herrstein Smith, a leading feminist scholar.[13]

This Goodmanite philosophy has filtered down from the ivory towers of academia by way of the media to Main Street USA, where, according to a 1991 George Barna poll, 67 percent of the American people believe there is no such thing as absolute truth![14]

When George Gallup asked Americans whether they agreed with the statement, "There are few moral absolutes: what is right and wrong usually varies from situation to situation," 69 percent agreed.[15]

So much for moral absolutes and truth. The Goodmanites and Donahueites have performed their operation with great success. The Donahueites anesthetized the patients, and the Goodmanites wielded the scalpel to complete the moral lobotomy.

As a result, the only stable virtue left in this relativistic world is unbridled tolerance: the modern broadmindedness which purports that any and all values, if sincerely held, are equally valid (except a value that claims allegiance to absolute truth, of course). There are no absolutes except the absolute that there can be no absolutes.

This is a frightening prospect, for ideas do have consequences. The views of life that engaged the minds of intellectuals and penetrated the imaginations of the masses have dramatically affected the currents of history. What we now know as recorded events are merely manifestations of these world-views.

For example, without the philosophy of Friedrich Nietzsche, which laid the foundation for resurgent German nationalism and the master race, there wouldn't have been an Adolf Hitler or a World War II. Without Karl Marx's utopian vision of the worker state, there would have been no Vladimir Lenin or Joseph Stalin. And without the moral consensus that sprang from the Greek philosophers and the enduring truth of biblical revelation, there would be no Western civilization.

Although the West is still called a "Christian culture" by some, it is not. It is a distinctly post-Christian, dominated by a relativistic world-view.

## The Prevailing World-view:
## Dancing with Wolves in Sheep's Clothing

Everyone has presuppositions, a general set of beliefs, a grid through which we perceive everything that happens—a general belief about what is true. Our presuppositions form the basis for our values, and these values determine how we behave.

What are the characteristics of the prevailing world-view in our culture, shaped as it is by relativism? It is critical that the Christian know and understand these characteristics, for they shape the environment in which the church must know, live, and defend its beliefs.

### The Prevailing World-view Is Secular

As an adjective, the word *secular* means merely "of this world," or "of the present age." As a world-view, however, it becomes secular*ism*, an ideology that places all emphasis on the here and now.

The anthem of modern American secularism is captured in the beer commercial: "You only go around this way once, so grab for all the gusto you can." Or as the t-shirts proclaim, "Carpe diem"—*Seize the day!*—the ultimate existential expression.

Such an attitude demands—no, exalts—instant gratification. Thus, sex, food, vacations, cars, wardrobes, drugs, whatever are the ends of life. Then there's the mid-life crisis, with plastic surgery or a sports car or a younger spouse to turn back the clock. As time passes, attempts to have it all become more desperate. Some don't wait; they move at once to the logical conclusion: crime—white collar, blue collar, any collar. *If I want what I want when I want it, why not take it?*

Translate this world-view into public policy, and it's easy to see why the nation is sinking in debt. If there is no tomorrow, why not triple the national deficit in just one self-indulgent decade?

And if there is no tomorrow, then there really is no value in yesterday either. For its own intellectual consistency, relativism cannot be content with exalting the momentary; it has to dispense with any belief in the objective reality of the past.

### The Prevailing World-view Is Antihistorical

During the last few decades, building on the growing skepticism about objective truth, a viewpoint known as deconstructionism has flourished on college campuses.* If there is no objective truth, there is no reason for objective interpretation of history, law, or politics. Deconstructionists contend, therefore, that past events or writings have no intrinsic meaning. What authors intended in literature, for example, is irrelevant. What matters is what we think of what they wrote. Authorial intent in historical documents suffers the same fate. So we freely revise the past to conform to current politically correct values.

Though born in the ivory towers of academia, deconstructionism first made its way into high culture and the courtroom. It is evident in current interpretations of the Constitution, where the original intent of the framers is considered irrelevant—or not considered at all; how we choose to interpret it in light of shifting social demands is what matters.

Now deconstructionism has invaded popular culture. The movies, for example.

When I come home from a trip filled with speaking engagements, prison visits, and meetings, I need to relax and unwind. One way I do this is to watch a good video. After *Dances with Wolves* swept the Academy Awards, Patty and I eagerly rented it one evening.

In the movie, Kevin Costner plays a sensitive Civil War hero sent to command a U.S. fort on the Western frontier. Gradually he makes friends with a nearby Sioux tribe and finds the Indians far more attractive than the white men he's known—as do the viewers.

The Sioux in this film are noble and humane. The white men, except Costner, are drunken, insane, perverted, or vicious. It's a relief when they get scalped. One movie critic wrote that he overheard a viewer say, "It makes you ashamed to be white."

That, of course, is the point.

---

*Deconstruction is literally the dismantling of language, texts, and discourse. It began in the realm of language and has since spread to other disciplines. It first manifested itself in English literature departments. If language, discourse, and thus, the intention of an author, can be called into question and doubted, then other realms can fall like dominoes. History, law, and politics proceed from an undermining of language, not vice versa. For those interested in reading further on this matter, we suggest John Ellis, *Against Deconstruction* (Princeton: Princeton University Press, 1984); Bruce L. Edwards, *The Suicide of Liberal Education: Deconstruction in Academia,* Heritage Lecture Series 277 (Washington, D.C.: Heritage Foundation, 1990); and Dinesh D'Souza, *Illiberal Education: The Politics of Race and Sex on Campus* (New York: Free Press, 1991).

While no one would deny that many white people committed abuses against the Native Americans, this movie totally ignores the historical fact that at the very time depicted in the film the Sioux were the most warlike of all the Plains Indian tribes, perpetrating some of the bloodiest massacres.

At one point in the film Costner brings bad news to his Indian brothers: More white men are coming. How many? they ask. Costner points to the star-packed skies above their campfire. "As many as the stars," he says. A subtle reference to the Abrahamic covenant?

It's clear in this movie that the real bad news is Western civilization. In both nuanced allusions as well as out-and-out caricature, the noble savage's enemy is Judeo-Christian civilization.

Deconstructionism at work.

Another popular film, also starring Kevin Costner, does exactly the same thing. It's the story of Robin Hood with some new twists.

First of all, the heroine is no maiden in distress; she's a 1990s-style Ms. Marian. Friar Tuck is a drunk whose Christianity is depicted as the same superstitious ignorance that fueled the horrific Crusades from which Robin has just returned. And the new hero, a character added to the original story, is Azeem, a Muslim Moor.

Repeatedly Azeem demonstrates the superiority of Muslim culture over the flawed Christianity of Crusade-era England. In one scene, Friar Tuck solemnly pronounces that a woman in difficult childbirth must die; it is God's will. Azeem quietly delivers the baby by Caesarean.

What's a Muslim doing in Sherwood Forest?

Deconstructionism at work.

Since white males aren't politically correct heroes in the 1990s, history—even the history of legend—has to be rewritten.

And then there's the infamous *JFK*, director Oliver Stone's $70-million re-interpretation of President Kennedy's assassination. With amazing skill, Stone has created an almost seamless montage of fact and fiction—real footage blended with re-created scenes. Historical realities about John Kennedy's assassination are merged with theories to fit Stone's political agenda. And once again the real enemy is "the Establishment"—which in this case includes the CIA, the FBI, the Mafia, the Dallas police force, and the whole "military-industrial complex" who conspired to kill the idealistic young president.

Deconstructionism at work.

Now granted, movies have never been known for their historical accuracy. John Wayne seldom got it right either. So all this might seem rather innocuous. After all, isn't this just artistic license—putting a new twist on an old tale? No, this is much more .

Nor is the issue here just concern over political bias or politically correct revisionism or even the trashing of Christianity. It is that the effect of these popular movies—and their underlying philosophy—erodes our sense of history altogether. And if history has no meaning, then a society has no tradition to draw upon, no lessons learned from or debts owed to the past.

Yet the very heart of our republican tradition is respect for the covenants of the past, for civic values and virtues passed from generation to generation, for the restraints the wisdom of the past imposes on today's behavior. Take away a society's common history, and you take away that which binds it together. Take away a sense of history, and you eviscerate the Christian faith, which is a religion of historical fact.

### The Prevailing World-view Is Naturalistic

For a generation, Christians have railed against the enemy called "secular humanism." So called because it was secular—of the moment—and humanistic, which meant that man, not God, was the center of the universe. But as the contemporary world-view has evolved, humanism no longer seems an appropriate term.

Because there is nothing beyond what we see and feel (there is no supernatural), the natural is supreme; therefore, all nature is equal and there is no longer a reason for humanity to be considered the center of the universe.

No surprise, then, that Earth Day would get more attention than Easter. Or that David Brown, former executive director of the Sierra Club, writes, "While the death of young men in war is unfortunate, it is no more serious than [the] touching of mountains and wilderness areas by humankind."[16]

So millions gather on mountaintops to wait reverently for the great moment when the planets pass in such a way as to create a "harmonic convergence." Naturalism enshrines nature with its own mystique and breeds its own form of worship, which partially explains the spread of pantheism and the proliferation of bizarre New Age cults.

One of naturalism's most influential advocates, television mogul Ted Turner, argues that we should replace the "outmoded" Ten Commandments with what he describes as the "Ten Voluntary Initiatives."

These include loving and respecting Planet Earth, supporting the United Nations, and everyone agreeing to have only two children so we don't overtax our environment.

In a totally relativistic world, of course, it is impossible to say that one creature has greater worth than another, or even that an individual has greater worth than nature. Since humans come from nothing and are going nowhere, there is no basis for human dignity and no logical reason to believe we are better than any other living thing. It is perfectly logical, therefore, that activists fight for the rights of endangered baby seals while not blinking an eye at the abortion of unborn humans. Or, as Ingrid Newkirk, president of People for the Ethical Treatment of Animals, puts it: "A rat is a pig is a dog is a boy."[17]

In a strange perversion of Darwin, some even hold that the higher species owe a special debt to the lower species. So animal rights terrorists poison products intended for humans to protest the alleged inhumane treatment of rats. And ecological terrorists booby-trap loggers in the Northwest to protect the owl.

All this is madness, of course, but perfectly logical. Since all life forms allegedly arose out of the same primordial slime, then it is no surprise that Stephanie Mills, co-author of *Whatever Happened to Ecology?* would describe humans as "debased human protoplasm."[18]

### The Prevailing World-view Is Utopian

In calling humans "debased," however, Mills has inadvertently exposed one of the inner contradictions of this modern view of the world.

In a naturalistic environment we have no intrinsic worth, but relativism, the reigning religion, holds all humans to be autonomous. God is dead, so we are our own masters. Thus we have the capacity to create our own brave new world. And we are basically good— the idea of original sin is anachronistic in the era of human autonomy. So good men and women are going to, with education and human progress, simply get better all the time.

The roots of this myth go back to Aristotle, who believed that education would in time erase sin and evil. This belief gained wide acceptance during the Enlightenment when the philosophical focus shifted dramatically from God to man. G. W. F. Hegel, for one, embraced and expanded the Aristotelian view.

The great architect of the Enlightenment myth, Jean Jacques Rousseau, argued that men and women were pure in their original state and that evil was the result of social structures and the oppression of civilization. "Vices belong less to man than man badly governed," he wrote.[19] So wise politics and social engineering could, he reasoned, achieve universal remedies for man's ills. Utopia on earth.

Karl Marx built upon that foundation, arguing that freeing the proletariat would lead to a classless society. As a result, government would "wither away."

But Marxism created no utopia. Rather, it led to a totalitarian state that slaughtered tens of millions of its own citizens and enslaved one-third of the world. And when it ran its course, the government didn't "wither away." It was trampled, torn from flags and toppled from monuments by the masses parading through the streets.

The twentieth century has produced the most staggering advances in knowledge, education, and technology in all of history. It also has given us Hitler and the Holocaust, the horrors of mass slaughter in two world wars, and countless other conflicts. It has given us brutal rulers, genocide, serial killers, greed, rape, horror, bloodshed, and evil of unimaginable proportions. Yet the myth of man's goodness endures.

In the 1960s, even as communist utopias were gripping the East, we in the West were experimenting with our own utopianism, with equally devastating results.

When President Lyndon Johnson declared war on poverty, the message went out that the poor were unable to extricate themselves from their plight. In a landmark speech at Howard University in 1965, he told black students that they were the victims of society's oppression and racism and that their government would rescue them.

LBJ, his compatriots in Congress, and the socially conscious elite who championed the war on poverty were well intentioned. They really believed that institutional programs could solve poverty. They really believed that the poor were victims.

Unfortunately, they were also very convincing. Up until then the work ethic had been strong among the inner-city minorities. Now all that changed. *If my condition is not my doing*, they now reasoned, *then why work to try to get out of it? And if society is at fault, then why not steal from it?*

The result is a crime rate that has soared since the 1960s and continues to rise; quadrupling of the prison population; five to thirteen million people on the public dole, unable or unwilling to work lest they lose their welfare benefits; a permanently subsidized underclass; and infrastructures of inner-city schools, families, and housing destroyed. We all saw one vivid culmination of this in the spring of 1992, when stripped of the sensibilities of moral restraint, stripped of the fragile inhibitions that regulate behavior, hundreds of citizens of Los Angeles's inner city broke loose in a rampage of burning and destruction, looting and violence that took dozens of lives and torched hundreds of millions of dollars worth of property.

But this deadly myth of utopianism affects all of society and creates our greatest modern dilemma: If we are basically good people, how do we explain the wrongs we do? We can't. So we simply deny that the wrongs are wrong—or else we blame them on sickness or on someone else. Thus, we all become victims.

So when a white-collar "looter mentality"—the logical consequence of secularism—gave us the S&L scandals and Wall Street insider trading, the perpetrators blamed the system. Except for their pinstripe suits, they were no different than the Los Angeles looters who blamed the system. Or when baseball star Wade Boggs was caught in adulterous affairs several years ago, he explained that he was just a victim of sexual addiction. Similarly, Pete Rose claimed he was addicted to gambling.

Former mayor of Washington, D.C., Marion Barry used the same defense, but with a new twist. When he was filmed by the FBI with his hand in the cocaine jar, he claimed he was the victim of a racist plot.

Militant gay activists suffering from AIDS rarely acknowledge that their disease might be a consequence of their own behavior. Instead, they angrily blame the government for not yet finding a cure.

This culture of victimization has resulted in numerous mind-boggling court cases. For example, a woman who developed lung cancer after smoking a pack and a half of cigarettes a day for forty years—despite all the well-publicized warnings by the government and the tobacco companies—sued the cigarette manufacturer.[20] And won.

Dan White, the disgruntled city employee who shot the mayor and city supervisor of San Francisco, raised what became known as the "Twinkie defense." He committed the murders, he said, because he was temporarily insane from a junk-food sugar high.

And then there was the case of a doctor arrested just outside of Washington, D.C. A state trooper stopped the doctor after watching her car weaving across the road's center line. The officer and his partner noted alcohol on her breath, and when they tried to take her in for testing, she kicked one of the troopers in the groin. Later, at the county jail, she drop-kicked the breath analyzer across the room. But in court the judge ruled her not guilty. Her successful defense? She was suffering from premenstrual syndrome.

If we are victims of PMS or crack or sexual addiction or racism or whatever, then somebody must be to blame. And whoever it is should have the pants sued off them. (So Americans have the highest per capita representation of lawyers in the world and spend $117 billion a year on insurance to protect against litigation.)

But sometimes blaming and suing aren't enough. So in this relative, naturalistic, utopian world when we can't blame something or sue someone, when our conscience finally convicts—when we are truly cornered by our sin—how do we respond? Filmmaker Woody Allen gives us a chilling answer in his movie *Crimes and Misdemeanors*.

The story is of Judah Rosenthal, a prosperous ophthalmologist and pillar of the community who happens to be cheating on his wife. He is enjoying his successful double life until one day when he opens a letter meant for his wife. It is from his mistress, and it threatens to unravel everything.

Judah goes first to a rabbi friend who urges him to repent and make a clean break with his past. Then he consults his brother who has ties to the mob and offers a cleaner way out. Murder.

Flooded with memories of his religious upbringing, Judah nonetheless tells his brother to go ahead and kill his mistress.

Most of the film deals with Judah's subsequent anguish. At first he is ravaged by guilt. Haunted by nightmares, he can talk with no one but his brother. He is close to a nervous breakdown.

Then something marvelous happens. No one discovers his crime! A burglar is blamed for the woman's death.

Judah's guilt fades. His life is rich and full, his business thrives, he lies to his rabbi friend. He feels wonderful, better than ever. The film ends with Judah back on top, at peace with himself and his world.

And the lesson is plain: Judah committed two murders; he killed not only his mistress but his own conscience as well.

In a culture where the tiresome vestiges of guilt still hang on, that's the answer. If there is no one else to blame and you still feel bad, then just kill your conscience. You'll feel so much better in the morning.

## The Prevailing World-view Is Pragmatic

If there is no objective truth, how are we to decide which of two possible actions is preferable? The answer is provided by the only philosophical system made in America: pragmatism.

It was in the late nineteenth century that William James, Charles Pierce, Oliver Wendell Holmes, and John Dewey, the father of modern education, met at Harvard and formed what was called the metaphysics club—although their philosophy began with skepticism about metaphysics and theology. In essence, they argued that one cannot know truth, so good can only be measured by what works, and what works is therefore good. As James said, "Truth is the cash value of an idea."[21]

Today, without a moral compass to gauge direction, "Does it work?" has replaced "Is it right?" as the question to ask in business decisions and lifestyle choices. If it works for you, then go right ahead. Thus, the only question about abortion is whether the pregnancy is "wanted" (read: convenient). If not, then flush it away. Is your marriage working? If not, then get out of it. Will an inside deal profit your business? If so, go right ahead. Good ethics is good business, as Harvard teaches. The 1960s adage, "If it feels good, do it," has been updated for the 1990s: "If it works, do it."

Your neighbor or friend or colleague won't necessarily articulate his or her world-view in such tidy categories. But make no mistake. Philosophical relativism, which is embraced by two-thirds of the American people, leads to the dominant secular, anti-historical, naturalistic, utopian, and pragmatic world-view. The Christian concept of truth—that ultimate reality is found in Jesus Christ—is held by a minority.

Modern man, as Schaeffer once quipped, has both feet firmly planted in mid-air, and modern society is lost in the cosmos, like an abandoned space vessel spinning randomly through the universe without meaning or purpose. Novelist Walker Percy must have had similar thoughts when he wrote his brilliant essay, "The Last Donahue Show," contained in his book entitled *Lost in the Cosmos: The Last Self-Help Book.*[22]

In Percy's fantasy, Donahue's guest panel one day consists of Bill, a homosexual who engages in sex with strangers in a San Francisco park; Allen, a heterosexual, married businessman who is a "connoisseur of the lunch-hour liaison"; Penny, a pregnant fourteen-year-old; and Dr. Joyce Friday, a well-known talk-show sex therapist.

In the midst of the dialogue about sexual preferences, techniques, choices, and nuggets of secular wisdom from Dr. Friday, the show is suddenly interrupted by three odd-looking strangers striding down the aisle to the front. The first is a tall, bearded man dressed like a sixteenth-century Reformer; indeed, it is John Calvin. The second is a clean-shaven, chivalrous young man who turns out to be Colonel John Pelham, one of Civil War hero Jeb Stuart's gallant officers. The third is a nondescript, 1950s-style person looking a bit like Lowell Thomas or perhaps Harry Truman.

"Holy smoke! Who are these guys?" exclaims Donahue, smacking his head, pushing up his glasses, and swinging around with a comic pan of the audience. Bedlam eventually ensues as John Calvin pronounces that the abominations being discussed merit God's eternal damnation unless those who espouse them cast themselves upon God's mercy.

"Wait a minute, Reverend," says Donahue. "You're entitled to your religious beliefs. But what if others disagree with you . . . what's wrong with two consenting adults expressing their sexual preference in the privacy of their bedroom or, ah, under a bush?"[23]

"Sexual preference?" responds Calvin.

Donahue quizzes Colonel Pelham, who expresses equal consternation and disdain for the hot topics the show has bandied about.

Then the 1950s person speaks, announcing to the puzzled audience that he is an alien who has assumed this shape so they can see him. The entire civilization the show represents is about to be destroyed by a mammoth nuclear device from beyond. He realizes that the idea of such sudden "judgment" will likely not be believed by the audience, lulled as it is by the titillation of the day. But for any who choose to believe the warning, he gives the site of one cave to which they can flee and be saved from the nuclear holocaust.

The essay ends with Donahue announcing that the show is out of time; tomorrow's segment will feature surrogate partners and a

Kinsey panel. There is a cut to commercials. Then a simple question for the reader: If you were in the studio audience, would you heed the cosmic stranger's call to judgment and retreat to the cave? Or would you ignore it?

That is precisely the question for our age . . . for all of those who scoff with disdain, "What is truth?" It is also at the root of the question that Pilate posed to the maddened crowd: "What then will you do with Jesus who is called Christ?"

# 15

## *The Pillar of Truth*

If everything that is, exists for the sake of God, then the whole creation must give glory to God.

*Abraham Kuyper*

$B$Y THIS TIME YOU MAY BE WONDERING what all this discussion of deconstructionism, relativism, Donahueites, and Goodmanites has to do with the Christian faith. Sadly, for many, not much.

Every week millions of believers settle into their church pews to worship and watch their cleric perform (not unlike "Donahue" audiences). We sing our favorite hymns, do our church duties, and study our Bibles. It's somewhat comforting to view a decaying world from the distant safety of our sanctuaries while we strive to strengthen our own personal relationship with God.

Not that striving for personal holiness is wrong; it is central to the Christian life. But the Christian faith doesn't stop on an individual level.

When believers recite the ancient baptismal confession, "Jesus is Lord," we refer to His rule over our own lives, of course, but we are also acknowledging His sovereignty over all He has created. That means we have the awesome responsibility of asserting that rule—of proclaiming His truth—in a world that is scornfully asking Pilate's timeless question: "What is truth?"

We cannot sit back in our sanctuaries and refuse to take up this challenge. We cannot forego the corporate consequences of Jesus' lordship. For we alone can provide the answer and point a weary and skeptical culture to the ultimate and only reality, Jesus Christ Himself.

**183**

His body—His church—is charged with the obligation to defend His truth. As the apostle Paul described in his letter to Timothy, the church is to be "the pillar and support of the truth."[1] That which raises up the truth and makes it visible to the world.

That means we must know the truth, as we discussed in chapter 13. And in order to effectively engage the mind-set of the scoffers we meet each day in the marketplace, we must understand their presuppositions or world-view, which we discussed in chapter 14.* And of course we must understand how Christ's lordship reigns over all of life, what it means to have a Christian world-view, and how to articulate that view.

For make no mistake—this clash of world-views is at the heart of the great cosmic struggle that rages for the hearts and minds and souls of men and women. How prepared are we for this great war of the worlds? How well-equipped are we to defend the truth?

Dismally. The Barna poll that revealed that two-thirds of the American people believe there is no such thing as absolute truth also revealed a shocking response from believers: 53 percent of those claiming to be Bible-believing, conservative Christians said there is no such thing as absolute truth.[2] A majority of those who follow the One who says, "I am the truth," profess not to believe in truth.

Equally chilling were Gallup's findings: Although 70 percent of all Americans believe it is important to do what the Bible teaches, two-thirds of this same group reject moral absolutes.[3] Schizophrenic.

---

*For one thing, as we will discuss later, it is impossible to know how to evangelize without first knowing the presuppositions upon which people base their view of life. For another, we cannot understand or deal with society's attitude toward us. Many believers seem bewildered at the growing antipathy toward the Christian faith. Yet the reason is obvious when we understand the dominant relativistic philosophy that exalts personal autonomy and elevates tolerance over truth. True Christianity threatens the world. Our beliefs challenge and clash with the reigning orthodoxy of secularism. (A recent Gallup poll found that 50 percent of all Americans expressed concern about religious fundamentalism; only 36 percent expressed concern about secular humanism. In one poll, 30 percent said they would not want a fundamentalist neighbor and 12 percent were doubtful; in another, 50 percent were concerned about religious fundamentalism, while 35 percent were concerned about secular humanism [PRRC (Princeton Religion Research Council) Emerging Trends (March 1989): 2; PRRC Emerging Trends (February 1992): 2]). Understanding this tension is essential to knowing how to behave intelligently and effectively present our case.

So how do we engage in this struggle? If we are to be, as commanded, the pillar and support of the truth, it seems obvious that the first thing the people of God need to do is understand what we believe and to recover the fundamentals of the Christian faith.

## Back to Basics

We must begin with a renewed commitment to the truth, for we must understand that Jesus' claim is the very foundation of our faith. That starts with Scripture, which we confess to be God's revealed propositional truth. We must be convinced by faith and by compelling evidence that Scripture is inspired by God, authoritative, and without error in its original autographs.[4]

Also, we must stand boldly in the tradition of those who have gone before us, many of whom have shed their blood in defense of the historic, orthodox confession of our faith. In theology, as in other areas of life, fads come and go, but truth is validated as it survives the assaults that come its way. Tested through the centuries, the central tenets of Christian orthodoxy have been passed on and entrusted to us. And here we must stand—without equivocation—even when the world hangs labels on us that represent everything considered ugly and backward.

A *New York Times* article, for example, labeled me a "theocrat" (if the author had bothered to read almost anything I've written, he would have discovered that I'm an outspoken critic of theonomy), implied that I was anxious and confused about my faith, given to apocalyptic visions, possibly a sadist, opposed to fiction, psychology, journalism, and assertive women. In short, a *fundamentalist*.

There's the dreaded word. It conjures up images of uneducated bigots, backward Bible-thumping preachers, and the Ayatollah Ruhollah Khomeni. But it's a bad rap.

"Fundamentalism" is really akin to Lewis's "mere Christianity" discussed earlier, or the rules of faith in the early church; it means adherence to the fundamental facts—in this case, the fundamental facts of Christianity. It is a term that was once a badge of honor, and we should reclaim it.

At the end of the nineteenth century, evolution and the new higher biblical criticism began to challenge biblical authority. This assault affected even great theological institutions such as Princeton Seminary, which, though once orthodox, began questioning fundamental doctrines such as the Virgin Birth and inerrancy of Scripture.

Meanwhile, a lively social gospel was also surfacing. Strong in good intentions, it was weak in biblical doctrine and orthodoxy.

So a group of theologians, pastors, and laypeople published a series of volumes titled *The Fundamentals*. Published between 1910 and 1915, these booklets defined what had been the nonnegotiables of the faith since the Apostles' Creed:

1. the infallibility of Scripture
2. the deity of Christ
3. the Virgin Birth and miracles of Christ
4. Christ's substitutionary death
5. Christ's physical resurrection and eventual return[5]

These were then, as they are today, the backbone of orthodox Christianity. If a fundamentalist is a person who affirms these truths, then there are fundamentalists in every denomination—Catholic, Presbyterian, Baptist, Brethren, Methodist, Episcopal . . . Everyone who believes in the orthodox truths about Jesus Christ—in short, every Christian—is a fundamentalist. And we should not shrink from the term nor allow the secular world to distort its meaning.

Whenever other believers ask if I'm a fundamentalist—and when they do, they usually lower their voices and look around to see if anyone is listening—I reply, "Certainly." When I then trace for them what it really means, my questioners often have said, "Well, that's what I believe! What a relief!"

We must get over our timidity. Secularists misinterpret it as insecurity and a weakness of faith. Some years ago the leading atheist spokesperson, Madalyn Murray O'Hair, was asked why so many people were afraid of her. "I'll tell you why some Christians are," she replied. "They are not sure what they say they believe is true. If they were, I wouldn't be a threat to them at all."[6] Precisely.

Nor should we be defensive about what we believe or the authority by which we believe it. The Goodmanites argue that church leaders who hold to orthodoxy are simply out of touch; doctrine should be determined by what the majority believe. That's the only way the church can be relevant, they argue.

What foolishness. Could there be anything more relevant than the spiritual salvation of each human being who, apart from Christ, is absolutely lost? The historic gospel is the most immediate, encompassing, and necessary news anyone could ever proclaim.

Besides, truth is not determined by majority vote. It is, by definition, objectively true whether anyone believes it or not. The world was still round even when most of its inhabitants believed it was flat. God is still God even when millions deny Him. His word is still His Word, notwithstanding all those who try to explain it away.

The church is not a democracy and never can be. We can change rules and practices and sing new hymns and use different styles of worship. We can change forms, but not our foundation. For the church is authoritarian. It is ruled over by Christ the Head and governed by a constitution that cannot be ignored or amended.

This is what galls the Goodmanites. This is why they portray the church as anachronistic and arbitrary. This is why their bashing of Bible-cleaving believers is so popular.

But Scripture and our orthodox confession teach us the truth, not only about God, but also about man. The Bible says that every person has sinned and fallen short of God's glory. Jesus said, "The things which proceed out of the man are what defile the man . . . these evil things proceed from within."[7] And this is where we really offend the modern mind; for this is a direct challenge to the dominant, secular, utopian view of men and women as innately good victims of corrupt social influences. Instead, Scripture teaches, men and women are independent moral agents who make moral choices and must accept responsibility for those choices.

For people to see their need for a Savior, they must first see this truth about themselves. And if the truth about God challenges the secular mind, the truth about man is terrifying.

In 1960, Israeli undercover agents orchestrated the daring kidnapping of one of the worst of the Holocaust masterminds, Adolf Eichmann. After capturing him in his South American hideout, they transported him to Israel to stand trial.

There, prosecutors called a string of former concentration camp prisoners as witnesses. One was a small haggard man named Yehiel Dinur, who had miraculously escaped death in Auschwitz.

On his day to testify, Dinur entered the courtroom and stared at the man in the bulletproof glass booth—the man who had murdered

Dinur's friends, personally executed a number of Jews, and presided over the slaughter of millions more. As the eyes of the two men met—victim and murderous tyrant—the courtroom fell silent, filled with the tension of the confrontation. But no one was prepared for what happened next.

Yehiel Dinur began to shout and sob, collapsing to the floor.

Was he overcome by hatred . . . by the horrifying memories . . . by the evil incarnate in Eichmann's face?

No. As he later explained in a riveting "60 Minutes" interview, it was because Eichmann was not the demonic personification of evil Dinur had expected. Rather, he was an ordinary man, just like anyone else. And in that one instant, Dinur came to the stunning realization that sin and evil are the human condition. "I was afraid about myself," Dinur said. "I saw that I am capable to do this . . . exactly like he."

Dinur's remarkable statements caused Mike Wallace to turn to the camera and ask the audience the most painful of all questions: "How was it possible . . . for a man to act as Eichmann acted? . . . Was he a monster? A madman? Or was he perhaps something even more terrifying . . . was he normal?"

Yehiel Dinur's shocking conclusion? "Eichmann is in all of us."[8]

I saw this myself in 1981 when I visited death row at the maximum security prison in Menard, Illinois, and one of the prisoners asked to speak with me alone. He was a middle-aged man with neatly brushed, silver-streaked hair, a warm smile, and intelligent eyes. Except for his shackles and chains, he could have been a genial high school principal or a friendly pharmacist. He could have been anyone.

In reality, he was John Wayne Gacy, Jr., the man who had sexually abused and murdered thirty-three young men. As we sat in a small interview room and talked, Gacy spoke quite rationally. And as I thought of his crimes, I kept telling myself that he had to be sick.

He was sick. Sick with sin that had erupted into horrific evil. Only as I reminded myself that he was sick with the same sin that dwells in us all was I able to spend one hour facing him across a table—and then to pray with him.

More recently, the trial of serial killer Jeffrey Dahmer revolved around the issue of his sanity. No one disputed that Dahmer had committed the unspeakably grisly crimes. But how could a sane person have done that? Yet a Milwaukee jury, confronted with ghastly murder, cannibalism, and necrophilia, concluded that Dahmer was not insane. Just evil.

The terrifying truth is that we are not morally neutral. A friend of mine who is a renowned psychologist and orthodox Jew often makes the point that left to their own devices, with the assurance they would never be caught or held accountable, individuals will more often choose what is wrong than what is right. We are drawn toward evil; without powerful intervention, we will choose it.

Eichmann is in all of us. And that sin can be cleansed only by Christ's shed blood.

That fundamental message sounds harsh and archaic in today's progressive society . . . even in many of today's "enlightened" churches. And it certainly doesn't conform to some of the strategies of the church growth movement.

As discussed earlier, most pastors are under pressure to grow their churches—that's how we measure success. In many instances the pastors' jobs are on the line if they don't. So they look to the great untapped market—the millions of Donahueites, who are daily conditioned not to think about the great questions and for whom pleasure is the chief aim of life.

Businesses penetrate new markets by giving people what they want. The temptation is great for the church to do the same: to offer pleasure, but in a spiritualized form. "If you think the world can give you a high, wait until you see what God can do."

Give people what it takes to get them into the tent; then let them have the whole message. This is good strategy, goes the argument. And many innovative churches have developed excellent techniques for drawing in the unconverted. But while it is true that we shouldn't frighten people away, there is a fine line here—one that is very easy to cross.

Because once we do have the pews filled with Donahueites, it is not going to get any easier. We cannot trifle with the truth—and truth is not comfortable or pleasant. Which leads us to the second requirement necessary if the church is to be the pillar of truth.

### Expose the Myth

"The true Christian . . . is not only to teach truth but to practice truth in the midst of such relativism," said Francis Schaeffer, and this will "bring forth confrontation—loving confrontation, but confrontation."[9]

Yet confrontation is something most Christians seem to want to avoid. Not only because we want people to come to our churches, but because of our fear of offending and being rejected.

Christians want to be nice people. Kind of like those pastel "Precious Moments" figurines sold in so many Christian bookstores. Nice Christians are genial and well mannered, wrote novelist Walker Percy, but one would barely know they are Christians at all.[10] Nice means not ever offending anyone with a gospel that is, by definition, offensive.[11]

But when we speak the message boldly, with love, God often surprises us, as I discovered several years ago when I met with a prominent business leader in a southeastern city.

Mr. Abercrombie, as we shall call him, was not only a pillar of the community and an active church member, but he also hosted a weekly Bible study luncheon at his office. Since I was in the city to speak at the governor's prayer breakfast, Mr. Abercrombie invited me to attend the study-luncheon.

Nineteen men in all, dressed in dark suits, conservative ties, and white shirts, filed in at the appointed hour. They filled the large conference room, which was paneled on one side in beautiful rosewood and on the other with plate glass windows offering a breathtaking view of the city that these men ran and owned. Although this was the city's power establishment, each man showed deference to our host, who had recently been featured in a national magazine as one of the up-and-comers of the corporate world.

Mr. Abercrombie had asked me to speak at the luncheon and then allow time for questions. Somewhere in my talk I referred to our sinful nature. Actually, "total depravity" was the phrase I used. I noticed at the time that a few individuals shifted uncomfortably in their leather chairs, and, sure enough, it must have hit the mark. Because after I finished, the first question was on sin.

"You don't really believe we are sinners, do you? I mean, you're too sophisticated to be one of those hellfire-and-brimstone fellows," one older gentleman said, eyeing my dark blue pinstripe suit just like his. "Intelligent people don't go for that back-country preacher stuff," he added.

"Yes, sir," I replied. "I believe we are desperately sinful. What's inside of each of us is really pretty ugly. In fact we deserve hell and would get it, but for the sacrifice of Christ for our sins."

Mr. Abercrombie himself looked distressed by now. "Well, I don't know about that," he said. "I'm a good person and have been all my life. I go to church, and I get exhausted spending all my time doing good works."

The room seemed particularly quiet, and twenty pairs of eyes were trained on me.

"If you believe that, Mr. Abercrombie—and I hate to say this, for you certainly won't invite me back—you are, for all of your good works, further away from the kingdom than the people I work with in prison who are aware of their own sins."

Someone at the other end of the table coughed. Another rattled his coffee cup. And a flush quickly worked its way up from beneath Mr. Abercrombie's starched white collar.

"In fact, gentlemen," I added, drawing on a favorite R. C. Sproul shocker, "if you think about it, we are all really more like Adolf Hitler than like Jesus Christ."

Now there was stony silence . . . until someone eased the pain and changed the subject.

When lunch ended and I was preparing to leave, Mr. Abercrombie took my arm. "Didn't you say you wanted to make a phone call when we were finished?"

I started to say it wasn't necessary, then realized he wanted to get me alone.

"Yes, thank you," I said.

He led me down the corridor to an empty office. As soon as we were inside, he said bluntly, "I don't have what you have."

"I know," I replied, "but you can. God is touching your heart right now."

"No, no," he took a step back. "Maybe sometime."

I pressed a bit more, however, and moments later we were both on our knees. Mr. Abercrombie asked forgiveness of his sins and turned his life over to Christ.

Martin Luther was right. "The ultimate proof of the sinner is that he doesn't know his own sin. Our job is to make him see it."[12]

Of course the sledgehammer that worked with Mr. Abercrombie might not be quite right for everyone. That's okay. Approach the issue lovingly and gently and tactfully, if you wish, but one way or another, *do it*. Conviction must precede conversion. You cannot present the gospel truth until you have also presented the fact of sin.

Without this message we are simply offering our own brand of therapy. And therapy can only modify behavior. It is the gospel that transforms character.

The object is not to make people able to live with themselves; it is to make them able to live with God.

Yet the huge gulf between the Christian and the secular view of man is sometimes underestimated because there are so many people with a Christian veneer. Many of our neighbors and co-workers don't seem so different from us—on the surface. But their world-view is utterly in conflict with Christian values, and their relativism is dominating a culture that was, until recently, at least nominally Christian.

The scandal is that we in the church have allowed this to happen. We have failed to stand for truth, failed to articulate, defend, and advance an intelligent and coherent Christian world-view.

Which brings us to the third and perhaps, because it is little discussed, the most daunting challenge of all—to develop and live out a biblically informed view of life.

### A Biblical World-view

It is impossible to read the Scriptures from Genesis to Revelation and not see the clear pattern of God's sovereignty and His charge that the people of God be His body, doing His work as stewards of His entire creation. This is a matter of obedience.

According to the Genesis account, God created the world and was pleased with His creation. Then He ordered Adam to "cultivate and keep" the garden. "To cultivate" means increasing creation's bounty, while the Hebrew verb *shāmar,* translated "keep," means literally "to guard." Adam was to guard the garden against anything that might jeopardize its reflection of God's goodness.

The Fall did not negate this mandate. It just made it harder to obey. The curse extended into every arena of life. But so did Christ's redemption.

Eventually, because of Christ's completed work on the cross, all creation will be restored to its former glory. Until His return, however, Christians must persevere in their role of "cultivating and keeping" the garden of a fallen world.

Even before Christ came, the men and women of the Old Testament understood this. The Psalms are filled with King David's exultation over God's rule and His mandate to us. David's son Solomon understood his father's words: His Proverbs touch on everything from child raising to neighborly relations to work to economic justice to international relations.

Later, the central message of the prophets was to call God's people to account for their failure to apply His truth to every aspect of their lives. They decried Israel's cavalier attitude toward the family, the tendency of the wealthy to treat the poor with injustice, and the self-serving ways of government officials.[13] They also led the people in carrying out their educational responsibilities to the generation to come.[14] And the prophets looked forward to a day when the application of God's truth to all of life would shape the nations of the world.[15]

Throughout His public ministry, Jesus evoked the kingdom mind-set that consciously takes "every thought captive to the obedience of Christ."[16] Likening the kingdom of heaven to leaven, Jesus described God's rule as having a transforming effect on everything it touches.[17] And in the parable of the talents He taught that God expects a "return on investment" from His faithful stewards,[18] who are to bring glory to Him as they cultivate and keep that which He has entrusted to them.*

Not surprisingly, the apostles took pains to teach the church not to be conformed to this world but to be transformed by the renewing of the mind, to guard against being taken captive by the empty deceptions and philosophies of the world or cleverly devised tales, and to seek truth according to Christ.[19]

What is clear from this, from creation onward, is that God's rule extends to everything. From our bank accounts to our business dealings to our educational curriculum to our social justice issues to our environmental concerns to our political choices in the voting booth—everything must reflect the fact that God's righteous rule extends to all of life.

*In obedience to this mandate, we must affirm that truth involves all of life and then define and teach a Christian world-view.*

That eloquent defender of the Christian mind, Harry Blamires, has written, "As a thinking being, the modern Christian has succumbed to secularization. He accepts religion—its morality, its worship, its spiritual culture; but he rejects the religious view of life, the thing which sets all earthly issues within the context of the eternal."[20]

---

*Jesus did not intend to reform the immediate structures of His day. His mission was greater than that, and He did not succumb to Satan's attempts to sidetrack Him. Yet Christ in no way changed God's mandate that we exercise dominion over the earth. To the contrary, He taught His followers in imagery and metaphors based on the most comprehensive world-view of all: the kingdom of God.

When Christians set all issues in the context of the eternal, when we shape our view of all of life in light of the truth, what does that view look like? Point by point, it is the antithesis of the dominant world-view described in the previous chapter:

- The world's view is shaped by relativism; the Christian's view is formed out of the objective, revealed truth of Scripture. It rests on absolutes.

- The world's view is secular; the Christian's view is eternal. What we do now is not passing and unimportant; it counts forever.

- The world's view is antihistorical; the Christian's view acknowledges the historical account of God's work from the beginning. History is treasured and respected.

- The world's view is naturalistic; the Christian's view is based on the *super*natural.

- The world's view is pragmatic—do what works; the Christian's view is idealistic—do what is right by objective standards.

One man who saw clearly this clash of world-views and the scope of God's call was Abraham Kuyper, a scholarly Dutch pastor. Following his sermon one day at a country church, an old woman from the congregation approached him.

"Dr. Kuyper," she said, "that was a brilliant sermon, but you need to be born again."

While the learned doctor was stunned at her words, he later discovered what she meant, gave his life to Christ, and became a towering figure in Christendom. For twenty-five years he edited a Christian journal, wrote, preached, ultimately led a Christian political movement, and became prime minister of Holland in 1900. He also became one of the great modern exponents of a Christian world-view.

"If everything that is, exists for the sake of God, then the whole creation must give glory to God," Kuyper argued. And after intense study of Scripture, he realized that the holy writings disclose "not only justification by faith but the very foundation of life and the ordinances that regulate human existence."[21]

*Understanding the antithesis between the secular mind-set and the Christian world-view, the people of faith need to look critically at every area of life and measure each area from this perspective.*

Nothing should be "too secular" to escape sacred scrutiny. For example, many Christians contribute to causes out of nostalgia or habit, never considering what those institutions or organizations really stand for. I've done it myself.

For years I gave to my alma mater, Brown University, out of gratitude for my undergraduate education. Then I woke up and realized that Brown, like its Ivy League cousins, is a bastion of the relativistic world-view. While I was contending for a Christian world-view in books, speeches, columns, and radio commentaries, I was also financially supporting a school committed to an opposing belief system. I stopped giving to Brown.

Christians must measure their involvement and activities, their use of time and money against one yardstick: Is it consistent with a biblical view of life, and does it bring glory to God? Instead, Monday through Saturday, many have become accustomed to measuring what they see and do by community standards rather than by Scripture.

Take the case of the conservative Presbyterian church elder in Florida who found himself foreman of the jury in the trial of the rap group Two Live Crew. The state of Florida had charged that the group's lyrics violated the state's obscenity laws, and most observers believed that the jury would convict; it didn't take a genius to see that the lyrics in question advocated violence, torture, and were grossly degrading to women. Not exactly a freedom-of-speech issue. Yet the jury voted to acquit because, as the Presbyterian elder announced in his role as foreman, "Representing a cross-section of the community as we do, we did not feel it was obscene."[22]

Is this man typical of the many who are unaware of the role their faith plays in everyday life? Who vote one way on Sunday and another way the rest of the week? Apparently so. A survey of mainline denomination members found that only 32 percent believed their faith had anything to do with their life outside of church.[23] It's a deadly form of schizophrenia.

Secular society does everything possible to encourage this split personality, arguing that religious influence doesn't belong in public life or conscience. Secularists have attempted to rid every public institution of any religious influence. That's simply being neutral, they argue, in the name of separation of church and state.

Nonsense. To leave religious references out of textbooks, for example, isn't neutrality. It is bad history. Also, it says to our schoolchildren that religion, one of the primary shaping forces of human experience, is irrelevant.

The mature Christian must constantly challenge these values of the culture. Fyodor Dostoevsky, the great Russian novelist, was eulogized at his funeral for perceiving the "falsehood that is prevailing in society and then dedicat[ing his] life to a struggle against that falsehood. . . . If we cannot rise above the material life one cannot ever become a citizen in the kingdom of the Spirit."[24]

*To do that, we need to defend what we believe.*

Many Christians suffer from an inferiority complex. Whether evangelicals or conservative Catholics or mainliners . . . we have been caricatured so often as reactionary, simpleminded bigots by the media and entertainment complex that we have almost come to believe it.

So when a discussion of abortion politics, or natural law, or politically correct education arises around the office coffee pot or at the lunch table, many of us clam up. Either we assume that the Christian perspective will lose in any debate, or we haven't done our homework.

When I speak on the need for a Christian apologetic, I'm often approached afterward by those who say, "I wish I could make the arguments for the historical fact of the Resurrection, but I just don't have time to read up on the issues."

Sure, studying how to best articulate a Christian apologetic takes time. But didn't the apostle Peter command *all* of us *to always be ready to give a defense of our faith?*[25]

It is inexcusable for mature disciples to allow themselves to be intimidated. The Christian world-view is not unscientific or simpleminded or anti-intellectual. It is the only plausible explanation for the universe.

And when it comes to a defense of the gospel, personal experience is not enough. Secularists believe that religion is private, cannot be affirmed by evident reason, has no public role or relevance; when we say it's true because we've experienced it, we simply let them off the hook. "Each to his or her own," they'll say.

So we need to equip ourselves to offer a reasoned, coherent, thoughtful defense of the biblical world-view.

*Finally, we need to actively contend for Christian truth in the marketplace.*

In describing the burden that God placed on his life, Kuyper, who might have been speaking for the church today, said, "[Our call] is this: that in spite of all worldly opposition, God's holy ordinances shall be established again in the home, in the school and in the state for the good of the people; to carve as it were into the conscience of the nation the ordinances of the Lord, to which Bible and creation bear witness, until the nation pays homage again to God."[26]

We do this not by attempting to usher in God's kingdom now—the mistake triumphalist, overzealous believers have made since the time of Augustine; nor by capturing control of political structures—although Christians should certainly seek office. Rather, we should be contending for truth in every area of life. Not for power or because we are taken with some trendy cause, but humbly to bring glory to God.

For this reason, Christians should be the most ardent ecologists. Not because we would rather save spotted owls than cut down trees whose bark provides lifesaving medicine, but because we are mandated to keep the garden, to ensure that the beauty and grandeur God has reflected in nature is not despoiled.

We should care for animals. Not because whales are our brothers, but because animals are part of God's kingdom over which we are to exercise dominion. Francis of Assisi should be our role model, not Ted Turner or Ingrid Newkirk.

We should care for human life. If we are concerned about baby seals, we should be far more concerned for unborn humans. Not because of some prudish Victorian morality or a desire to interfere in people's private lives, but because every human being is created in the image of God. When necessary, we take a stand against the world because lives are at stake.*

Thus, the Christian world-view is what makes the church a passionate defender of human liberty and civil rights. The very term our founding fathers used, "endowed by their creator with certain *unalienable* rights," reflects a Christian view of human liberty that is nonnegotiable. Governments can neither confer nor take away human rights; these rights are given by God. It is this conviction that put Christians in the forefront of the campaign for the abolition of slavery, the civil rights movement, and the crusade for human rights in oppressed nations around the world.

---

*To be consistent with the Christian world-view, the church may need to engage in peaceful civil resistance. For a more in-depth discussion of this complex issue, see Colson, *Kingdoms in Conflict*, 246–51.

Thus, Christians zealously seek reforms in the prisons and in criminal justice laws. Not because it's part of some party platform or vague humanistic idealism, but because our view of institutions must always be measured by God's clear standard of justice.

Thus, Christians celebrate the arts—painting, music, dance, drama—and all creative expressions that bring glory to God, the Great Artist. It's sad that the National Endowment for the Arts controversy has siphoned off so much attention in this area. Obscenities parading as art are pathetic abominations designed to shock and profane; they express a world-view that thrives on moral chaos rather than the delight of God's created order.

In the same way, Christians must champion ethics. Not because it is good business—the dominant pragmatic view—but because moral norms come from God. Objective truths are neither arbitrary nor irrational; they are just and enduring, reflecting God's just and unchanging nature.

Thus, Christians are not enemies of academic freedom, but true defenders of education. Because the purpose of learning is the pursuit of truth, open inquiry is critical.

And Christians see work as good, with all labor done to the glory of God.

Since no area of life is beyond the glorious rule of God, the Christian world-view embraces every arena of experience and opportunity. We need to get our heads out of the secular sand and stop being intimidated by the post-Christian culture that surrounds us. Only then will truth be heard above the chaos and discordant din of modern life.

## War of the World-views

We are engaged in the war of the worlds. The problem is that we neither understand the enemy nor hold our position well. At the very time when we are being attacked on all sides by powerful and wholly alien forces, the church is weakest.

Actually we have two enemies—both with fully developed, integrated, and coherent world-views.

One is the secularist—and his fellow pantheists and naturalists—we discussed earlier. This world-view is stealthy, subtle, and sometimes well camouflaged. Supported by intellectuals in every walk of life, this relativistic world-view can afford to be subtle because, by its very nature, it appeals to the weakest and most vulnerable aspects of human nature. People are naturally drawn to it. They throw their arms around it and surrender, as the majority of Americans have.

The other enemy, Islam, actually a perversion of Christianity, is far more aggressive. Islam is a theocratic religion which teaches that all areas of life are within its reign. Being submitted to Allah means being fully integrated into a society with rules, values, and standards.

Islam is appealing to men and women in prison because in those moral jungles it provides order and concern for the whole person and a strong community (as we should but often don't). It has a similar appeal in countries where men and women live with the constant chaos of coups and revolutions, and for the same reason is thriving in America's inner cities.

Because of Islam's monolithic structure, its officials can—and do—carefully plan evangelization campaigns from country to country. Christians, on the other hand, rush off in a hundred different directions, arguing over which methods to use, and end up giving a truncated message.

Not since the barbarian hordes overran Europe has the influence of Christianity been weaker. We hear all about church growth in various parts of America or Christianity exploding in African countries, but look at the cold, hard facts. Look at what we really are up against.

There are approximately 1.7 billion members of various Christian churches: 900 million Roman Catholics, 300 million Orthodox, approximately 300 million mainline Protestants, and perhaps 200 million conservatives, Baptists, Pentecostals, and assorted evangelical sects. And the heart of the church—those with serious, alive faith? No one knows the number for sure, but they are spread throughout myriad denominations and traditions, scattered in various corners of the globe, widely separated by theology and tradition, and in some cases not even speaking to one another.

Compare that with one billion, well-organized, relatively well-disciplined Muslims. Or with 2.5 billion pantheists—the forces from the Great Deep of which Calvin and Kuyper spoke.

We often hear Christianity spoken of as the dominant world religion. Not so. The church of Jesus Christ is a minority, and the odds against it overwhelming. Which is why it is so crucial for the members of the Body to put aside their less significant differences and join forces around our integrated world-view to defend the truth.

But the church must not only stand together; it must stand free. Remember, ideology constantly changes; it is from man. Truth is immutable; it is from God. So if the church is to be the pillar and support of the truth, ideology and truth can never be mixed.

And wherever and whenever it has stood for the truth, independent from tyrants who would enslave it, the church has demonstrated a power nothing on earth can contain.

Historians are still writing the tumultuous history of the most astonishing development of the twentieth century: the fall of Communism. As the 1980s ended and the 1990s began, one by one the nations of the Eastern bloc cast off their Communist oppressors. Yet even the best of Western intelligence did not see the changes coming nor discern the real inner workings of these quiet revolutions.

But as historians now sift the evidence, if they are honest, they will have to conclude that at the heart of this globe-shaking shift was the church: that body of persecuted Christians who stood apart from the culture around them, fearing God rather than men. They kept their independence. And, in the end, they made history.

When you talk with these brothers and sisters . . . in a drab apartment in Romania . . . over a cup of tea in a cold Polish flat . . . during a walk through the streets of Prague . . . you realize that they are ordinary people. But the faith of these ordinary people fueled the greatest story of the century.

# 16

## *Between Two Crosses*

*I*N SOME WAYS THE STORY BEGAN IN the town of Nowa Huta, Poland, soon after World War II.[1]

Planned in the late 1940s and constructed in the 1950s as a living monument to Communist utopianism, Nowa Huta, or "New Town," was originally designed as a center for the workers who would make up the backbone of the new Poland. Adjacent to the medieval city of Krakow, ancient seat of Polish kings and golden centerpiece of Polish art, culture, and spirit since the thirteenth century, Nowa Huta was an industrial center; its only artifacts were mammoth steel works and ugly chimneys spewing smoke and sulfuric fumes into the skies of southern Poland.

Early in the town's construction, an open square attracted the workers' attention. It testified to the vacuum the Communists had left in all their frenzied urban planning.

"We need a church," the workers said. "A place to worship."

What was the problem with these troublesome Poles? the authorities wondered. After all, their new housing was the best planners could design (discounting the fact that in a typical flat the kitchen was so narrow that a woman could barely enter it sideways after her sixth month of pregnancy). And now they even had hot and cold water. Why in the world did they need more? Especially a church!

The Communists bought time, however, by nodding agreeably. "Fine," they said. "No problem."

So several young Christians and a Polish priest nailed together two rugged beams and pounded the rough timber cross straight and solid into Polish soil to mark the site where their chapel would be built.

Soon, however, the authorities returned with a different verdict. "We are sorry," they told the workers. "This space is needed for something else. You cannot build a church here."

But the people wanted their church. Night after night they gathered around the cross. Priests offered mass, and the people sang and celebrated communion with one another and their Lord.

The authorities retaliated with water cannons, but this forceful baptism didn't faze the faithful. Then the Communists tore down the cross, as if sundering its heavy beams would somehow cleave the people. But the citizens of Nowa Huta were determined, and in the morning the cross was once again stretching toward heaven for all to see.

This went on for years—the authorities tearing down the cross and the people restoring it. And in the midst of the struggle the people came to a realization that would steel their faith in a way that Communism could never steal their souls.

"The church is not a building," they said to one another. "The church is us, celebrating the presence of our Lord among us! Praise be to God!"

Meanwhile, students in Romania were discovering the reality of the choice Communism posed for them.

In a small classroom in Cluj the temperature was cold and the lighting low as a philology teacher finished his lecture. Joseph Tson shifted uncomfortably in his wooden chair. Earlier he had asked a question that seemed to enrage his teacher—something about the historicity of biblical literature. Now Joseph felt the professor's attention return to him.

"We no longer need the old fables," the teacher said abruptly. "And you watch. Within a generation, the church will die out."

At first his vehemence startled Joseph. But, he reasoned, people don't usually become angry unless they feel threatened. Then he thought about the words of Jesus Christ in the Gospel of Matthew: "Upon this rock I will build my church; and the gates of hell shall not prevail against it."[2]

What Joseph had seen of Communism seemed a fair translation of "the gates of hell." And paraphrasing the verse in his mind,

Joseph realized that to those like the professor and the present regime, the church did indeed pose a threat: "I will build my church in Eastern Europe, and Communism will not prevail against it."

When the class ended, Joseph stuffed his books into his battered briefcase and thought, *What I believe will determine how I act. So I have to decide who I will believe: this Communist professor—or Christ.*[3]

The same choice faced Hanani Mikhalovich, a major in the army of the Soviet Union, stationed at a remote compound near Vladivostok. Like his father before him, Major Mikhalovich was a good soldier and faithful Communist party member. His wife, in fact, was the local party secretary. Aligned with the state, their future looked bright.

But one day Major Mikhalovich heard a shortwave radio broadcast that changed his life. He heard the gospel, and the Holy Spirit touched his heart.

The Wednesday after his conversion, Major Mikhalovich went to the weekly, compulsory party meeting. Always he had sat at the front of the bare hall, focusing on the huge portrait of Lenin, straining to take in everything that came from the podium. But this night he took a straight wooden chair in the last row.

The following Wednesday he didn't show up at all.

The next morning the commanding officer and the political officer demanded an explanation.

"I have become a Christian," Mikhalovich said simply.

The commanding officer looked at him for a moment in shock, but the political officer jumped from his chair, his face red with fury. "Shut up!" he screamed. "You are never to say those words again! Get out!"

That evening orders were issued for a special parade to be held the next day; all personnel were to wear ceremonial dress.

The next morning the parade grounds were full. Even citizens from Vladivostok were there, Mikhalovich noted with surprise, filling long bleachers along the gray gravel square of the marching area.

Precise lines of troops passed the reviewing stand, followed by an array of tanks and heavy artillery. Then the loudspeaker system crackled, and Mikhalovich's name was called.

His throat suddenly dry, the major made his way to a raised platform in the center of the parade grounds on which the commanding officer and the political officer were standing. The band had stopped; the crowd was silent.

The political officer began shouting hoarsely into the microphone, reading an official charge accusing Mikhalovich of desertion from the Communist party because of indulgence in a religious belief. Then the commanding officer stripped the narrow crimson stripes off Mikhalovich's sleeve, ripped his navy blue tunic from top to bottom, and tore his cap from his head and tossed it to the ground.

Two armed soldiers stepped forward to escort Mikhalovich, not with their usual deference but with the cold distaste reserved for traitors. They marched him around the parade ground, his tunic gaping open to reveal his undershirt. From the troops he sensed a chill wave of derision; in the bleachers he could see civilians laughing and poking one another. In the front row his wife sat tight-lipped, furious. His older son kept his eyes down. The young one, oblivious, waved happily.

That afternoon Mikhalovich was handed a stiff-bristled push broom.

"This is the last time I will ever address you," the commanding officer said. "Your job is to clean."

The Communists were also subduing their opposition in the German Democratic Republic.

In June 1953, tanks ground through the streets of East Berlin, armed with the party's indignation. In this workers' state, fifty thousand laborers had dared to protest when the government announced a 10 percent increase in production quotas without a corresponding raise in pay.

Now, as masons and carpenters crowded the streets, throwing rocks at tanks and tearing up boundary markers between East and West Berlin, the Soviets sealed the border. Mine, factory, and rail yard workers all over the German Democratic Republic joined the protest in support of their comrades in Berlin. But tanks and guns carried the day.

The Soviet commandant declared martial law, and police herded the people into their homes. Premier Otto Grotewohl urged "loyal citizens" to join the search for workers leading the insurrection, and the party purged thousands of "doubters" from its ranks.

Two years later, a group of grim, gray men gathered around a fragile Queen Anne table to sign the Warsaw Pact: the military unification of the Soviet Union, Poland, Czechoslovakia, Hungary,

Romania, Bulgaria, Albania, and East Germany. With this counter-balance to NATO, the world was officially divided. The Cold War had begun.

Two years later, in the fall of 1956, the Hungarians revolted. Demonstrators in Budapest cheered wildly at the sight of a decapitated statue of Joseph Stalin, even as they demanded the heads of their current rulers and an end to Hungary's hard-line Communist regime.

Secret police opened fire on the crowds. Hundreds fell, dead or wounded. But by this time the protesters had won the regular army's heart, and many troops joined the rebels, distributing arms to students and workers.

During the weeks of the rebellion, two reform-minded Communists who had been jailed and tortured under Stalin, Imre Nagy and Janos Kadar, were made prime minister and first secretary by the people. These new leaders declared Hungarian neutrality and disbanded the secret police.

At this, the Soviets throttled Budapest with two hundred thousand heavily armed troops, a thousand tanks, and an armada of planes. While the Hungarians hurled sticks, stones, and Molotov cocktails at the invaders, the advancing weapons leveled buildings and hundreds of Hungarian patriots.

At 9:00 on the morning of November 23, Soviet troops marched into Budapest's elegant parliament buildings to arrest Prime Minister Imre Nagy and most of his government. At 9:30 the Soviets opened fire on the American embassy, where Hungary's spiritual leader, Joseph Cardinal Mindszenty, had taken refuge just days earlier after being released from seven years in a Communist prison.

By the end of the day, the streets of Budapest were littered with rubble, bodies, and broken dreams. Some estimate that ten thousand Hungarians were killed, thirty thousand wounded. But Janos Kadar emerged unscathed. In the midst of the uprising he changed sides, denounced the freedom fighters, and was made puppet prime minister by the Soviets as they put Hungary back together again—their way.

In Berlin the authorities responded to the people's quest for freedom not with bullets, but with concrete blocks.

By now, two thousand people were escaping from East Germany to the West every day. So on the morning of August 13, 1961, soldiers left their barracks in East Berlin before dawn, driving trucks loaded with tons of concrete blocks and coils of barbed wire. By the time most Berliners awoke, an ugly barrier was snaking its way through the heart of their city.

While soldiers with machine guns spiraled barbed wire over the Berlin Wall, battle-ready Soviet divisions surrounded the city, poised to enforce the point: No more East Germans would cross to the West.

Around the same time in Poland, Karol Woytyla, bishop of Krakow, looked out over the sea of people and grinned, his rosy face shining with pleasure as he prepared to celebrate the triumph of the Christians of Nowa Huta.

Communists or Nazis, he sighed inwardly, in the end Poland's oppressors had all been the same, with their hard, narrow minds that shut out love and shut up people. He himself had been conscripted by the Nazis during World War II, forced to break up rocks in a stone quarry in Zakrzowek. In his labor camp work he had seen the toughest stones broken by sustained pressure and precise blows. But he had also seen stones, built together in a wall, resist even the mightiest of opposing forces.

It was like what the apostle Peter had written about the church: "You are living stones, being built up as a spiritual house for a holy priesthood, to offer up spiritual sacrifices acceptable to God through Jesus Christ."

Karol Woytyla believed the words of Scripture. And he believed his country would withstand the Communists—and in the end prevail. Just as this beloved church of Nowa Huta had prevailed.

The struggle had gone on for years: the workers of Nowa Huta demanding their church, erecting their cross, and the authorities tearing it down, only to have the cycle repeated. Perhaps the Communists had just worn down and given up. Whatever it was, Woytyla himself had finally led the church building campaign and set the cornerstone. And today fifty thousand people packed the square to consecrate and celebrate the result of their years of faithfulness.

"This city of Nowa Huta was built as a city without God," Bishop Woytyla shouted to the people, as many of them wept with joy. "But the will of God and the workers here has prevailed. Let us all take the lesson to heart. This is not just a building. These are living stones."[4]

Such moments of triumph were sweet during the Communist occupation. Like the spring of 1968, when the Czech people enjoyed a season of hope during Czechoslovakia's "Prague Spring."

Students flocked to the Balustrade, Prague's avant-garde theater, to see the works of the artistic director, playwright Vaclav Havel, which mirrored socialism's absurd impositions on his country.

Czech leader Alexander Dubcek, determined to break the Soviet grip on his land, had stirred his countrymen with the vision of "socialism with a human face"—a loosening of policy that did not please Leonid Brezhnev, the heavy-browed face in the Kremlin.

The crushing Soviet response came quickly, as troops from obedient Warsaw Pact members—Poland, Hungary, Bulgaria, and East Germany—moved in to help subdue the Czechs.

Soon the resisters were gone and so was Alexander Dubcek, removed from power and replaced by a more reliable socialist with a less human countenance.

Five months later Jan Palach, a Czech student, stood in Wenceslas Square before the statue of Czechoslovakia's great saint and drenched himself in petrol, protesting the Soviet invasion of his nation. A match, a flame, and he was gone.

A few years later, a young woman with as fiery a passion stood before a KGB court in Lithuania.

As a schoolgirl Nijole Sadunaite had been taken on tours of old cathedrals. When she insisted upon genuflecting at the altar, she was ordered to stop. She did not. Likewise, her parents refused to stop attending mass, even though her father was threatened with the loss of his job. And when the Communists threatened to throw Nijole and her brother out of school for refusing to join the party's youth league, their mother told the authorities that her children would never be "hypocrites and compromisers." And they weren't.

Nijole underwent a profound experience of the Holy Spirit at eighteen and then joined an underground order of nuns. In the early 1970s she published and distributed the *Chronicles of the Catholic Church,* which detailed the Soviet persecution. In 1974 she was caught and tried, but turned the courtroom into a forum against her accusers.

"Are you happy with your triumph?" she asked. "What have you triumphed over? Over the moral ruins of the country, over millions of unborn children whom you have killed, over people robbed of their human dignity, poisoned by fear and evil passions?" And then she made a defiant prophecy. "Every day your crimes are bringing you closer to history's junk heap."

The flustered, angry members of the tribunal sentenced her to the Gulag.[5]

In Romania, the threat to Christians was as constant, but perhaps more subtle. Doru Popa was a young chemical engineer when he met some Christians from the West connected with Campus Crusade for Christ. By law all Romanians were required to report any contact with Westerners within twenty-four hours. Popa neglected to do so, and his relationship with these believers resulted in extended theological training and his decision to become a pastor.

Popa became very influential among the Baptists in Arad, a city of three hundred thousand near Romania's Hungarian border. One day the secret police approached him and asked if he would like to travel all over Western Europe and the United States at their expense. All he needed to do was cooperate with them.

The idea of the Securitate as his personal travel agents didn't appeal to Popa, a fiery, passionate preacher who loved Christ a lot more than he loved the dictator, Nicolae Ceausescu. He declined the invitation—and soon found himself transferred from the guest list to the hit list.

Agents broke into his apartment, bugged his phone, stole his work permit, and regularly arrested him for questioning. His car sometimes did strange things while he was at the wheel, and one day the steering mechanism failed to respond. Popa ran off the road and into a tree. Two of his passengers were injured, and Popa found himself at the center of a government-rigged lawsuit designed to put him in prison.

Vaclav Havel's books and plays had been banned in Czechoslovakia since the crackdown during the 1968 Prague Spring uprising. Havel continued to publish outside of the country, but he was still writing in his homeland as well. With a group of writers and intellectuals he drafted the declaration of the 242-member Charter 77 movement.

The document, released on New Year's Day, 1977, called for "freedom of religious belief," "the right to freedom of expression," and an end to "tapping telephones, bugging homes, opening mail, carrying out house-searches, setting up networks of neighborhood informers."[6]

The Czech authorities didn't care for this New Year's resolution, and by January 2, Vaclav Havel was in prison.

In October of the following year, an election took place that would profoundly affect the battle between the cross and Communism. At the Vatican, the College of Cardinals announced the name of the 262nd successor to the throne of St. Peter.

Karol Woytyla, archbishop of Krakow, planter of crosses, was now Pope John Paul II. He was the youngest pope in 132 years, the first non-Italian in 456 years, the first pope from Poland, and the first pope with direct experience of life under totalitarian atheism.[7]

The following year when Pope John Paul II joyously returned to his beloved homeland, Warsaw's Victory Square—named for the Communists' triumph over the Axis powers in World War II—was packed with hundreds of thousands of Poles, crowded shoulder to shoulder to welcome home their own. Standing before an altar erected for the occasion, an immense cross in place behind him, the sturdy pontiff with the rosy complexion and the smile crinkles around his eyes raised his arms into the air.

"Holy Spirit, descend upon this ground," he shouted in a loud, exultant voice. "Holy Spirit, descend upon this ground! Holy Spirit, descend upon this ground!"

The people looked at one another with a sense of wonder. "Where are the Communists?" they asked. "Here we are. So many of us! Together with our pope!"

And in an instant came the realization that this truly was "victory square." Not the stale victory of one rival atheism supplanting another, but a spiritual victory. Gathered together that summer day the people saw with the eyes of their hearts; in the cross raised high they saw hope for the future.[8]

That hope would stand them in good stead in the dark days to follow. For life in Poland was bleak. The land had been bled of its fruitfulness, the heart and blood pressed from its workers. Conditions in the mines and factories were atrocious, and unions were outlawed. Food was scarce and lines were long.

Then at the end of the 1970s came *Solidarnosc,* or Solidarity. Many in Poland say it began more as an ideal than as a workers' union—a concept of oneness rooted in the spiritual values the Polish people clung to in those times of physical and spiritual repression. But what the world first saw of Solidarity appeared dramatically in the summer of 1980 when workers in Gdansk's Lenin Shipyard, in northern Poland, went on strike.

It began after Anna Walentynowicz, a thirty-year shipyard employee, was abruptly dismissed on August 7. The management did not care for Anna's activity in the Free Trade Union, a movement she had cofounded with Lech Walesa, a former shipyard electrician.

At six in the morning on August 14, sections of the Lenin Shipyard went out on strike. By the next day the strike had spread to fifteen other plants. That afternoon the authorities cut telecommunication links between Gdansk and the rest of Poland. Yet word of the strike seeped throughout the country, even as rumors flew of Soviet troops poised to enter Polish soil.

On August 17 workers erected a timber cross in front of Gate 2 of the Lenin Shipyard. Workers' families brought food, and priests entered the locked-in yard to celebrate mass.

As the tense days and nights of August ticked by, strikers and government representatives continued to negotiate, and on August 31 came the miraculous: the "Gdansk agreement" was signed. The strike was over, and the workers had won twenty-one new rights. Lech Walesa, the young electrician, had become an international name, and Poles had a new sense of hope in their national movement.

But Solidarity's summertime hopes dimmed in the dark days of December 1980.

The Soviet leadership, concerned about the party's authority in Poland, had put Defense Minister General Wojciech Jaruzelski in charge. And in the early hours of December 14, Jaruzelski's government declared martial law. Tanks, troops, water cannons, and guns hedged in Poland's citizens, while police rounded up the leaders of the trade union and hustled them off to jail. By morning, the country had become one vast prison.

But something else was happening in the gray light of dawn: Priests across the nation were announcing that anyone who wanted to be of help in this terrible situation should make themselves known. Thus, only hours after the crackdown, the people were once again resisting—all over Krakow, all over Poland.

The first act of these "committees of social help" was to serve as information networks, finding out where people were imprisoned and informing their families. Then they gathered care packages—

soap, toothpaste, warm clothing—and assisted prisoners' families who were left with no means of income. And as the people connected with one another to help, they broke the barrier of fear and isolation that martial law imposed.[9]

In seeing Solidarity as merely a trade union, the authorities had miscalculated. Solidarity was not simply an organization; it was a movement, a linkage of hands and hearts across Poland. And the Communists could not stop it, no matter how many troops they shuttled through the streets of Warsaw and Krakow.

But the linkage of hands and hearts didn't stop at Polish borders. Even as Soviet tanks massed outside of Poland, ready to quell any uprising, Pope John Paul II defied their oppressive authority. He announced to the press that if the Soviets invaded his homeland, he would return to stand with his people.

The tanks did not invade.

Hours after marital law began, a Warsaw priest named Father Jan Sikorski was knocking on the doors of the city's prisons to celebrate mass for the incarcerated. He encountered resistance, but Father Sikorski, a dramatic, good-natured priest whose father had survived Auschwitz, had a blunt, amiable, if unorthodox way of dealing with prison guards. After staring down more than one prison officer and dousing more than one guard with holy water, he was given permission to celebrate mass in the prisons. They didn't want to tangle with Father Sikorski, so he soon got his way.

Another Warsaw priest, Father Jerzy Popieluszko, dealt with the troops with his own brand of ecclesiastical love. On Christmas Eve he slipped away from his church, St. Stanislaw Kostka, and went into downtown Warsaw. There he give the thin Christmas Eve wafers—a traditional gift the Poles give friends and family to celebrate the coming of Christ—to the soldiers enforcing the hated martial law. "Be not overcome with evil, but overcome evil with good," was his creed.

Meanwhile, in the Soviet Union, the former Major Mikhalovich thought often of the suffering Christ on the cross. For decades, since he had been publicly demoted because of his conversion, he had cleaned the soldiers' barracks in Vladivostok.

At first the soldiers had harassed him, urinating on floors he had just swept, kicking over his water bucket while he mopped. His wife had left him, taking the children with her. He had only his faith to cling to.

But as the years went by and the soldiers were transferred, those who had known Mikhalovich as an officer dwindled. The commanding officer was killed in a train accident; the political officer was appointed to a key post in Moscow.

Hanani Mikhalovich was allowed to retire the year he turned seventy. He had no money, so he could not leave Vladivostok, but after all, his home was there—Dhom Baptista, a house church filled with sixty fervent Christians sharing three Bibles. Among these men and women, Hanani was a white-haired saint, his once-square shoulders now bowed, his hands gnarled from years of scrubbing floors, his black peasant's pants a bit tattered, but impeccably clean, as if he were expecting inspection at any time.

In Poland, Father Jerzy Popieluszko was walking his own pilgrimage of suffering. Father Jerzy's lifelong hero, Maximilian Kolbe, had given his life for another inmate at Auschwitz during World War II.* Now Father Jerzy felt a call to lay down his own life for his brothers.

Soon after the birth of Solidarity, Father Jerzy preached among the striking workers in Warsaw's huge steel works. He showed them how alcohol contributed to their oppression: If their drinking caused absenteeism or mistakes at work, it could be used to blackmail them. After that, alcoholism dropped dramatically. "Somehow we felt they owned us," said one foundryman, "and we became their slaves. Father Jerzy changed that."[10]

Not long after martial law was imposed and his foray into the night with Christmas peace for the soldiers, Father Jerzy instituted a monthly "Mass for the Homeland," dedicated to all victims of the repressive regime. Eventually thousands, then tens of thousands, attended these services at St. Stanislaw Kostka, with Father Jerzy ministering from a balcony and the people fanned out in the courtyard and streets below.

The pale, gaunt priest spoke without flair or passion. Yet his words themselves were filled with power:

*"A man who bears witness to the truth can be free even though he might be in prison. . . . The essential thing in the process of liberating man and the nation is to overcome fear. . . . We fear suffering, we fear losing material good, we fear losing freedom or our work. And then we act*

---

*See chapter 23.

*contrary to our consciences, thus muzzling the truth. We can overcome fear only if we accept suffering in the name of a greater value. If the truth becomes for us a value worthy of suffering and risk, then we shall overcome fear—the direct reason for our enslavement.*

*"A Christian must be a sign of contradiction in the world. . . . A Christian is one who all his life chooses between good and evil, lies and truth, love and hatred, God and Satan. . . . Today more than ever there is a need for our light to shine, so that through us, through our deeds, through our choices, people can see the Father who is in Heaven."*[11]

Father Jerzy's influence did not escape the notice of the authorities. He was far too popular, far too independent, far too threatening to the regime's control. He must be silenced.

The secret police followed Father Jerzy everywhere. He received unsigned, threatening letters. On the first anniversary of martial law, a pipe bomb sailed through the front window of his small flat, exploding in his sitting room.

Then, on October 19, 1984, while driving back to Warsaw from Bydgoszcz where he had celebrated a special mass and delivered a homily called "Overcome Evil with Good," Father Jerzy disappeared.

Thousands prayed for him in churches all over Poland. The steelworkers stopped their work in order to pray and threatened a national strike if their priest was not returned to them. The universities smoldered with unrest.

On the last Sunday of October, as fifty thousand people filled St. Stanislaw Kostka in an emotional Mass for the Homeland and listened in tears to a tape of Father Jerzy's final sermon, Father Antoni Lewek, one of the thirty priests at the altar, received word: "Just a moment ago it was announced on television that Father Jerzy's body has been found in the Vistula River."

Months later Father Lewek recalled the scene as he told the people the dreaded news.

"I shall never forget what happened," he said. "In a second people went down on their knees, crying and shouting; what we had feared most, the worst, had happened. . . .

"And then something very moving happened. This crying crowd managed to show that they could forgive. Three times they repeated after the priest: 'And forgive us our trespasses as we forgive them that trespass against us.' It was a Christian answer to the unchristian deed of the murderers."[12]

The secret agents had done their job with deadly expertise: the body pulled from the Vistula, bound tightly and weighted with stones, was unidentifiable. Only when his brother saw the birthmark on the corpse's chest could he be sure it was Father Jerzy. His body was covered with deep wounds and horrifying bruises. Hair had been ripped from his scalp; his eyes, nose, mouth, and skull were gouged and smashed. His teeth had been broken to bits, his tongue reduced to pulp, as were his inner organs. His final agonies were unimaginable.

Yet on November 2, the day of Father Jerzy's funeral, people marched the streets past the secret police headquarters bearing banners reading, "We forgive."

Regardless of their expertise in murdering the body, the executioners could not kill the soul. Father Jerzy had taught his people well.

Five months later there was another funeral, this one in the Soviet Union.

Konstantin Chernenko, leader of the USSR, lay in a mound of roses, medals, and scarlet bunting, flanked by Soviet flags. Somber funeral music played on television and radio stations across the vast nation as the Communist leaders gravely deliberated over the choice of a new general secretary, sobered by the fact that they were burying their third leader in three years.

In the end, they chose Mikhail Sergeyevich Gorbachev, former KGB deputy and Politburo member who, even as he led Chernenko's funeral procession, vowed to free the Soviet Union from its own rigor mortis.

In Romania there were no new vows. Just Nicolae Ceausescu's relentless grip on his nation, where Christians continued to endure persecution.

Joseph Tson, the student who had heard his teacher's prophecy that the church would die out in a generation, had purposed to use his life to equip and strengthen the church for its battle.

Trained first as a philologist, Joseph taught Romanian literature for a decade. In 1969 he was able to travel abroad and subsequently studied theology at Oxford. Returning home in 1972, he taught for two years at the Baptist Seminary in Bucharest, but was fired when he wrote about the persecution of believers in Romania. He then became pastor of the Second Baptist Church of Oradea, the largest Baptist congregation in Eastern Europe.

Over the years, Joseph was arrested many times and beaten for his faith. By September 1981, the authorities presented him with a choice: prison in Romania or exile. Tson chose the latter.

He also chose to go to America, where he founded the Romanian Missionary Society and began to translate Christian books to smuggle back into Romania.

Back in his homeland, Christians who weren't exiled were hounded mercilessly.

Peter Dugulescu, a Baptist pastor in Timisoara, was warned by the Romanian secret police, "If you don't obey us, don't be surprised if a truck or a bus crosses your path."*

On September 30, 1986, Peter, his wife, and their thirteen-year-old daughter were driving down a one-way street when a large bus, empty except for its driver, ran a stop sign and appeared in the intersection before them, perpendicular to their car. Peter tried to stop, but it was too late.

After seeing that his wife and daughter appeared to be all right, Peter sat there stunned in his wrecked car, his right arm hanging useless by his side, but feeling the Holy Spirit nudging his mind back to a sermon he had preached three weeks earlier. That morning he had exhorted his congregation that the Christian must give thanks to God for everything that happens, even problems, troubles, and accidents.

"I tried to concentrate," Peter said later. "I tried to use my last strength to say, 'Oh, Lord, I don't understand what has happened. But I want to thank You—because You reign over all these things.'"

The police arrived, but neglected to question the bus driver, measure Peter's skid marks, or do any of their usual accident investigations. They just took Peter and his family to the hospital, where they were treated for shock, bruises, and broken bones. Two days later, they took Peter's driver's license away from him.

Peter knew the Communists had murdered other outspoken church leaders—like Jerzy Popieluszko in Poland—so he asked a friend to visit the bus driver. "Look deep into his eyes, without blinking, and ask him, 'Was it just an ordinary accident, or were you ordered to kill Pastor Dugulescu?'"

Peter's friend visited the driver, and when he asked the question, the man looked away. "I can't talk to you about that," he said. "Go away!"

---

*See chapter 4.

Later, after he left the hospital, Peter visited the driver himself. "I forgive you," he said. "Take this Bible, in Jesus' name."[13]

Two years later, in 1988, Nicolae Ceausescu stood on the balcony of the Central Committee headquarters in Bucharest, smiling the best smile his unpleasant face could muster, waving as the parades passed below him.

"Ceausescu, Peace!" read one bright banner. Schoolchildren carried another reading simply "Romania!" The crowd, swelled by thousands of Securitate agents and compliant citizens dressed in colorful native costumes, marched and sang of Romania's glory.

*Forty years of Communism,* thought Ceausescu. *And the greatest glories of Romania are yet to come.*

Meanwhile, Christian leaders across the nation were acknowledging the anniversary as well. "Look at the newspapers," one told his congregation, noting the authorities' emphasis on this forty-year mark and comparing the believers' situation with that of the ancient Israelites. "The newspapers are preaching to you that your time in the desert is almost over. Get ready!"

In January 1989 a small group of Czechoslovakian students peacefully made their way to St. Wenceslas's statue in Prague to commemorate another anniversary: the twenty-year anniversary of Jan Palach's suicidal protest of the Soviet invasion of their country. Before they could reach their destination, however, a group of policemen moved toward them with water cannons and tear gas.

As the officials advanced, a short, fair-haired man watched in disgust from the other side of the square. A plainclothes agent grabbed the man and shoved him into a police van—only to find that this was Vaclav Havel, known throughout the West as Czechoslovakia's greatest human rights champion. No matter. A judge sentenced Havel to nine months in prison for inciting the demonstration.

When he was released on parole five months later, pale and thin, Havel met with Alexander Dubcek, deposed hero of the 1968 Prague Spring uprising. It was the first time the two visionaries had met. But it would not be the last.

Meanwhile, Poland's problems, including a $38.9 billion debt and continuous consumer shortages, had driven the government to desperation. As a result, the authorities did the unthinkable: They opened avenues for discussion with their longtime opponents. Solidarity representatives who had spent time in jail during martial law now found themselves being wooed by party members offering to reinstate the union and give it a share of parliamentary power—if Solidarity would, in turn, assure the government's continued control of the parliament.

Like boxers in the ring, the leaders of the government and the leaders of Solidarity sized one another up, probing for strengths, tricks, and weaknesses.

The Soviet Union was attempting an equally surprising exercise in democracy, with general elections held in March 1989—the first nationwide, competitive election since the autumn of 1917.

When the votes were tallied, Communist party officials, including those who ran without opposition, found themselves ousted. A substantial number of independent and reform-minded candidates swept into office, including a bold, opinionated iconoclast named Boris Yeltsin.

In June, Poland's elections made it clear that Solidarity had won everywhere. Many leading Communists, running unopposed, had failed to get enough votes to win. The power struggle continued through the summer, however, since the party still controlled a portion of the government. But by August 19, President Jaruzelski had appointed Tadeusz Mazowiecki as prime minister of Poland.

Mazowiecki, a journalist, a devout Roman Catholic, and an adviser to Solidarity leader Lech Walesa, had the heady distinction of being the first non-Communist to head a government in Eastern Europe since Stalin had imposed his Soviet-style Communism there after World War II.

In Hungary, during that same summer, processional music filled Budapest's largest square as Imre Nagy, who had led the nation's 1956 uprising against the Communists, was buried. Again.

Thirty-one years after he had been hanged and flung in a common grave with hundreds of other rebels, the former prime minister was honored by a state funeral—the type of tribute usually reserved for top party officials. Four companions who had led the revolt with Nagy were reburied with him, and the government network broadcast the proceedings.

Though the nation's top leaders marched solemnly behind the coffin in the funeral procession, Nagy's former ally, Janos Kadar, the turncoat leader who had been Hungary's Soviet-backed leader for thirty-two years, was not present. Deposed in 1988, Kadar was said to be physically and mentally ill.

Then, in September, came another procession, when Hungarian troops tore down their barbed-wire fences and watchtowers on the border with Austria. Since early 1988 the Hungarians had been able to travel more freely, but this physical opening of the border crossing meant that it was now possible to walk from Hungary into Austria—and on into West Germany.

And at midnight on September 13, 1989, the Hungarians went further, formally suspending their agreement with East Germany and officially opening their western border. According to the East German penal code, "flight from the republic" meant long prison terms. But within three days, fifteen thousand East Germans had headed for freedom.[14]

Meanwhile, the unimaginable happened: A thirty-five-year-old Lutheran pastor, Gabor Roszik, challenged a sitting member of parliament. For his impertinence, Roszik was defrocked by his Communist-sympathizing bishop. Undeterred, Roszik preached all the harder and campaigned to a stunning upset, making him the first non-Communist to win a seat since the Soviet occupation of the Eastern bloc.

As more and more special trains were added to the freedom railroad from east to west, the hundreds of thousands who chose to remain in East Germany took to the churches and the streets.

In Leipzig, Dresden, Halle, Weimar, and Wittenberg, churches were filled. Monday evening prayer services at St. Nikolai's in Leipzig overflowed, and after the services, the people spilled out to the Karl-Marx Platz to march for freedom.[15]

Fifteen hundred people crowded into Leipzig's Evangelical Reformed Church on Monday evenings, though the building seated only 550. Meanwhile, people were spilling out of the doors of the larger churches in the city centers. The huge Church of the Cross in Dresden was packed, as was Gethsemane Church in East Berlin.

During that time, says Juergen Weidel, pastor of Peace Church in Leipzig, "People saw that the church was a living and viable organism, not the decaying institution Marxism said it was."[16] The church had indeed survived the Communists.

Yet, maintains Johannes Richter, pastor of St. Thomas Church in Leipzig, "We didn't encourage disobedience. The responsibility would have been too great. What we did was encourage obedience to God. We said, 'Do you want to be free and obey the Ten Commandments? Or do you want to be a slave and have a car and a good job?'"[17]

Clearly the people of East Germany had had enough of slavery, and Communism's triumphal forty-year anniversary celebration on October 7 was not quite the event the party had planned. In East Berlin, Lutheran bishops boycotted the affair, and riot police broke up a peaceful candlelight vigil of some fifteen hundred protesters. In Dresden, Leipzig, and other cities, police used water cannons and swung riot sticks to beat back the crowds.

On October 9, after the usual Monday night prayer meeting at Leipzig's Nikolai church, 150,000 people took to the streets.

"We are the people!" they shouted.

State security forces and riot police stood by with live ammunition. Tanks sat ready in the garage of the state university, and armed troops surrounded every church in the city.

But this time, at least, blood was not shed. Church leaders pleaded with government leaders for nonviolence, and the order to fire was never issued.

On October 19, Bishop Leich arrived at the party offices for his scheduled meeting with Communist leader Erich Honecker. After the mass demonstrations of October 9 and the averting of disaster, Honecker had sent for the bishop to discuss the church's role in the protests erupting all over East Germany. Instead of meeting with Honecker, however, Bishop Leich found himself the first official visitor of a new prime minister.

Secretly, the day before, the man who had been the leader of the East German Communist establishment for eighteen years had fallen from power, but not before replacing himself with his protégé, Egon Krenz. No matter, thought Bishop Leich. All would soon be changed. He could feel it coming.

Krenz hastened to present himself as a younger, more sophisticated leader, aware of the people's discontent. Within a day or two, however, angry citizens were bold enough to shout down the East German party chief.

"You are finished!" they cried. "Give us free elections!"

A few weeks later, on the first Sunday of November, all of the Romanian Baptist churches spent the day in prayer and fasting for their nation.[18] As they had for years, they prayed for religious freedom in their country. They had heard rumors about upheaval in Eastern Europe, but they dared not dream such changes could come to Romania.

For his part, Pastor Doru Popa had had enough of the petty Communist oppression. He was due to preach at a funeral service in a small town north of Arad, and now the ever-troublesome secret police had called him to Timisoara, the university town south of Arad, for questioning regarding his case. Popa went to the prosecutor in Arad to explain his situation.

"Sir, you can arrest me if you want," he said, "but today I have to go to a funeral service. I am a pastor, and that is where I am needed. I will stay here only if you arrest me. But know this: You will stand before God one day."

The official blanched, then responded in typical bureaucratic fashion.

"Reverend Popa, I have nothing to do with this," he said. "Your case was given to me, and you will be in prison. That is the plan. It's not up to me. It's beyond my powers. The case will go before the court in December."

Popa went on to preach at the funeral. And by December, events the officials had not foreseen had overtaken Romania. Doru Popa did not go to prison.[19]

On November 9, work crews in Germany embarked on a deconstruction project the people had awaited for twenty-eight years. Several days earlier the entire Communist cabinet of the German Democratic Republic had resigned, and this time the army crews did not come at night while the people slept. They came openly, their progress marked by cheers and tears of joy and watched with amazement and celebration around the world.

The Berlin Wall was coming down!

Many chipped away souvenirs of a past they prayed would never return. And as the wall broke open, citizens of East Berlin poured through. Crowds of West Germans waited to greet them with uncharacteristic fervor, hugging strangers and throwing bouquets of flowers. Friends who had not seen each other for twenty-eight years were reunited. East Germans gleefully picked up their 100-mark "welcome money," hungrily eyeing the sights in the sumptuous West German shop windows.

Whatever lay ahead, it was a celebration they would never forget. Nor would the rest of a watching world.

"We Germans are now the happiest people on earth," declared the mayor of West Berlin.

The people of Czechoslovakia were also on the road to freedom. During the third week of November, all of Czechoslovakia seemed to be in the streets, shouting for change and demanding the resignation of Milos Jakes, Czechoslovakia's hard-line Communist leader.

Those not crowding Wenceslas Square watched in fascination as the rallies unfolded on television. There was Vaclav Havel, with hundreds of thousands cheering him madly. A worker named Honza Lexa, interviewed by a reporter, was saying openly that she thought the government had been lying. "What is the government afraid of?" she asked.

Suddenly their screens went black. The voice of an announcer soon came on, explaining that some unidentified television workers had disagreed with Lexa's statement. Thirty-five minutes later the broadcast was reinstated and the people heard the strong voice of Father Vaclav Maly from Wenceslas Square.*

"There can be no confidence in the leadership of a state that refuses to tell people the truth," shouted Maly, a Catholic priest whose propensity for truth telling had annoyed the government for years. Long barred from performing priestly duties, Maly was reading from an open letter from Cardinal Frantisek Tomasek, who had prayed for the day when the people would no longer accept lies.

Maly had prayed for this day as well. Not for his own advancement, but for the proclamation of gospel truth against the government's lies. After his clerical license had been revoked in 1979, he had cleaned toilets in the Prague subways and worked as a coal stoker in a hotel.

When a religious foundation in the West heard about him and began sending a small stipend, he was able to quit stoking coal and study theology instead—sitting at a small kitchen table in the tiny apartment he shared with his widowed father. Maly knew the police listened in on his conversations through a microphone hidden in a ceiling light fixture; he hoped they paid special attention when he prayed out loud to God for his nation.

---

*See chapters 9 and 22 for more on Vaclav Maly.

Ironically the priest found that his tormentors' harassment helped, rather than hindered, his devotion to Christ.

"They stripped our faith of all the superfluous things," he said. "They took away church property. Only someone willing to make a personal sacrifice could make a confession of faith. Young people entered the church because they understood this sacrifice."[20]

And in a demonstration along the Letna Plain, the huge riverfront park bordering the northern edge of downtown Prague, Father Maly had an unexpected opportunity to practice the faith he had learned from years of sacrifice.

As Maly was speaking before a crowd of half a million demonstrators, a young police officer pushed his way forward, climbed the steps to the podium, and explained to the shocked crowd that he had been among the police officers who had beaten a group of student protesters several weeks earlier. "I am sorry," he stammered. "Please forgive me."

Maly put his arm around the weeping officer, then spoke firmly to the crowd about the Christian duty to forgive. "Let us pray," he shouted.

And in a voice five hundred thousand strong, they affirmed the faith the Communists had not been able to steal: "Our Father, who art in heaven . . . Thy will be done on earth, as it is in heaven . . . forgive us our trespasses, as we forgive those who trespass against us. . . ."

By now the people in Wenceslas Square had cheered themselves hoarse. Yet still singing, dancing, screaming, 350,000 protesters welcomed back a man they had not seen in public since 1968: Alexander Dubcek, leader of the Prague Spring uprising. For the past two decades he had worked in an obscure state forestry office.

As he stood on the balcony, Dubcek's eyes filled with tears. "An old wise man said, 'If there once was light, why should there be darkness again?'" he shouted. "Let us act in such a way to bring the light back again!"[21]

Soon after his speech, the people received the news that Czechoslovakia's Communist party leadership had resigned, including Milos Jakes.

Their long-ago springtime dreams were finally coming to harvest.

In Romania, Nicolae Ceausescu was open to no such dreams. On November 20 he harangued his way through a five-hour speech in Bucharest. His party delegates chanted slogans, jumped up, applauded, and sat down in unison, uniformly—too uniformly—affirming their support for Ceausescu's disdain for democratic changes elsewhere in Eastern Europe.

Meanwhile, from his exile in the West, Dr. Joseph Tson had stepped up his assault on Romanian airwaves via Radio Free Europe.

"Change is coming to Romania," asserted Dr. Tson. "Christians, be ready!"

Believers in western Romania heard his challenge with a mixture of joy and wonder.

There was joy and wonder at the Vatican, too, as media from around the world recorded the culmination of an unprecedented event: the first encounter between a Soviet leader and a pope. Clasping hands at the close of a tumultuous decade, John Paul II and Mikhail Gorbachev stood at a crossroads.

During the historical meeting the pope pressed for religious freedoms for Soviet Catholics. In response, the Soviet leader acknowledged that all believers "have a right to satisfy their spiritual needs" and that his country had made the mistake of treating religion in "a simplistic manner."[22]

The ironies of the meeting were not lost on the *New York Times,* which observed, "At an earlier time, Stalin had scornfully asked how many divisions the pope had. Now, a successor intent on undoing Stalin's legacy has crossed St. Peter's Square in open recognition that he must reckon with the Vatican as a moral and political force."[23]

Three days later the Soviet Union and the four Warsaw Pact allies that had taken part in the invasion of Czechoslovakia in 1968 issued a joint statement condemning the Soviet-led military suppression of the popular Prague Spring uprising.

Back in Prague, a prisoner from that uprising was on his way to becoming president.

For years Vaclav Havel's most common form of transportation had been paddy wagons and police cars. Now, during the first week of December 1989, people had glimpsed him riding in government limousines. What was going on?

Then came the announcement the people had hoped for: Havel was willing to become president of Czechoslovakia.

"I have repeatedly said my occupation is writer," the dissident told an American reporter. "I have no desire to be a professional politician. But I have always placed the public interest above my own. And if, God help us, the situation develops in such a way that the only service I could render my country would be to do this, then of course I would do it."[24]

At the same time, though heartened by the democratic changes coming elsewhere in Eastern Europe, the people in Romania could not believe that such changes might possibly come to their own land. Nicolae Ceausescu was too powerful, his Securitate too insidiously pervasive.

Nevertheless, believers in Timisoara spent hours in prayer. Lying prostrate on the cold floors of their small flats, they were warmed by a spiritual passion that caused them to thunder a bold and unlikely prayer: "Lord, help our nation. Turn Your face to our land. Bring revival to Romania—and bring it through Timisoara!"[25]

God answered that prayer. And help for Romania did indeed begin in Timisoara as Pastor Laszlo Tokes's eviction from his church swelled into a protest that filled the city's central square. Christians from all over the city rallied and prayed that this might be the beginning of the end of the godless tyranny of Ceausescu's regime.*

Some believers held back from the protest demonstrations at first. Was this their answer to prayer? Surely they would give their lives for Christ and the cause of the gospel—but was this that time? Or was it merely a political situation? They were ready, but they wanted to be wise.

As they prayed for wisdom, they also brought tea and soup and blankets to warm the people in the square. And as they did so, they believed God was leading them to join these demonstrations against a dictator who had despised His name. For the sake of the university students with whom they worked, the ones who would ask in the future, "Were you there?" they had to be able to answer, "Yes, we were there. We were in solidarity with those who stood for the cause of freedom and justice."

Gelu Paul, his wife, Rodica, and Peter and Gina Bulica were part of the small group that fasted and prayed over their decision to join the people. They also prayed, as they had for years, for the downfall of Nicolae Ceausescu.

Meanwhile, in Bucharest, Ceausescu convened a meeting of the Political Executive Committee of the Romanian Communist party,

---

*See chapter 4.

furious that the military had yet to open fire on the Timisoara demonstrators.

"Why didn't they shoot?" he asked Defense Minister Vasile Milea. "They should have shot to put them on the ground, to warn them—shot them in the legs."

Addressing the group, Ceausescu continued, "Everybody who doesn't submit to the soldiers—I've given the order to shoot. They'll get a warning, and if they don't submit, they'll have to be shot. It was a mistake to turn the other cheek. . . . In an hour, order should be reestablished in Timisoara."[26]

Supposing the situation resolved, Ceausescu left for a three-day trip to Iran, leaving his army and faithful Securitate agents to carry out his violent measures. What he didn't realize was that his army was not entirely with him.

Marius Miron was on the streets of Timisoara on the evening of December 17 after Ceausescu had given his order to shoot. Miron saw cars driving the wrong way down one-way streets, and near Laszlo Tokes's church he saw tear gas canisters and water cannons. On the city square a huge bonfire raged in front of a bookshop: People had broken the windows and were dragging out books by and about the Ceausescus, throwing them into the flames. Near the opera house he saw soldiers firing their guns into the air; he heard the sounds of breaking glass and people shouting slogans.

He was at the corner of Liberty Square and Karl Marx Street when he saw a group of ten people shot down by soldiers. Miron, a trained medical assistant, ran and bent over the man closest to him; the man's femoral artery had been severed by a bullet, and he was bleeding to death.

When Miron stood up to take off his belt to make a tourniquet, he saw a soldier take deliberate aim at him and fire. He felt no pain. His leg just suddenly blew up. He hit the ground, his limb shattered, and began to drag himself backward by his elbows until someone picked him up and took him to the hospital.[27]

The shooting continued.

Gradually hundreds, then thousands, of people flooded the streets, making their way toward Timisoara's main square, carrying signs and banners. One held a stick aloft with a shoe on top—a reference to Ceausescu's original vocation.

"Down with the shoemaker!" he cried.

"Liberty!" shouted others. "Freedom!"

Adina Jinaru, watching the procession go by her home, felt as if the whole of Timisoara had been in prison—"and now they were all to be released at once."

Rumors spread everywhere in the bullet-torn city: Nicolae Ceausescu had given the order to level Timisoara and annihilate everyone in it. Elena Ceausescu had urged the use of chemical weapons. The army's special code, "Blue Rain," was about to be activated and would signal the city's utter destruction.

During the night Adina and her family huddled in their basement with a few provisions while the air raid siren wailed across the city. Somehow Adina got an open phone line and called her friend Nellie Iovin in Arad.

"I don't know what will happen to us," she cried into the phone, "but if we are wiped out, call my brother in Germany and tell him what happened!"[28]

Nellie Iovin lived in a small, detached house in Arad on Scolii Street, just off the main highway through town. Like Nellie, most of Arad's citizens knew about the drama being played out in neighboring Timisoara. Then their own uprising began as a hundred thousand people gathered in Arad's main square in front of the city hall, where they were soon ringed by tanks and soldiers.

As Nellie and other Christians approached the square, they had to pass these tanks and a line of soldiers. Would they shoot? Fearful but determined, Nellie and the others knelt in front of the guns and began to pray; some stuck flowers into the gun barrels. The soldiers let them pass.[29]

Here, as in Timisoara, the crowds were shouting, "Down with Ceausescu! Down with Communism!"

And here, as in Timisoara, the Christians in the crowd added other slogans. For forty-five years the citizens of Romania had been told there was no God. Now a hundred thousand people were shouting as one, "God exists! God is with us!"

Across the street from city hall, Baptist pastor Mihai Gongola was given a microphone, wired with electricity from the tram lines. His main theme was the people's slogan: "God is with us!"

Pastor Doru Popa preached to the crowd as well. "Finally we are free," he shouted. "But some of us here were free already: we had been made free by God."

Then Popa gestured toward the Communist headquarters, a building where he had been searched and interrogated many times.

"We will write on this building three words," he said. "*Via, veritas, vita:* the way, the truth, the life. We need a way: for forty years we had no leadership. We need the truth: for forty years all we heard were lies. And we need life: for forty years we have had only an existence."

Popa closed his sermon with a traditional Romanian carol that people had not sung in public for forty years: "What wonderful news is coming from Bethlehem, that we have now a Savior."

Holding candles aloft in the night, a hundred thousand people took up the melody. A song of good news in a land that had known only bad for so long.

On December 21, with Romania on the verge of total upheaval, Ceausescu staged a rally in Bucharest. Such rallies had been the staple of his regime for years: pro-Ceausescu banners displaying carefully retouched, attractive portraits of the unattractive dictator and his wife; the Ceausescus on a balcony high above the people, who obediently brayed their shouts of approval and adulation.

But this time something went awry.

When Ceausescu appeared on the balcony, he intoned with unintended irony, "I would like to extend to you . . . warm revolutionary greetings."[30]

At first the usual cheers and applause came back to him: "Ceausescu! Ceausescu! Romania!"

Suddenly there was a movement in the crowd, as if people in the back of the throng were pushing those in front of them. Undistinguished shouts. A sense of confusion.

Then a faint cry began: "Timisoara!" "Timisoara!" and several young people unfurled a banner they had hidden under their coats: "Down with Ceausescu!" Some in the crowd began to run away.

Perplexed by the disorder, Ceausescu began waving his arms, muttering into the microphone, "Hello? Hello?" assuming something was wrong with the sound system. Elena Ceausescu strode forward, shouting for silence, and then her husband resumed his speech.

But it was too late.

Even as a few supporters still cheered the dictator, a group of people began singing "Romanians, Awake," the same song the crowd had sung outside the church of Laszlo Tokes. And then came the cry: "Yesterday Timisoara, today Bucharest!"[31]

As Nicolae Ceausescu tried once more to speak to the crowds, his once-docile people booed and threw shoes at him. Furious, the ugly little man turned back into the Central Committee building and ordered the army to fire.

By this time, however, many members of the army had defected to the people. Also, Vasile Milea, minister of defense, refused to give the firing order to his troops; soon after, his death was announced as a traitor's suicide. Milea had shot himself rather than carry out Ceausescu's lethal order.[32]

When a crowd stormed the Central Committee building, Ceausescu, his wife, and a few aides fled by helicopter from the roof.

Just as the news of Ceausescu's flight reached Timisoara, Pastor Peter Dugulescu was poised to speak to the two hundred thousand people assembled in the city square. For hours speakers had been addressing the crowds from the balcony of the opera house—the same balcony from which Ceausescu had spoken to the people during his annual visits to Timisoara.

On this night, just hours before Christmas, people in the crowd had requested that a pastor come to preach to them. A committee of sorts was reviewing each speaker's material. When Dugulescu told them his plans, they nodded. "Just end with the words, 'Down with the tyrant,'" they said. "I can do that," Dugulescu replied.

"I'm Pastor Peter Dugulescu from the First Baptist Church, Timisoara," he began as he took the microphone, "and I have come to speak to you in the name of God, as you wanted. For almost forty-five years—my age, unfortunately—we have been told there is no God. The Communists wanted to take God away from our hearts, from our minds, from our families, from our schools. I want to speak to you in the name of this God."

From the balcony Dugulescu could see thousands of upturned faces, hear the shouts of voices hoarse with tears.

"God exists!" they shouted. "There is a God. There is a God. God is with us!"

Dugulescu continued. "The Communists tried to kill me a few times—but I am still alive, because God protected me. And I have asked the government to bring Pastor Tokes back to Timisoara; we must have real religious freedom in Romania!"

Cheers interrupted him periodically as he continued for a few minutes, then asked the people to pray with him. "This is a historic moment. Let us turn our hearts to God. Please follow me in the Lord's Prayer."

He hadn't asked the people to kneel, but as he looked out he saw a sight he would never forget.

On this square where people had been forced to sing the praises of Ceausescu for years, before this balcony that had been an altar to the Communist regime, now, as far as he could see, a tidal wave of people knelt on the pavement. And sentence by sentence, with one voice, they thundered out the ancient prayer: "Our Father, who art in heaven, hallowed be Thy name. . . ."

Believers in the crowd looked at those beside them and sensed a unity that set their hearts afire. They could see hope on the faces of young people who had known nothing but socialism for their entire lives; they saw joy on the faces of old people who had long yearned for Romania to return to God, long prayed for God to turn His face back to their beleaguered nation. In their eyes was the wonder of the truth, the life, the way: *God is sovereign. It is His kingdom, His power, and His glory.*

As Christmas dawn crept across the land of Romania, the church bells rang for the first time in forty years. Good news blared from television sets across the country: "God has turned His face back to Romania!" Christians who had not sung carols in public during their lifetimes sang out the good news of Christ's coming: "Immanuel, God with us!"

Since Nicolae Ceausescu had denied that fact during his entire political career, to many Romanians it seemed fitting that his execution came on Christmas Day.

For Ceausescu and his wife had been captured almost immediately after their flight from Bucharest and kept in army custody for several days. Then on December 25, having been tried by a military tribunal for crimes against the people, they were convicted of genocide. Hundreds volunteered to serve on their firing squad.

Video images of the dictator and his wife sprawled in pools of blood were transmitted across Romania—and around the world.

*What a man sows, so shall he reap,* thought Pastor Mihai Gongola as he saw the fallen tyrant. Then he went through his forty-four-unit apartment block distributing New Testaments and wishing his neighbors a merry Christmas, relishing his extraordinary new freedom to do so openly.

The bells ringing in Romania rang across the rest of Eastern Europe as the people gathered in the streets, hugging each other and weeping for joy, singing Christmas carols with the fervor of newfound freedom.

And even as the citizens of the East shook off their bonds, the pundits of the West lost no time in analyzing the story.

*Time* magazine held nothing back in its enthusiasm for the end of the Cold War, declaring Mikhail Gorbachev "Man of the Decade." Ignoring the complexities and the heart of Eastern Europe's revolutions of 1989, the journal effused, "A catalyst for reform from Moscow to Bucharest, Gorbachev has transformed the world."[33]

Surely Gorbachev's policies created an atmosphere wherein change seemed more accessible than at any time in the Eastern bloc's history. But had the glasnost cowboy riding the buckling brontosaurus of his ailing nation really pulled off such a miracle?

No. Even as they affirmed the wonder of the Cold War ending, not with a bang or a whimper but with shouts of joy in the streets, the media missed the heart of the biggest story of the century.[34] Surely bad politics and dismal economics played their part in fueling the unrest. But man does not live by bread alone, and in Eastern Europe the people were not marching for bread alone. They were marching for a freedom that transcends the physical—the freedom of the human spirit.

While the "Man of the Decade" issue filled Western newsstands, President Vaclav Havel adjusted his glasses, took a deep breath, and began his New Year's Day address to the people of Czechoslovakia. His theme was the same one that had gotten him arrested thirteen years earlier.

The worst thing about the legacy of Communism, he told the people, "is that we are living in a decayed moral environment. We have become morally ill, because we have become accustomed to saying one thing and thinking another. We have learned not to believe in anything, not to have consideration for one another, and to only look after ourselves. . . .

"When I talk about a decayed moral environment . . . I mean all of us . . . all of us are responsible, each to a different degree, for keeping the totalitarian machine running. None of us is merely a victim of it, because all of us helped to create it together."

Shocking words for people accustomed to forty years of Communism, but words they had staged a revolution to hear. Then Havel took it further:

"Our first [pre-communist] president wrote, 'Jesus and not Caesar.' . . . This idea has once again been reawakened in us."[35]

Christ or Caesar?

This was the choice made all across Eastern Europe. And what began in Nowa Huta with the raising of the cross in the public square came to its denouement three decades later in, of all places, the heart of the Communist behemoth . . .

It was May Day, 1990. The place, Moscow's Red Square.

"Is it straight, Father?" one Orthodox priest asked another, shifting the heavy, eight-foot crucifix on his shoulder.

"Yes," said the other. "It is straight."

Together the two priests, along with a group of parishioners holding ropes that steadied the beams of the huge cross, walked the parade route. Before them had passed the official might of the Union of Soviet Socialist Republics: the usual May Day procession of tanks, missiles, troops, and salutes to the Communist party elite.

Behind the tanks surged a giant crowd of protesters, shouting up at Mikhail Gorbachev. "Bread! . . . Freedom! . . . Truth!"

As the throng passed directly in front of the Soviet leader standing in his place of honor, the priests hoisted their heavy burden toward the sky. The cross emerged from the crowd. As it did, the figure of Jesus Christ obscured the giant poster faces of Karl Marx, Friedrich Engels, and Vladimir Lenin that provided the backdrop for Gorbachev's reviewing stand.

"Mikhail Sergeyevich!" one of the priests shouted, his deep voice cleaving the clamor of the protesters and piercing straight toward the angry Soviet leader. "Mikhail Sergeyevich! Christ is risen!"

In a matter of months after that final May Day celebration, the Soviet Union was officially dissolved. Christ is risen indeed and is building His church, ". . . *and the gates of hell shall not prevail against it.*"

# 17

## The Church in Captivity

Here's the great evangelical disaster—the failure of the evangelical world to stand for truth as truth. There is only one word for this—namely, accommodation.

*Francis Schaeffer*

𝓜ANY OF THE HIPPIES AND YIPPIES OF the sixties are today's boomers and yuppies. VW bugs emblazoned with "Make Love Not War" have been replaced by Volvos with bumper stickers reading, "My child is an honor student at Suburban Elementary School." Love beads, peace signs, and Woodstock memorabilia are collectors' items; former Black Panther Bobby Seale now presides over that middle-class icon, the Weber grill, marketing his cookbook, *Barbecuing with Bobby*.

But the sixties aren't completely history. The University of California at Berkeley still clings to vestiges of that turbulent decade. Twenty-five years ago Berkeley was a haven for flower children, simmering with anger, protests, and anti-establishment fervor. Today, as many students opt for business degrees and public relations courses, notorious Berkeley strives to keep its avant-garde image alive.

Walk up University Drive, the long hill that leads you toward campus. You'll still see shops with tie-dyed t-shirts and peace-symbol earrings, although most establishments are now stocked with crystals, herbal tea, and New Age gear. On campus, however, one sixties tradition remains intact: Sproul Plaza, the famous square that celebrates free speech, where students once spewed their most furious venom against the Vietnam War.

Students can still sign up to speak at Sproul, and during most lunch hours you can hear passionate diatribes on everything from Chinese politics to reincarnation to lesbian sociopolitical agendas. And in the spirit of the great legacies of pluralism and free speech that Americans hold dear, most of those who gather at the plaza are tolerant toward speakers, whatever the subject. It's a free country, isn't it? People have a right to believe and to express in the public square whatever they want, don't they?

Of course they do. Except when a Christian is on the program. Then the mood changes. The general goodwill among listeners eating their pita sandwiches and swilling their organic apple juice slowly gives way to clenched teeth.

All this comes to a head in the form of one campus celebrity. If a Christian is slated to address the crowd, even more students than usual will mill around Sproul Plaza just to see if this guy will show up. And usually he does, pushing his way through the crowd to get nose to nose with the speaker.

It's Hate Man.

Hate Man has been around Berkeley for years, so he's probably in his fifties now, with a graying beard. And he's no caped crusader; most often he wears a dress. He's the type of person you would probably avoid if you saw him talking to himself on the subway. But if he is insane—the jury is still out on that—he is also extremely intelligent and articulate.

So before they venture into the public square, Christians at Berkeley are warned to prepare well. For if they proclaim their faith in Sproul Plaza, Hate Man will be in their face, raising objections, punching holes in their logic, eloquently rebutting everything they say. All at the top of his lungs.[1]

Most of us never confront such an obvious foe. Certainly not the way the first-century Christians did. Nothing too hard about identifying the bad guys back then: the Caesars, the Pilates, the fertility goddesses. The early church challenged those reigning powers head-on.

And surely the Christians we've just read about stared down their oppressors. Christ or Communism. Choose. Official doctrine spelled it out clearly: siding with Christ meant you were against their world.

But most of us in America aren't confronted by a Caesar or a Ceausescu or even a Hate Man. No, in our corporations, in our neighborhoods, at the PTA, in the media, the challenge to the Christian world-view is far more subtle. So subtle we often don't even recognize it.

Maybe if Hate Man were on every corner, challenging us as we come out of church—even threatening our lives—we would understand the dangerous forces around us. But that's not the way it works. The voices of culture are smooth, personable, and oh, so reasonable.

That the threat is subtle makes it no less menacing. In fact, the dangers of compromise are made the more insidious by their subtlety.

### In League with Caesar

In the East the pressure to conform to the state came frontally and brutally. In the West we have ensnared ourselves in the coils of politics. Not that it is wrong to address or involve ourselves with political issues; that's a Christian duty, as we discuss elsewhere. But political involvement is different from marrying one political agenda or putting that agenda ahead of our primary calling.

That's what happened to the mainline denominations in the sixties. Genuinely outraged by racial discrimination in our country, the major denominations joined the civil rights movement with fervor. As they should have. The moral passion for human rights is compelled by Christian conscience.

But many church leaders moved from there into a political agenda. Motivated by compassion for the poor and believing that justice would roll down through Lyndon Johnson's public policies, they embraced the grand visions of the Great Society. And in the political world they quickly became just another special interest group for politicians to court.

Enjoying their newfound access, church bureaucracies began sliding down the slippery slope of politics, churning out press releases on every possible political issue, including ones such as economics and defense on which they seemed especially ill informed. In a short time, many mainline churches were politicized to the core. Issuing position papers, marching in anti-war protests, and lobbying Congress for particular agendas took precedence over their higher call to worship the Lord, preach the gospel, and make disciples.

The leftward slide continued even as the pews emptied.* So much so that liberal churches, holding fast to their socially relevant agenda, have been among the last to recognize the moral vacuum of socialism. Long after most of the world had recognized that behind Daniel Ortega's designer sunglasses was nothing more than a small-time Marxist thug, he was still welcomed into the pulpit of New York's famed Riverside Church. The National Council of Churches endorsed him and the Sandinista party in the 1990 Nicaraguan election—notwithstanding his brutal persecution of Christians in that country.

Today, minister James Forbes has replaced the well-known activist William Sloan Coffin at Riverside, but many parishioners—including the denominational bureaucrats who worship there—believe Mr. Forbes should "spend more time critiquing capitalism than citing Christ."[†]

It was no surprise that when the Persian Gulf crisis erupted in 1990, so did the printing presses at the National Council of Churches. Even before the debate developed in Congress, church leaders were pontificating on national television. A monsignor from the U.S. Catholic Conference and Joan Campbell, secretary of the NCC, declared that the "just war" doctrine, first defined by Augustine and

---

*One study, done by the Lilly Foundation, found that 40 percent of those people who attended confirmation classes in the 1950s and early 1960s no longer belong to or attend church regularly, yet still consider themselves religious (Michael Hirsley, "Mainline Protestants Trying to Stem Losses," *Chicago Tribune,* 7 May 1991, 12); the United Methodist Church has dropped about 2 million members since its glory days of the 1950s and 1960s (ibid., 11) and went from 10.5 million in 1970 to 9.1 million in 1988 (Marjorie Hyer, "Church Council May Seek New Alliances," *Los Angeles Times,* 12 November 1988, 23). Presbyterians went from 4 million to 3 million between 1970 and 1988; in the same period, Episcopalians went from 3.3 to 2.5 million, and the United Church of Christ from 2 million to 1.7 million (ibid.). "The politicized church generally becomes unloving in its attitudes toward society, particularly toward those who are part of its structures," says Dr. Charles S. MacKenzie (Charles S. MacKenzie, "Deformation of the Church," in *Church on the Wrong Road,* ed. Stanley Atkins and Theodore McConnell [Chicago: Regnery Gateway, 1986], 37).

[†] Twice in 1990 groups of parishioners stormed Rev. Forbes's office to voice "anger that Riverside Church was not doing enough," and the former head of Riverside's disarmament program said: "I personally like the politics, and for me, being politically active is being spiritually aware" (R. Gustav Niebuhr, "Prayer and Politics: A Landmark Church Famed for Activism Faces Tougher Times," *Wall Street Journal,* 1 August 1990, A-1, 6).

defended through the centuries, was no longer applicable because of nuclear weapons. (No one bothered to mention that nuclear weapons were not at issue.) The presiding bishop of President Bush's own denomination paraded in front of the White House, surrounded by an assortment of anti-war protesters.

And when Communism crumbled in the East and oppressed peoples danced in the streets of Prague, Bucharest, Warsaw, Budapest, and Berlin, where was the religious left? Conspicuously silent. The last holdouts against the worldwide discrediting of Marxism seemed to be Cuba, North Korea, and, as Michael Novak has acerbically noted, American universities and the mainline church.[2]

This politicization of the church is not limited to the United States. On the thirtieth anniversary of the "liberation" of Cuba, Cardinal Paulo Evaristo Arns of São Paulo, Brazil, commended Fidel Castro for his example of social justice and proclaimed that "Christian faith discovers in the achievements of the Revolution signs of the kingdom of God, which are made manifest in our hearts and in the structures which permit us to make of political familiarity an act of love."[3]

Could the ecclesiastic not hear the echoes of the groans and rattling chains from the cells of Castro's wretched political prisons?

Some of this politicization was the result of infiltration. Perhaps one of the saddest disclosures in the newly opened KGB files is that the World Council of Churches was penetrated by Communist agents. That they manipulated the WCC, including electing a general secretary and issuing eleven messages corresponding to the socialist line, is now well documented.[4] As Charles MacKenzie, president of Grove City College, has reminded us, Lenin once urged his followers to work to politicize the church if they wanted to neutralize its effect in society.

But for the most part the liberal churches didn't need to be infiltrated. They eagerly promoted leftist political alliances.

Those on the conservative side have no reason to gloat, however. Evangelicals and fundamentalists who for decades had carefully separated themselves from politics—so much so that many went to an equally wrong extreme and didn't even vote—reversed themselves dramatically in the seventies by sliding down the right side of the slippery slope.

And they, too, started with a noble goal: elect to office those Christians or moralists who would reform a decadent America. But political agenda soon overcame spiritual focus. Organizing Christians in "get out and vote" campaigns, these conservatives published scorecards that rated the voting records of senators and representatives on issues ranging from abortion to national defense. Morally upright individuals who voted "wrong" on, say, the Panama Canal or trade legislation scored low; thieves and knaves who voted "right" scored high.

While the Moral Majority and others did awaken many Christians to the fact that involvement in the political process is part of their stewardship, they also led many to naively put all their faith in that process. One prominent Christian leader even warned that there could never be revival until Christian conservatives gained control of the Congress.

But the lions who helped put Ronald Reagan in the White House did not roar long. Conservative Christians enjoyed access to the Oval Office, state dinners, and the like, and in the process they were quickly tamed. So much so that by the time George Bush invited a homosexual activist group to the White House for a bill signing—the first time an American president had officially recognized gay militants—there was hardly a growl of protest.

One evangelical leader was outraged but didn't want to say anything. "I'm going to have dinner with the president next month," he explained. He knew that those in power dump those who rock the boat. In fact, shortly afterward the White House liaison to the evangelical community, who did protest the bill-signing invitation, was fired.[5]

Disillusionment has a way of bringing enlightenment, and the Christian conservative movement began taking other directions in the nineties. And there have been some encouraging signs in those instances when Christian leaders have refused to be manipulated by the state, even when the cost of taking their stand was very great.

For example, in 1989 the Salvation Army told the city of New York that they would withhold their services to the city—services that amounted to $4.5 million in contracts—because they refused to agree to New York City requirements not to discriminate in the hiring of homosexuals. Cardinal O'Connor, impressed with the stand that the Salvation Army took, aligned himself with the cause and decided to throw the $90 million worth of contracts with the New York archdiocese into the kitty.

One can imagine the temptation to rationalize: the money was for a needy cause . . . the organizations could maintain a great witness . . . yet both organizations stood their ground, willing to forfeit the funds. And the city was forced to back down!

Much of our earlier book, *Kingdoms in Conflict,* is devoted to the difficult issues of church and state; so for our purposes here, it suffices that we be reminded of the lessons the church has learned the hard way over the centuries. When Christianity was made the official religion of Rome in the fourth century, the church became socially and politically acceptable. People with halfhearted faith flocked to churches that could no longer disciple them. Soon the word "Christian" became meaningless. And when the empire that sanctioned it collapsed, the church nearly went down too.

In the Middle Ages, the unholy alliance of church and state resulted in bloody crusades and scandalous inquisitions. And in our own day, one of the most inglorious examples can be found in the church's failure to stand solidly against Hitler in Germany during the 1930s.[6]

The church must stand apart from the state. Independence from the culture is what gives the church its reforming capacity and enables it to point society toward the truth. The church must be free to address issues biblically across the spectrum and to speak prophetically, regardless of who is in power.

Ironically, political flirtations and dalliances have threatened the church's independence in the West even more than the direct oppression of the Communists in the East.

## In the World and of the World

A second and even greater threat to the church's independence is the one that sidles in the door on Sunday morning unnoticed because it wears a familiar face. It is the subtle, gradual acceptance of cultural values and practices. Accommodation always dulls the gospel's sharp edges.

The church needs to be sensitive to cultural attitudes. Evangelistic methods will differ according to the understanding and background and age of one's audience. In this decade it may well take some unorthodox techniques to reach jaded Americans with the orthodox truth.

But there is a crucial distinction here: The church must never confuse technique with truth. Times change; truth doesn't. What was orthodox nineteen centuries ago is orthodox today. The church stands or falls on its adherence to Scripture and its historic confessions. This may offend, but the scandal of the cross of Christ has always offended.

Rather than offend, however, the church has gradually, almost imperceptibly, slipped into accommodating the culture. It begins with a small step, something almost unconscious. Like the pastor who never quite gets around to teaching about sin and repentance, or the one who simply smooths the edges off some of the hard sayings of the gospel. Or those who shade the message, subtly equating the "abundant" life with upper middle-class affluence. Or the church leaders who are unwilling to confront sin or challenge sinful behavior.*

These small seeds of accommodation may well ripen into the therapeutic gospel we described in chapter 3. While the culture unrelentingly focuses on self-esteem, the church struggles to catch up with "Christianized" therapy—and in the process loses much of the truly freeing distinctive of the Christian message.

Sometimes we simply want to keep up with what is perceived to be culturally sensitive and politically correct. No one likes to appear bigoted or indifferent to the feelings of others. This can affect the language we use.

Some mainline denominations have eagerly embraced secular fashions, reworking hymn books and even changing liturgy. Lest we offend anyone by talking about the *Father*hood of God, some have rewritten prayers to address "our Creator" rather than "our Father," "our Redeemer" rather than "Jesus," and "the Sustainer" rather than "the Holy Spirit." A church in which one of my evangelical friends worships now offers a unisex service at one of its three morning services, during which prayers are offered to "Our Father and Mother in heaven." Another mainline church has gone all the way over, beginning worship with the invocation: "May the God who mothers us all bear us as the breath of dawn and make us shine like the sun and hold us in the palm of Her hand."[7]

And evangelicals are being herded in the same direction, only less overtly. In 1987 I was invited to give an address on the sanctity

---

*This phenomenon is not peculiar to America; enculturation has been taking place in Europe and Great Britain, too. According to a recent poll in Great Britain, while 85 percent of those polled professed to be Christians, only 34 percent knew what happened on the first Easter Sunday (*National Christian Reporter*, 12 April 1991).

of life at a symposium held at an evangelical Christian college. My remarks were transcribed for later publication, then edited by one of the professors. When I reviewed the draft, I discovered that all references to "man" and "mankind" had been changed to "human" and "humankind," which made for some very awkward constructions, to say the least.

I returned the draft, changed back to its original wording. I knew the professor wouldn't like it, but I was unprepared for his reply, in which he accused me of advocating "Christian Archie Bunkerism."

Another time, I was not quite so vigilant. An evangelical publisher excerpted a chapter from one of my books, and I failed to read the proof sheets. When the copy was in print I discovered that the publisher had substituted inclusive language throughout. After my protest, subsequent printings were returned to the original language.

I dismissed these as isolated incidents—until the thought police struck with a vengeance.

A few days before I was scheduled to address a large evangelical gathering, I received a letter from one of the event organizers, a professor at a leading evangelical seminary, sternly warning me against the use of sexist words such as "mankind." They were, the professor said somewhat imperiously, the equivalent of racist slang and violated "ethical biblical guidelines." (I'm still searching for these guidelines . . .) I was also told that if the translation of the Bible I used contained such offensive references, I was to substitute "correct" wording when reading those verses out loud during my presentation.

This was more than I could stomach. I changed what I had planned to speak about and, in language straight out of the "insensitive" Scripture, argued for the inerrant Word of God and the need to guard orthodoxy. One of the event organizers later told me, "You just don't understand how strong some people's feelings are." And, not surprisingly, the organization has not invited me again.

But the issue here isn't feelings; the issue is objective truth.

There is nothing wrong with crafting one's speaking or writing to show respect and courtesy for both sexes, for people of color, for the disabled—to be sensitive to and include all one's listeners or readers. We should do that, and over the years I have sincerely tried to become more "inclusive" with my language.

Also, women have not been treated as equals in the workplace, in the culture, or in the church. That inequity needs to be changed.

But the politically correct movement is interested in much more than achieving equality, fairness, or sensitivity. Lurking just beneath its surface is an angry, militant agenda that is not really concerned with the words themselves. Rather, the words are part of a litmus test that separates those who agree with the agenda from those who don't. Sort of a not-so-secret handshake or a campaign button that neatly identifies the wearer. These are code words of what one writer calls "a feminist orthodoxy"—and this inclusive language represents subscription to the entire agenda.[8]

The issue, then, is not whether the word "mankind" is incorrect; it is not. It still remains the generic term for "the human race: the totality of human beings" according to Webster. The issue is whether we agree with militant feminist orthodoxy. For when people are forced to use the feminist dialect, they are being forced to signal agreement with the agenda, and if they don't use it, they're accused of being bigots.

When Christians uncritically take up the language of the movement, they are, perhaps without even realizing it, embracing an ideology that inevitably raises serious attacks on biblical authority. For what the militants seek is not equality, but the elimination of all gender distinctives. This despite the empirical fact that there are biological differences; that's the way we're made. And this despite the clear distinctions in Scripture: Men and women are created by God as equal partners, but with different gifts and roles relating directly to the biblical character of the family and the patriarchal character of God Himself.

Thus, while it may parade under the banner of sensitivity and relevance and other benign terms, the militant feminist agenda is actually an assault on the revealed, propositional truth of God and His plan for men and women. And the tragedy is that it has duped a lot of people, preying on the understandable resentment of many evangelical women and imposing unwarranted guilt on evangelical men.

So believers must not be intimidated. We must make sure our language is loving and respectful, recognizing the God-given dignity of every person. But we need not, in a headlong effort to seem relevant, salute the god/goddess of political correctness and his/her/its underlying opposition to the biblical world-view.

Another area where the church has just as eagerly rushed to embrace the latest trends of modern culture is sexual morality. x

Recently, for example, openly homosexual candidates have been ordained into the Episcopal priesthood.* It would be foolish to suggest that there haven't been homosexuals in the clergy before. The difference is that while in the past homosexuality was dealt with as sin, today there is a growing movement to celebrate it as simply an alternate lifestyle choice. John Shelby Spong, Episcopal bishop of Newark, who never fails to say or write exactly what the trendy, cultural elite want to hear, has even argued that the apostle Paul, though unfortunately repressed, was a homosexual.

And one can only wonder what John Calvin and John Knox, founders of Presbyterianism, would have thought had they returned in the summer of 1991 to witness the deliberations of the Presbyterian Church USA's General Assembly. Before it were the recommendations of its task force on human sexuality: The church has to adjust to cultural norms. That means optional celibacy for those who are unmarried. Sex is okay if it is "full of joyful caring"; adultery is okay if it meets the same criterion; ordination of homosexuals is okay too. It is time, the task force argued, to dump "the pervasive fear of sex and passion . . . [and] embrace the erotic as a moral good."[9] (Another subtle twist on God's design: It was God, after all, who invented the physical relationship between man and woman and pronounced it "very good." But the church, huffing and puffing to keep up with culture, now goes outside His design to proclaim "good" the perversions that God specifically outlawed.)

The proposal was soundly defeated, but the denomination's leaders commissioned a new study to be returned to the next assembly. It's an old technique: Propose something positively outrageous and then "compromise" later with something slightly less outrageous, but which by then seems almost reasonable by comparison.

The Evangelical Lutheran Church is right on the heels of the Presbyterians. In December 1991 it issued a study on human sexuality,

---

*A resolution was passed at the 1979 denominational convention that stated it was "not appropriate to ordain practicing homosexuals." Only in the last three years have openly gay priest candidates been ordained. The Episcopal (homosexual) group Integrity, Inc., numbers about eight hundred people; fifty priests are members.

"Human Sexuality and the Christian Faith," to be considered at the governing assembly in 1993. While the paper is slightly more restrained than the Presbyterian version—describing in sympathetic terms committed relationships, heterosexual and homosexual, within or without marriage—it is second to none in rationalizing away biblical fidelity.

The paper argues that "Christians view all structures, including those that order our sexual life, as historically conditioned and subject to change. . . . We must be open to the possibility that faithfulness to Christ's mission in our day may cause us to question some moral rules and practices we have inherited. We are part of *a living, dynamic tradition*."[10]

So much for orthodoxy. And all this from those who bear the name of Martin Luther, who called homosexuality "an idolatrous distortion instilled by the devil."[11]

Once a movement like this begins, it gains a certain momentum and life of its own, and similar discussions are now going on among Methodists, Episcopalians, and some Baptists. In fact, in June 1992, the governing board of the American Baptist Churches voted down a resolution which called for an affirmation of the Bible "as the only sure rule of faith and practice" and which rejected homosexual practices as unscriptural.[12]

It has also reached evangelical circles. Seattle Pacific University was rocked when it was discovered that in a course on human sexuality, two homosexual lovers had been invited to explain their relationship to the class, and one textbook used in the course endorsed homosexuality. The university defended the course; the early retirement of the president was, the school said, unconnected to protests over the incident.[13]

But in some denominations it is no longer even accommodation. The battle is over and the church has gone to the other side. Consider the United Church of Christ, which recently ordained a self-professed lesbian graduate of Harvard Divinity School who was also a witch. "I found that some of the same sense of empowerment that I got from the coven, I would get from the church," she enthused.[14]

And at a recent UCC conference the "creation spirituality" theologian, Matthew Fox, led four hundred worshipers in a Native American tribal dance, singing, "I walk with beauty before me, behind me, above me, all around me." Seminars on inner-healing through meditation followed, during which Scott Peck, whose books until recently were all the rage among evangelicals, told the gathering: "We have the technology to welcome God into our organizations." How gracious of us![15]

Nor is there much encouragement from the emerging generation. Our schools have little distinctive Christian perspective; some even fund anti-Christian activities. More and more seminaries, even evangelical ones, have succumbed to modernity and abandoned the high view of the inerrant Scriptures.

What is so ironic about the church's mad quest for relevance is that though believers seem to be oblivious to our compromise, those we seek to impress are not. Consider the following—a minor example, but perhaps not an unfair metaphor for the church at large.

It was the 1991 commencement of Fairfield University, a coed, Jesuit institution located in a New York bedroom community at the southern tip of Connecticut. And the commencement speaker and recipient of Fairfield's highest honor, the Honorary Doctor of Humane Letters, was none other than songwriter William M. (Billy) Joel.

Honoree Joel gazed out over the excited throng of students, alumni, and faculty, many of them priests. Then, to the accompaniment of clattering camera shutters and popping flashbulbs, he asked the question the school should have asked before he was invited: "What makes me qualified to do this? What relevance do I have to the future lives of these young people?"[16]

The obvious answer? He was a celebrity and his presence brought media attention to Fairfield, which has since its founding in 1951 lived in the shadow of its more illustrious sister institutions, Holy Cross and Georgetown. But beyond that, what qualified this high school dropout to receive an honorary doctorate and impart wisdom to the exultant seniors was his music. Like his 1973 hit "Only the Good Die Young," an ode to a young man's attempts to seduce a Catholic girl in which he disparages the young girl's virginity, cross, and church.

It wasn't as if the compliant commencement crowd had forgotten the song; just a week earlier there had been publicity in the school paper when someone protested the appropriateness of a Catholic school honoring a person who had ridiculed the ancient verities of the church. *No matter,* the school administration must have reasoned. *There are always cranks around to write such letters. And after all, Billy Joel is such a big name.*

After the commencement, one woman in the crowd was heard to say, "He's a class act, such a class act." When a reporter asked whether she thought it was odd that Joel hadn't explained why he wrote "Only the Good Die Young," the woman replied, "Oh, he's too classy for that."[17]

Apparently Fairfield's Christianity is a veneer. But it's an example that should convict many an individual believer and many a church. We are fearful of appearing out of touch with the times, but if the church (which includes its schools) does not defend unchanging truth and fixed moral standards, who will?

To stand for right and wrong, to defend truth in today's culture is admittedly a trying task. Daily, in a hundred different ways, by little things we scarcely notice, we are subtly enticed to accommodate the culture.

Of course our fellowship must be loving and attract those who hunger and thirst. But we must never forget that the early church did not explode because it was a comfortable haven for those weary of life's pressures or because it accommodated the culture's values. The early church turned the world upside down because the believers confessed that Jesus, not Caesar, was Lord. They didn't embrace the culture; they scandalized it.

And, lest we forget, the early Christians were seen not as enlightened and progressive folks. One charge hurled against the church was cannibalism: Opponents said that Christians gathered to eat and drink the flesh and blood of their Savior.[18] Their contemporaries were shocked, but the believers made such a dramatic and bold witness that no one could ignore them.

The church will again be the church—for the world, against the world—not when it's applauded for being politically correct or sexually liberated, but when it is slandered for "cannibalism"—for consuming a truth so bold and vibrant that it makes the world's poor wiles pale by comparison.

Today the church is in Babylonian captivity, like the ancient Jews in Old Testament times or the church in Martin Luther's day. Not that it is in the clutches of a pagan emperor or a corrupted ecclesiastical hierarchy, but rather in its easy acquiescence to the values of a thoroughly secularized culture.

We mock authentic faith and trivialize the sacred. We are captives of our own doing, dying a slow death, at peace with our enemies, feeding on ourselves.

But there is hope. Always hope. The church can break free of its cultural captivity. It did once before, and we are still seeing the repercussions in our world today—though it happened nearly five hundred years ago.

# 18

## The Terror of the Holy

*H*E WAS LIKE A MAN CLIMBING IN THE *darkness. Higher and higher he made his way up the narrow, spiraling staircase of an ancient cathedral. If he paused, he heard the sound of his own heart pounding, the creaks and groans of the antique structure. He wiped the sweat from his face, resolve renewed in his quest toward the heavens.*

*He climbed faster. What had been dread now turned to certainty: he would reach the apex, climb out the steeple window and see the stars, feel the fresh breeze on his neck. Faster. Around and around the narrowing spirals he went until suddenly, dizzy in the blackness, he reached out to steady himself. And was startled to hear the clanging of a bell.*[1]

Martin Luther did not set out to reform the world—or even the church for that matter. In the beginning he was simply a near-mad, maddening monk searching for sanity. Throwing inkwells in his cloister cell, he wept and ground his teeth in frustration and fear because he sensed too little of God's presence, too much of the Devil's.

The medieval world lent itself to such terrors. People lived short, brutal lives. Which was worse, they wondered, the plagues and pestilence of this life, or the hell and purgatory of the next? To attempt to ward off the evil spirits, they mingled the gnomes and witches of old German paganism with elements of Christianity.

Churches dotted every town, and religious processions routinely passed through the narrow, muddy streets. Crippled men dying of pneumonia stationed themselves near churches, hoping to be cured by the ringing of the vesper bell. Beggars shouted for coins and consigned passersby to the fires of hell for their lack of charity. The dying saw fiends that tempted them to abandon faith.

Playing upon these tensions between terror and hope, the church reinforced images of hell, despair, and ghastly purgatory so that people might be driven to the sacraments of the church. Artists carved the Great Judgment into their woodcuts. Christ the Judge sat on a rainbow, with a lily emerging from his right ear—symbol of the saved, taken by angels into paradise. From his left ear shot a sword—symbol of the damned, dragged from their tombs by devils and cast into the flames of hell. Young Martin Luther would stare at these pictures, fascinated in fear: Christ the Judge was coming for him.[2]

His father wanted Martin to be a lawyer so he could provide for his parents in their old age. But while he was attending the University of Erfurt, a July thunderstorm altered his path forever.

Returning to school after a visit with his parents, sturdy young Martin was startled by a bolt of lightning. The flash, the heat, the crash of power flung him to the ground, scattering his books like ashes. And that instant he saw in the power of the storm all that his soul feared in the dark hours of the night: God could incinerate him in a moment.

In his terror he cried out for the surest safety he knew. "Saint Anne, help me!" he screamed. "I will become a monk."

Singed, scared, and sobered, Luther was off to the monastery. And there, after a quiet first year of study, spiritual discipline, and austerity, his struggles began in earnest.

The crisis came the day he celebrated his first mass. It was a family celebration as well; his father had ridden into town in a company of twenty horsemen. The cloister bells chimed, the music of the glorious psalm ascended to the heights of the cathedral: "O sing unto the Lord a new song." The young monk, robed for ecclesiastical duty, took his place before the altar.

But as he approached the bread and wine of the holy rite, Luther's senses began to spin. In this ceremony the sacrifice of Calvary would be reenacted, and he, a spurious worm, was to handle the holy host. When he came to the words, "We offer unto Thee, the living, the true, the eternal God," he was suddenly filled with terror.

*Who am I that I should lift my eyes or raise my hands to the divine Majesty?* he thought. *The angels surround Him. At His nod the earth trembles. And shall I, a miserable little pygmy, say 'I want this, I ask for that'? For I am dust and ashes and full of sin, and I am speaking to the living, eternal, and true God.*

His knees buckled at the thought. After all, the God of the Old Testament had smitten those He deemed unworthy. Sinai had rumbled with His fury; no man could look on His face and live. And now he, Martin Luther, dared stand before the altar. Pale and shaking, he remained standing. Barely.

During the winter of 1510–11, Luther journeyed to Rome. There, the basilica of St. Peter's was just being built. From his swaying scaffold, Michelangelo was painting the Sistine Chapel's grand ceiling. An elderly Leonardo da Vinci was still designing and inventing. And Vasco de Balboa was preparing for the voyage that would lead him to discover the Pacific Ocean.

Yet it was not the Renaissance splendor of Rome nor her past pagan glories that interested Luther; it was her Christian history. The city of the martyrs. The holy city of the church. He visited the catacombs, venerated the bones of the saints, prayed and fasted and performed the daily devotions of his order. But he was shocked by the Italian clergy. They rattled through prayers and masses as quickly as possible. They mocked the bread and wine of the holy sacrament. And they mocked the young monk for caring. They mocked him for his fear of the Lord.

Luther returned to Erfurt downcast over what he had seen, but he was soon busy enough to put it behind him. That same year, 1511, he was transferred to the village of Wittenberg, invited by Frederick the Wise, prince and elector of Saxony, who had high hopes for his university there.

Luther lived in the Augustinian cloister at one end of the town; less than a mile away, at the other end, stood the Castle Church. At the cloister, once again, he wrestled with his old fears: How did a man know he was saved from the yawning pit of hell? How did he meet the demands of an utterly holy God?

Others struggled with such fears as well, but they found a miserable degree of solace by purchasing pieces of grace called indulgences. The church sold its people these dubious favors, based on a kind of spiritual banking system.

Their premise was that the goodness of the saints of old, as well as Christ and the blessed Virgin, created an inexhaustible store of goodness—sort of an immense bank account from which the spiritually needy of this world could draw. If your personal account of goodness was low, depleted by sin's withdrawals, then you could draw from the account of the saints. All you had to do was view a holy relic belonging to one of them, pay the prescribed price, and you could count on a specific deposit in your own account.

In one of Rome's great storehouses, a single crypt held the bones of forty popes and seventy-six thousand martyrs. Among thousands of other items, Rome also had a piece of Moses' burning bush, the chains of St. Paul, and one of the coins paid to Judas for betraying Christ. Just viewing the coin ensured fourteen hundred years off one's sentence in purgatory.

In Wittenberg, Frederick the Wise had amassed his own storehouse of relics, with more than five thousand items listed in a 1509 catalog. Among these were a tooth of St. Jerome, four pieces of St. Augustine and six of St. Bernard, four hairs from the Virgin Mary, a piece of Christ's swaddling clothes, one piece of the Wise Men's gold, one strand of Jesus' beard, one of the nails driven into His hands, one piece of bread from the Last Supper, and, not to be outdone by Rome, one twig from Moses' burning bush.

By viewing these relics on the designated day—the Eve of All Saints, October 31—and making the proper contribution, people could receive indulgences to reduce time in purgatory by up to 1,902,202 years—either for themselves or for others.

For his part, Martin Luther fastened his dim hopes on penance, seeking absolution from confessors who wearily heard his painstaking reviews of his soul and conduct. One such session lasted six hours as Luther, fearful of missing some blot of sin that would cast him into perdition, worked his way through the Ten Commandments and the seven deadly sins several times over.

In order for sins to be forgiven, Luther reasoned, they must be confessed. And to be confessed, they must be remembered. If not remembered, not confessed, then they were not forgiven. Frantic that he had not recognized or remembered every transgression, he would lie awake at night, hearing fiends in the dark coming to bear him to hell. The moaning of the wind stirred terror in his soul. His vitality drained away.

"Your problem is not so much sins as sin," his mentor Staupitz counseled. "It is not single wrongdoings that damn men, but their nature itself. The whole nature of man must be changed."

Luther could no longer look at a crucifix without seeing Christ seated on the rainbow, judgment emanating from Him as men were tossed into hell. To him it seemed that God capriciously titillated men with the hope of heaven, then hardened and damned them, as if He delighted in tormenting the wretches for eternity. *I wish I had never been created*, he thought. *Love God? I hate Him!*[3]

The unsayable had been said, and Luther haunted Staupitz, wondering if he was the only man alive plagued by such doubts and fears. "No," responded the vicar dryly. "But I think they are your meat and drink."[4]

Perceiving that the troubled monk needed to focus on Scripture rather than his own struggles, Staupitz gave Luther the chair of the Bible at the university. As an Augustinian monk, Luther was required to do frequent Bible readings; now, in his focused study, the Scriptures themselves pointed him to two central truths about their Author.

The first spike to pierce Luther's heart was his study of Psalm 22: "My God, my God, why hast Thou forsaken me?"

Christ had cried these very words from the cross, knowing despair, desolation, and the withdrawal of God's presence. Spiked by rough nails, bloody sweat pouring off his brow, He had cried out in desperation.

But Christ was not Luther, the monk thought. Christ was without sin; no ashy worm He. Why, then, had God turned away His face?

Then the answer hit him like a lightning bolt.

By becoming man, Christ had taken upon Himself the sins of the world—an alienation He did not deserve. The Judge upon the rainbow had chosen to be the helpless man dangling from a bloody cross. Christ was forsaken and damned. For him.

Luther saw that his desire to repent was right, but it was sin itself that must take a singular death blow. The old self must perish altogether.

"When lightning strikes a tree or a man," he mused, "it does two things at once—it rends the tree and swiftly slays the man. But it also turns the face of the dead man and the broken branches of the tree itself toward heaven." As Christ had died, so must he; as Christ was raised, so would he be. Because of Christ's righteousness.

If Psalm 22 crystallized in Luther a new understanding of Christ the Savior, Paul's epistle to the Romans cured his confusion about Christ the Judge.

"I greatly longed to understand Paul's Epistle to the Romans," he later wrote, "and nothing stood in the way but that one expression, 'the justice of God,' because I took it to mean that justice whereby God is just and deals justly in punishing the unjust.

"My situation was that, although an impeccable monk, I stood before God as a sinner troubled in conscience, and I had no confidence that my merit would assuage Him. Therefore I did not love a just and angry God, but rather hated and murmured against Him. Yet I clung to the dear Paul and had a great yearning to know what he meant.

"Night and day I pondered until I saw the connection between the justice of God and the statement that 'the just shall live by his faith.' Then I grasped that the justice of God is that righteousness by which through grace and sheer mercy God justifies us through faith. . . . I felt myself to be reborn and to have gone through open doors into paradise. The whole of Scripture took on a new meaning, and whereas before the 'justice of God' had filled me with hate, now it became to me inexpressibly sweet in greater love. This passage of Paul became to me a gate to heaven."[5]

Justification by faith! Luther's heart thumped with the liberty of his discovery. No longer a slave to fear, but freed by faith in Jesus Christ!

"If you have a true faith that Christ is your Savior," he wrote, "then at once you have a gracious God, for faith leads you in and opens up God's heart and will, that you should see pure grace and overwhelming love."[6]

As Luther began to revel in his new freedom in faith, he could not help but look around him and see that many others were bound by the same fears that had fettered him. And he saw that the church fueled those fears. If men and women were in bondage, it was the church that was selling the bonds. The indulgences.

His heart was pained. People were paying for nothing. They were being robbed—most heinously; they were being spiritually plundered to line the coffers of the church. The indulgences of Rome were funding St. Peter's new basilica. And Pope Leo X seemed to relish hunting, gambling, and devotion much more than assuaging the fears of his flock.

A Dominican monk named Johann Tetzel was the most notorious of the pope's indulgence peddlers. Tetzel was not allowed in Wittenberg because the church could not sell indulgences without the consent of the civil authorities, and Frederick the Wise was not interested in having his own collection superseded. But Luther's parishioners could easily cross the border when the Dominican was nearby and return with all kinds of spiritual benefits—for a price.

Whenever Tetzel entered a town, he was met by dignitaries who ushered him down the main street with great fanfare. A cross bearing the papal arms preceded him, then was planted in the marketplace, where people quickly gathered to seek peace for their souls.

"Listen to the voices of your dear dead relatives and friends beseeching you and saying, 'Pity us, pity us. We are in dire torment from which you can redeem us for a pittance,'" Tetzel would shout. "Open your ears. Hear the father saying to his son, the mother to her daughter, 'We bore you, nourished you, and you are so cruel and hard that now you are not willing for so little to set us free. Will you let us lie here in flames? Will you delay our promised glory?' Remember that you are able to release them, for *as soon as the coin in the coffer rings, the soul from purgatory springs.*[7]

Tetzel was not much of a poet, but he was quite a salesman. The people flocked to him, and he fleeced them mercilessly.

Luther, meanwhile, mourned for the sheep and knew he could not remain silent.

On October 31, 1517—Eve of All Saints, the day that Frederick the Wise would again display his holy collection of bones, teeth, hair, and twigs—Martin Luther fired his warning shot. It was in the form of a placard posted on the thick door of the Castle Church in Wittenberg: Ninety-five Theses, or propositions, for debate. Written in the heat of anger, they were designed to expose the business of selling grace.

One, for example, crisply pointed to the underwriting of St. Peter's basilica with German funds from anxious souls: "First of all, we should rear living temples, not local churches, and only last of all St. Peter's, which . . . we Germans cannot attend. . . . Why doesn't the pope build the basilica of St. Peter out of his own money? He is richer than Croesus. He would do better to sell St. Peter's and give the money to the poor folk who are being fleeced by the hawkers of indulgences. If the pope knew the exactions of these vendors, he would rather that St. Peter's should lie in ashes than that it should be built out of the blood and hide of his sheep."

Luther's posting was nothing unusual. Such signs were a routine means of provoking debate or making a point of view known. And he had penned his affirmations in Latin, the language of the clergy and the collegiate. This was not necessarily a matter to put before the people, and Luther took care at this point not to bring them into the debate. In his introduction to his points, he said he spoke "out of love and zeal for truth and the desire to bring it to light."[8]

But Luther did send a copy of the theses to Albrecht of Mainz, his archbishop, humbly writing, "Forgive me that I, the scum of the earth, should dare to approach Your Sublimity. The Lord Jesus is my witness that I am well aware of my insignificance and my unworthiness."*

Such pleasantries dispensed with, he warmed to his subject as he wrote the archbishop about indulgences. "God on high, is this the way the souls entrusted to your care are prepared for death? It is high time you looked into this matter. I can be silent no longer."

Luther could not have known that his challenge would rock the very foundations of the church. He had not even intended his theses for wide distribution. But scholars translated them into German and reproduced them, and soon people everywhere were taking sides in the growing battle between the reluctant reformer and the assembled powers of the church.

Originally, Pope Leo X was not particularly concerned, reportedly telling an aide, "Luther is a drunken German. He will feel differently when he is sober."[9]

Perhaps Luther was drunk—in the Spirit. At any rate, the years between 1517 and 1521 found him defending his growing convictions before church councils, in the face of a papal bull or official pronouncement, threats of excommunication, and more warnings of assassination than he cared to note.

Luther's prince, the earnest and pious Frederick the Wise, was devoted to the church but also to Luther, who spoke with the authority of one who knows truth.

Meanwhile, the monk had another ally in his old mentor, Staupitz, who wrote to him: "The world hates the truth. By such hate Christ was crucified, and what there is in store for you today

---

*Albrecht did not attain his archbishopric by means of his piety or commitment to Christ. Rather, he had paid Rome the equivalent of $250,000 to become archbishop. The bulk of these funds were recouped through the sale of indulgences.

if not the cross I do not know. You have few friends. . . . Leave Wittenberg and come to me that we may live and die together. The prince [Frederick] is in accord. Deserted let us follow the deserted Christ."[10]

In 1520, after appealing in vain to the pope, Luther put his case before the civil authority of his day, Emperor Charles V: "I prostrate myself before your Imperial Majesty. I have published books which have alienated many, but I have done so because driven by others, for I would prefer nothing more than to remain in obscurity. For three years I have sought peace in vain. I have now but one recourse. I appeal to Caesar."[11]

Luther would later assert that no one had so championed the civil state as he. He believed that the civil magistrate was ordained of God to punish evildoers, and that the state had the power to protect citizens from ecclesiastical corruption. The church's claims to theocracy must be repulsed.[12] Hence his appeal to the emperor.

As the months passed, Luther's books were burned in Rome and other cities. Theological students, however, threw the papal bull, or edict, condemning Luther into the river Elbe, calling it a "bulloon" and seeing if it would float. All the while, Luther continued to write books and articles furiously.

Finally, in the spring of 1521, he was requested to appear at an assembly in the town of Worms to answer questions regarding his books and teachings. The emperor and church officials assured him safe conduct, but Luther, well aware of the dangers of the meeting and the possibility that it could end with his execution, set his face toward his own Jerusalem. He would enter Worms "though there were as many devils as tiles" on the roofs of the city.[13]

Late in the afternoon of April 16, Luther and a few companions entered Worms by oxcart. An imperial herald escorted them, and two thousand of the town's citizens turned out to march with the monk to his lodgings. Whether hating or admiring, few were neutral about Luther or his cause.

The following day, Luther was escorted to the assembly where, gaunt and pale in his Augustinian habit, he stood before the resplendent Charles V, heir of a long line of Catholic sovereigns and scion of the house of Hapsburg, lord of Austria, Burgundy, the Low Countries, Spain, and Naples, Holy Roman Emperor.

The examination began when an official of the archbishop of Trier pointed to a pile of Luther's books resting on a wooden table. Among them were his *Address to the German Nobility*, a treatise presenting his strategy for the reform of the church; *The Babylonian Captivity of the Church*, which examined the sacraments of the medieval church; and *On the Freedom of the Christian*, which poured out the heart of Luther's discovery of justification by faith in Christ alone.

"Are these yours?" asked the examiner.

Luther responded in a soft, low voice, "The books are all mine—and I have written more."

"Do you defend them all, or do you care to reject a part?" The examiner seemed to be giving him an out.

Luther paused, his heart pounding, then spoke: "This touches God and His Word. This affects the salvation of souls. Of this Christ said, 'He who denies Me before men, him will I deny before My Father.' To say too little or too much would be dangerous. I beg you, give me some time to think it over."

The assembly began to buzz. Think it over? Surely the man had had several years to think over his positions! Was this the fiery reformer who had so boldly challenged Rome? Where was the firebrand they had expected?

At the moment, the firebrand was shaking and sweating, experiencing a terror not unlike the holy fear he had experienced at his first mass. How could he, a lowly monk, challenge the assembled powers of his day? More important, his stand would affect, as he put it, "the salvation of souls." Whatever he said, there was no going back. He had to be sure. Was he?

Luther's request was granted, and the assembly reconvened the next afternoon. This time a larger hall had to be used, with a packed, standing crowd filling every space. Only the emperor was seated.

The examiner repeated the question of the day before. This time Luther was ready.

"They are all mine," he asserted. "But as to the second question, they are not all of one sort." This tactic gave him the opportunity to make a speech, rather than simply affirm or deny.

He went on to describe some of his books, telling how they dealt "with faith and life so simply and evangelically that my very enemies are compelled to regard them as worthy of Christian reading." A second class, continued Luther, denounced "the desolation of the Christian world by the evil lives and teaching of the papists. Who can deny this when the universal complaints testify that by the laws of the popes the consciences of men are racked?"

At this point, the emperor broke in, shouting, "No!"

Luther continued, describing a third class of his works that "contains attacks on private individuals. I confess I have been more caustic than comports with my profession, but I am being judged, not only my life, but for the teaching of Christ, and I cannot denounce these works either. . . . If I am shown my error, I would be the first to throw my books into the fire. I have been reminded of the dissensions which my teaching engenders. I can answer only in the words of the Lord, 'I came not to bring peace but a sword.' . . . God it is who confounds the wise. *I must walk in the fear of the Lord.* . . . I have spoken."[14]

"Martin, your plea to be heard from Scripture is the one always made by heretics," responded his examiner with passion. "How can you assume that you are the only one to understand the sense of Scripture? Would you put your judgment above that of so many famous men and claim that you know more than them all?

"You have no right to call into question the most holy orthodox faith, instituted by Christ, the perfect lawgiver, proclaimed throughout the world by the apostles, sealed by the red blood of the martyrs, confirmed by the sacred councils, defined by the church in which all our fathers believed until death and gave to us as an inheritance, and which now we are forbidden by the pope and the emperor to discuss lest there be no end of debate.

"I ask you, Martin—answer candidly and without horns—do you or do you not repudiate your books and the errors which they contain?"

Luther was sweating again, his legs trembling, as he spoke with the resignation of a man who has counted the cost and is ready to pay.

"Since then your majesty and your lordships desire a simple reply, I will answer without horns and without teeth. Unless I am convinced by Scripture and plain reason—I do not accept the authority of popes and councils, for they have contradicted each other—my conscience is captive to the Word of God. I cannot and I will not recant anything, for to go against conscience is neither right nor safe. God help me. Here I stand. I cannot do otherwise. Amen."

He had spoken in German. Now the examiner asked him to repeat his statement in Latin.

A friend called out, "If you can't do it, Doctor, you have done enough."

Then Martin Luther repeated his statement in the language of the church, threw his arms up into the air, and left the crowded hall . . . hisses and boos echoing behind him.

# *19*

## *Justice Unleashed: A World Transformed*

> The task of the people of God is, as far as possible in a sinful society, to reclaim the cosmos for God's created purpose.
>
> *Carl F. H. Henry*

*T*he day after Martin Luther strode out of the assembly hall at Worms, his valiant stand seemed likely only to make him a sitting duck for the powerful men who opposed him. Even Luther himself could never have dreamed of the consequences that would flow from his courageous—if perspiring—confession.

After pondering the monk's position, Emperor Charles V proclaimed his own: "I am descended from a long line of Christian emperors. . . . I have resolved to follow in their steps. A single friar who goes counter to all Christianity for a thousand years must be wrong. Therefore I am resolved to stake my lands, my friends, my body, my blood, my life, and my soul . . . I will proceed against [Luther] as a notorious heretic."[1]

And proceed he did, forbidding his subjects to offer Luther food, drink, or shelter and ordering anyone who came upon the beleaguered monk to arrest him.

But the emperor was distracted by convulsions elsewhere in his empire: revolts in Spain and threats from the Turkish ruler to the east, Suleiman the Magnificent. Meanwhile, the French king, Francis I, claimed a number of territories that Charles claimed as his own, and Pope Leo X often cast his lot with the French king over Charles. Thus, busy monitoring rebels, fighting infidels, squabbling with the pope, and trying to keep his own balance on the slippery slope of sixteenth-century politics, the emperor let Martin Luther slip away.

Immediately after the Diet of Worms, Luther was "abducted" by friendly forces and hidden in the castle at Wartburg, where he lived, disguised as a knight, until early in 1522.

Cut off from the heat of battle and shut up in the chilly, silent castle, Luther's natural disposition began to manifest itself again, as it had in the cloister. As he wrote furiously, producing nearly a dozen books and translating the New Testament from Greek into German, he also suffered from constipation, insomnia, and depression—woes even lesser writers know quite well!

Modern distortions—and reductions—of Martin Luther abound. Many lay Catholics know him only as the mad monk who broke up the Catholic Church and was somehow responsible for Protestantism. Many Protestants know him only as the dissident who nailed up the Ninety-five Theses, whatever those were, and composed "A Mighty Fortress Is Our God."

Secular observers see Luther as simply an odd textbook figure sandwiched somewhere in the midst of the Middle Ages and the Renaissance. Or they celebrate his autonomy as the new man, standing "counter to Christianity as it had been practiced for a thousand years," the modern man emerging from the stultifying domination of the superstitions of the Middle Ages.

But Martin Luther was more than a mad monk, a composer of theses, or an enlightened liberator. And this is why we tell his story. For Luther, one of the most significant figures in Christian history, profoundly shaped the character of Western civilization, and many of the structures of our modern world bear his stamp.

What compelled this man to take his stand and loom so large in modern history?

First, it was the flaming truth he saw: Christianity is no mere creed or confession; it is ultimate reality in Jesus Christ. The Scriptures are God's authoritative Word—the revelation of truth. Convinced of this, Luther had no choice but to stand for truth, even if it meant taking on the power structures of his day.

Second, it was the very nature of his radical discovery within the Scriptures. For as he sat in the flickering candlelight, poring over the Scriptures, Luther discovered that the central theme of all Scripture was the justice of God.

When Isaiah admonished the Jews to "do justice" and Amos thundered, "let justice roll down like living waters," the Hebrew word they used, *tsedeq,* literally meant "righteousness." It was God's declaration that men and women and social structures must be in conformity with the standards of a just and holy God.

The New Testament sets forth the same standard, but it is embodied in Jesus Christ, who pays for our sins, bearing God's just judgment in His own body. Thus the apostle Paul could write, "We are justified, *declared righteous* by our faith in Christ alone."*

The biblical theme is consistent from Genesis to Revelation: The justice anticipated in the Old Testament, called forth by the Law and the Prophets, is fulfilled in the New through Christ the Mediator. No dichotomy then between justice and faith.

So in that great moment when "the gates of heaven" swung open for him, Luther saw the whole biblical vision: God demands justice—that is, *righteousness*—in all of the created order, and He declares men and women *righteous* by their faith. The Christian, then, must see all the world through God's eyes: righteousness for the world, for the structures of society, and for people. This leads to the biblical world-view which affects all of life.

Our own age needs that same holistic view. In recent decades many Christian endeavors have divided into two camps: social activists in one and soul-winners in the other. Those seeking to right injustices and meet human needs have been accused of abandoning the classic Christian call to evangelize the lost. Meanwhile the social activists deride soul-winners for being concerned only with altar calls and notches in their Bible belts.

And failing to see the true definition of justice, many Christians slice the Scriptures in two, evoking images of an angry Old Testament God bringing vengeance upon those who disobeyed His laws (exacerbated by the King James translation of justice as "judgment"), or the New Testament caricature of a God who has discarded His law in favor of showering grace on everyone.†

---

*The connection is clear in the Septuagint, the Greek translation of the Old Testament, where the Greek word for justification, *dikaiosunē,* is the term used to translate the various cognates of *tsedeq,* the Hebrew term for justice.

†People further the confusion by defining justice in secular terms—everyone getting his or her due—then politicizing that interpretation depending on their partisan leanings. Conservatives often suppose that justice means punishing wrongdoers, while liberals assert that it means everyone getting a fair share of society's benefits. Both are embraced within, but fall far short of, the full biblical meaning.

How desperately the modern church needs to recapture the full biblical vision of justice! And we need also to take hold of Luther's third great contribution to the church: the unity of biblical truth and its relevance to all of life—an integrated Christian world-view.

In his monastery cell, Luther was reborn. The justice he had so feared as a tumbrel to God's gallows became the chariot to God's throne of grace. Galloping in that chariot with the winds of grace and freedom rushing through his head, Martin Luther cast his eyes over the landscape of his day and saw that it was all the Lord's. From the farmer tilling the soil, to the prince hearing the pleas of his people, to the merchant selling his wares, to the child singing a small song . . . all of it was to reflect the righteous justice of the Lord of heaven and earth. All of it was to reflect right relations between people and their Lord, and right relations between people and their neighbors. All of it was to proclaim the glory of God.

Luther's vision for biblical justice shaped not only his own perspectives and actions, but launched a movement that swept across Europe, its currents surging with new leaders. John Calvin . . . Ulrich Zwingli . . . Philip Melanchthon . . . John Knox . . . soon the entire continent was in the midst of a mighty—and far-reaching—Reformation.

Seized by this biblically informed view of life and the realization that Scripture made truth plainly known to men and women, these Reformers were moved by a holy passion. Filled with the fear of God—the deepest reverence of the Lord Almighty—their cry became *Coram Deo*, "in the presence of God."

And nothing could stop them.

As Luther sought to reclaim the faith from the cultural corruption his church had unconsciously begun to embrace over the centuries, his work was less a radical new beginning than it was a re-formation in the truest sense of the term—a return to the essence of what the church had been in its noble past.

But the Reformation was more than a cleansing of ecclesiastical structures. Nothing was left untouched: the arts, commerce, government, and education all came under its powerful influence. In chapter 13 we discussed the foundation absolute truth provided for the whole of Western history, but it was during the Reformation that the consequences of that belief had their most profound influence.

Consider just a few examples of that influence as we now see it from the perspective of nearly five centuries.

## Politics and Government

State and church had been wed in an unholy alliance since Constantine, each using the other for its own purposes. With the gospel held hostage, the church could bring little reforming influence on culture. But the Reformers, seeing God as sovereign and the church as the people of God, wrenched free from the emperor's clutches and enabled the church to make a profound difference in societal values and structures.

For one thing, the Reformers changed the view of man in relation to the state. Luther's belief in the priesthood of all believers—that men and women had direct access to God and need not go through any earthly mediator—provided the philosophical foundation for political change. All men and women, whether sovereign or peasant, were equal in God's sight. All were created in the image of God and imbued with intrinsic dignity. And all were fallen and in need of divine grace.

And since the rights of the individual came from God, the state's power could no longer be regarded as absolute, nor could a ruler's "divine" authority be a charter for arbitrary rule.

One who expounded such radical ideas with particular cogency was the Scottish minister Samuel Rutherford, a great scholar and disciple of John Knox's ministry.

Rutherford wrote the classic work, *Lex Rex* ("The Law Is King") in 1644, arguing that the truth of Christ could never be subordinate to Caesar. Only Christ's authority is absolute and arbitrary. God is the true seat of government; rulers are merely trustees and stewards of God-given authority. The sovereign must administer law—not break, abrogate, or dispense with it. Public magistrates are public servants. Even the king, highest authority in the land, is a servant.

*Lex Rex* laid the philosophical foundation for a constitutional republic—the form that best balances man's intrinsic dignity with his inherent sinful nature that demands restraint. These principles were soon transported across the Atlantic.

John Witherspoon, president of what would become Princeton University and the only clergyman to sign the Declaration of Independence, advanced Rutherford's ideas in America's great constitutional debates.

Thomas Jefferson also drew on Rutherford—indirectly—when he borrowed from John Locke. Locke, one of the Enlightenment's great thinkers, had himself been influenced by *Lex Rex*, secularizing

Rutherford's concepts into his view of a social contract: inalienable rights, separation of powers, consent of the governed, and the right of revolution. Though not a Christian (he composed his own Bible, excising with scissors all references to miracles), Jefferson nonetheless brought Christian-based ideas to the New World debate.

So two streams—one from the Scottish reformers, the other from Enlightenment thinkers—drew from the common reservoir of the Reformation and converged in America with the first truly constitutional republic.

Meanwhile, the forces unleashed in the Reformation were producing massive political and social reforms in England. The Reformation's biblical world-view and vision of justice drove John Wesley, William Wilberforce, Lord Shaftesbury, Elizabeth Fry, and thousands of others in their crusade for the abolition of the slave trade, the reform of values, and the prevention of exploitation of children and workers in the mines and prisons.

And the influence of those democratic ideals—unleashed by the Reformation—are still being felt, not just in Europe and America but around the world, in the closing years of this century.

## Vocation

While the priesthood of all believers influenced the political sphere, Luther's view of God's sovereignty altered established concepts of work and vocation. For one thing, it rent the veil between the sacred and the secular. In God's sight, Luther wrote, the work of monks or priests was "in no way whatever superior to the works of a farmer laboring in the field, or of a woman looking after her home."[2] All work was noble and worthy if it was done to the glory of God.*

His reasoning here was that God's creation was good, and human beings were to be stewards of it; so work took on a holy character. In the Reformation era, vocation was considered one of the first steps of discipleship.

People were to discern their skills and use them fully, to seek excellence and shun idleness. The belief that people should pursue their individual callings broke down the rigid caste system, not only

---

*In this, radical though it sounded at the time, Luther was simply restoring the teaching of the early church fathers that work had dignity and was a Christian virtue and duty, an act of service to God as master.

in the church but in society as a whole, paving the way for new economic and social freedoms.

By the seventeenth century, those whose religious convictions made them unwelcome in the Old World fled to the New and brought with them this high view of work, later known as the Protestant work ethic. The virtues of industry, frugality, respect for property, and duty to community were firmly planted in the soil of the new colonies and produced the most vibrant and productive economy in human history. In time, that distinctively Christian ethic was secularized; until recent years its virtues remained ingrained in the American character.

## Economics

The church had long embraced Thomas Aquinas's teaching that most work carried on for profit was immoral. But the Reformers' insistence that all work could and should be done to the glory of God legitimized successful commerce and profit. Thus, in a very real sense, the Reformation made possible the emergence of what we know today as democratic capitalism.

This recognition of legitimate commerce could not have been more timely. The plagues of the Middle Ages had decimated much of Europe's population, but by the 1500s there was a population surge—an 80 percent growth in Germany, for example, in one century. Increased forms of mobility aided commercial expansion, and the craft guilds shifted to more capitalistic modes of production. Banking, trade, and commerce prospered. All of which set the stage for the great Industrial Revolution with all that meant to the development of Western society.*

But along with this high view of work and commerce, the Reformers demanded stewardship and social responsibility. "Man does

---

*Sadly, as Francis Schaeffer points out, the church at large did little to actually guide the tide of increased wealth during the Industrial Revolution. While there were individual attempts to do so, for the most part the church ignored biblical principles regarding the use of wealth. This lack of Christian compassion was partially responsible for the abuses of the day: the slums in industrial towns, the exploitation of children and women in particular, the vast gulf between the wealth of the few and the misery of the many, and the growth of the slave trade. Reform-minded Christians eventually woke up and addressed these abuses (Francis Schaeffer, *How Shall We Then Live? The Rise and Decline of Western Thought and Culture* [Old Tappan, N.J.: Revell, 1976]).

not live for himself alone . . . he lives also for all men on earth," wrote Luther, while John Calvin encouraged workers to produce more than they needed so they could give to those less fortunate.

It has taken five hundred years, but the fruits of the Reformation are once again being witnessed around the globe. Apart from a few intellectual strongholds and holdout tyrannical governments, where is socialism not in retreat today? The Marxist vision has been thoroughly discredited; the welfare state is an acknowledged failure.

In one of the wonderful turns that history often takes, the head of the church against which Luther and others rebelled is today one of the most articulate defenders of democratic capitalism—more articulate, ironically, than the present-day spokespersons for mainline Protestantism. In a 1991 encyclical, Pope John Paul II powerfully defended the free market and private profit.[3]

## Education

Protestantism has often been described as "the religion of the word," with an emphasis on oral instruction. Protestants used both press and pulpit to propagate their message, and wherever Lutheranism and Calvinism spread, new schools were founded.

The study of history was particularly important to the Reformers, who took seriously the obligation to examine original sources. This also affected their attitude toward ancient languages. The Renaissance had already focused on classical literature and languages; the Reformers broadened the intellectual horizon of the day, calling attention to the ancient world, arguing that the chronology of history was the evidence of God's sovereign working.

These convictions directly affected the spread of education. At the popular level, Luther wanted to end illiteracy so people could be instructed in the Scriptures, so he advocated mandatory education for all children. And Luther's colleagues from the University of Wittenberg, including Philip Melanchthon and student Joachim Camerarius, championed classical learning in various German universities.

William Tyndale, among the first generation of English reformers, skilled in seven languages, translated and published a vernacular Bible in Britain. In Scotland, John Knox, influenced by both German and Swiss Reformation teaching, drew up the *First Book of Discipline,* which essentially provided the basis for a national system of education in Scotland.

The Reformation restored the university to the cultural leadership it had known in the thirteenth century and stimulated popular education throughout the West.

## Science

In 1530 the publication of scientific books outnumbered that of religious books. This was no passing phenomenon, but a mirror of the sixteenth century's fascination with nature. The spiritual awakening created a hunger to understand the wonders of the universe, the work of the Creator.

During this period, as we noted in chapter 12, science claimed no conflict with religion, contrary to what is popularly thought today. Instead, the notion of an orderly universe provided a context for the development of the scientific method, and progress was made in a number of fields.

The Reformation was a golden age for the increase of knowledge. Astronomy's burgeoning views of the universe challenged conventional medieval myths. The fields of botany, zoology, and geology flourished; musicians were learning the mathematics of harmony; anatomy, metallurgy, plants, inertia, polar magnetism, optics, and acoustics were being studied; pendulum clocks, refractor telescopes, and air pumps were invented.

## Art

Bursting forth in the midst of the glorious Renaissance, which had inspired grand religious iconography in European cathedrals, the Reformers saw art of all types as a means to give glory to God and to reflect the goodness and beauty of His creation, and this view had widespread influence.*

Among the best known of the artists influenced by the Reformation is the Dutch painter Rembrandt van Rijn. His famous

---

*Some zealous Reformers were known to destroy invaluable works which they saw as graven images, so the Reformation gained a reputation among some as being anti-art. What is not known—or at least not stated—is that the destruction was often carried out by those who had donated the art to the churches in the first place, and the smashing, say of an image of a saint, was not done to denigrate its beauty or the saint per se, but was a statement by the donor that donations to the church could not buy salvation—and that no other gods came before the holy Lord.

*Raising of the Cross* includes a self-portrait, in which he painted himself wearing a painter's beret and a cruel look on his face, helping to erect the cross. *My sin,* proclaimed the great artist, *sent my Lord to the cross.**

Luther, himself a hearty singer with an excellent voice, considered music the noblest of the arts. "Next to the word of God, music deserves the highest praise," he wrote.[4] His love for music reflected his holistic view of life: All art reflected theology.

As with other aspects of the Reformation, Luther's focus on music was truly reforming, bringing the church back to the practice of the early centuries. (Ambrose, fourth-century bishop of Milan, for example, had written hymns and then taught them to his congregation.) And in providing music and hymns to be sung by the common people, not just the priests, Luther reinstated a tradition that went back as far as the early apostles singing in their house churches in Jerusalem.

The German Reformation in particular stressed music and singing, giving rise to the chorale, which led to the cantata and oratorio of the baroque period.

The baroque era mirrored the exuberance of a "golden age" in European history, and many of its artists, composers, and writers were products of the Reformation heritage. In architecture, it appealed to impressiveness and grandeur. In literature, it came to expression through Shakespeare. In music, it was dominated by German Protestants.[†]

Johann Sebastian Bach was the zenith of the composers emerging from the Reformation. Inscribing his scores with the letters

---

*Schaeffer points out that Rembrandt's work shows the tensions and balances of the Reformation spirit: He neither idealized nature nor demeaned it. As he portrayed both man's potential for greatness and his proclivity to evil, Rembrandt's world-view encompassed both man's sin and God's grace.

†For Luther, Christians, of all people, should be in tune with God's creation, using their hearts and minds and bodies for the fullest for His glory. Part of this entailed "recovery of the external world" which had been obscured as a result of the Fall. E. W. Gritsch, author of *Martin—God's Court Jester: Luther in Perspective* (Philadelphia: Fortress, 1983) argues that "Luther's sense of wonder at God's creation is sorely needed among Christians who are often blinded by the forces of anxiety, guilt, and self-righteousness. Luther helped later generations embrace a holistic view of life contrary to the bifurcated view of theological and philosophical anthropologies dominated by dualistic separations of mind/body and flesh/spirit."

*S.D.G.—Soli Deo Gloria,* "To the Glory of God alone"—Bach wove the words and chords of music in a conscious effort to please and exalt the God from whom his gifts had come.

## Ecclesiastical

While the Reformation went far beyond Luther's original focus, we cannot ignore the theological reform it sent throughout the body of Christ. For here again history has made one of its great sweeping circles.

To see this, we must stand back from our partisan passions and view the past five hundred years with some detached perspective. When we do, the picture is remarkable.

The Reformers, for example, assailed the corrupt practices of indulgences; today they are gone (save for the modern-day equivalent practiced by some unscrupulous television hucksters, ironically mostly Protestants, who promise healing and blessing for contributions).

And consider the view of the church. Calvin insisted it was not an institution that stood between man and God as it had become in the Middle Ages, but that it was the very people of God. Today's Catholic doctrine describes the church as the people of God, saying, the lay faithful should be conscious "not only of belonging to a church but of *being the church.*"[5]

Or take the central issue for the Reformers: *Sola Fides* ("by faith alone"). The widest and deepest chasm was opened between Protestants and Catholics over this issue.

In recent decades, however, Catholic and Protestant doctrine has dramatically converged. In the fall of 1991, Pope John Paul II and Lutheran bishops from Scandinavia joined in an ecumenical celebration—not ignoring differences, but emphasizing growing unity on matters of orthodoxy, including justification. In his message, the Swedish primate said: "Dialogue has proven the existence of a basic unity for instance in the question of justification by faith," to which the pope agreed that both sides were "very close" to a common understanding.[6]

And Cardinal Ratzinger, whose Vatican task it is to guard church doctrine and who has written powerfully on the orthodox principles of Christianity, elaborates on the issue of justification. Faith in Jesus Christ, writes Ratzinger, is "truly 'personal faith'" which comes from hearing.[7]

One would be hard-pressed to find instances today in which the Catholic Church has been coopted by the state, a condition the Reformers rightly assailed. In fact, the church's heroic refusal to bow to the state in Eastern Europe helped to bring that corrupt and oppressive regime to its ruin.

In the larger sweep of history, any dispassionate observer would have to conclude that although the Reformation fractured church unity, it has brought profound renewal and reform to the church as a whole. The final chapters are yet to be written, but even today there are signs of an emerging movement, crossing traditional lines, bringing together conservative, confessing believers in a new expression of orthodox unity.

## *What If . . . ?*

What if Martin Luther had not been inflamed by holy passion, had not taken his courageous stand? What if he had retreated to the cloister, cowed by the mighty forces arrayed before him? What if he had turned away, feeling helpless or indifferent?

One thing is certain. Our modern world would look distinctly different.

This is a fact of which many of today's sharp-tongued critics of Christianity's influence in public matters seem unaware. In their oblivion, they are sawing off the limb on which they sit. For it was the religious influence of the Reformation that secured the very civil liberties they enjoy and which permit them to attack religion.

Viewed in its full historical perspective, we can now see why Luther's stand was so important.

First, the church of his day was in captivity, just as the Jews had been in Babylonian captivity two thousand years earlier. The movement Luther spawned broke the church free, gave it an evangelical thrust, made it an instrument of justice and compassion in the great awakenings that followed, and restored its theological heart.

Second, the movement influenced all of culture, with its effects still being experienced to this very day. The Reformation provided the most sweeping political, economic, and cultural benefits ever for Western civilization.

What would it take to free today's church from its own Babylonian captivity—the twentieth-century enculturation we described earlier? Some of the very same things that characterized the Reformers.

First of all, it would require *a commitment to the truth*—the One who says He is ultimate reality—and from this a renewed passion for what God has propositionally revealed, His inerrant Word, and the orthodox confession of faith by which the truth has been preserved and passed through the centuries.

It would mean *an awakening to the fact that the church is the people of God and that the church must be the church.* Away with consumer religion, the edifice complex, slick marketing plans, and syrupy sermons. Equip the people of God with spiritual weapons so they may serve the living God in the world.

It would mean *a healthy fear of God.* No trivializing of the sacred, but a sense of living in the day-to-day, hour-to-hour, minute-to-minute presence of the holy, majestic God.

It would require *the realization that God is sovereign over all and that we must, therefore, have a biblically informed view of all of life.*

It would demand a passion for the blazing scarlet ribbon running through the whole of Scripture: *A commitment to be agents of God's justice in society at large and to see His whole world from the perspective of His truth.*

It would require us *to have Luther's courage, to declare our independence from culture and to take our stand.* To let truth infiltrate every area of life, to let God's righteousness roll down on societal structures and the people who live within them.

And what if we did all this? . . . The world would once again be turned upside down.

But the vision of another reformation is blurred. One might even be forgiven for thinking that the church today could not possibly have a fraction of that kind of impact on the world.

Admittedly, when we survey the state of that world, it often seems hopeless. Indeed, it would be hopeless . . . except for the awesome secret Jesus left with us.

# 20

## *The Body*

The holiest moment of the church service is the moment when God's people—strengthened by preaching and sacrament—go out of the church door into the world to be the Church. We don't go to church; we are the church.

*Ernest Southcott*

*I*T WAS AN ASTOUNDING EVENING—the last supper Christ shared with His disciples. The men who had followed Him for three years ran the gamut of emotions. Christ washed their feet, broke their Passover bread, and passed them the common cup. He spoke of His death. He comforted them, confused them, and challenged them.

We who follow Christ today read the biblical account of that remarkable meal and feel some of the same emotions. But we know, as His disciples soon discovered, that "last supper" was not an end, but a beginning. The beginning of a whole new era. For within the extraordinary words Christ spoke to them is one of the most powerful secrets of His plan for us and for the world.

"I tell you the truth," said Jesus to the followers gathered at the Passover table "anyone who has faith in me will do what I have been doing." The disciples must have looked at one another in bewilderment. They had seen the Master cast out demons and raise the dead. How could they possibly do that?

But then their Teacher went even further, adding, "He will do even greater things than these, because I am going to the Father."[1]

*Greater things than these?* How could this ragtag lot of powerless men do more than Jesus? What in the world was He talking about?

Consider the context. Christ was poised at the juncture between the conclusion of His earthly ministry and His death, resurrection, and ascension into heaven. Confined in the human experience—God incarnate in a human body, with the limitations of time and space—He had for thirty-three years done the works and ministry to which God had called Him. Now He was preparing to return to the right hand of the Father.

"I will ask the Father," Jesus promised them that night, "and he will give you another Counselor to be with you forever—the Spirit of truth."[2] God would send in His place the Holy Spirit, who would enable His people to do all Jesus had commanded them to do.

True to Christ's promise, the first disciples were empowered with the Holy Spirit a few weeks later, at Pentecost. And from then on they began to fulfill His commission to them, carrying out His plan for His new earthly body: They proclaimed the Good News; they baptized new believers and gathered them into communities; and under the seal of the Holy Spirit, the church began to grow.

Hundreds, then thousands, then millions of believers became part of that body. Generations of Christians, gifted in a thousand different ways and empowered by the same Holy Spirit, invaded *every* arena of human life, *every* country, *every* field of endeavor, bringing the truth to bear on their surroundings.

In His earthly ministry Jesus was limited to one human body; now the body of Christ is made up of millions and millions of human bodies stamped with His image—His followers. That includes you and me, for Jesus prayed for *us* that last evening, not just for the disciples who were with Him. "My prayer is not for them alone, " He told His Father. "I pray also for those who will believe in me through their message."[3]

What an astounding thought! Jesus ascended. But His Spirit descended to empower His body—the church—to do more than He could accomplish as one Person.

In light of this awesome truth, it is scandalous that so many believers today have such a low view of the church. They see their Christian lives as a solitary exercise—Jesus and me—or they treat the church as a building or a social center. They flit from congregation to congregation—or they don't associate with any church at all. That the church is held in such low esteem reflects not only the depths of our biblical ignorance, but the alarming extent to which we have succumbed to the obsessive individualism of modern culture.

Of course every believer is part of the universal church. But for any Christian who has a choice in the matter, failure to cleave to a particular church is failure to obey Christ.* For it is only through a confessing, local body of believers that we carry out the work of the church in the world.

It is within the church particular that we commit ourselves to intimate relationships with fellow believers and submit ourselves to accountability, duties, and responsibilities. In this community our Christian character is shaped; it is the context in which our spiritual gifts are developed and exercised. It is the family whose ties cannot be broken. It is the training camp that disciples and equips believers to be God's people against the world and for the world.

If we don't grasp *the intrinsically corporate nature of Christianity* embodied in the church, we are missing the very heart of Jesus' plan.

But when we do understand that the church is Christ's body, what next? What does this one body with many parts look like? What does it do? What is its mission in the world? These are questions we will examine in the next section of this book.

One of our favorite pictures of the church comes from Richard Halverson, a friend and mentor. Dick is chaplain of the U.S. Senate, but before his Senate service he was pastor of Washington D.C.'s large Fourth Presbyterian Church. He had been pastoring Fourth Presbyterian for years, when suddenly, Dick says, he saw his church clearly for the very first time.

He was flying into Washington one day at dusk. Since the approach path to Washington's National Airport happened to pass directly over Fourth Presbyterian Church, Dick pressed his face against the window to catch a glimpse of the building from the air. But everything on the ground was shrouded in the shadows falling over the city as the sun set. Dick could not find his church.

He leaned back in his seat, watching the fast-approaching Washington skyline, always an inspiring sight. As his eyes followed the Potomac River, Dick could see the skyscrapers of Rosslyn, just across

---

*While there are exceptions—like prisoners who come to Christ in solitary confinement but are not able to become part of a church particular, even though they are part of the church universal—it is normative for believers to gather together, and some in hostile circumstances do so under great hardship. Former hostage Terry Anderson has written movingly of his fellowship with his Catholic and Protestant brethren—the Church of the Locked Door—during his captivity in Lebanon (see "How They Survived," *Newsweek*, 16 December 1991, 34–37).

Key Bridge from Georgetown. Then, in the distance to the left, the White House, the lights of the Labor Department, the distant glow of the Capitol dome.

As he stared out the window, he began mentally ticking off the names of members of his congregation who worked in those office buildings and government bureaus. Disciples he had equipped to live their faith. And suddenly it hit him.

"Of course!" he exclaimed to the startled passenger in the next seat. "There it is! Fourth Presbyterian Church!"

The church wasn't marked by a sanctuary or a steeple. The church was spread throughout Washington, in the homes and neighborhoods and offices below him, thousands of points of light illuminating the darkness.

And that is the way the church should look in the world today. The people of God—one body with many different parts—spread throughout every arena of life, twenty-four hours a day, seven days a week, doing even "greater things" than Christ Himself!

# *Part 3*

## *The Church in the World*

Every Christian mind is a seed of change so long as it is a living mind, not enervated by custom or ossified by prejudice. A Christian has only *to be* in order to change the world, for in that act of being, there is contained all the mystery of supernatural life. It is the function of the church to sow this Divine seed, to produce not merely good men, but spiritual men—that is to say, super men. In so far as the church fulfills this function it transmits to the world a continuous stream of spiritual energy. If the salt itself loses its savor, then indeed the world sinks back into disorder and death.

*Christopher Dawson*

# 21

## Equipping the Saints

> Every member of the Body has the potential to be—and should be fed and led toward functioning as—a fully equipped agent of Jesus Christ, as His minister.
>
> *Jack Hayford*

*A*SK ABOUT THE LOCAL CHURCH'S ROLE IN THE WORLD, and most Christians immediately begin hauling out mission statements, action plans, and strategy schemes. They are already lacing up their Nikes, asking, "What should we do?"

That eagerness is wonderful, and mission statements are important. But first, like Dick Halverson, we need to see the church from a higher perspective. We need the big-picture view of the Body, alive and vibrant—the *holy* presence in the world. For the church's role in the world is not a series of independent items on an action checklist. Instead, the church's role (what it *does*) is dependent on its character (what it *is*) as a community of believers.

*What we do, therefore, flows from who we are.*

Remember the bold believers in Eastern Europe? They had no Moral Majorities, no carefully designed church-growth strategies. Their strength derived not from what they did, but from who they *were*—the church. Their very presence invoked a power that even the most ruthless government could not repress.

The same was true of the early church. The first Christians worshiped God and lived as a holy community, conforming their character to the demands of Christ rather than Caesar. They didn't purpose to turn the first-century world upside down. They did so because of *who* they were.

This character-oriented perspective is totally foreign to our achievement-oriented society, however, where we look at what people do rather than who they are. And it goes against everything in our consumer-oriented religious culture, where we pick and choose churches on the basis of fellowship or outreach programs or music or location or convenient parking. Rarely do we hear believers say, "I decided to join this church because of its character as a holy community." Nor do most choose a church on the basis of its capacity to disciple and equip them for ministry.

Yet that should be our very first consideration. If the church is the Body, the holy presence of Christ in the world, its most fundamental task is to build communities of holy character. And the first priority of those communities is to disciple men and women to maturity in Christ and then equip them to live their faith in every aspect of life and in every part of the world.

### The First Task: Making Disciples

The most familiar of our mandates is the Great Commission: "All authority has been given to Me in heaven and on earth," Jesus said. "Go therefore and *make disciples* of all the nations, baptizing them in the name of the Father and the Son and the Holy Spirit, teaching them to observe all that I have commanded you."[1]

Note that this is not a charge to individuals. It is a commission to the church. Baptism, which, as we said in chapter 12, is the public witness of faith in Christ and the visible sign of entry into the church, can only be carried out by the church. And only the church can truly teach all that Christ has commanded, equipping believers to grow in maturity and to be the people of God.

And note also that "making disciples" involves more than evangelism. Though the church must be passionate in its duty to introduce people to Jesus Christ (who came into the world to save the lost), that is only the beginning, only a part of God's commission to us. Evangelism must be fully integrated with discipleship in order for the church to truly be obedient to Scripture.

This may sound almost heretical to some. Ask evangelicals what the first priority of the church is, and most will invariably answer, "Evangelism."

I vividly remember hearing a visiting missionary use his entire message one Sunday morning to berate the congregation for failing to win souls. "The *only* purpose of the church is soul winning," he charged, pounding the pulpit and glaring at the worshipers before him. "Each and every one of you are failing if you are not out there winning souls for Christ."

And even as we were in the throes of finishing this book, Ellen took time away from her computer to attend a meeting at Prison Fellowship's headquarters with a group of consultants who had been brought in to advise the ministry on its fund-raising procedures. To do this, they needed to catch a sense of the vision behind PF and its programs.

"What is Chuck particularly excited about these days?" they asked Ellen.

She paused, her head still spinning with the themes we were writing about. "Well," she began, "he is excited about Christians bringing a biblically informed world-view to bear on all arenas of life . . . and about Christians getting out of their pews and living their faith . . . about the call of the church to equip its people for ministry—"

One of the men leaned forward intently. "How does Chuck feel about evangelism?" he asked.

"He loves evangelism!" said Ellen. "But Prison Fellowship's mission isn't just to introduce people to Christ. It is designed to equip the church to make disciples. This is a ministry of discipleship."

The conversation continued as one of the other men at the table asked several questions on another theme. But the first fellow looked troubled. Finally he broke in.

"I don't mean to sound jaded," he said. "My heart is really with you guys and what you do. But we have to look at this from a fund-raising point of view—what raises money. What people want to hear. And what they want are stories of changed lives. Evangelism! Discipleship doesn't sell."

This very capable man, a committed believer, was no cynic. He was simply stating the realities of direct-mail solicitation.

People do want to hear about decisions, about souls coming to Christ. And that is certainly how transformation begins. A person becomes "a new creature in Christ" in the instant of regeneration. The Holy Spirit moves in the hidden places of the soul, bringing spiritually dead men and women to repentance and a new life in Christ.

But conversion is a process. The process of growth in holiness: sanctification.

The nurturing and maturing of character, of putting off the old habits and putting on the new, takes a lifetime. And it takes place in the context of the community of saints, the church, through discipleship.

### Building Up the Body

Similarly, it is also a process for the people called by God to be the Body. Paul described it succinctly in his letter to the church at Ephesus when he sketched the anatomy of a healthy church:

> And He gave some as apostles, and some as prophets, and some as evangelists, and some as pastors and teachers, for the equipping of the saints for the work of service, to the building up of the body of Christ; until we all attain to the unity of the faith, and of the knowledge of the Son of God, to a mature man, to the measure of the stature which belongs to the fulness of Christ. As a result, we are no longer to be children, tossed here and there by waves, and carried about by every wind of doctrine, by the trickery of men, by craftiness in deceitful scheming; but speaking the truth in love, we are to grow up in all aspects into Him, who is the head, even Christ, from whom the whole body, being fitted and held together by that which every joint supplies, according to the proper working of each individual part, causes the growth of the body for the building up of itself in love.[2]

Paul is speaking here of the whole body, the church universal. But since the process described can only take place in an actual community of faith, T. M. Moore, president of Chesapeake Theological Seminary, uses this passage as a model for the progression of healthy development for the church particular—and discipleship is the key to that process.

Moore breaks down the major elements in Paul's description of how God builds up the church:

- *Unity of the faith.* The church must have a oneness of confessional creed: common understandings, vision, goals, and aspirations. And it must have a oneness of experience: shared lives.

- *The knowledge of the Son of God.* The church must have full assurance of salvation, grounded in right doctrine.

- *A mature man.* The church must manifest maturity in critical areas of discipleship: committed to growth achieved through the Word of God, prayer, worship, and fellowship; producing the fruit of the Spirit, demonstrating love, keeping God's commandments, and bearing witness to the Lord.

- *No longer children.* The church must be able to discern false doctrines and to distinguish truth from error. To put it in terms we've already discussed: believers must be equipped with a Christian world-view.[3]

- *Speaking the truth in love.* The church must articulate the truth of Christ to one another and to those outside the Body (unbelievers). But it must confront error with love rather than condescension.

- *Every joint supplies.* The individual members must cultivate their spiritual gifts, using them to the glory of God in ministry to one another and for the community.

- *The growth of the Body.* All of this increases the church both quantitatively and qualitatively.[4]

But note the role Paul assigns to the pastor in the process of building the Body.[5] Contrary to popular impressions today, the pastor is not paid to do our work (service) for us. Pastors and teachers are to equip the saints—that's us—to serve, to build the Body, to be the church in the world. Every layperson is to be equipped as a minister of the gospel.

French social critic Jacques Ellul puts it well: The channel through which the Holy Spirit brings truth to the world is the pastor, who teaches it to the laity, who in turn translate it and put it to work in the marketplace, infiltrating the world. The problem in the modern church, however, Ellul says, is that the channel is blocked. The pastor doesn't engage in the secular world on a day-in, day-out basis, and the laypeople, who do, tend to keep their faith in a compartment separate from the rest of their life.[6]

So Sunday after Sunday congregations sit passively—like spectators watching the entertainment up front—missing the fact that they should be absorbing the truth and applying it to their lives, training to be effective soldiers of the Cross.

I cannot help but see parallels here with my own military experience in Marine officers' basic training. The Marines, if you'll pardon an old leatherneck's pride, do it right, and I've never forgotten those lessons.

During the first grueling weeks we were put through intense physical training on death-defying obstacle courses. We learned to handle and clean a rifle, and to disassemble and reassemble it blindfolded. We memorized the Marine handbook of military rules and regimen (and no one argued about whether the rules were relevant or accepted by a majority of Marines). Our hearts and minds were imprinted forever with the meaning of discipline. (I remember once cracking the slightest smile during inspection: "Fifty push-ups, Colson!")

From there it was on to the rifle range and small-unit tactics. Then field maneuvers. And while all of this was simulated warfare, no one treated it like a game. When I was in training, the Korean War was at its bloodiest; young men just out of school were leading other young men in deadly combat. Many came home in pine boxes. So we were serious not only about surviving combat, but about winning it.

It should be the same for the soldiers of the Cross. Yet rather than being well-trained, well-disciplined, functioning members of the Body, many of us act more like reserve units: weekend warriors whose real jobs occupy them during the week and who just turn out for occasional drills or to hang out in the officers' club on Sundays.

If we take our Handbook seriously, we have to conclude that the church is the basic school of discipline and training for all Christians. And shouldn't our training be at least as serious as the military? After all, we are in warfare. None of us can have any illusions about that. And the battle is not just for flesh and blood; it is for eternal souls.

Every part of the church has to be geared for the training (discipling and then equipping) of the local units that fight this battle. Evangelistic ministries should be directing new believers into the church particular. Discipleship ministries should be working hand-in-hand with local congregations. Specialized ministries—such as service to the disabled, to youth, to executives, to the inner city, to prisoners—should be guiding those they reach into local congregations, even as they are equipping those same local churches with the skills, resources, encouragement, and education they need to do effective ministry in these unique areas.*

In fact, whether these ministries are building up the Body is perhaps the best test of their biblical fidelity. Those that aren't endeavoring to do this, cooperating with the work of local churches, run the risk of ending up promoting their own cause over the good of the Body and thus being out of God's plan. (This has been a real problem among evangelicals. One great strength of the movement is its vitality: independent, dynamic leaders raising up powerful organizations to do important work. But human nature being what it is, this can also be a weakness when those same leaders become protective of their turf or fall into the trap of the personality cult.)

So the church must first build strong disciples and then equip its men and women for battle in the world.

### Training for Battle

Since a biblical world-view involves all of life, the church must equip its members for all of life. Like the military, this begins with the basics and moves on to building the mature character of the seasoned warrior. There are hundreds of diverse and creative ways to train Christians to be the people of God so they, together, can do those "greater things" to which Christ referred—and the service for which they are trained varies from church to church. What is needed in suburban Atlanta, for example, might well be different than tactics employed in inner-city Detroit.

We cannot cover all of the areas of equipping, let alone include even a fraction of the particular churches doing a great job preparing their people for ministry. For our purposes here, we can only touch upon those training areas that should be a part of every church—and a few representative examples.

---

*Para-local church ministries, or what we often call parachurch organizations, are ministries and movements that come alongside the local church to equip members with specialized skills for ministry. Prison Fellowship, for example, exists to "exhort and assist the church in its ministry" to those affected by crime, seeking to equip believers with expertise and resources for ministry to prisoners, ex-prisoners, victims of crime, and their families that local churches would not ordinarily have at their disposal. Dozens of ministries do the same thing in a variety of different arenas of need.

*At the most fundamental level, the church must equip its members to know and defend their faith and to apply it in the world.*

The ministry of the Word—the first mark of the church, discussed in chapter 10, is the beginning. The Christian disciple must be grounded in the Word and historic Christian truth. Without this basic training, we are unable to give a reasonable defense for the hope within us.

Most churches do a good job with Sunday school and Bible studies, but they can also make use of parachurch resources like the Navigators, which produces excellent discipleship material. Or they might take advantage of Walk Thru the Bible, which gives Christians a big-picture perspective on the Old and New Testaments. And I personally have profited greatly from Ligonier Ministries' seminars, tapes, and videos on doctrine.

Those seeking more advanced skills can take advantage of lay seminary training like that offered by the Seminary of the East, located in New York and Philadelphia, or Chesapeake Theological Seminary in the Baltimore-Washington area; the latter, for example, offers three master's level programs for laity, as well as courses in Christian education, Christian heritage, and evangelism. Some larger churches like Elmbrook Church in Waukesha, Wisconsin, provide similar courses, enabling students to receive credit through nearby Trinity College and Trinity Evangelical Divinity School. A number of Catholic dioceses do the same thing, as in Washington, D.C. where Education for Parish Service (EPS) requires two years of academic study combined with practical work in the attendee's parish.

And we can be discipled to apply a biblical perspective to current events. Some friends in Florida initiated a tough-minded "life issues" course in their parish. They met weekly to study timely issues—from just-war theory to the New Age movement to abortion to the question, "Does truth exist?" One hundred people turned out for that last one.

Why leave it to the League of Women Voters or the local university to lead discussions on the concerns of the day? The church should be aggressively training its people to be discerning and to speak out of the convictions of an equipped Christian mind.

*In this same vein, the church should equip its members to lead exemplary lives in the marketplace.*

Who in society should be teaching ethics? Not value-free schools. Not bottom-line businesses. And surely not the media. Ethics training should be a prime task of the church.

Since ethics is basically how one applies one's world-view, the church should be equipping its members to understand the biblical world-view and then training them to live by the range of standards created by that perspective.

In this regard, for example, the church can provide invaluable help to Christian businesspeople and professionals. One ministry designed to do this is the Executive Leadership Foundation, a resource center that teaches Christians how to apply absolute values in tough, realistic scenarios. The goal? That Christians "would have an impact" in their sphere of influence, whatever it is.[*]

***The church must also equip its members to build strong marriages and families.***

The family, the most basic unit of civilized society, is the institution that may well be under the greatest attack in society today. Unless we insist on counseling and training before marriage and then provide a full range of services to build and strengthen the family thereafter, the church cannot say it is making disciples and fulfilling the Great Commission. This is why the ministry of Jim Dobson's Focus on the Family is so critical, and every church can profit from it.[†]

In doing its part to equip its members, the First Baptist Church of Modesto, California, urges "seriously dating couples" to take "relationship instruction." These sessions are aimed at promoting spiritual maturity, building trust, and learning self-control. The couple agree to be held accountable to the instructor and also sign a contract stipulating that they will limit their time together and that they will remain chaste.

---

[*]ELF, established in 1986 by twelve Christian business executives, trains people to think through situations like these: You're a young career person ranking in the top 10 percent of your company's sales. In order to boost sales in a depressed economy, the company has asked you to engage in questionable tactics. What do you do? You are a high school teacher. One of your students is under extreme pressure from home to make good grades and is abused verbally, and possibly physically, when she makes anything lower than a B. She has worked hard, but her average in math turns out to be three points short of a B. What do you do? Other resources include Gordon College in Wenham, Mass., which conducts ethics seminars and offers course material. So does Biola University in La Mirada, Calif., Ligonier Ministries in Orlando, Fla., and the C. S. Lewis Institute in Washington, D.C.

[†]See also Keith Fournier, *Bringing Christ's Presence into Your Home: Your Family as a Domestic Church* (Nashville: Thomas Nelson, 1992), which deals with the themes of the family as domestic church and the church as family.

Sound tough? It is. In the period between 1976 and 1985, four hundred couples signed the contract. More than half of the relationships broke up before marriage. But the 196 who did marry are still married. Compare that with the 50 percent failure rate that is the national average!*

In Rhode Island, the Catholic Church instituted a similar program. Couples must wait six months to a year before marriage, taking intensive marriage instruction conducted by 250 "coordinating couples" trained by the church to provide strong guidance. The churches have noticed a conspicuous decline in divorce among those who have enrolled.†

Every church must provide its people with the training, counseling, biblical instruction, and encouragement they need to build godly marriages as beacons of light in a dark world.

*Similarly, the church needs to equip its members to "train up their children in the way they should go."*

It is every Christian parent's responsibility to raise his or her children in the fear and admonition of the Lord, and it is the responsibility of every church to equip its parents to do that. The

---

*Dr. Jim Talley, coordinating with the originator, Mike McManus, drafted a "Community Marriage Policy" that purposed to strengthen marriages in the entire Modesto area by putting couples through stringent, accountable preparation for their marriage vows. One hundred pastors from all the major denominations signed the covenant. After three years, although its population had increased, Modesto's divorce rate had dropped. Dr. Talley has since moved to Oklahoma City, where he is developing this program on a nationwide basis. He uses the material in his book *Too Close Too Soon* to weed out relationships that are too weak for marriage, and *Friendship Instruction,* designed to help couples maintain healthy relationships; along with a book called *Reconcilable Differences,* which helps separated and divorced couples toward reconciliation.

† At the First Evangelical Free Church of Fullerton, California, Associate Pastor Dave Carder heads a ministry for church members called New Foundations. When the program was first announced, twenty-seven couples admitted they were on the verge of divorce and needed help and were put through a ten-week course designed to help them work through the issues threatening their marriages. To prevent divorce, the church has also organized a program called "An Ounce of Prevention." Members of the church who are divorced go to Sunday school classes and tell their stories to married couples. Most of them say they had no idea their own marriage was falling apart—and then it did. After this honest discussion of the anatomy and pain of divorce, many married couples sign up for counseling or simply for a "marriage tune-up"!

Body itself must also take part in training young people to grow in Christian character.

Part of that training means equipping parents to be discerning in educational issues. Vigilance is the essential watchword for families whose children attend public schools.

When the Fairfax, Virginia, County School Board proposed a study program called "Family Life Education," parents at McLean Presbyterian Church examined the curriculum. What they discovered was a serious undermining of family and moral values in the "value-free" curriculum designed for kindergarten through twelfth grade. So McLean laypeople organized an "information night" at which members could be alerted, and then helped organize parent groups to attend school board meetings. While they did not get the curriculum changed, Christian parents did wring some concessions from the school—and many have taken their children out of offensive classes.

Sometimes the church needs to help children who have been forced to grow old before their time. In designing their program to work with children of divorced parents, the First Evangelical Free Church of Fullerton found a good model in the Catholic Church's "Rainbows for All God's Children." So fifteen people from First Evangelical were trained by a group of nuns in a nearby parish, who seemed to particularly delight in anointing their Protestant brothers and sisters with oil and ashes at the dedication service.

Fifty children were part of the first group at Fullerton, and church volunteers taught them Bible memory verses to help comfort and strengthen them in times of need as well as helping them learn how to express their feelings and work through their emotions.

The program deals with children like Brandy, eight years old, who had locked up her feelings tightly after her parents' divorce.

The first time he met with Brandy and her younger brother, Stephen, Pastor Gary Richmond said, "It's really hard to go through a divorce, isn't it, kids?"

"Man, it's the pits!" responded Stephen right away. "I hated it!"

Brandy looked up, a bored expression on her face. "Oh, I didn't think it was so bad," she said. "You just get more moms and dads. No big deal."

Stephen glared at his sister. "You're lying to a pastor, Brandy!"

"Yes," she said, "but I don't like to talk about it . . . I just take the sad thoughts to my secret place and then I lock them up."

*What a thing for an eight-year-old child to say!* Gary thought.

"Brandy," he asked, "is your secret place getting full?"

"Yes," she said, tears welling into her eyes.

"What happens when you can't fit any more into it?"

"I don't know," she said. She paused for a moment, then said suddenly, "I don't say the F-word any more."

*Now what?* thought Gary. "What word is that?" he asked.

"F-a-m-i-l-y," she said. "I don't say it because it hurts too much."*

At Faithful Central Missionary Baptist Church in South Central Los Angeles, Christian Education Minister LaVerne Tolbert and her volunteers provide Christian education in a real combat zone. The neighborhood is overrun by gangs and drugs, and teen pregnancy is commonplace. There, through role plays, frank Friday night discussions, and Bible study, the church equips kids not only to say no, but to call on the power of the Holy Spirit to enable them to do so.[†]

***The church should equip its members to fulfill their vocation.***

In the Reformation era, helping believers find their vocation was considered a first step of discipleship. Since our work is to bring glory to God, the church needs to teach a high view of work and the Christian character traits of diligence, thrift, creativity, and excellence. If the church doesn't teach a healthy work ethic, who will?[‡]

---

*Whittier Area Baptist Fellowship, a few suburbs away from Fullerton, has a similar support group system called "Confident Kids," designed to equip elementary age children to communicate clearly. "They need to get out of the bondage of the 'don't talk, don't feel' messages of dysfunctional families," says Pastor Lee Eliason. There are one hundred children involved in this program at any given time.

[†] At Fullerton's Evangelical Free Church, kids confront similar temptations and problems in a very different environment. They see their parents' expensive lifestyles and the peer pressure and temptations are all around them. So in equipping these kids to avoid the attitudes of the world, Youth Pastor Eric Heard focuses on the antidote to materialism: service. "We offer a lot of service ministries to show them that there's something bigger in life than making a buck," says Eric. Over the past eight years the youth group has built an orphanage in Mexico and in the process established a strong relationship with the children. They put up a small house for a woman and her two children who were living in a shack beyond description. The kids also visit convalescent homes and minister to the inner-city homeless at the L.A. Mission. "We are committed to helping kids see that they don't have to buy into what the culture is saying," says Eric. "It's tough, but it's definitely worthwhile."

[‡] For a more detailed discussion of the work ethic and its loss in America today, see Chuck Colson and and Jack Eckerd, *Why America Doesn't Work* (Dallas: Word, 1991)

The church is also the natural place to provide vocational counseling. To do this, a number of congregations across the country use "gifts analysis inventories," which not only highlight an individual's spiritual gifts but also focus on his or her vocational strengths and aptitudes.

In Los Angeles, Victory Outreach, which evangelizes and disciples heroin addicts, provides an outstanding example of the church equipping believers with a healthy work ethic. Once clean of drugs, the participants spend nine months in intensive Bible study and training, breaking the old patterns of the streets and establishing basic Christian character and behavior. After that, they enter a nine-month reentry phase, during which they develop their work skills.

Clear Vision is a building maintenance service operated by the graduates. Since smog and pollution are huge problems in downtown Los Angeles, who better to make windows gleam and hallways shine than men and women who have been rescued from the streets and are now living clean for Christ?*

*The church should equip its people to be good stewards of financial resources.*

The Presbyterian Church in America is one denomination that regularly offers seminars at individual churches to help believers manage their resources and determine how to maximize their charitable giving. And Ron Blue of Atlanta is well known in evangelical circles for his expertise in financial planning, investment management services, and estate and tax planning. Blue's books, including the *Personal Financial Planning Guide,* and his six-part videotape series, "Master Your Money," are excellent tools for church groups seeking to be good stewards.

Another resource is Larry Burkett's Christian Financial Concepts. CFC runs seminars for business people on how to manage their companies based on Christian principles, seminars for married couples on how to budget, as well as conferences and financial management training sessions for laity. It also publishes a

---

*In a very different context, Christ Church of Oakbrook, Illinois, offers a ministry of help and facilitation to people who have been laid off or are looking for employment. Oakbrook provides regular training sessions to equip people in skills analysis, résumé writing, job-search marketing plans, and job interview preparation. The program combines basic job-search skills with Christian principles, reinforcing a positive view of how God specifically gifts and equips people for various vocations.

monthly newsletter, *How to Manage Your Money,* dealing with questions about the economy, tithing, business ethics, budgeting, and getting out of debt.

*The church should equip its people to be effective bearers of the Good News.*

To say that evangelism is not the first call of the church is not to diminish it. As we will see in chapter 23, all believers are called to be witnesses, both in word and in deed. Thus, the church needs to train laypeople to identify their own evangelistic gifts and use them effectively in the marketplace.

Willow Creek offers a seminar called "Network," designed to help members of that huge congregation identify spiritual gifts. Those with the gift of evangelism are directed into a training seminar where the first lesson "is called 'Being Yourself.' We want people to understand that they don't have to be Billy Graham in order to be salt and light," says Director of Evangelism Mark Mittelberg. "They can be themselves and reach people that Billy Graham can't."

Another powerful ministry is Evangelism Explosion, which started in the Coral Ridge Presbyterian Church in Fort Lauderdale, Florida, but has spread across the country, training laypeople to share their faith comfortably and effectively.* But, as Dr. James Kennedy, pastor of Coral Ridge, emphasizes, evangelism is not an end in itself. Rather it exists in the context of loving discipleship relationships. So EE includes three levels of discipleship: trainer and trainee, EE participants and other members of the church, and new believers and their spiritual parents. The program consists of sixteen units of class instruction, homework assignments, and on-the-job training.

And finally, *the church must equip its people with specialized training that enables them to reach out to those in particular types of physical and spiritual need.* As believers grow in Christian maturity, the words of Matthew 25 become more and more compelling:

> For I was hungry, and you gave Me something to eat; I was thirsty, and you gave Me drink; I was a stranger, and you invited Me in; naked, and you clothed Me; I was sick, and you visited

---

*As many as seven hundred people have gone out weekly from Coral Ridge to proclaim the Good News to unbelievers, and the church has grown from seventeen people to a congregation of eight thousand members with a missions budget of nearly $30 million annually.

Me; I was in prison and you came to Me. . . . Truly I say to you, to the extent that you did it to one of these brothers of Mine, even the least of them, you did it to Me.[7]

And if we are to reach out to a world of hurting people with complex needs, we need specialized training in a variety of different areas. (Again, keep in mind that a particular church's ministry will vary depending on location, cultural context, and the unique vision and burdens of its members.) Compassion ministries are tough, front-line work, and many churches have developed great programs for training believers to do them well.

At Eastside Foursquare Church in Kirkland, Washington, Pastor Doug Murren and his staff have created "cluster ministries," driven and shaped by laypeople with a particular vision. Small groups of five to fifteen people focus on such needs as a medical mission, a Romanian orphanage, and a nursing home Bible study team. They even have a mechanics cluster that repairs cars for needy families!

Eastside requires these clusters to attend various church training sessions, appoint a recognized leader, raise their own funds, be responsible to the oversight of a church elder, meet as a "home group," agree to have their ministry reviewed every six months, and present a twelve-month plan and strategy to the church leadership team.

Churches and ministries across the country are applying these same principles. Begun in the late 1970s by a Missouri Synod Lutheran pastor, Dr. Kenneth Haugk, the Stephen Ministry is an interdenominational effort that equips Christians with "care-giving" skills for people in crisis situations. Those who seek training must pay a fee for the fifty-hour core course in which they develop counseling and other practical skills. Upon graduation, "Stephen ministers" work in every area of need.

---

*HOPE began when Pastor Bob Russell was thinking about three women in his church who had tried to commit suicide. Two were paralyzed from their attempts; yet all three had found new life in Christ, and where there was once hopelessness, God had opened a door of hope. Impressed by their joy, Bob asked if they would be willing to conduct a seminar for people struggling with depression. They agreed, one hundred people showed up for that meeting, and out of it grew HOPE, an ongoing support group. Many of these people have also been going through specialized training at the church that equips them to reach out to others with various kinds of problems and situations related to depression. For example, members of HOPE go into the Kentucky Correctional Institute for Women on a regular basis, helping inmates there.

At Southeastern Christian Church in Louisville, Kentucky, a group called HOPE—He Offers Peace Everlasting—reaches out to people struggling with depression.*

Another area of need is crime. And in Prison Fellowship's work with churches across the country, we've clearly seen the importance of solid training. Loving Christians can, with the noblest of motives, make a mess of prison ministry. They may buttonhole prisoners with tracts, respond naively to prisoners' requests, or promise things they can't deliver, which amounts to just another "rejection" in the prisoner's life. Training is critical. So PF requires laypeople to complete twenty hours of training courses in order to be certified as volunteers.*

Since 1989, Prison Fellowship has also equipped local churches to minister to victims, one of the most ignored sectors of society.†

And what about the tiniest victims? In South Central Los Angeles, the Faithful Central Missionary Baptist Church is training volunteers to work in the neonatal intensive care unit of the overburdened and underfunded Martin Luther King Hospital. After completing their training, these "Rock 'n Hold" volunteers spend hours in the hospital nursery. Swathed in hospital greens, they sit and hold the twitching, afflicted babies who have been born addicted to the crack their mothers consumed. They rock and hold the babies who have been born with AIDS, loving them, singing them lullabies. And the Christian witness of these volunteers is not lost on the hospital staff.

As the church equips its people to minister to the living, it needs to train them as well to deal with death and disease. Many churches have done this with a variety of special ministries. One is "Love That Heals," a cancer support group of Elmbrook Church. Members pray together, help one another with practical concerns, and shepherd

---

*Since 1976 more than forty thousand volunteers have received training on how to communicate, care, and serve in prisons, and how to help inmates and their families take responsibility for their own lives through the power of the Holy Spirit and the help of the local church.

†Through "Neighbors Who Care," local church volunteers have received specialized training to work with victims of property crimes. Volunteers spend time with victims who may well be afraid to be alone in their homes; they help change locks, replace screens, repair doors or windows, bring food, and assist them in talking through their feelings about the crime . . . and the volunteers share Christ, the One whose caring love they model.

each other through the rough times that affect both the individual sufferer and the family. They also seek to discern the spiritual opportunities that come through suffering.

Another vital ministry in our hurting society is outreach to homosexuals—an arena where Christians are greatly needed. Harvest is just such a ministry in urban Philadelphia.

Tenth Presbyterian Church, led by well-known pastor James Montgomery Boice, is located in the middle of a downtown neighborhood that caters to gay bars and homosexual meeting areas. Recognizing the need mission field in its own backyard, in 1984 the church began a Bible study for anyone interested in being healed from homosexuality; they began running a two-line advertisement in the *Philadelphia Inquirer,* "Homosexuals and Lesbians Can Change," followed by the Harvest phone number. Crank calls aside, Harvest heard from hundreds of people who had almost lost hope, and the ad now garners several thousand calls a year.

Dozens of men and women trapped in homosexual lifestyles have been delivered. Hope, a companion ministry, seeks to help those who have contracted AIDS, tenderly offering them real help and spiritual healing. The church has been sensitized and equipped to articulate a godly response to one of the great crises of our day.

Harvest's full-time director, John Freeman, understands the church's role: "It is within the church that healing, fellowship, growth, and maturing in Christ are to take place. It is therefore one of our goals to transfer dependence of an individual from Harvest to a caring local church as soon as we can.

"Speaking the truth in love," he adds, "this ministry brings the resources of the church to bear on the problem of homosexuality. It is an important part of any effort to reach modern America for Christ."*

---

*Harvest staff and volunteers speak to adult Sunday school classes, Sunday evening services, youth groups, annual missions conferences, and seminarians regarding issues of homosexuality and AIDS. All their training is intended to equip believers to better understand sexual brokenness and the specific means of healing God offers through the power of His Holy Spirit. Regeneration, a ministry of a number of churches in the Baltimore, Maryland, and Northern Virginia areas, fosters support groups for prayer, discipleship, and reorientation.

Regeneration also sponsors a twenty-one-week, intensive discipleship program called "New Directions," to help those struggling with homosexual temptations and to challenge them to become an integral part of a local church.

New Beginnings, a ministry of Whittier Area Baptist Fellowship, is designed

We wish there were space to profile more of the wonderful churches and ministries across the country that are effectively equipping believers to be the Body in the world today. The apostle John wrote at the end of his Gospel, "Jesus did many other things as well. If every one of them were written down, I suppose that even the whole world would not have room for the books that would be written."[8] And if the people of God, being His body, are doing "even greater things" than Jesus did, then certainly there is not room here—or in many books—to recount their acts!

But as the church equips believers to do these "greater things," we must also remember that our model is none other than the Head of the Body, Christ Himself. For we can do all the right things, reaching out in the name of Christ to meet spiritual, physical, and emotional needs, but if we do so with the wrong attitude, all of our good works are for naught. This is why the church's primary focus must always be on developing the character of its people.

When members of the church at Corinth were squabbling about their various gifts, the apostle Paul told them that the greatest gift—that which characterized their Lord—was love. So as we serve one another in the Body and reach to those beyond, we are to do so with the same loving, humble attitude as Jesus Himself. We must think more of others than of ourselves, caring most for "the least of these."

Nothing could be more at odds with the way of the world, where in today's celebrity-mad culture we are impressed by power and position, fame and influence, not selfless service. I was reminded of this vividly one evening at one of Washington's most glittering gatherings.

---

for gays and lesbians who want to go straight and live under the lordship of Christ. One member of the group was a pastor from a nearby church. He was struggling with bisexuality, but rather than firing him, his church put him under discipline and told him that if he would deal with the issue, they would consider keeping him on. The pastor agreed and attended the New Beginnings group for a year. At the end of that time he had made so much progress that the church brought him back as their pastor. "It was a story of remarkable spiritual and personal breakthrough," says Whittier Baptist Fellowship Pastor Lee Eliason.

# 22

## Let This Mind Be in You . . .

We have too many people who have plenty of medals and no scars.

*Warren Wiersbe*

$I$N 1990 A GOOD FRIEND, A JOURNALIST for *Time* magazine, invited me to the White House correspondents' dinner. Attended by the president and vice-president, members of the cabinet, the Supreme Court, and the Congress, network anchors, national columnists, reporters and journalists of every stripe, as well as Hollywood luminaries, the dinner is one of Washington's most prestigious annual events.

On the appointed evening I was enjoying a pre-dinner reception hosted by *Time,* renewing old friendships with a number of congressmen, senators, and columnists. Nearly everyone in the room was a public figure, so there was no pushing or shoving to rub shoulders with the mighty, no autograph seekers.

Suddenly I heard a huge commotion in the corridor, obviously a thundering horde of people. *It has to be George Bush,* I thought. *No one other than the president would attract such attention in this crowd.*

A mass of bodies hove into sight, flashbulbs popping, microphone cords dragging. It looked like a rugby scrum, except in the center was a person, not a ball.

The tangle pressed through the door, and the room blazed with klieg lights. Amid the oohing and aahing, I strained to see past the cameras and into the center of the group.

It wasn't the president. It was a young blonde woman, hard to identify behind all the bobbing heads and shoulders. One young man nearly knocked over Supreme Court Justice Antonin Scalia to get a better view. Then I got a good look and recognized the center of all this attention: Marla Maples, smiling coyly into the cameras.

Her claim to fame? She was tycoon Donald Trump's girlfriend, the other woman in his recently fractured marriage.

I stood against the wall, arms folded across my chest. "What a sad commentary on our media-crazed culture," I told my friend. Then I added smugly, "Can you imagine, some poor soul is going to have to spend four hours sitting with her tonight."

A few minutes later my host went to check on the seating arrangements.

"Chuck, I have good news and bad news," he said when he returned. "The good news is we're at table twenty-six, best table in the place, right down front. The bad news is we're sitting with Marla Maples."

As it happened, dinner conversation was no struggle. Marla spent the entire dinner greeting an unending procession of governors, senators, and Hollywood stars who stopped at the table, many deferentially asking for her autograph.

Later, as the speaker opened his remarks with a string of off-color jokes about Donald and Marla, a huge spotlight fell on our table. Marla smiled and waved for the applauding crowd.

And in the next morning's newspaper stories covering the event, most of the pictures were of Marla.

### Celebrity Syndrome and Pedestal Complex

Celebrities have long been a part of American life. It used to be, however, that people became celebrities because they were admired—for making the first solo flight across the Atlantic, hitting 714 home runs, or inventing penicillin. But today people are celebrities simply because they receive attention. As someone has quipped, people are well known for being well known. Fame has little to do with worth or character or achievement. So Marla Maples gets more press than the president, and no one questions it.

In large part, television is responsible for this obsession. Just appearing on the small screen confers big status. And audiences are so mesmerized by media that it matters little what one says or does.

Because of this uncritical acceptance, television celebrities have inordinate influence. The rappers and rockers of MTV are childhood heroes, while adult role models emerge from sitcoms and late-night talk shows.

Thus, when Los Angeles erupted into riots in the late spring of 1992 following the Rodney King verdict, people didn't clamor for the president or Mayor Bradley. They wanted talk-show host Arsenio Hall. "He showed more leadership than any of the elected officials," enthused one radio commentator. "He was . . . one of the few that people would listen to."[1]

Why? Because Arsenio knows the frustrations of urban poverty firsthand, or could authorize relief aid? No, because he is famous.

But this is the secular world, you may be saying. Christians aren't caught up in this kind of slavish adoration before the flickering screen. Oh, no?

After I guest-hosted a television talk show for two weeks, everywhere I went people stopped me, excited to tell me they had seen me on television.

"What was I talking about?" I would ask, curious about which segment they had seen and what they thought of it. But not one person could tell me what had been said. I could have been selling bongo drums or preaching some perverted gospel. All that mattered was that I was "famous"; they had seen me on the tube.

Not only are we as attracted to these new national icons as our secular neighbors, but we also have our own heroes. The fact that a television show or network is "Christian" doesn't alter its fundamental character. And for many Christians, watching our stars on television has become a substitute for participation in the local church. Why get involved with all those troublesome people down on the corner when we can just sit in our family room and listen to smooth preaching and wonderful music, all within range of remote control? So millions of believers remove themselves from the fellowship of the Body and begin living their spiritual lives vicariously through the religious celebrities they venerate.

Hence the blind devotion of thousands of Christians who continue sending their hard-earned ten- and twenty-dollar checks to televangelists who wear Rolex watches and live in palatial ministry-provided homes—and even to those who have publicly disgraced the gospel.

These larger-than-life figures do more than entertain; they also affirm us. The fact that "our" person can be right up there with Dan Rather eases the insecurity of many Christians. Because we want to be like the world, we create our own superstars out of honey-tongued preachers, World Series heroes, converted rock stars, and yes—sometimes even former White House aides.

All the blame can't be put on television, of course; it only plays to our human tendencies. Remember the ancient Israelites? Not satisfied with Yahweh as their king, they demanded a human leader—someone in the flesh they could admire. Even when warned of the consequences, they insisted.[2] And, for the most part, lived in misery thereafter, exploited by one tyrant after another.

Today this mentality translates into what we call the pedestal complex; it is rampant throughout the church. Too many clergy and parachurch organizers see themselves as leaders, not servants, and their parishioners and followers eagerly reinforce that attitude.

Thus we have the pastor who announces with a great sweep of his arm—like Charlton Heston parting the Red Sea—that God (pronounced, "Gawd") has told him to preach on this verse. A hush falls over the congregation. And after the service the people give him just a slightly wider berth as he passes in the corridor. Everyone calls him "Doctor," even when his degree is from East Overshoe Bible School.

This pedestal complex carries over to leadership posts throughout the church—even to the Sunday school teacher who, filled with his or her own importance, patronizes those lesser souls who sit silently in their chairs.

In fact, this attitude can infect the whole church. Not in the celebrity sense perhaps, but in pride and self-important preoccupation—the sense that we are the righteous ones, a little better than others. The tidy congregation of Riverton Community Church in our opening chapter was guilty of this: Failing to see themselves as servants of "the least of these," they became impotent as a church.

### Consequences for the Church

It is unfair to generalize, of course, for many of our Christian leaders do exhibit the qualities of servanthood. But if we are honest, we have to admit that the pedestal complex has embedded itself firmly in the church—and it can have disastrous consequences. Consider the most obvious.

*First, exalting leaders encourages spiritual Lone Rangers.* The Bakker case, though extreme, makes the point. When Jim and Tammy's multimillion-dollar excesses were exposed, everyone asked, "How could they do that?" But few asked, "Why did the

PTL board of directors allow them to do it?" Where was the accountability?

The sad fact is, Jim Bakker's closest advisers not only allowed the excess, they approved and encouraged it. Apparently they were glad to see their leader getting the same fame and reward as his secular counterparts—which also, by association, filtered down to them. I remember in 1980, long before the scandal, meeting a PTL board member on a plane flight; he bragged at the time that the board had just given Jim a six-figure salary. My expression must have betrayed my feelings, because the man quickly added, "Well, look, do you know what he'd be making if he were running NBC?"

But PTL wasn't NBC.

The celebrity syndrome destroys accountability. "God told me to build this," announces the visionary leader. "Just look at all the stations God has put this program on," respond the loyal followers. Who can argue with that? And once the enterprise is launched, jobs depend upon it and the spreading of the gospel supposedly hangs in the balance. So we'd better do whatever the leader wants.

The strong leader who builds a large and successful church is often not held to strict account either. For this reason, more and more pastors seem to be falling into temptation. One, a man I had often cited as a model pastor, suddenly revealed that for eight years he had been carrying on an adulterous relationship. Eight years! It's almost inconceivable. Not only his hypocrisy in leading the congregation while continuing in his sin, but the apparent blindness—or unwillingness to confront—of his elders and deacons.

*Many of these moral failures are the result of burnout, the second consequence of the pedestal complex.* We expect the pastor to be a shrink in the pulpit, a CEO in the office, and flawless in every area of his life, says Os Guinness. Unfortunately, the conscientious pastor who tries to live up to such unrealistic expectations can be swallowed up in his own frustrations and threatened by exhaustion, burnout, and even secret immorality.

Recently a group of megachurch pastors met with Gordon MacDonald, author of several excellent books on burnout. As pastor of a large church, he knew the problem well; he had fallen, repented, and been restored. The pastors asked his views on the megachurch in this regard.

The jury is still out, he told them. It depends on what it does to the individual. Chief executive officers in business last an average of six years.

Actually, the jury may already be in. The divorce rate among clergy is increasing faster than in any other profession. Statistics show that one in ten have had an affair with a member of their congregation, and 25 percent have had some illicit sexual contact.[3] One friend who operates a ministry for pastors with burnout told me he cannot keep up with the demand for help.

**Third, the celebrity syndrome leads to a distorted view of people's worth.** The late Max Cadenhead, when he was pastor of First Baptist Church in Naples, Florida, riveted his congregation one day with a bold confession.

"My message today is on the parable of the Good Samaritan," Max announced. "Let me start with an illustration.

"Remember last year when the Browns came forward to join the church?" he asked. Everyone nodded; the Browns were a very influential family. "Well, the same day a young man came forward and gave his life to Christ. I could tell he needed help—and we counseled him." No heads nodded; no one remembered.

"We worked with the Browns, got them onto committees. They've been wonderful folks," Cadenhead said to muffled amens. "And the young man . . . well, we lost track.

"Until yesterday, that is, as I was preparing today's message on the Good Samaritan. I picked up the paper, and there was that young man's picture. He had shot and killed an elderly woman."

Chins dropped throughout the congregation, mine included, as the pastor continued. "I never followed up on that young man, so I'm the priest who saw the man in trouble and crossed to the other side of the road. I am a hypocrite."

More of that kind of sober honesty in the church would be very healthy. For God's kingdom is just the opposite of ours. We go after the rich or the influential, thinking if we can just bag this one or that one, we'll have a real catch for the kingdom. Like the folks profiled by the apostle James, we offer our head tables to the wealthy and well dressed and reserve the back seats for those we consider unimportant.

We forget that it was an ordinary Sunday school teacher who dropped into a shoe store one day and began a process that changed the world. Few remember the name of the teacher who witnessed to the young shoe clerk that day—it was Edward Kimball—but they surely do remember the shoe clerk, Dwight L. Moody, who went on to evangelize two continents and shake nineteenth-century America to its roots.

*Fourth, the celebrity syndrome skews the theology of the church.* Adulation feeds on itself—as most politicians discover. It's addictive; once people taste it, they crave more. The pastor or Christian leader who is constantly the object of adoring crowds soon can't live without it and, often unconsciously, begins to shape his message to assure continued adulation. No more prophetic messages or challenges to the congregation.

*The fifth, and in some ways most destructive, consequence of the pedestal complex is that it lets everyone else off the hook.* We pay our leaders to do our spiritual service for us. They are like performers—and the better they perform, the more we pay.

Part of my responsibility at Prison Fellowship involves visiting PF ministries abroad. I do this not because I especially enjoy overseas travel (I don't), but to encourage those far-flung brothers and sisters—and to be encouraged. For I often find more real church vitality in places like Sri Lanka than here at home. Why? Because there the church is a tiny, embattled minority—and it has no superstars. So when the church wants to evangelize, for example, it can't depend on a celebrity or bring in Billy Graham for a crusade. The people have to do the work themselves. Which means the church functions as the church—not a bunch of observers watching someone else perform.

When we sit passively in our pews, paying some charismatic leader to do our job for us, we do much more than miss the task of the church. When we mimic the world with our pedestal complex, we offend a holy, all-powerful God—the most grievous consequence of all.

Of course we should respect those who are invested with spiritual authority. That's biblical. But there's a difference between respect and adulation. With the latter, we are always in danger of stepping over the line—giving glory to man rather than God. But God will not be mocked.

### The Biblical Model

It's easy to see how the world's fascination with fame has snuck into our tents and sapped our effectiveness. Yet this attitude runs absolutely contrary to that which Christ modeled when He, the King of the universe, came to live among us as a suffering servant.

Jesus said that the rulers of this world may lord it over their subjects, but if His followers wish to become truly great, they must be servants. Embodying this, the Messiah Himself washed His followers' feet.

The leader serves.[4] The mandate could not be clearer. We are to serve—and to reach out to the "least of these" to do it. That lesson first hit me while I was in prison.

During my early days as a federal prisoner, I experienced my share of self-pity. It had been a steep fall from an office next to the president of the United States to a prison cell, and I had been a very self-righteous man—one of the deadliest sins. And even though I was now a Christian, I still felt I was better than the car thieves, dope dealers, and murderers who shared my incarceration.

It was while sitting in a dreary prison day room, studying a Navigators' discipleship Bible study, that I read the words of Hebrews 2 for the first time:

> But we do see Him who has been made . . . lower than the angels, namely, Jesus . . . that by the grace of God He might taste death for everyone . . . for which reason He is not ashamed to call them [us] brethren.[5]

The God of the universe was made like us, undeserving sinners that we are, so He could save us! And He wasn't ashamed to call us His brothers?

As I wrote in *Born Again*, this was a life-changing moment. Suddenly the men around me looked entirely different. I was no better, nor more important, nor less deserving of punishment. They were my brothers.

Years later I would read Warren Wiersbe's comment that heads this chapter—"We have too many people who have plenty of medals and no scars"—and realize that right then that fit me to a T. I had been so proud of my accomplishments, bedecked with all the "medals" the world could offer: education, power, influence. Now I began to see, in the light of eternity, how hollow they really were. And at that point, God started tenderizing me, making me malleable for His purposes—in preparation for the call He had for my future.

The humbling process is not a one-shot thing, of course. If we stay in His Word, God continues to remind us of our dependence on Him and the dangers of pride. One chapter of Scripture particularly convicts me, and I often find myself repeating the words over and over like a hymn. They were written by the apostle Paul from his own jail cell:

> Let this mind be in you, which was also in Christ Jesus: Who, being in the form of God, thought it not robbery to be equal with God: But made himself of no reputation, and took upon him the form of a servant, and was made in the likeness of men: And being found in fashion as a man, he humbled himself, and became obedient unto death, even the death of the cross.[6]

But hard as we try to live out what we know to be the truth, our old selves often reemerge. It's a particular problem for someone like me, by nature assertive, strong-willed, and prideful. So God from time to time has to break our wills. That happened to me in an unforgettable experience and through the witness of Mother Teresa.

It was Christmas 1985, and I was scheduled to preach in several prisons in Raleigh, North Carolina. Arriving late on Christmas Eve, I checked into a hotel and, while preparing for bed, flipped on CNN to catch the late news. On the screen was Mother Teresa. The little nun with the love-lined face had her arms around two emaciated young men, advanced AIDS sufferers who had been released that very day from a New York state prison to enter a home established by Mother Teresa's order.

When a reporter demanded to know "why we should care about criminals with AIDS," Mother Teresa explained that these young men had been created in God's image and deserved to know of His love.

I sat on the side of the bed staring at the picture on the screen. How could she do it? Embrace those men who were dying of that deadly virus? I had to admit to myself that I wouldn't have the courage to do what this little ninety-pound woman was doing.

I went to sleep that night thinking about Mother Teresa, and at the same time thanking God that I didn't have to deal with AIDS patients.

The next morning I preached to several hundred women prisoners. As I was getting ready to leave, the warden asked if I would visit Bessie Shipp.

"Who is Bessie Shipp?" I asked.

"Bessie has AIDS," said the warden. "She's in an isolation cell. It's Christmas and nobody has visited her."

I reacted instinctively with, "I'm running late for the men's prison." *Besides,* I thought to myself, *I don't want to take the chance.* Much less was known then about how the virus was transmitted, and, frankly, I was afraid. Then the face of Mother Teresa flashed before me, and I heard her words: *These boys deserve to know of God's love. . . . Have this mind in you . . .*

"Well, all right," I said, "take me to Bessie Shipp."

As the chaplain escorted me through two secured areas, he explained that a petition had been presented to the governor for Bessie's release, that it hadn't been acted upon, and that she was feeling particularly depressed. The doctors had given her only a few weeks to live.

A chill came over me as we swung open the gate to the isolation cell, where a petite young woman sat bundled up in a bathrobe, reading a Bible. She looked up, and her eyes brightened as the chaplain said, "I promised I'd bring you a Christmas present, Bessie."

We chatted for a few moments, and since there wasn't much time for either of us, I decided I had better get to the point.

"Bessie, do you know Jesus?" I asked.

"No," she said. "I try to. I read this book. I want to know Him, but I haven't been able to find Him."

"We can settle it right now," I said, taking her hand. The chaplain took her other hand, and together we led Bessie in prayer. When we finished, she looked at us with tears flowing down her cheeks. It was a life-changing moment for Bessie—and for me.

Outside the prison, television crews were waiting to cover the "Christmas in Prison" story. Instead of my planned words, I made a plea for the governor to release Bessie Shipp, and that night on the plane flying back to Washington, I dictated a long letter to him. But the letter never had to be mailed. Two days later, Governor Jim Martin released Bessie, and she went home to Winston-Salem.

There Bessie studied the Bible, was baptized into a local church, and was visited regularly by Al Lawrence, our Prison Fellowship area director at the time. She told Al that those were the happiest days of her life because she knew that God loved her and God's people loved her as well.

Three weeks after her release, Bessie joined the Savior she had so recently come to know.

I shuddered later when I thought how close I had come to avoiding that visit. And since that day I have never hesitated to walk into an AIDS ward and embrace dying men and women. No heroics or courage on my part—just obedience. And in this case, through Mother Teresa's example, He took away the unholy fear that had gripped me.

The attitude Christ modeled for us is one that should typify every Christian, whether in pulpit or pew, whether leader of a vast organization or solitary prayer warrior. Not puffed up with self-importance, but poured out for others.

Speaking to a fractured German church in the post-Hitler era, the great pastor Helmut Thielicke eloquently put it into perspective:

> The church must be a mother to all who are weary and heavy laden, to all who have strayed and gone wrong, even to those who have forsaken their mother in the last decade and fallen victim to strange ideas. And therefore its task is not to look to the great and powerful, to the Americans or the English, but rather to visit the prisoners and preach the gospel to those who cannot help the church because they have no privileges to bestow.[7]

### Servant Leadership

How do we tear down the pedestals? How do we vigorously assert the biblical mind-set of servant leadership, so radically at odds with the celebrity-crazed culture in which we live?

Like everything else, it begins with each of us coming under the conviction of God's truth. All of us—pastors and lay leaders and parishioners—need to take a hard look at ourselves.

*First, we must reassess our objectives.* Is our goal to be the biggest and most powerful church in town? Is it to get on television and influence the community? Those things may happen, but they should be the fruit of faithful service, not the overarching goal.

The church, as a witness to the kingdom of God, is to be a community that worships God and equips men and women to be disciples, growing in holiness and service. How can the church fulfill these functions if it is not a servant church—from pulpit to pew? And this being the case, the principal job of the pastor is to serve: to equip others to serve.

But we are human and weak. So while we know the biblical model, it is easy to stray.

***Our second task, therefore, is to consciously strive to avoid the snares.*** This is not easy. Temptations surround us every day—both our natural inclinations and the world's style of authoritarian leadership. But there are ways to protect ourselves.

Bob Russell can attest to this. Pastor of one of the fastest-growing and most successful churches in America, Southeast Christian in Louisville, Kentucky, Bob has by all accounts been unaffected by success. But it hasn't been without real effort.

For one thing, Bob chose and trained an associate, a very capable, bright, young preacher named Dave Stone who takes the pulpit one Sunday out of four. ("Name" preachers in major churches do not readily share their pulpits. I know of one who brags he's done it only twice in thirty-five years.) This mentoring process both lessens the risk of the personality cult and trains a successor.

Bob delegates as well. For example, he took a gifts test and discovered, as many pastors eventually do, that he was a poor administrator; so Bob and his governing board appointed a business manager and have given him almost free rein.

Finally, Bob does little things to remind himself of his role as well as signal it to others. For example, Southeast has outgrown its parking lot and must use a satellite area a mile away for the overflow. Instead of reserving a "senior pastor" parking slot next to the church, Bob parks in the overflow lot and takes the shuttle bus.

Another pastor who understands the need not to lord it over others is Mihai Gongola in Arad, Romania. When freedom came to Eastern Europe and the church emerged from underground, Westerners poured in, showering money on those pastors who had lived on next to nothing for so long. Some of them now sport silk ties and drive Mercedes. But when Mihai Gongola was offered a new German car, he refused. His people drove old cars or took trams, and he would not elevate himself above them.

Another church leader from the East has shown the same spirit. Vaclav Maly, the young Czech priest who played such a key role in

---

*See also chapter 16.

the fall of Communism in his country, had heard crowds of nearly a million people shouting his name in the streets: "Maly! Maly!" After the revolution, power and position were his for the taking. Vaclav Havel, the new president of Czechoslovakia, offered him any post in government. Maly declined.*

When I visited him in his simple, one-bedroom apartment in Prague in 1991, I told him he was a great hero to many of us in the West.

"Oh, no," Maly replied. "I am no hero. A hero is someone who does something he doesn't have to. I was just doing my duty."

Change in government was important, he said, and Vaclav Havel was doing vital work. But the work to which he, Maly, had been called, was the work of changing hearts. He must continue in that call, preaching the gospel and living among the people he served. Like his role in the revolution, it was not a matter of choice. He was simply doing his duty. And he did not want to get diverted from his duty by the seductions of power.

For sometimes it is the trappings of power that trap us.

A few years ago I agreed to fill in for Pat Robertson, hosting "The 700 Club" for two weeks. During my stint, a driver arrived every morning to take me to the studio; in the car were papers to read before the morning program (all reminiscent of White House days). When I arrived at the studio I was greeted by the makeup artist, the wardrobe person ready to press my jacket, more briefing papers, coffee, anything I wanted. Everyone showed deference to the "star."

I found the old adrenalin surging. And I found, worst of all, that I was beginning to enjoy it. The attention. The excitement of the countdown to broadcast. After the second week I fled Virginia Beach. I knew I could never do this kind of thing again—and I haven't. I know some of my own weaknesses, and I don't trust myself.

Some can handle television—Billy Graham, Pat Robertson, and others do it beautifully—but there are more who cannot.

That doesn't mean we shrink from responsibility. God calls each of us to a particular task. But when the temptation of pride comes knocking . . . as it will . . . we must lock the door against it— whatever that takes.

But the toughest question is, How do we know? Because usually the knock is very faint, and we don't listen for it. The best protection I have discovered is accountability. Since we all have blind spots, we must, as we mentioned earlier, submit ourselves to those who can see the logs floating in our eyes.

How often does your church governing body review 1 Peter 5:2 with the pastor and elders: "Shepherd the flock of God among you, . . . not under compulsion, but voluntarily, according to the will of God; and not for sordid gain, but with eagerness"? Or Paul's first letter to Timothy? We must constantly check each other on how well we are measuring up to the clear biblical requirements of leadership.

In addition to the biblical passages, I have found one book especially useful for Christian leaders and workers: *Spiritual Leadership* by Oswald Sanders. I give it to every colleague, particularly for the twenty-two questions Sanders poses for every Christian's self-examination.[8]

*As we develop the characteristics of biblical leadership, we begin to fulfill the third task, which is to identify with those to whom we minister.* Missionaries soon learn this is vital for compassionate, intimate ministry. Like the Baptist missionary couple who went to Sri Lanka a few years ago, taking with them four rooms of furniture. When they set up their home in Colombo, it looked just like the one they had left in America, including a deep freezer, television, and microwave. After two years and many urgent appeals for funds from the faithful in the States, they had two or three converts. Disillusioned, they shipped themselves and their possessions home.

William Booth, founder and first general of the Salvation Army, sent a command to all of his missionaries in India: "Go to the Indian as a brother, which indeed you are, and show the love which none can doubt you feel . . . eat and drink and dress and live by his side. Speak his language, share his sorrow."[9]

And Count Zinzendorf, the great reformer, sent missionaries around the world with the same instruction: Do not lord it over the unbelievers but simply live among them; preach not theology, but the crucified Christ.[10]

Those are good instructions for all of us. For in a post-Christian culture, the church in America is not unlike a missionary outpost.

As Dietrich Bonhoeffer put it: "The church is herself only when she exists for humanity. . . . She must take her part in the social life of the world, not lording it over men, but helping and serving them. She must tell men, whatever their calling, what it means to live in Christ, to exist for others."[11]

If the church can only be the church when it exists for others, then the Christian can only be truly Christian when he or she is willing to be emptied out for others. There are no harder words in all of Scripture than Jesus' commandment that we love one another as He loved us—which means love that lays down its life for another.

Sometimes that is a commandment we must take literally.

# 23

## Who Are You?

*H*AVE YOU BEEN TO AUSCHWITZ?

From Warsaw, take the early train south to Krakow. A few blocks from that city's central square, find the small bus terminal and buy a ticket to Oswiecim, the proper Polish name for the pleasant town the Nazis turned into a killing field. An hour and a half later, you disembark at Oswiecim's even smaller bus station and cross the street to catch a tram, which takes you directly to Auschwitz.

On the tram you meet tourists. Two backpackers from Finland. A handful of university students from New Zealand. A retired couple from Detroit. You enjoy chatting together. But then, as the tram nears the camp entrance, you are all suddenly bound by a common curiosity and a common dread. Auschwitz does not encourage conversation.

It is autumn, and dead leaves skitter across the long path to the entrance. You cannot quite believe you are here in this notorious place. The double rows of barbed-wire fencing, the railroad tracks that transported millions to their deaths, the famous iron-arched gate with its ironic motto spelled out above in foot-high letters: ARBEIT MACHT FREI. *Work makes freedom.*

The camp is silent now, its brick barracks a museum, with rooms full of the ordinary items people brought to their imprisonment: a huge case of eyeglasses, another of shaving brushes and bowls; stacks of suitcases; and a giant case piled with thousands of shoes, heaped on top of one another.

The shoes alone tell the tales of millions of lives. Like that pair of black high heels over there, now fifty years old but still festive. Purchased for a special occasion, rarely worn, they happened to be on the feet of their owner the day the Gestapo rounded up her family.

You imagine her—call her Anna—getting off the train in Auschwitz, on edge because of the brutal discomfort of her journey in the cattle car yet not fully aware of what is happening. The knock on the door had come suddenly during dinnertime on the Sabbath; they, like other Jewish families, were to be resettled, the German officer said. But first they would spend some time in a work camp; after all, a war was raging, and the government needed laborers.

They had given Anna time to pack only a small bag: some clothes, the baby's medicine, a toy for her little boy, the prized, silver-framed photograph of her husband's parents. The soldiers also told them to bring their valuables, so she had her mother's gold necklace around her neck and her own wedding ring on her long, pale hand.

Now, as she stumbled off the train holding little Wiktor's hand, watching her husband Jan jump down with the baby, Biruta, in his arms, she laughed a little to herself. Here she was, detained away from home for who knew how long, and she was wearing her good shoes. In the fear and flurry of departure, she had forgotten to change. It would be a funny story to tell when the war was over—how she came to the work camp wobbling in high heels. Perhaps they would issue her a pair of work shoes.

But as you stand before the glass case fifty years later, you know what happened to Anna and her shoes.

As they came off the train, the Jews were divided into two groups, one large, the other small. Auschwitz was already crowded with non-Jewish prisoners—Poles who had displeased their Nazi rulers. No need to make room for Jews, except for the strongest of potential workers. Women and children were sent to one side, as were all but the most vigorous-looking men.[1]

Then the large group was herded along, clutching their suitcases, to another section of the camp. Here they found a scene both soothing and perplexing: a small orchestra of young women, each with her hair tied back with a bright ribbon, clothed in white blouses and navy blue skirts. They were playing a light, cheerful tune.

As the music continued, a camp matron made a general announcement: because of the threat of disease, delousing showers would be necessary. The Jews were shown where to put their belongings for retrieval later. They carefully folded their clothing and left it with the family suitcase on a table.

Then, naked and shivering and trying to concentrate their attention elsewhere to escape embarrassment, they walked toward the large, low building with a sign reading "BATHS." It was dug into a hill, and above its roof were plots of grass and tidy flower borders.

As the last of the large group—as many as two thousand—entered the shower rooms, the doors slid shut with a metallic click. Then, through mushroom-shaped vents hidden in the grass and flowers on top of the building, Nazi orderlies dropped a small quantity of blue crystals into the sealed rooms below, and perforations in the ceilings began to exude a deadly mist: Zyklon B, a potent poison produced by a German firm called Deutsche Gesellschaft zur Schädlingsbekämpfung—the "German Society for Combating Pests."

The crystals of hydrogen cyanide made quick work of those in the showers: The panicked victims vomited, suffocated, and emptied their bowels on the concrete floor. Within twenty-three minutes, workers wearing gas masks and rubber boots opened the door and begin unloading the corpses, a grim tangle of arms and legs.

Workers shaved the heads of the female corpses, snipped off long braids, then transported the bodies to large brick ovens, where they were fed to flames so intense that they would emerge as ash within the hour, to be sprinkled on the flower beds and dumped into the river Sola.

This was the fate of the owner of those high-heeled shoes you see in the case before you. Multiply her suffering by that represented by the small red shoes with the broken strap, the gentlemen's shoes with the dark brown laces, the old-fashioned boots, the soft baby booties—and multiply those by thousands, then millions of souls, and you begin to perceive the horror of Auschwitz.

At another exhibit you see rather ordinary bolts of cloth standing on end—a linenlike fabric in a neutral brown color. Look closer: there are braids of human hair wound over the bolts, hair that was found in Auschwitz storage rooms by Allied troops after the war. Eight tons of it. Forensic scientists found that the hair was full of cyanide. These ordinary bolts of tailor's lining were made from human hair.

You have stared long and hard at Anna's shoes; no reason not to believe you are now looking at her hair.

Touring the rest of the camp, you visit the prisoners' quarters where many non-Jewish inmates somehow survived in spite of crowding, disease, and starvation; the Wall of Death, where twenty thousand political prisoners were shot; the square where roll call was held each day; the gallows where insubordinate prisoners were hanged; the barracks where perverse medical experiments were carried out on children and pregnant women; and the gas chambers themselves, the crematorium, where the ovens are now cold, save for a single flame of remembrance.

What was it like then? you wonder. It's unimaginable to us, this surreal concentration of evil. How could anyone here have held onto hope of any sort? Could good ever overcome evil in a place of such cruel despair? Were there any flickers of faith in this darkness?

Father Maximilian Kolbe was forty-five years old in the early autumn of 1939 when the Nazis invaded his homeland. He was a Polish monk who had founded the Knights of the Immaculate, a Franciscan order whose headquarters was in Niepokalanow, a village near Warsaw. There 762 priests and lay brothers lived in the largest friary in the world. Father Kolbe presided over Niepokalanow with a combination of industry, joy, love, and humor that made him beloved by the plain-spoken brethren there.

Maximilian Kolbe had a global vision for evangelism, and he saw the budding technology of his day as powerful potentials to be harnessed in his work. Radio, publishing, mass media—he dreamed of having the resources to use them all, without limit, to spread the Good News. Whereas St. Francis, his predecessor, had loved all living things, exclaiming his delight in "Brother Son" and "Sister Moon," Kolbe roamed through his friary print shop reveling in the ministry made possible by what he called "Brother Motor" and "Sister Press."

In his simple room at Niepokalanow he sat each morning at a pigeonhole desk, a large globe before him, praying over the world and focusing on the many opportunities for the gospel seed to be sown. He did so tortured by the fact that a far different seed was being spread in those dark days of the late 1930s.

A pale man with arresting blue eyes and a terrifying power of manipulation had whipped the people of Germany into a frenzy. Whole nations had already fallen to the evil Adolf Hitler and his

Nazis. Storm troops were already marching in the streets of Austria and Czechoslovakia.

"An atrocious conflict is brewing," Father Kolbe told a group of friars one day after he had finished his prayers.

> We do not know yet what will develop. In our beloved Poland we must expect the worst. During the first three centuries, the Church was persecuted. The blood of martyrs watered the seeds of Christianity. Later, when the persecutions ceased, one of the Fathers of the Church deplored the lukewarmness of Christians. He rejoiced when persecution returned. In the same way, we must rejoice in what will happen, for in the midst of trials our zeal will become more ardent.[2]

Father Kolbe was right. Poland was next. And his zeal did become more ardent. On the last Sunday in August 1939, he preached an impassioned homily on the three stages of life: preparation, activity, and suffering.

As a young boy, Kolbe told the brothers, he'd had a dream in which he was offered a choice between two crowns: one white to symbolize purity, the other red for martyrdom. He had chosen both. All of his life he had practiced purity; perhaps the Nazis would now provide the opportunity for him to receive the second crown.

Were that to be the case, he said, one thing was sure: *Greater love hath no man than this, that he lay down his life for his friends.* He smiled as he said the words, and those in the small church would carry that phrase to their graves, their zeal for ministry inflamed by the boldness of this bearded, unassuming brother in his rope-belted black robe.

On September 1, 1939, the Nazi blitzkrieg broke over Poland. The skies above Niepokalanow were filled with bombers on their way east toward Warsaw.

Soon, however, Niepokalanow itself was a target. As flames roared in the night and glass shattered, the brothers in the friary prayed. When the skies cleared temporarily, Father Kolbe sent many of them home to their families; he encouraged others to join the Polish Red Cross. Thirty-six of the number remained with Kolbe at the friary, which now became a hospital and haven for refugees.

But not for long.

On September 19, a group of Germans arrived at Niepokalanow on motorcycles and arrested Father Kolbe and all but two of his friars. The monks were loaded into trucks, then into livestock wagons, and two days later arrived at Amtitz, a prison camp.

Conditions were horrible, but not horrific. Prisoners were hungry, but no one died of starvation. One day the camp administrator's wife, touched by Father Kolbe's grace in suffering, sent him a cake; he gathered all the brothers together and each received a thin slice.

The monks slept on prickly beds of straw in barracks overrun by rats. One night a brother named Juraszek woke from his troubled sleep, aware that someone was touching him. In the dim light he saw that it was Father Kolbe, tenderly tucking his feet into the dirty rag that served as his blanket. Kolbe smiled at Juraszek, then moved on through the barracks, praying over each brother, sharing a quiet word with those who could not sleep.

Strangely, within a few weeks the brothers were released from prison. Back at the friary, they found the buildings vandalized and the Nazis in control, using the facility as a deportation camp for political prisoners, refugees, and Jews.

The situation was a tremendous opportunity for ministry, and Father Kolbe took full advantage of it, helping the sick, comforting the fearful, and even publishing his magazine, which he now had to deliver by hand.

Sensing the anxiety of some of the brothers, he gathered a group of them before a chalkboard.

"I insist that you become saints," Kolbe said with a smile, "and great saints! Does that surprise you? But remember, my children, that holiness is not a luxury, but a simple duty. It is Jesus who told us to be perfect as our Father in heaven is perfect. So do not think it is such a difficult thing. Actually, it is a very simple mathematical problem."

On the blackboard he wrote "w = W," grinning widely as he did so.

"A very clear formula, don't you agree? The little 'w' stands for my will, the capital 'W' for the will of God. When the two wills run counter to each other, you have the cross. Do you want to get rid of the cross? Then let your will be identified with the will of God, who wants you to be saints. Isn't that simple? Now all you must do is obey!!"[3]

While the monks used their time for such lessons, the Nazis used theirs to decide just how to impose their will on the rest of

Europe. Their goal was clear: a Nazi-ruled Europe whose people would be slaves of the German master race and whose "undesirable elements" would be exterminated.[4] In their drive to achieve that goal, they lit a conflagration that would decimate cities, destroy cultures, and kill forty-five million people.

To the Nazis, the Jews and Slavic peoples were the *Untermenschen* (subhumans). Their cultures and cities were to be erased and their industry appropriated for Germany. On October 2, while Father Kolbe prayed for his nation, Adolf Hitler outlined a secret memorandum to Hans Frank, the Governor General of Poland. In a few phrases he determined the grim outcome for millions:

> The [ordinary] Poles are especially born for low labor . . . the Polish gentry must cease to exist . . . all representatives of the Polish intelligentsia are to be exterminated. . . . There should be one master only for the Poles, the German.

As for Poland's hundreds of thousands of priests, spiritual leaders in a land nearly 100 percent Catholic?

> They will preach what we want them to preach. If any priest acts differently, we shall make short work of him. The task of the priest is to keep the Poles quiet, stupid and dull-witted."[5]

Maximilian Kolbe was clearly a priest who "acted differently" from the Nazis' designs.

In early February 1941, the Polish underground smuggled word to Kolbe that his name was on a Gestapo list: He was about to be arrested. Kolbe knew what happened to the loved ones of those who tried to elude the Nazis' grasp; their friends and colleagues and families were taken instead. He had no wife or children; his church was his family. And he could not risk the loss of any of his brothers in Christ. So he stayed at Niepokalanow.

At nine o'clock on the morning of February 17, Father Kolbe was sitting at his pigeonhole desk, his eyes and prayers on the globe before him, when he heard the sound of heavy vehicles outside the thick panes of his green-painted windows. He knew it was the Nazis, but he remained at his desk. He would wait for them to come to him.[6]

After being held in Nazi prisons for several months, Father Kolbe was found guilty of the crime of publishing unapproved materials and sentenced to Auschwitz. Upon his arrival at the camp in May 1941, an SS officer informed him that the life expectancy of priests there was about a month.

Kolbe was assigned the timber detail; he was to carry felled tree trunks from one place to another. Guards stood by to ensure that the exhausted prisoners did so at a quick trot.

Years of slim rations and overwork at Niepokalanow had already weakened Kolbe. Now, under the load of wood, he staggered and collapsed. Officers converged on him, kicking him with their shiny leather boots and beating him with whips. He was stretched out on a pile of wood, dealt fifty lashes, then shoved into a ditch, covered with branches, and left for dead.

Later, having been picked up by some brave prisoners, he awoke in a camp hospital bed alongside several other near-dead inmates. There, miraculously, he revived.

"No need to waste gas or a bullet on that one," chuckled one SS officer to another. "He'll be dead soon."

Kolbe was switched to other work and transferred to Barracks 14, where he continued to minister to his fellow prisoners, hearing their confessions, praying with them, comforting them.

His eyes ringed by weary shadows, he would hug thin shoulders beneath gray striped uniforms and nod his understanding as men poured out their hearts. Then he would raise his emaciated arm and make the sign of the cross in the foul air of the packed barracks.

*The cross,* he thought. *Christ's cross has triumphed over its enemies in every age. I believe, in the end, even in these darkest days in Poland, the cross will triumph over the swastika. I pray I can be faithful to that end.*

Then priest and penitents lay down on their pallets, bone-tired yet so tortured by hunger they could not sleep.

By the end of July 1941, Auschwitz was working like a well-organized killing machine, and the Nazis congratulated themselves on their efficiency. At first, they admitted, there had been some doubt that they could find a utilitarian way to dispose of the undesirables. Early methods of execution—mass shootings, gas dispersed in vans, lethal injections—all made it too difficult to effectively dispose of the corpses or dispatched people in too-small quantities.

But Auschwitz—ah, it was going well. The camp's five chimneys never stopped smoking. The stench was terrible, but the results were excellent: eight thousand Jews could be stripped, their possessions appropriated for the Reich, gassed, and cremated—all in twenty-four hours. Every twenty-four hours.

About the only problem was the occasional prisoner from the work side of the camp who would figure out a way to escape. When these escapees were caught, as they usually were, they would be hung with special nooses that slowly choked out their miserable lives—a grave warning to others who might be tempted to try.

Then one July night as the frogs and insects in the marshy land surrounding the camp began their evening chorus, the air was suddenly filled with the baying of dogs, the curses of soldiers, and the roar of motorcycles. A man had escaped from Barracks 14.

The next morning there was a peculiar tension as the ranks of phantom-thin prisoners lined up for morning roll call in the central square, their eyes on the large gallows before them. But there was no condemned man standing there, his hands bound behind him, his face bloodied from blows and dog bites. That meant the prisoner had made it out of Auschwitz. And that meant death for some of those who remained.

After the roll call, Camp Commandant Fritsch ordered the dismissal of all but Barracks 14. While the rest of the camp went about its duties, the prisoners from Barracks 14 stood motionless in line. They waited. Hours passed. The summer sun beat down. Some fainted and were dragged away. Some swayed in place but held on; those the SS officers beat with the butts of their guns. Father Kolbe, by some miracle, stayed on his feet, his posture as straight as his resolve.

By evening roll call the commandant was ready to levy sentence. The other prisoners had returned from their day of slave labor; now he could make a lesson out of the fate of this miserable barracks.

Fritsch began to speak, the veins in his thick neck standing out with rage. "The fugitive has not been found," he screamed. "Ten of you will die for him in the starvation bunker. Next time, twenty will be condemned."

The rows of exhausted prisoners began to sway as they heard the sentence. The guards let them; terror was part of their punishment.

The starvation bunker! Anything was better—death on the gallows, a bullet in the head at the Wall of Death, or even the gas in the

chambers. All those were quick, even humane, compared to Nazi
starvation, for they denied you water as well as food.

The prisoners had heard the stories from the starvation bunker
in the basement of Barracks 11. They said the condemned didn't even
look like human beings after a day or two. They frightened even the
guards. Their throats turned to paper, their brains turned to fire,
their intestines dried up and shriveled like desiccated worms.

Commandant Fritsch walked the rows of prisoners. When he
stopped before a man, he would command in bad Polish, "Open
your mouth! Put out your tongue! Show your teeth!" And so he
went, choosing victims like horses.

His dreary assistant, Palitsch, followed behind. As Fritsch chose
a man, Palitsch noted the number stamped on the prisoner's filthy
shirt. The Nazis, as always, were methodical. Soon there were ten
men—ten numbers neatly listed on the death roll.

The chosen groaned, sweating with fear. "My poor wife!" one
man cried. "My poor children! What will they do?"

"Take off your shoes!" the commandant barked at the ten men.
This was one of his rituals; they must march to their deaths bare-
foot. A pile of twenty wooden clogs make a small heap at the front
of the grassy square.

Suddenly there was a commotion in the ranks. A prisoner had
broken out of line, calling for the commandant. It was unheard-of to
leave the ranks, let alone address a Nazi officer; it was cause for execution.

Fritsch had his hand on his revolver, as did the officers behind
him. But he broke precedent. Instead of shooting the prisoner, he
shouted at him.

"Halt! What does this Polish pig want of me?"

The prisoners gasped. It was their beloved Father Kolbe, the
priest who shared his last crust, who comforted the dying, who
heard their confessions and nourished their souls. Not Father
Kolbe!

The frail priest spoke softly, even calmly, to the Nazi butcher.
"I would like to die in place of one of the men you condemned."

Fritsch stared at the prisoner. #16670. He never considered them
as individuals; they were just a gray blur. But he looked now. #16670
didn't appear to be insane.

"Why?" snapped the commandant.

Father Kolbe sensed the need for exacting diplomacy. The Nazi
never reversed an order; so he must not seem to be asking him to do

so. Kolbe knew the Nazi dictum of destruction: the weak and the elderly first. He would play on this well- ingrained principle.

"I am an old man, sir, and good for nothing. My life will serve no purpose."

His ploy triggered the response Kolbe wanted. "In whose place do you want to die?" asked Fritsch.

"For that one," Kolbe responded, pointing to the weeping prisoner who had bemoaned his wife and children.

Fritsch glanced at the weeping prisoner. He did look stronger than this tattered #16670 before him.

For the first and last time, the commandant looked Kolbe in the eye. "Who are you?" he asked.

The prisoner looked back at him, a strange fire in his dark eyes. "I am a Catholic priest."

"Ein pfaffe!" the commandant snorted. He looked at his assistant and nodded. Palitsch drew a line through #5659 and wrote down #16670. Kolbe's place on the death ledger was set.

Father Kolbe bent down to take off his clogs, then joined the group to be marched to Barracks 11. As he did so, #5659 passed by him at a distance—the soldiers wouldn't let them come near one another—and on the man's face was an expression so astonished that it had not yet become gratitude.

But Kolbe wasn't looking for gratitude. If he was to lay down his life for another, the fulfillment had to be in the act of obedience itself. The joy must be found in submitting his small will to the will of One more grand.

As the condemned men entered Barracks 11, guards roughly pushed them down the stairs to the basement.

"Remove your clothes!" shouted an officer.

*Christ died on the cross naked,* Father Kolbe thought as he took off his pants and thin shirt. *It is only fitting that I suffer as He suffered to gain the glory He gained.*

In the basement the ten men were herded into a dark, windowless cell.

"You will dry up like tulips," sneered one of their jailers. Then he swung the heavy door shut.

As the hours and days passed, however, the camp became aware of something extraordinary happening in the death cell. Past prisoners had spent their dying days howling, attacking one another, clawing the walls in a frenzy of despair.

But now, coming from the death box, those outside heard the faint sounds of singing. For this time the prisoners had a shepherd to gently lead them through the shadows of the valley of death, pointing them to the Great Shepherd. And perhaps for that reason Father Kolbe was the last to die.

A prisoner named Brono Borgowiec, who survived Auschwitz, served as attendant to the death cells. Each day he had to remove the corpses of those who had finally withered away. He also was supposed to empty the waste bucket, but each day the bucket was dry. The inmates had drunk its contents in a futile effort to slake their thirst.

On August 14, 1941, there were four prisoners still alive in the bunker, and it was needed for new occupants. A German doctor named Boch descended the steps of Barracks 11, four syringes in his hand. Several SS troopers and Brono Borgowiec were with him—the former to observe and the latter to carry out the bodies.

When they swung the bunker door open, there, in the light of their flashlight, they saw Father Maximilian Kolbe, a living skeleton, propped against one wall. His head was inclined a bit to the left. He had the ghost of a smile on his lips and his eyes wide open, fixed on some faraway vision. He did not move.

The other three prisoners were on the floor, unconscious but alive. The doctor took care of them first: a jab of the needle into the bony left arm, the push of the piston in the syringe. It seemed a waste of the drug, but he had his orders. Then he approached #16670 and repeated the action.

In a moment, Father Kolbe was dead.

Have you been to Auschwitz?

If so, you know there *is* a flame of hope burning in that place of death and despair. You see it when you descend the basement stairs of Barracks 11 and make your way to the cell at the end of the dim hallway, where countless men died. There on the floor next to a large spray of fresh flowers burns a steady flame. Like the candle in the crematorium, it is a flame of remembrance.

But this is not just a vow of remembrance that Nazi atrocities might never happen again. No, this flame celebrates the fact that men and women, even in the greatest of horrors, can demonstrate the greatest of loves.

Nor is it a monument to Father Maximilian Kolbe alone, hero though he was. For those with eyes to see, it points to the Man who laid down His life for His friends, on the cross. To the Master who came not to be served, but to serve those He loved. To the only King in history who died for His subjects.

# 24

## Being His Witnesses

The goal of evangelism is to persuade men and women to become disciples of Jesus Christ and to serve Him in the fellowship of His Church.

*Lausanne Committee on Evangelism*

𝒲HAT WENT THROUGH MAXIMILIAN KOLBE'S mind when he volunteered to lay down his life for prisoner #5659?

No one knows, but the decision was instantaneous, the natural consequence of a character shaped by a lifelong commitment to Christ. *What he did resulted from who he was.*

Few of us will find ourselves in Maximilian Kolbe's shoes. But the moral of his story applies to every believer: *What you do emerges from who you are.* Being precedes doing. At the core of our Christian witness in the world lies the reality of who each of us is in relationship to God Himself and in relationship to one another in the new society of God's people—the church.

Kolbe didn't have to witness to the guards who marched him to the death chamber. He was a witness. And this is exactly what Jesus calls us to be. Just before His ascension, He told His disciples: "You will receive power when the Holy Spirit comes on you; and *you will be my witnesses* in Jerusalem, and in all Judea and Samaria, and to the ends of the earth."[1]

So many Christians interpret those words as *to* witness, rather than *be* a witness. And so they see it as an activity instead of what it really is: the state of our very being. Particularly is this so among evangelicals, for whom "witnessing" has become the supreme duty. And a source of enormous pressure.

Like the time my friend Charlie and several others, armed with copies of the "Four Spiritual Laws," set out to witness in a

Charlottesville, Virginia, bar. Charlie struck up a conversation with a well-dressed young professional who soon admitted his own spiritual emptiness. As Charlie told the man of his own experience with Christ, the rapport between them deepened. Sensing that the man was not ready for a commitment, Charlie got his phone number and made plans to contact him later.

After they left the bar, one of Charlie's companions queried him excitedly, "Did you go through the book with him?"

"No," Charlie replied. "He wasn't ready. We're going to talk again later."

The young man was furious. "I can't believe it!" he exploded. "Here we are trying to witness, and you didn't even go through the book!" Six months later this same young man had a nervous breakdown.

While we may have many occasions *to* witness, as God's Spirit leads, Jesus charges us to *be* witnesses. To understand this—that we don't always have to assault people with our tracts or gospel plans—is wonderfully liberating. But it is also intensely demanding. For *being* Christ's witnesses involves every aspect of what we are and do, individually and collectively as the community of faith. Remember Francis of Assisi's challenge: "Preach the gospel all the time; if necessary, use words."

How are we Christ's witnesses? By our whole being—in both word and deed. This involves responsiveness to the Holy Spirit, our best judgment, and sensitivity to other people. Often we miss this balance, however, tilting to one extreme or the other.

At one extreme are those who say plenty about God but don't live out their faith with the same vigor. Their lives lack love. Or purity. Or hope.

Unfortunately, they are the ones the world stereotypes as the church: the blatantly hypocritical Jimmy Swaggart; the worker who sips coffee from a Jesus mug and showers colleagues with Christian platitudes but does the shoddiest work in the office; the businessman who prays before every meeting and then cheats his customers; the pro-life activist who wears a "God Loves You" button while hurling hateful invectives at women entering abortion clinics.

For the watching world, it is difficult to separate the message from these messengers. Or, as Sheldon Vanauken put it:

> The best argument for Christianity is Christians: their joy, their certainty, their completeness. But the strongest argument

*against* Christianity is also Christians—when they are somber and joyless, when they are self-righteous and smug in complacent consecration, when they are narrow and repressive, then Christianity dies a thousand deaths.[2]

At the other extreme are those who earnestly live their faith but never articulate the reason for the hope that is in them. While people may look at us and see a reflection of Christ, and even admire the reflection—"You're such a good person"—unless we tell them about Him, they may never know the source of that goodness.

Thus we must always keep in mind that our first calling is to *be* a witness. That is our very nature. But included within that calling is the duty to *proclaim* a witness. And because the gospel is propositional, proclaiming the Good News is a primary task of the church.

### To Proclaim the Good News

The word *evangelism* comes from the Greek noun *euangelion*—meaning "good news"—and the verb *euangelizomai,* "to announce or proclaim or bear good news."

Every believer is called to evangelize—to bear the Good News of God's saving love for men and women. But not all are called to be evangelists. The latter is a specific office commissioned for the good of the church as a whole and filled by those called and gifted by God for that task. This was clear in the beginning when Timothy was called an evangelist and when Philip was given that specific charge.[3] The Book of Acts is full of the evangelistic fervor of the early church, including the travels, trials, and travails of the greatest evangelist of them all, the apostle Paul.

One of the most remarkable evangelists in the history of the church was a man whose memory is associated more with green beer and leprechauns than the proclamation of the gospel—Patrick of Ireland.

Kidnapped by pirates as a teenager, Patrick was taken from his well-to-do home in Roman Britain in A.D. 405, transported to Ireland, sold to a farmer, and given responsibility for the man's sheep.

Patrick had grown up in a Christian home; his father was a deacon in the church, his grandfather an elder. But the faith had not been real to him until one day, tending sheep in the barren hills of Ireland, he encountered the Great Shepherd and purposed to follow Him.

Eventually Patrick escaped from slavery and returned to Britain, where he became a priest. Then in a dream he heard an Irish voice pleading with him: "Holy boy, we are asking you to come home and walk among us again."

Return to the land of his servitude? An unlikely mission. But Patrick was a slave to Christ now, and the Lord gave him a sense of compassion for the Irish. "I was struck to the heart," he wrote later.

Patrick returned to primarily pagan Ireland, determined to bring the gospel to people enslaved by superstition and Druid worship. Traveling throughout the land, he baptized thousands of new converts and discipled new believers, trained church leaders, ordained pastors, exerted discipline on unrepentant church members, and commissioned more evangelists. He started scores of churches and witnessed to kings and their courts, farmers and peasants. He also forcefully protested injustices against the common people. By the time he died, about A.D. 461, he had started a movement of the church that transformed ancient Ireland.

Through the centuries God has raised up many uniquely gifted evangelists to proclaim the truth to a lost world. That the calling of evangelist is a specific gift conferred by God has never been more evident than in the life of an upstate New York lawyer named Charles Finney. Converted to Christ in 1821 when he was twenty-nine years old, Finney left his successful law practice to become a Presbyterian minister. He told his family and friends that he now had but one client, with "a retainer from the Lord Jesus Christ to plead His cause."[4]

After Finney began preaching among settlers in upstate New York during the spring of 1824, a series of revivals broke out in that area and around the state, spreading to Rochester, New York City, Philadelphia, and Boston. And later in the century, one of the greatest evangelists of them all, Dwight L. Moody, set two continents aflame with his preaching, as well as profoundly influencing ministry to the needy of his day.

The greatest evangelist of this century—perhaps the greatest since Paul—is Billy Graham, who has fervently, yet humbly, preached the gospel to more than 100 million people in eighty-four countries. What accounts for his astonishing influence? Like Patrick and Finney and others, it is the anointing of the Spirit and his single-minded devotion to his call from God.

I was among the friends who a decade ago urged Billy to give up strenuous crusades and spend more time writing and perhaps teaching. It's the only time I have seen the man agitated.

"No," he said. "My call is to preach the gospel, and I will do that as long as God gives me the breath to preach."

Graham has been equally unswerving in his commitment to the church, both to the unity of the whole body (he's taken plenty of criticism, but invariably includes all traditions on the platforms of his crusades) and to the local confessing congregations.

There are also men and women in the body of Christ who may not be called to full-time evangelism, but who are gifted in winning others to Christ. The late Arthur DeMoss, insurance company founder, was surely one.

When Art and his family traveled by air, they often did not sit together. Scattered through the plane, the children would witness to their seatmates. Art himself would engage anyone and everyone in conversation, and before long he would have shared his own testimony, often leading the person to Christ. Of all the people I've known in my life, he was the best in such one-on-one encounters.

At Art's memorial service in 1979—one of the greatest celebrations I've ever witnessed—the pastor asked those who had come to Christ through Art's ministry to stand. Throughout that packed congregation, men and women rose to their feet. What a legacy!

Another close friend, Dave Cauwels, a businessman and a colleague on Prison Fellowship's board of directors, has a similar calling. Dave has a gentle, sensitive heart for Christ and an innate sense of how to lovingly share Him with others.

Once Dave and I were traveling together, visiting Prison Fellowship International's ministries in the Far East. After ten arduous days on the road, we were resting in the lounge at the Singapore airport, awaiting our flight home. I was exhausted, my stomach in knots from too many exotic foods; all I wanted to do was slump in the corner, drink a Coke, and dream about home. I didn't want to talk to anyone, not even myself.

But Dave and another businessman traveling with us, Jim Zanios, noticed a fellow sitting despondently at the bar. Without exchanging a word, Dave and Jim simultaneously moved across the lounge, sat near the man, and engaged him in conversation. Within minutes, they were telling him about Jesus Christ.

But what about the rest of us? Those who don't have a special gift and boldness for sharing the faith? Are we off the hook? No.

For while God does specifically and uniquely gift some of His followers to proclaim His truth, all of us in the community of faith have a responsibility to be bearers of the Good News. So even if we are uncomfortable—or reluctant—about doing it, we'd better be obedient when the Holy Spirit nudges us. I'm especially sensitive to this because that's how I came to Christ.

Whenever I tell the story of my conversion, I give my own perspective on how Tom Phillips told me about Christ. Only years later did I learn what was going through Tom's mind at the time.

Tom Phillips is a shrewd executive and a strong Christian. He also is the type of person who feels awkward and uncomfortable creating a scenario solely for the purpose of sharing his faith. So it was unusual that he set his sights on me. Actually, he didn't want to. God just wouldn't let him off the hook.

At the time, the spring of 1973, Tom was president of Raytheon, one of the largest and most successful companies in America. I had recently left the White House and was planning to return to Raytheon as legal adviser, but Tom was nervous about meeting with me. It was the early days of Watergate, and I was in the midst of the controversy; that could hurt the company. Besides, since he had become a Christian, he had changed a lot. We had known one another before on altogether different terms.

So, as he tells it, he prayed the night before our scheduled meeting, "God, make Chuck Colson go away." And the Lord seemed to say to him, "No, you tell Chuck about Me. He needs a friend."

Tom didn't want to tell me about Christ. But he was the one the Holy Spirit had tagged—and empowered—for that particular task. He was the one chosen to break through my resistance and tell me about Jesus.

Tom was miserable. I was miserable. Yet it was God's appointed hour—and how eternally grateful I am for Tom Phillips's obedience.

While there will always be great evangelists, God uses people in every walk of life, people who thrill to tell about Christ, and even those who do so while dragging their feet.

The verb tense of the commissioning of the disciplines in Matthew's Gospel allows us to render Jesus' words literally, "*as you are going* make disciples." *As you go.* That means evangelism should flow naturally out of the context of our everyday lives. It's not a set of formulas, techniques, or memorized scenarios. It can't be put in a box. Evangelism is a consequence of holy living, of our own personal passion for Christ, and naturally flows out of the healthy life of the church.

### Concerns for Today's Church

Since this is not a book about evangelism, it is not our intention to deal with the subject exhaustively.* But if the church is to be effective in evangelizing today's world, there are a few critical concerns we need to discuss. For when we do have the opportunity to share our faith, we face formidable barriers.

***First of all, we need to recognize that we live in a post-Christian culture.***

During World War II, after Hitler blitzkrieged his way across France, demanding the unconditional surrender of the Allied forces in the European theater, thousands of British and French troops dug in along the coast of northern France in a last-ditch effort to hold off the German forces. Trapped on the beaches of Dunkirk, they knew they would soon be obliterated by the Nazis.

During that agonizing period, it is said that the British soldiers broadcast a terse message across the English Channel. Just three words: "And if not."

"*And if not*"? Was it code?

No. It was a reference to the Old Testament episode when Shadrach, Meshach, and Abednego stood before King Nebuchadnezzar's fiery furnace. "Our God is able to save us, and He will save us," the young men had said, "*and if not*, we will remain faithful to Him anyway."

And, as astonishing as it seems today, the oblique message was immediately understood by the British people. In the days that followed, a ragtag flotilla of fishing boats, pleasure cruisers, yachts, and rowboats set out from the shores of England, managing to rescue 338,000 Allied troops.

---

*We seek to examine the specific task as it relates to the church. For further reading, we recommend: J. I. Packer, *Evangelism and the Sovereignty of God*; Michael Green, *Evangelism in the Early Church; Who Is This Jesus?; Evangelism Then and Now; Evangelism and the Local Church*; John Stott, *Basic Christianity*; Paul Little, *Know What You Believe and Know Why You Believe*; Becky Pippert, *Out of the Saltshaker into the World*; Robert Coleman, *They Meet the Master*.

If the same message came to America today, it would be greeted with raised eyebrows and blank stares—even from many Christians. The tie that binds us is no longer common religious belief or heritage. The closest we come to a shared experience or common language are the messages that flow out of our television sets. So old phrases like "Where's the beef?" . . . "I don't get no respect" . . . the current, "Uh-huh, you got the right one, baby," and the adventures of Wayne's World and the Teenage Mutant Ninja Turtles become our common bonds of communication within American culture.

Yet expressions Christians have used for decades, like "God loves you and has a wonderful plan for your life," no longer necessarily connect. Christians understand them, but few others can relate. For example, proclaiming that "The Bible says . . . " commanded respect in the 1930s and 1940s, even into the 1960s—when 65 percent of all Americans believed the Bible to be literally true. Today only 32 percent believe the Bible is true.* The majority find it an interesting collection of ancient legends and stories, but they don't believe it. So if you say, "the Bible says," only one out of three Americans is even ready to listen.

As we discussed earlier, the prevailing world-view denies the existence of absolute truth. The existential, not the historical, conditions the American view of life. So when the Christian message, which is essentially historical and propositional, is proclaimed, modern listeners hear what they interpret as simply one person's preference—another autonomous human's choice of lifestyle or belief. *If Christianity works for you, that's great. But it doesn't mean much for me.* Thus, even sharing your personal testimony may not necessarily be convicting.

I discovered this recently when talking with an acquaintance who happens to be a prominent journalist. He had told me he was intrigued by my commitment to Jesus Christ, and we met for dinner to discuss it further.

---

*"In 1963 . . . 65 percent of Americans said they believed in the absolute truth of all words in the Bible. Within 15 years, by 1978, the proportion of the population holding this belief had declined to 38 percent. The current figure of 32 percent represents a new low in literal belief in the Bible" (*PRRC Emerging Trends* [January 1992]: 1). The same thing has happened in England. The proportion of people who believe in a personal God has declined from 36 percent in 1981 to 31 percent today. Those who believe that Jesus Christ was the Son of God has fallen from 52 percent in 1981 to 48 percent today (*International Christian Digest* [July/August 1992]).

I was armed with all sorts of arguments, ready to tell him about my own experiences. But when I started talking about what Christ had done in my life, he cut me off.

*It's wonderful that you've found peace and fulfillment through Jesus,* he said in effect, *but I don't believe in Jesus.* He told me he had friends in the New Age movement who had found spirituality too; it had worked for them as well as Christ had "worked" for me.

So I shifted gears and began to talk about eternal life. This man had had some health problems in the past; surely he had done some thinking about his own mortality.

Again he cut me off. Death was simply the end, he said. When we die we are just like a tree or an animal: we return to the dust. No such thing as an afterlife.

I talked about the Bible. He put his hand up, palm outward. "All legends," he said firmly.

What could I say? He didn't care about God's plan for his life, getting into heaven, or what the Bible said.

Perhaps it's when we are caught short—when our canned answers don't work—that God uses us most effectively. For even as I was fumbling with my fork and my facts, an idea popped into my head.

"Have you seen Woody Allen's *Crimes and Misdemeanors?*" I asked.

He had, and we talked about it for a few minutes. Then, catching him off guard, I asked, "Are you Judah Rosenthal?"*

He laughed, but it was a nervous laugh.

"You may think this life is all there is," I said, "but if so, then there is still an issue at hand—how do you live with yourself while you're here? I know you have a conscience. So how do you deal with that when you know you do wrong?"

He picked at his food and told me that very issue gave him a lot of problems. Then somehow we moved into a discussion of Leo Tolstoy's novel, *War and Peace,* in which Pierre, the central character, cries out, *Why is it that I know what is right but do what is wrong?* That in turn led us to C. S. Lewis's concept of the natural law ingrained in all of us, and then to the central point of Romans 1: That we all are imbued with a conscience, run from it though we might, and that conscience itself points to questions which can only be answered outside of ourselves.

---

*See chapter 14.

I don't know what's going to happen to this friend. My hunch is he's going to come to Christ, because I believe the Holy Spirit is hounding him. But I know one thing: without Woody Allen, Leo Tolstoy, and C. S. Lewis, I wouldn't have found a common ground and language with which to discuss the spiritual realm.

What does this tell us? Well, first of all, it does not mean that we must all run out to the video store and rent *Crimes and Misdemeanors* or slog through *War and Peace.* But it does mean that to evangelize today we must address the human condition at its point of felt need—conscience, guilt, dealing with others, finding a purpose for staying alive. Talking about the abundant life or life everlasting or Bible promises often just won't do it.

Like the young man referred to in chapter 14. When he stood up in a Donahue show and said "Jesus is the answer," he drew blank stares and frowns from the audience; not only because religious zealotry is scorned, but because the audience didn't even know there was a question to be answered!

The knowledge of God is in each of us, and through the power of the Holy Spirit the Word of God can penetrate even the toughest human heart.[5] So we are not suggesting that we cannot present the truth directly and frontally to our listeners. Nor do we suggest that we should not share our testimony; of course we should, and God will often use it to convict others.

But on a purely rational level, apart from the benediction of the Holy Spirit, the secular person's existential mind-set precludes his or her understanding us. As George Hunter, dean at Asbury Seminary, has argued, we are in much the same situation as the first-century church, needing to educate in order to witness.*

---

*George Hunter III, dean of Asbury Seminary's School of World Mission and Evangelism, maintains that we have four things in common with the early church and thus should take a lesson from them: (1) Because they faced a population with no knowledge of the gospel, early Christians had to inform people of Christ's claims and His offers. They had to educate them before they could witness to them. (2) Because the early Christians faced a hostile populace and persecution from the state, they had to influence people to have a positive attitude toward the Christian movement. (3) Because they confronted an empire with several entrenched religions, early Christians had to convince people of the truth of Christianity, or at least of its plausibility. (4) Since entry into the faith involves an act of the will, Christians had to invite people to make a clear choice and adopt this faith, join a community of believers, and follow Jesus as Lord (George G. Hunter III, "Can the West Be Won?" *Christianity Today,* 16 December 1991, 43–46).

So we must be familiar enough with the prevailing world-view to look for points of contact and discern points of disagreement.

It is no different than if you or I were talking with a Hindu, for example, about issues of life and religion. We wouldn't assume that he or she was coming from a Judeo-Christian perspective. We would start from the Hindu presuppositions about the world, probe their world-view, find the points of contact and concern, and then begin to challenge or question those presuppositions. Only then could we begin to present our case effectively.

In a post-Christian age we must approach our culture in the same way. This is a tremendous challenge to the church, and to evangelicals in particular. Almost all of our evangelistic messages and methods were developed in the 1940s and 1950s, some in the 1960s, at a time when Christian presuppositions were commonly understood, when two-thirds of the people believed the Bible. Today all that has changed. So we must examine and perhaps drastically overhaul our tracts and techniques to engage the modern mind.*

For our handy prepackaged God-talk won't do. Before we tell them what the Bible says, we may have to tell them why they should believe the Bible (there is a great case to be made). And we need a Christian apologetic that doesn't just make the case for *us;* it must touch chords within our unbelieving friends and neighbors and begin to alter their view of reality.

***And this leads to a second point. To reach the modern world demands that we be both sensitive and creative.***

Odessa Moore, a Prison Fellowship volunteer and member of the Faithful Central Missionary Baptist Church in South Central Los Angeles, is a good example.

Eight years ago when Odessa was visiting the juvenile jail, she met a teenager waiting to be tried as an adult for first-degree murder. His eyes chilled her, they were so full of hate and anger.

"I don't care about anything," he said defiantly. "I don't feel no shame."

A familiar story emerged as they talked—father a drug user, mother an alcoholic, both parents abusive. They would beat the boy

---

*The Christian Businessmen's Committee (CBMC), in conjunction with NavPress, has put together just such materials, seeking to communicate the gospel in ways accessible to people today. See Jim Peterson's books, *Living Proof* (Colorado Springs: NavPress, 1989) and *Church Without Walls* (Colorado Springs: NavPress, 1992), and the accompanying video teaching series.

and tie him up in the closet for hours. All of his life he had been told he was nothing. No one cared about him. But that was all right, he said.

"I don't care about nobody."

"There is Someone who loves you," Odessa told him.

"No way," he responded. "Nobody."

"You're in here for murder, right?" asked Odessa.

"Yes, and I'd do it again," he said.

"How would you like it if Someone came in here tonight and said, 'I know you committed the murder, and they are going to give you the death penalty, but I am going to take your place for you.' How would you like that?"

For the first time the boy showed a spark of life. "Are you kidding? That would be great!"

Odessa went on to tell him about Jesus, the Prisoner who did take his place, who had already paid the price for his wrongdoing. Using word pictures the young man could understand— he had obviously never heard anything about the gospel—she walked him through the steps to a growing understanding of sin, repentance, forgiveness, and freedom—true freedom—in Christ.

By the end of the evening the stone-cold teenager had melted, weeping tears of repentance. He committed his life to Christ that night.

I have experienced the same thing on hundreds of occasions. Christianity seems remote to prisoners, but when I talk about the historic Jesus who was executed for a crime He didn't commit, on a cross between two thieves, their eyes light up. This they can relate to.

Many churches are doing this same kind of "translating" in their communities. Perhaps the best-known example is Willow Creek Community Church in South Barrington, Illinois.

In the summer of 1975 Youth Pastor Bill Hybels and a couple of his buddies conducted a door-to-door survey throughout the west Chicago suburbs. They simply asked, "Do you regularly attend a local church?" If the answer was yes, they thanked the respondent and moved on. If it was no, they asked the follow-up, "Why not?"

They got an earful. But essentially there were four reasons people had no interest in attending church:

1. Churches are always asking for money.
2. Church services are boring and predictable.
3. Church is irrelevant to real life.
4. Pastors make people feel ignorant and guilty.

Targeting the huge population of unchurched baby boomers in those Chicago suburbs, Hybels and his colleagues began a church that would, while faithfully preaching the gospel, address these four objections. They also listened carefully to the people who came, discovering their expressed needs and discerning the unexpressed, and they designed a church experience that would feel comfortable but also intrigue and challenge: "a safe place to hear a dangerous message!" The new local body, meeting in a movie theater, began to grow.

By the early 1990s, fourteen thousand a week were gathering at Willow Creek. But not just on Sunday morning. The facilities hum with activities all week, from the weekend "seeker services" on Saturday evenings and Sunday mornings, designed to draw in unbelievers, to the midweek worship services on Wednesday and Thursday evenings, designed for believers to grow deeper in their faith.

A good illustration of how the process works is Lee Strobel, once legal affairs editor of the *Chicago Tribune*. Confirmed in a mainline church as a child, Lee felt no need for God as an adult. When questioned about spiritual things, he would simply respond that he was an atheist.

Then in 1978 Lee's wife, Leslie, became friends with a neighbor who was a Christian. Gradually the neighbor began to talk about Christ and invited Leslie to come to Willow Creek. There Leslie was comfortable but also confronted, and committed her life to Christ in November 1979.

*Oh, isn't that cute,* thought Lee when his wife told him about her conversion. "If that's good for you, if you want to believe it, that's okay," he told her. "I'm certainly not going to get involved with it."

But Leslie kept urging Lee to come to Willow Creek. "The music's great," she said. "You'll like the music. Come on and check it out."

In January 1980 Lee finally gave in. The music *was* great, he discovered. And the pastor, who was his own age, used an overhead projector during his message. He talked about grace. Lee had heard about grace back in the dim religious mist of his childhood, but this seemed new. *What a fascinating concept!* he thought. *What if it's true? But of course it's not . . .*

So Lee, with his legal and journalistic background, began to investigate. For almost two years he researched other religions, read the Bible, while continuing to attend Willow Creek. Then, on November 8, 1981, Lee Strobel realized he had run out of questions. He surrendered to Christ, and he is now one of the teaching pastors in the church.

Willow Creek isn't for everyone, nor does it claim to be. And, like all churches, it has its warts. It's been accused by some of bending the gospel and being too market-oriented. But Willow Creek strives to keep its purpose clear.

"Willow Creek is evangelical," says Mark Mittelberg, director of evangelism. "We believe in the fundamentals of Scripture . . . and we don't want to mess with them at all. But we want to translate them for the society we live in."

And what that means, adds Strobel, "is that we're not using entertainment to pacify people, helping them to have fun. We are taking contemporary art forms—music, drama, dance, multimedia, video—to communicate Christ. We take the historic Christian message and translate it into language twentieth-century Americans understand; in that way, a suburbanite like me, a cynic, can come in and be hit right in the heart with the gospel."[6]

Willow Creek is only one of hundreds of churches consciously endeavoring to evangelize in ways modern men and women can understand. But its fervor for evangelism doesn't blind this local body to its proper priorities, as its objectives clearly show:

1. To exalt God in worship.

2. To evangelize, bringing people to a saving knowledge of Christ, with a church attitude that is outward oriented rather than a holy huddle mentality.

3. To edify, taking new Christians and maturing them in the faith.

4. To extend, reaching out into the community to meet physical, spiritual, relational, and emotional needs.

*Right priorities lead us directly to the third point about evangelism, which is that evangelism flows out of worship.* When evangelism is based on the biblical model, it naturally follows worship and fellowship; it is a byproduct of spiritual life flowing from a healthy body being nourished by the Head. For this reason, the worship service itself should not be primarily evangelistic.

Too often Baptist churches (and others)—as a Baptist, I think I can fairly say this—treat the worship service as the church's weekly evangelistic outreach.* As a result the members never really get a sense of worship. When the whole service is geared to an altar call—when that becomes the emotional high point, and when the pressure is put on and the invitation hymn is played endlessly—the purpose of the worship service can be distorted.

In a healthy church body, worship leads to evangelism, which leads to discipleship.

*Which leads to the fourth point. Evangelism should always be designed to bring the convert into the local church, where the work of discipleship can be done.* Evangelicals fall short on this score. We are forever organizing highly publicized campaigns to win people to Christ. We pick up some catchy name, "mission this or mission that," raise money on the promise of a new Great Awakening, barrage some area or group, count the hands raised—which, particularly overseas, may be nothing more than a polite response—and then boast about the number of conversions.

Although well conceived in structure, many evangelical efforts become a kind of hit-and-run extravaganza. And when they do, they are often little more than a superhype fund raiser for some enterprise or an ego trip for the charismatic leader.

I've been in this kind of meeting. For every hundred decisions that the promoter trumpets, two individuals may show up for the follow-up. In fact, I've become so dismayed with this kind of scalphunting that I will not give an invitation unless I know in

---

*Willow Creek has dealt with this issue in a novel way: The Saturday night and Sunday morning services are expressly designed for non-Christians, since that is when they are most likely to visit. As such, though they are respectful and reverent, they are short on what we would call true worship. But how much can a seeker truly worship God anyway? So these services are designed to create an environment in which the nonbeliever will get some of his or her questions answered. Then, on Wednesday and Thursday nights they hold worship services, designed for Christians to come together to exalt their King. In fact, these services are called "New Community." As seekers become believers, they are incorporated into this discipleship/worship track of the church.

advance there is a follow-up mechanism in place. It is a gross dis-
service to unsaved people—as well as an impediment to the cause
of Christ—to get them excited, lead them into some emotional response, and then dump them on the doorstep. Unless evangelism
brings converts into the visible body of Christ, it is like assisting
at a baby's birth and then leaving the infant out in the cold alone.

When evangelistic efforts are not integrated with the local
church, they run the grave danger of being out of the will of God.
For the Great Commission by definition involves baptism and disciple making, and this can only be done in the context of a local
confessing congregation. So while individuals certainly—and
rightly—introduce people to Christ, or people come to Him alone
in a prison cell or in areas where the church is banned, the normative practice has to be to evangelize and then immediately bring
the new convert from the church universal into the fellowship and
discipline of the church particular.

This is why the fourth-century Patristic Fathers went out to proclaim the gospel in small groups, rather than as individuals. As
people responded to their message and became believers, the monks
could act as the church, baptize them, and get them started in community and discipleship.

J. C. Harris, who is pastor of a Baptist church as well as chaplain in a North Carolina prison, has taken pains to do the same. In
the prison he is constantly seeking to bring inmates to Christ. But
when a prisoner does make a profession of faith, J.C. counsels the
new convert about choosing and joining a local church in his hometown—even though he's still in prison.

"We don't baptize people," he says. "Baptism is an ordinance
of the church. We want our men baptized into the fellowship of a
church in their hometown, and then to become a long-distance part
of that particular congregation, just as if they were away in the Army
or something. Then, when they get out, they go back home and their
church families are waiting for them, ready to help with clothes,
food, a job—and accountability."

This focus on the local church has been one of the great hall-
marks of Billy Graham's crusades. They are always held at the request of local churches, are meticulously planned in cooperation
with those churches, and are designed so those who make decisions
at a crusade are then integrated into a local church where they can
be discipled and grow in Christian maturity.[7]

As one of Graham's biographers has put it:

> The fundamental objective of Graham's follow-up program was not merely to get a person to come forward and register a decision for Christ, but to help solidify that decision and insure that the individual became an integral part of a local congregation. There his Christian life would be nourished, and his spiritual gifts developed and employed. . . . Recognition must be paid to Graham's early discernment that the true object of evangelism, in the context of the Great Commission, is discipleship.[8]

Important words: *The true object of evangelism, in the context of the Great Commission, is discipleship.* And that discipleship takes place in the church particular. But the church congregation also needs to understand that its mission is not just to get people through the doors and onto membership rolls and call this evangelism.

**Which leads to our fifth point. Evangelism is to be directed to the non-Christian.** Sounds obvious, doesn't it? But surveys show that as much as 85 percent of church membership growth is made up of people who church-hop. Other surveys show that there has been no real growth in church membership in recent years; increase in some denominations is simply offset by decrease in others.*

We cannot compete with neighboring churches or scoop up the church shoppers and then boast about successful evangelism. Though evangelism will sometimes touch people within a local congregation who have never been truly regenerated, as a norm it should be reaching outside of the church community and bringing in the unsaved.

Churches across the country are doing this in thousands of creative ways. Consider just a few examples:

• The Whittier Area Baptist Fellowship in Southern California sponsors quarterly "Teddy Bear Parties," where three- and four-year-olds from the neighborhood are invited to bring their favorite

---

*Gallup says 81 percent of those who have changed are Protestant, and one out of four have changed faiths or denominations (23 percent). He writes: "A superficial view of the statistics on religious life in America would suggest that there is little change over the decades" (this, in spite of what he calls "constant denominational shifting") (*PRRC Emerging Trends* [May 1991]: 1).

stuffed bear to a church tea party. Their mothers come too and, in the process, learn about the church's children's programs and other ministries. Juice, cookies, and teddy bears have become, for a number of young families, a gateway into church fellowship.

• During the Christmas season each year, McLean Presbyterian Church, just outside of Washington, D.C., hosts evangelistic teas. These small gatherings of neighbors, hosted by a church member, offer morning coffee and Christmas goodies and a refreshing pause in the Christmas rush. The hostess asks everyone to share a special Christmas memory or family tradition; then a lay speaker from the church gives a short talk about the Christ whose arrival Christmas celebrates.

• At the St. Stephen's Church of God in Christ in San Diego, California, evangelistic teams called "block-busters" hit the streets of their drug-ridden inner-city neighborhood on Friday evenings. For the groups of young people loitering on the street corners smoking pot, drinking beer, and killing time, the block-busters are a diversion. They talk to the kids one-on-one and give them appropriately designed tracts they can read later.

But more important, a number of the block-busters are living tracts: They themselves have been delivered from drugs, hopelessness, and a life without Christ. Over the past fourteen years many young people have come to Christ, been discipled in the church, and gone back out to the streets to bring in their peers.

• Southeast Christian Church in Louisville, Kentucky, sponsors a yearly outreach to the community called the "Drug House Odyssey," a full-scale dramatic event. The production begins with a depiction of a drug deal. The hundreds of kids who attend see shadowy figures in the dark, then police cars screeching to the scene, officers with guns drawn; then a police helicopter hovers overhead, shining lights down onto the drug bust. The drama then moves to a courtroom scene and concludes in a penitentiary. Afterward, police officers are standing by to answer questions and pass out literature. So are church members and staff.

The church has been entrusted with the truth in an age that knows not truth. We've been entrusted with a message of hope in an age that puts its hope in temporal toys and transient things.

Believers of the first-century church, when challenged or told to cease proclaiming the Good News by the authorities of the day, burst out, "We cannot stop talking about what we have seen and heard."

In the same way, modern-day evangelism must exuberantly flow from our character as a worshiping, godly community; it must be done in the context of the corporate body; and it must articulate the gospel in language twentieth-century men and women can understand.

But as we said at the outset of this chapter, we will not always *proclaim* the gospel. Sometimes, in order to be heard, we must first be *seen*. We must *be* the gospel!

Lights shining out in the darkness, like candles that illuminate and warm and draw others toward the one true Light.

# 25

## *Being the Light*

Be of good comfort, Master Ridley, and play the man. We shall this day light such a candle, by God's grace, in England, as I trust shall never be put out.

*Bishop Hugh Latimer to Nicholas Ridley*
*as they were being burned at the stake in 1555*

SOME PEOPLE SAY CALIFORNIA IS A strange place. Actually it's no more peculiar than the rest of America, but it is a place of unlikely juxtapositions.

Take a trip to downtown Los Angeles. During the week it is a matrix of towering buildings and grand, paved canyons humming with people busily making money; on the weekends it is an empty glass-and-steel hive whose workers have buzzed home to the suburbs. Just a few blocks from the center of the hive, however, the neighborhoods start to change. Drive south, under the Santa Monica freeway, and you'll soon be in another world. Clusters of low-rise buildings scrawled with graffiti, razor-wire looped over parking lot fences, littered streets crowded with life.

And death. For this is where the gangs rule, and where drugs provide both an income and a way out. Many of the young men in this primarily Hispanic area are in prison, on drugs, or in the cemetery.

In the middle of it all stands a white building that winds its way around the corner of a horseshoe-shaped street off Grand Avenue. "VICTORY OUTREACH" reads the bold sign.

Victory Outreach is one of the many ministries that sprang from David Wilkerson's famous "cross and switchblade" work in New York in the late 1950s. One of the gang toughs converted through

**349**

Wilkerson's ministry was Sonny Arguinzoni, who later started a ministry to drug addicts: Victory Outreach, now active in hundreds of locations.

Robert Alverado, who pastors Victory Outreach in this South Central Los Angeles neighborhood, is typical of the men and women this ministry reaches; he himself is a former drug user with a rap sheet eleven pages long who came to Christ through Victory Outreach. At this branch, where about forty men live at any given time, an atmosphere of peace and purpose prevails—at odds with the chaos on the streets.

Since they come here as addicts, those helped by Victory Outreach must first go through a cold-turkey detoxification. During that period Christians hold their hands and pray them through the violent agony as the drugs exit their systems. Most come to Christ during this time. They then enter a nine-month rehabilitation period, tightly structured with Bible studies, worship, classes, work, and prayer. And after that comes a nine-month reentry program, during which they are trained in skills and deeper Christian discipleship, equipping them to reenter society as whole, contributing individuals.

Photos on the walls of an upstairs conference room tell the story. Smiling shots of Sylvia and Jose, for example. She was a member of the Playboys, and he was part of the inner circle of one of Los Angeles's largest gangs, the Eighteenth Street Gang, which has about six thousand members. Then they met Christ, dried out, were discipled, got married, and now they run the Victory Outreach women's home several blocks away.

Living photos walk the halls. One is Lupe. He is thirty-seven but looks twenty years older, with gray in his short-cropped hair. Tattoos cover his body; a tear is tattooed at the corner of his left eye.

"I have been a drug addict since I was thirteen," he says. "My mom was a drug addict. My uncles overdosed on heroin. My brothers are in prison. I have been in prison. I have been in gangs all my life. I thought that was where the love was. I was trapped. I couldn't get out. I knew I would die with a needle in my arm.

"Some brothers here came to me. I was living in the street in downtown L.A., pushing a shopping cart. These brothers had been addicts. They told me, 'Come home now. We got a place for you.' I thought that God was telling me, 'This is your last chance.'

"But I stayed on the street. Then I burned some drug connections. They were looking for me. I was running like a dog, running like a chicken. No way out. I locked myself in a motel bathroom for two days. They were waiting outside for me. I was scared. I realized I didn't want to die.

"'God,' I prayed, 'if You are real, give me a way out. I will serve You. I will give You my whole life. Everything.'

"The next thing I knew, there was like a bright light. It directed me out of the motel. The people looking for me didn't even see me come out. I came out the back and came to Victory Outreach. I know His presence is real. I kicked heroin. I am serving Him. He has shown me the good things in life. I have already seen the bad."[1]

After you bid farewell to Lupe, you spot a group of men in a lunchroom, eating apples and laughing as they break from their morning work. Others are sweeping, cleaning, whistling.

Then you pass the chapel. Inside, a young man is lying prostrate in front of the cross. He is alone, praying out loud, interceding for a brother who is still out there, still on drugs, still in danger. "O Father," he cries, "You know His heart. Only You have the power to save him. Bring him to Yourself!"

As you leave you hear a voice singing. It is a young black man mopping the pavement at the entrance. He waves and smiles as you go past. The strains of "I once was lost, but now am found, was blind but now I see" float over you like a benediction.

Driving away from Victory Outreach, you are full of the hope of that hymn of joy. Then, changing gears, you look at your watch. You have some time before your next appointment. How about a break from the mean streets? How about a spin through Hollywood?

You careen down the Hollywood Freeway to Hollywood Boulevard. Soon you're at the corner of Hollywood and Vine, where celebrities star the sidewalks. It's seedier than it used to be, but it still marks the entry to that glittering pinnacle of all that our narcissistic, materialistic culture has to offer. This is the world of Rodeo Drive, the kleig lights of the television and movie studios, all those long white limousines snaking around the curved drive of the pink Beverly Hills Hotel. This is the world of "Entertainment Tonight," where everyone is fit, famous, and fabulous.

And here, on the corner, towering over the traffic, is a huge sign that serves as well as anything to define life in Hollywood: LIFE IS SHORT. PLAY HARD.

You gasp. It is only an ad for Reeboks, but you've just come from a neighborhood where people are dying every day because they have lived out the logical consequence of that mind-set.

*Life is short. Play hard.* For the inhabitants of Hollywood—or Chicago, or Washington, or your hometown—the drug of choice may not be heroin. It may not be a drug at all, just a world-view that says, *this life is all there is.* This view even has its own commercials: tanned young people windsurfing or playing volleyball in their bathing suits, then quaffing a lite beer or three: *Grab for the gusto.* The view even has its own bumper sticker: *Whoever dies with the most toys wins.*

In these two neighborhoods the choice is clear: Either we remain blinded by the bright lights of the world that mask a heart of darkness, or we choose the Light that dispels the darkness.

Darkness. Light. Jesus made some bold claims about these, although perhaps they have become so familiar that we have forgotten just how radical they are.

"I am the light of the world," he said to the Pharisees. "He who follows Me shall not walk in the darkness, but shall have the light of life."[2]

Light is one of the great metaphorical themes and theological realities running through Scripture. At the very beginning, at the outset of creation, God commanded, "Let there be light." And as the story closes in Revelation with an eternal beginning, we see a glorious city bathed in light where "there will be no more night. They will not need the light of a lamp or the light of the sun, for the Lord God will give them light."[3]

Christ was the Light who had been prophesied for centuries— the revelation of truth to nonbelievers. And in Matthew 5 He charged His disciples: "*You* are the light of the world."

Then He added: "A city on a hill cannot be hidden. Neither do people light a lamp and put it under a bowl. Instead they put it on its stand, and it gives light to everyone in the house. In the same way, let your light shine before men, that they may see your good deeds and praise your Father in heaven."[4]

His followers are, He said, by their very character, the light of the world. They are to do the same works He did—and, as we mentioned earlier, even greater ones—in order that God in heaven might be glorified.

The key thing about light is that its radiance can best be seen in the darkest places. It's difficult to see a candle flame in a brightly lit room, but strike even a single match in the darkness, and every eye will be drawn to it.

"You *are* the light," Jesus said. Not, "You need to become the light." We already are, by virtue of His presence within us. So as we come together, we form communities of light, like Victory Outreach. And from these communities, which the world cannot help but see, we then take the light to the needy and hurting places where the gospel flame is not already lit. That can be a mansion in the Hollywood hills or an inner-city crack house. And as we are faithful, wherever we go into the dark we bear the light of Christ's love.

Millions of Christians are doing just that. Consider a few examples.

### Shining Like Stars, Lighting Up the Skies

Annie Howard tools down Interstate 60 in her bright teal Honda, one hand on her appointment book, one hand on the steering wheel, one hand on the car phone . . . wait a minute, does Annie Howard have three hands?

Yes, she does. At least three, sometimes four or five. Anyone who spends any time with her knows she has more energy than ten people, and she expends it all in Christ's service. In 1991 she was awarded one of President Bush's "Thousand Points of Light" awards for her Prison Fellowship volunteer work in the Kentucky Correctional Institute for Women (KCIW). But back to the car . . .

As Annie turns down the narrow lane that leads toward the prison, she dials her home. "Bill," she says when her husband answers, "I'm turning into the prison now. We'll have inmate choir practice, then evening Bible study, then six of the volunteers will be coming home for dinner. There's a big salad in the refrigerator, a loaf of raisin nut bread on the counter, and a pot of stew on the stove. At 8:45, could you turn the burner on medium low? We should all get there by 8:52. Thanks, Honey!"

She's hanging up the phone as she pulls into the parking lot of Kentucky's state facility for women offenders, which houses about 340 inmates—and most of them know Annie Howard. She strides up to the gate (Annie is short, but people with much longer legs have to run to keep up with her), signs in, gets her badge—"volunteer #1"—and stands back as the long, rectangular electrified gate slides open.

As she hurries toward the chapel, Annie is a bouncing, bright spot in the prison drabness. Brilliant blue eyes, big blonde hair, and usually wearing pink or purple, bright teal or blue, with perhaps a giant polka dot bow in her hair, or rabbit earrings in her ears, or sparkly gold laces in her tennis shoes. Annie looks like a bright birthday package, and when the inmates see her, they open right up.

Along the way, she waves and calls to the inmates walking around the prison's central green. Women rush up to her. "I got a letter from my daughter!" one confides happily. Another drags on a cigarette nervously as she talks about her upcoming parole hearing. A third proudly tells Annie she has passed her high school equivalency exam.

In the chapel, Annie cheers the choir on as they practice their Sunday selections, gathers women in who arrive for the evening Bible study, listens and watches while her volunteers for the evening, Linda and Judy, teach a session on grace.

Linda Childress and Judy Daniel have been teaching at the women's prison for about a year. They attend different churches than Annie but have responded to her city-wide appeal to local congregations for people burdened for prison ministry. Now they help strengthen this church behind the walls.

So do their husbands. Tom Childress and Dick Daniel attend the study faithfully, and the quiet way they support and affirm their wives in ministry is a silent, powerful testimony to these women prisoners, the majority of whom have been abused, betrayed, or put down by men much of their lives.

Linda and Judy have both taught women's groups in their own churches. "I hate to say this," says Judy, "but the women here in prison are more excited to have us teach than our church members. They are so anxious to learn."

There is another difference between prison and the outside, though, adds Linda. "I have always known there is evil in the world, that there is a Satan," she says. "But in prison you can sense the presence of evil in an almost tangible way. You can feel the heaviness of the battle for people's souls . . . like a battle between darkness and light."

"I have seen the result of [Christian volunteers in the prison]," says Warden Betty Kassulke, who has served at KCIW since 1964. "It's been an extremely important process in an institution where . . . we were very concerned about satanic worship. We felt like there was a tremendous amount of evil out there; we were training our staff to recognize the symbols, the writing, the colors . . . there has been a whole change in attitude."

Much later, after the volunteers have gone home and Bill has gone to bed, after she has cleaned up the kitchen and fed the cat, Annie's creative adrenalin kicks in. After all, she has a volunteer training conference coming up this weekend, and there are still parts of the curriculum she wants to personalize for the people who have signed up. So as the moon rises and her neighborhood sleeps, Annie sits clattering away at her computer keys, turning biblical truths and her ideas and experiences into concepts the other volunteers can use.

Over the twelve years Annie has been a volunteer at KCIW, she has learned a lot from experience, mistakes, and study. She has prayed and wept and searched her Bible for the needs of particular women, and she has seen many come to know Christ while in prison. And she has multiplied herself by training and involving more than 150 volunteers from local churches.

"Every morning when I wake up, I go into my bathroom. That's kind of my special time with the Lord," she says. "I'm concentrating my thoughts, thinking about the day, praying as I shower. Then I look in the mirror and say, 'Lord, what are You going to do with me today?'

"The women in prison know I represent Jesus Christ," she continues. "His love works through me. So what they see is Christ's love in action, a whole lot more than words! I believe that even if I don't see it, at some point that love will make a difference in their lives.

"I know that I'm a vessel, that I'm weak," she adds. "But God has shown me that He could use me in spite of my weakness. The first time I went into prison, I read this verse in the *Good News* translation they were using in the chapel: 'You must shine among them like stars lighting up the sky, as you offer them the message of life.'[5]

"That Scripture continues to be my focus. We are that light in a dark world where there seems to be little hope . . . lighting up the skies with His hope."

The award Annie received from President Bush is a heavy medallion with a stylized candle on it. It's on a gold chain, designed to be worn around the recipient's neck. Not the sort of thing you'd wear to the grocery store, although a lovely, significant honor.

But Annie doesn't need to wear a big gold candle for people to see her light. They know she represents Jesus. They can see Him shining through her.

## *Doing the Light Thing*

While Annie Howard and her volunteers brighten a drab prison campus, Sherry Woods and her colleagues at the UNIQUE Learning Center in Washington, D.C., are penetrating the dark shadows of the inner city.

When Sherry Woods was a little girl, a kid from a blue-collar white family in Minneapolis, she attended an inner-city school where the majority of her classmates were Native Americans, African Americans, and Irish Americans. She loved the diversity of her school.

Sherry was a precocious kid; at the time her parents even thought she was a bit odd. Her hero was Martin Luther King. Each day when she came home from school she searched the newspapers for stories about the preacher from Atlanta, clipping and pasting them carefully in a large scrapbook. Her father, a bit of an Archie Bunker, would snort with annoyance.

Then came King's famous "I have a dream" speech. And when Sherry heard her hero passionately proclaim, "I have a dream that my four little children will one day live in a nation where they will not be judged by the color of their skin but by the content of their character. . . . I have a dream that . . . little black boys and black girls will be able to join hands with little white boys and white girls and join together as sisters and brothers," she thought to herself, *Of course. That's how God wants it to be.*[6]

Today, a grown-up Sherry has given her life to the call she sensed as a child: that God would have her demonstrate the reality of King's dream, and that she could help to bring justice, equality, and opportunity to children of the inner city. To do this, Sherry manages the UNIQUE (United Neighbors Involved in Quality Urban Experience) Learning Center, a ministry of the Third Street Church of God, a dynamic, three-hundred-member, primarily black church located in D.C.'s Shaw neighborhood.

It's a tough place. You can see the Capitol dome from the streets of Shaw, but the decisions of Congress don't seem to have much effect on the citizens of this neighborhood. They're just trying to survive the dangers of their everyday lives: drugs and shootings and hopelessness.

Drugs cost money and lives. But Third Street Church offers something the kids from the neighborhood can have for free. In the evening when the lights come on at Third Street, neighborhood kids are there, along with Christian volunteers. This is the one time during the week that these kids have an adult's full attention, says Sherry. It's also the only opportunity many of them have to see a healthy lifestyle consistently lived out.

On Tuesday evenings at seven o'clock the warm yellow lights shine out of the church's large multipurpose room, where you find thirty neighborhood kids matched up with thirty Christian tutors. The tutors come from Third Street and its sister church, the primarily white, diplomat-and-politician stocked National Presbyterian Church.*

Many of the "graduates" of the learning center are now in college. Like Tinisha, who "escaped" in more ways than one. When she was still part of the group of older high school kids that meets on Fridays, she was standing outside of her school one afternoon when two boys on motorbikes buzzed past and sprayed bullets from rapid-fire weapons into the group of kids on the curb. Tinisha was hit in the heart and lungs. The learning center kids and tutors prayed earnestly for her—and Tinisha lived. She's in college now.

Krushae, Tinisha's brother, is working on his master's degree at Howard University. Years ago he was a street-wise kid without much direction, but the tutoring program changed his life. Now Krushae is a tutor himself, helping at the center on weekends and working in the computer program in the summer. When Krushae talks to the little kids, they listen—whether about staying away from drugs and sex, living with integrity, or giving their lives to Christ. He's a positive role model for black kids who have been disappointed time and again by the likes of their city's former mayor, Marion Barry, imprisoned after he was busted for smoking crack, or sports hero Magic Johnson, whose dubious message of "safer" sex through condoms still left them in mortal danger.

---

*Third Street and National Presbyterian have worked hand in hand for years, discipling many who came to Christ during Billy Graham's Washington, D.C. Crusade in 1986, feeding homeless people breakfast every morning, and mentoring the youth of this risky neighborhood. The kids aren't the only ones who learn from the partnership; the tutors and both congregations have found that denominational differences as well as racial and cultural contrasts tend to melt away when people are shoulder to shoulder on the front lines of spiritual battle.

The Tuesday evening tutoring is just one component of a whole menu of opportunities for the neighborhood kids which, says Sherry, also teach the children they must give as well as receive. Several times a year they do service projects, and she includes them in the decision making. Gathered into groups by age, they are asked, "What would you like to do to help others?"[7]

At one of these idea sessions, a group of fifth and sixth grade boys said, "It's so cold outside now. Let's collect blankets for the homeless!"

As the idea grew and took shape, with Sherry moderating, the group eventually decided they would fix sack meals and gather blankets, then have them available at the church so people in need could come help themselves.

One kid in the circle, a boy named William, frowned at that. "Why should they have to come to us?" he asked. "We should go to them."

Some would say that William and his friends are so deprived that they shouldn't even have to think about helping others. The welfare mind-set that funds many in Shaw's community would have these residents believe they are dependent on handouts in order to survive. But people—even young ones—are helpless only if they are treated that way.

William and company pooled their resources, enlisted volunteers, and made dozens of ham-and-cheese sandwiches. Then, on a snowy Washington night, with a volunteer driving the van, the kids visited the grates and doorways where the homeless sleep.

Some of the girls were afraid to approach one very large, very dirty man huddled in a doorway. So one of the boys, Dominick, squared his shoulders and took the man a blanket and a sack dinner. "God bless you!" the man said, his smile showing his toothless gums.

The next night Sherry quizzed Dominick on what he had learned.

"Well," he said, "it's like this. Just like God loves us, and we know it because people showed us He does, well, the homeless people need to know that He loves them too. So we have to show them!"*

---

*Since this first contact, the kids have delivered food to the homeless every month. They've even developed relationships with some of the "regulars" they visit. At Christmas, they raised funds by selling African-American-theme Christmas cards in their neighborhood so that they were able to take not only sack dinners, including Christmas cookies they made themselves, but also socks, hats, scarves, and mittens.

## *Meals and Squeals*

Like the kids and tutors of Shaw, two women on the other side of the country have discovered that letting your light shine sometimes means miracles will happen. After all, if Jesus once multiplied loaves and fishes, there's no reason why He wouldn't do the same thing today with groceries and gasoline. At least that's what Beverly Barnwell and Jackie Russell have found.

Every Saturday morning, Beverly and Jackie deliver food to people in the needy neighborhoods around their church, the Faithful Central Missionary Baptist Church in South Central Los Angeles. Their ministry is just one of this community of light's dozens of outreaches, but it is distinct in that it has Beverly and Jackie.

Ask these two women about their work and their faces light up, they start laughing and crying and talking so fast they can barely breathe, telling all that God has done in providing for them and for those they help; they finish each other's sentences, nod as they talk, and in general make you feel exhilarated about just being part of the same body of Christ that they are.

Beverly and Jackie pick up food on Saturdays from a Christian organization, "the Spirit Mercy ship," that provides wholesale groceries for relief ministries. On a typical morning, Jackie will load her rickety old car with fifty bags of groceries, sticking parcels in every available corner. When she finishes, she slams the doors and the trunk shut, praying they will hold. Somehow they do.

San Pedro, where Jackie and Beverly pick up their groceries, is only nineteen miles from Jackie's destination, but she can't take the freeway when her car is fully loaded. It won't go faster than forty miles an hour, and the rear end fishtails like a drunken brontosaurus.

"I've had times when *I've* been out of work," says Jackie, "I don't have any money, and I leave for my delivery route with a quarter of a tank of gas in the car, deliver all the groceries, drive home, and realize that I still have a quarter of a tank of gas in my car! And I know people are praying for me."

Jackie and Beverly never know quite what they'll find when they arrive at the twenty or so different homes on their regular route. "We pray," says Beverly, "and we meet whatever needs we can."

As they drive up to the curb, tooting their horn, people will usually be waiting for them. At one place, which houses fifteen children and eight adults, everyone comes running out, helping to carry in the bags, hugging Jackie and Beverly excitedly. Even the two-year-old lugs in a loaf of bread. It's the highlight of their week.

"It's such a thrill just to see their faces light up. You know they have prayed for things to change. And when they see their needs met, see God on the move in our crazy cars, then they learn, bit by bit, how to trust Him. It gives them hope. They see the gospel in action."

If they can help it, the delivery ladies don't let it stop there, though. "I take real good notes on Sundays," says Beverly. "On the route, I'll end up preaching Pastor Ulmer's sermon four, maybe five times."

Beverly and Jackie's weekly deliveries have become a lifeline for needy families. They provide food, shoes, clothing, social services help, and encouragement—and at Christmas, even Christmas trees. But most of all, they demonstrate to those who feel hopeless and forgotten that the church has not forgotten.

"People aren't going to get real help unless we do it," says Jackie. "Government can't do it! It's time for the church to regain its rightful place. We've got to stop being so comfortable, and we've got to come out and help our brothers and sisters in need! The church has got to be the community that sees people like Jesus did when He was on earth—so they can see Him today."

### Candles on Winter Mornings

Since 1973, Christians across the country have also shone the spotlight of God's truth on one of the ugliest social ills in our country. Unlike hunger, however, abortion isn't perceived as a problem in our culture; it enjoys political prominence and legislative protection. All the more reason why believers like John Aker have had to faithfully stand for righteousness against the night.

John Aker simmers, the Holy Spirit bubbling within him. When you meet him, you sense that he keeps himself tightly reined—passion yoked with discipline. It is this that has made him such a strong pastor and leader.

John and his church, the First Evangelical Free Church of Rockford, Illinois, have been involved in a multitude of enthusiastic, creative ministries.* They have also been on the front lines of Rockford's

---

*At the time of this story, Rev. John Aker was pastor of the First Evangelical Free Church of Rockford, Ill.; he is now president of the Slavic Gospel Mission.

abortion debate, joining with area Catholic and Protestant churches to picket the Turner Clinic, where abortions are performed three days a week.

At daybreak every Friday morning volunteers from John's church carpool to the clinic, where they join the others marching around the facility, carrying candles, signs, and softly singing hymns or praying silently, until it is time to go off to work or school. The clinic itself used to be an elementary school, and the horrible irony is not lost on the protesters. This place where children once skipped and recited their lessons is now a place where babies are killed.

But John always tries to ensure that Christians in Rockford protest in a godly way. "We need to stand for what is right," he says, "but not in a negative, reactive way. We need to be positive and proactive."[8]

He understands the temptation to become angry. But, he asks, how will non-Christians ever believe that God loves unborn people when those who claim to serve Him are hateful to people who have already been born?

If ever there was a person it was easy to fear or hate, however, it was Fred, the security guard at the abortion clinic. Fred's face was scarred, the result of a high school chemistry explosion years earlier. He was also a heavy drinker, and the dissipation combined with his rough appearance and general ill will made him frightening to the children who came with their parents each Friday to march outside the clinic. His face would get all red sometimes, and he would yell words the younger children had never heard before. Words that made their mothers wince.

But as the weeks passed, some of the children began to lose their fear of Fred. For one thing, his language got better.

Perhaps because Pastor Aker had crossed the picket line one day and approached the guard. "Excuse me," he said mildly, "may I talk to you?" Fred nodded skeptically.

"My name is John," he said, "and I want you to know that though I'm on the other side, I want to be your friend. I'm not going to turn my back on you when I see you in the supermarket. But I need you to know that my mother is marching in this line, and I have two little girls out here with me. I would never talk the way you're talking in front of your mother. I'd like to ask you to watch your language and be careful, especially for the children."

"Humph," said Fred.

Soon the cool autumn mornings gave way to Rockford's winter prairie wind, fluttering the small white candles the children held in their mittened hands. On these cold mornings, some would bring thermoses of hot cocoa and boxes of doughnuts to share. Christmas was on its way.

By now the older children's fear of Fred had been replaced by pity. They had heard he had no family. "We need to get him a Christmas present!" they decided.

So they saved and pooled their allowances and accosted their parents for funds. Then one Friday morning, just before Christmas, several of the girls asked Fred for permission to cross the line. One was carrying a cup of hot cocoa, another a doughnut wrapped in a napkin. A third held a large box, wrapped in bright paper with red ribbon.

"Merry Christmas," they said. "This is for you."

Fred carefully set down the cocoa and doughnut and opened the package, handling the three gifts as if they were gold, frankincense, and myrrh. Inside was a thick wool sweater, cabled in rich colors, with a Marshall Field label.

"Thank you," he said huskily. "Thank you very much."

Following the Christmas holidays, the group kept up their peaceful, steady, pressure at the clinic, though they were often harassed by the clinic's owner and by angry bystanders. But John noticed that when he and the children were around, Fred watched his language.

One night as John was conducting the usual Tuesday evening elders' meeting at church, there was a knock at the conference room door.

"Fred from the clinic is here to see you, Pastor," a staff member said. "And he's been drinking."

"Tom, I'll probably need you the rest of the night," John said to his associate pastor, Tom Clinton.

Fred was waiting outside the front door of the church, his breath reeking of whiskey. John and Tom loaded him into John's car and drove to one of their favorite restaurants. Tom had a muffin and plenty of coffee. John had a Diet Coke. Fred devoured a gigantic platter of catfish.

By midnight, about four hours after he had first appeared at the church, the alcohol had run its course, and the three men had talked for hours about Christ's power to change lives, forgive sin, and give hope. Then, as John and Tom each held one of his large, calloused hands, Fred bowed his head and asked Christ to be his Savior.

Fred quit his job at the abortion clinic, and John and others continued to meet with him, encouraging him in the faith. The church welcomed him, and John lined up several businessmen from the church who were willing to offer Fred a job; all he needed to do was choose one. Fred started to work on his alcohol problem. John paid off some debts Fred had incurred, obligations that were holding him hostage to his former life, and things were looking good.

But everyday life doesn't always do a happy-ending fade-out. And most of us can attest to that keen twentieth-century ballpark wisdom, "It ain't over till it's over."

Fred's old employer, the clinic landlord, started coming around to visit, bringing a bottle with him. And gradually Fred slipped away—back into booze and back into his old job at the abortion clinic. John wanted to weep when he saw him there.

But there wasn't a statute of limitations on loving Fred. So John still called him, and Fred occasionally phoned John. Sometimes when John was out of town, Fred would even call his wife, Rose, to make sure that she and the kids were okay. And John and Fred still met for lunch at their favorite restaurant, where people marveled at the improbable sight of the abortion clinic guard and the pastor sharing a plate of catfish.

"I wish this was a great success story," says John. "But the success is that the relationship is intact. People need to see Jesus, God in us, enfleshed again. So with Fred, I've built a friendship, a bridge of kindness he can walk over. I'll meet him on it any time."

In a world full of shadows, it is sometimes difficult for us to believe we can really make a difference. Sometimes our little lights seem small indeed. Sometimes the darkness looks overwhelming. But throughout history the church has always shone as a community of light that cannot be quenched. In a thousand dim arenas of need around the world, *the light still shines in the darkness—and the darkness cannot extinguish it . . .*

# 26

## *Being the Salt*

We have filled everything you have—cities, tenements, forts, town, exchanges, yes! And camps, tribes, palace, senate, forum. All we have left you is the temple.

*Tertullian*

*I*N THE SAME SERMON ON THE MOUNT where Jesus used the light metaphor, He also said, "You are the salt of the earth," describing His disciples.[1] Since then, many have lumped these two images together to describe good works—such as "salt and light ministries." But salt and light are not projects we undertake; they are descriptions of the character of the people of God living in biblical faithfulness. We *are* light; we *are* salt.

We've already discussed what it means to be light. But what does it mean to be salt? Jesus clearly differentiated between the two. But how are they different?

For one thing, light is visible. Thus, wherever the people of God bear visible witness in a darkened world, this light is seen by all. It can't be hidden, and it glorifies God.

Salt is not so obvious. In fact, when used properly it isn't visible at all—at least not in the same sense.

In the ancient world salt was a vital staple, both as a preservative and as a seasoning.[2] The first function was particularly critical, since it was the only preservative available. Farmers would slaughter animals, carve the meat, and then rub raw mineral salt into it until the flesh was penetrated and the salt was dissolved. This prevented the meat from decaying.

When it came to seasoning with salt, the principle of penetration also applied. If it was to flavor the food, salt had to penetrate and be absorbed.

Just as meat exposed to the natural elements of air and sun will decay, so society exposed to the elements of the evil in this world will decay. For this reason, Christians are to be "rubbed" into culture, penetrating every aspect of life and preserving and seasoning the society in which we live. (But two words of caution: Often Christians are so busy building visible institutions—buildings and retreat centers and places for fellowship—that we are in danger of becoming pillars of salt. The object isn't for the world to see how glorious our institutions are; instead the world should feel our presence in its midst. And second, we must be careful not to lose our saltiness. To be a preservative, it is essential for salt to keep its quality and character intact.)[3]

The church as salt is not only a biblical mandate, it is also particularly applicable in our modern world. The 1980s certainly demonstrated that in most instances confrontation doesn't work; on virtually every issue where we've launched a frontal assault on the culture, we've lost. For, as we discussed earlier, we are dealing with a culture that has lost its fundamental Christian presuppositions, and the guardians of that culture—the gatekeepers of television, radio, newspaper, and other public forums—are for the most part Goodmanites, unsympathetic to a Christian perspective.[*]

Frequently we can't even get a hearing. Cal Thomas, the articulate Christian columnist, discovered this when he was scheduled to appear on a morning network show. During the preliminary interview, when it appeared that he might quote Scripture on the air, Thomas was politely told that would not be acceptable and was subsequently scrubbed from the show.

That's no exception. I've encountered the same reaction many times. Over and over in public debate we are told that religious issues are private matters. Those who dare mention their faith are mocked, or at the very least their motives and reliability are suspect.

Besides, frontal assaults only mobilize the opposition. Start an organized campaign against pornography, and before long the ACLU and the pornographers will marshal a better-funded defense.

---

[*]One study of 100 leading television and film producers found that only 6 percent attended church. In another survey of 240 leading U.S. journalists, 54 percent responded that they saw nothing wrong with adultery, 75 percent considered homosexuality an acceptable lifestyle, 86 percent seldom or never went to church or synagogue, and 90 percent believed that abortion was a woman's fundamental right (study done by Stanley Rothman, Linda Lichter, and Robert Lichter, *The Media Elite: America's New Powerbrokers* [Adler and Adler, 1986], quoted in David Aikman, "Press Is Missing the Scoop of the Century," *Christianity Today*, 4 March 1988, 12).

They've often bragged that they can tie that kind of legislation up in courts for an indefinite time—and they've done so.

Now this doesn't mean that there shouldn't be confrontation. There always is when the Word is proclaimed and lived in a lost world. And there are times when Christians need to courageously stand against evil and present a world-view informed by Judeo-Christian truth. Abortion clinic protests are one example; another is religious liberty litigation, where we must fight repressive laws; or instances when we have to prophetically critique immorality or debate ethics. But as a general strategy, we will be more effective when we penetrate behind the lines, influencing the culture from within—which, by the way, does not mean we lose our character. Salt is still salt.

How does an army fight behind enemy lines? It doesn't move its forces en masse; it can't. Rather, it infiltrates small units to disrupt the enemy's communication and attack strategic targets. And that's exactly what Christians must do in a post-Christian culture.

### From the Inside Out

There are thousands of ways we can infiltrate the camps of those who are hostile to Christian truth, thousands of ways we can bring a Christian perspective to the public arena. Sometimes that means infiltrating a command post by gaining a position of influence.

A young Christian communicator, for example, works as an assistant producer for a network news program. In some ways she is like a secret agent, slipping articulate Christians onto the show whenever possible. Another young person we know, a speechwriter for a cabinet officer, laces speeches with biblically informed values whenever possible.

Although people outside Washington deride it as a haven of power-crazed excess and godlessness, there are many believers salted away in the halls of Congress, in government agencies, even in the White House. Bright young Christian men and women influence lawmakers through staff positions on Capitol Hill; Christian attorneys in the Justice Department wrestle through the tough issues of drugs, crime, and pornography from godly perspectives; and key aides in the Department of Education influence educational policy. (So if you think Washington is bad now, just think how much further decayed it would be if the preserving influence of these people was not present!)

In fact, Christians have infiltrated the government arena in every state. One of our favorite examples comes from North Carolina.

In 1984, when North Carolina Governor James Martin asked Aaron Johnson to join his state government team, he said that he wanted this Secretary of Correction to be different from all the rest. Governor Martin got what he was looking for.

Aaron Johnson was the first black to be appointed to the position in North Carolina—and the only ordained minister in the nation to hold such a job. And from his first day in office, he made God's presence felt.

When he arrived in Raleigh in January 1985, Aaron Johnson walked into his large, gracious office, stared at the huge desk, the official insignia, the trappings of power, and dropped to his knees. *Lord,* he prayed, *here I am. Use me however You want to.* Then he got up and called in his chief legal adviser.

"Tell me," said Johnson, "how much power does a secretary of correction have?"

"As much as you want," responded his aide.

"I mean from a statutory standpoint, how much authority do I have?"

The adviser looked him in the eye. "Mr. Secretary," he said, "you can do what you want in these prisons."

"Well, then," responded Johnson, "I want to stop the cursing in them, taking the Lord's name in vain. The profanity in these places is horrible."

"Are you serious, Mr. Secretary?" the aide stammered.

"I am dead serious. I want the very first order I send out to be an anti-cursing ordinance. You find a way to do it."

The aide left, shaking his head. He returned a few hours later, dust from old law books covering his sleeves. "I found it, Mr. Secretary!" he said. "There's a statute against cursing in public—and we can use it to issue your order!"

And thus profanity was prohibited within the North Carolina prison system.

Soon after that, Aaron Johnson discovered that soft-core pornography magazines were being bought at state expense for inmates. He called in his legal counsel.

"How much authority do I have?" he asked.

By now the adviser was ready for anything. "What do you want to do?" he asked.

"I want to stop *Playboy* magazines from coming into the prisons," said Johnson. "Can I do that?"

"You're the secretary!" responded the aide.

And so, by official order, *Playboy* magazines were barred from North Carolina prisons.

Now this doesn't mean that never a foul word nor a lascivious thought exits the mouths or enters the minds of North Carolina inmates. But it does show that a Christian can be a direct, righteous influence on his or her environment.*

In Indiana during the 1980s, my colleague Dan Van Ness and I worked with a group of Christian legislators who did just that in the halls of legislative power.

It began in 1981 when we met with Indiana Governor Robert Orr, a simple courtesy call. During our time together the governor mentioned that he had proposed a $200 million prison construction program. He intended to show that Indiana was doing something about criminal justice issues—but I was appalled.

I told him that roughly half the offenders in his prison system were confined for nonviolent offenses. It would be a far better use of state funds, not to mention a more redemptive punishment, for these offenders to serve their time in nonprison retribution, rather than being warehoused among violent offenders.

That "chance" conversation with the governor led to the establishment of the Indiana Task Force, made up of state officeholders, judges, attorneys, a probation officer, insurance agents, an advertising executive, a homemaker, a real estate developer, a cabinetmaker, and a PF staff person. Key to the task force's development were several Christian policymakers, including Ed Simcox, Indiana's secretary of state; Les Duval, the chairman of the senate judiciary committee; Steve Stoughton, who served on the House Ways and Means Committee; and Bill Long, who chaired that same committee.

The task force decided to back the Community Corrections alternative sentencing programs which had just been passed, were woefully underfunded, and which most of the local criminal justice

---

*Johnson was also the first official to throw open the doors of all the prisons of his state and challenge Prison Fellowship to do ministry like it's never been done before. Through a program called "Just Common Sense," PF has trained four thousand Christian volunteers across North Carolina to carry the gospel into the state's ninety-four prisons, an intensive ministry that has resulted in a great spiritual revival in these prisons.

officials either didn't know or didn't care about. The task force argued for restitution and other alternatives, wrote articles, made speeches, and spent hours meeting with legislators, judges, and corrections officials. They visited prison after prison, then reported what they had seen to state and local officials. And they prayed—gathering regularly in Ed Simcox's capitol office.

In 1983 those prayers were answered when the state legislature enacted the first of what would be many reforms. And in 1985 the Indiana legislature approved a budget of $6 million for alternatives instead of new prisons (a far cry from that $200 million Governor Orr had originally cited).

Working inside the system, this team of concerned Christians had done the "impossible," saving their state tens of millions of dollars, raising public awareness on a key social issue, and bringing biblical justice to bear.

Wherever they work and live, Christians must provide the conscience and caring that makes a neighborhood a community. That can be true even in the most desperate of places. Like Austin, a neighborhood in inner-city Chicago.

Years ago, Austin was a solid, stable community. But after the 1960s riots the "white flight" began, as it did in urban centers across America. Property values plunged; Sunbeam Corporation, Shell Oil, and small businesses all moved out. So did the Christian churches.

Today Austin is a broken community, its streets controlled by the crack and cocaine generals of the local gangs, the Four-Corner Hustlers and the Vice Lords, who wear heavy gold necklaces and carry Uzi submachine guns under their leather jackets, drive Cadillacs with car phones, make a twenty-thousand-dollar exchange of drugs or cash in fifteen seconds, and kill each other with horrific regularity.

But not all of Austin is caught in this cycle. At the intersection of Central and Washington streets, a sprawling brick building houses the Rock of Our Salvation Church and Circle Urban Ministries, where blacks and whites live, work, and worship together, infiltrating and reclaiming Austin. They provide a health clinic, legal clinic, individual and family counseling, food distribution for the hungry, shelters for the homeless, low-rent housing, high school equivalency education, job training, and placement.

The effectiveness of Rock and Circle Urban Ministries is reflected in its leaders, Raleigh Washington, who is black, and Glen

Kehrein, who is white. Take a car tour of the neighborhood with them and you won't necessarily see Christians preaching on the street corners, but you can see the effects of this Christian community's presence salted throughout these decaying blocks.

Circle Urban has been buying up dozens of properties in the neighborhood—former crack dens, abandoned shells, vacant lots—and renovating them as low-rent housing for needy families and shelters for the homeless. A dirty, rundown tenement has become a clean apartment complex with bright flowerpots at the entrance.

Turn another corner and you see a dusty vacant lot with weeds sprouting everywhere. Glen Kehrein looks at it and sees a health clinic. Next door stands a deteriorated building with broken windows that will become housing for senior citizens and the handicapped.

This used to be called the "murder building," Glen tells you cheerfully. "They hauled bodies out of there all the time. This block was crack city. The drug trade was so heavy they had curbside service. But we just purchased this building and the empty lot, and we'll be getting this other one in a couple of months from the city."

Glen is a visionary, but his dreams come true; all around you see buildings reclaimed and lives rehabilitated through the ministries of Circle and the Rock church.

"Basically what we're doing here," says Glen, "is taking back the turf, block by block. We've carved out a target area of forty square blocks and we've claimed that turf. We can't buy it all. But we can buy enough so Christians can move in and by their presence preserve the rest of it. Already we can see folks waking up and saying, 'Hey, maybe there is some hope here.'"[4]

Radically different from Austin, but equally in need of infiltration is corporate America—particularly since scandals and excesses have ripped through Wall Street and corporate headquarters across the country.

Over the years I've known many able Christian businessmen and women, but none more committed than the man who led me to Christ in the summer of 1973.

For twenty years Tom Phillips was CEO of Raytheon, the large electronics firm best known in recent years for manufacturing the Patriot missile. One of the many ways Tom brought Christian influence into the marketplace was by creating an ethics office that reviewed company policies and offered guidance to managers and employees on a confidential, case-by-case basis. Employees were encouraged to consult the office about their own decisions, ask questions, and report any violations they witnessed. Since the ethics officer reported only to Tom, they were assured total confidentiality and no recrimination.

The standard was "absolute integrity," Tom said bluntly in a message to all employees. "Even if you think you are serving your company by bending the rules, let me be absolutely clear: Don't do it. Don't even think about doing it." Competitive pressures were great, he acknowledged, but more important than winning was playing by the rules. Tough rules: Submit honest bids, nothing inflated; charge honest hours to the right job; don't pad any figures for any purpose; never pay except for services performed; never give or receive a favor.

People need a moral code to live by, and they need to know it is being enforced. It's healthy—and biblical—to provide a check on natural human dispositions.

To what extent was this motivated by Tom's faith? "Virtue is a natural consequence of one's faith," he says, citing 2 Peter 1:5. He has always seen it as part of his witness to not only seek to be righteous but to encourage virtue in those around him.[5]

No large company—and Raytheon has seventy-six thousand employees—can avoid conflicts and ethical failures, but during Tom's tenure the company enjoyed a remarkably clean record, something observed even by outsiders. He was cited by *Time* magazine for his spiritually dynamic leadership, along with a list of other chief executives and businessmen known for their Christian commitment. "Flocks of businessmen are born-again Christians, and many run their companies according to biblical principles. Putting service to the Lord in first place gives them peace of mind but doesn't stop them from racking up some glorious earnings."[6]

Being salt is not just for corporate executives. Chris Thompson, a petite, energetic mother of four, has quietly salted her suburban neighborhood for years. She believes you've got to build relationships if you're going to change hearts. Since her family responsibilities keep her hopping most of the time, she focuses on relationships within her neighborhood and her children's school, Willow Spring Elementary in the Washington, D.C. suburb of Fairfax County.

Willow Spring has an uplifting motto—"If it is to be, it's up to me!"—and endeavors to teach kids everything from self-esteem to how to deal with death to stress and relaxation techniques. When Chris and her family moved to Fairfax County four years ago, she quickly learned that some of the school's teachings didn't square with her Judeo-Christian values. The school's "Family Life Education" curriculum, for example, teaches so-called value-neutral concepts to children from kindergarten through the twelfth grade.

Many local Christians had protested the curriculum when it was first introduced and continued to monitor classes, exercising their right to "opt out" their children from questionable courses. Chris and her husband, Pete, took part in the protest, but Chris decided to infiltrate as well. She did so by becoming "basically a servant" to the staff and building relationships with them.

Chris asked her daughter's first-grade teacher if she could help him in the classroom once a week. Though reluctant at first, he agreed, and Chris began spending every Thursday doing whatever odd jobs the teacher needed done, energetically and pleasantly.

As they talked from time to time, Chris took the opportunity to explain how she was trying to equip her children to live in a world where the lack of absolute values is actually destroying society and why self-esteem isn't dependent on how much we like ourselves, but on the fact that we are created in the image of God . . . and gradually, bit by bit, a friendship and trust developed. Soon the teacher was checking with Chris regarding any films he planned to show the class. She also noticed that he wasn't sticking to the value-free curriculum courses.[7]

One day a little boy brought a picture book with the David and Goliath story to the class for Show and Tell. Chris's little girl, Claire, raised her hand and asked the boy if the story was true. ("I just wanted to see if he knew," she told her mother later when she explained what had happened.) The teacher told the class that it was not a true story.

The next Thursday as she helped out in Claire's classroom, Chris mentioned to the teacher that she was teaching her children at home that the Bible was true and that it didn't seem appropriate for him to label a biblical account fictitious.

The next day, Claire's teacher pulled her aside. "It's really good that you tell your mom everything that happens," he told her. "And you're right. David and Goliath is a true story!"

No huge victory. But think what a difference it would make if thousands of Christians were salting our culture in similar ways.

## Shaking the Salt

Being salt demands discernment of our environment and imaginative, innovative, strategic infiltration and influence. Writers have been doing this for centuries, with the result that much of the classic literature of the past three hundred years contains Christian truth. The great Russian works of Dostoevsky, Tolstoy, and Pushkin, for example, with the Christian message salted in their pages in such a way that the Communists forgot to ban them, were the books that led Irina Ratushinskaya toward Christ.

In many ways, literature has the most lasting power to shape ideas. Great books are read, reread, passed around, discussed, debated, and then passed on to succeeding generations.

Today, many writers reveal in their work the incoherence, shattered logic, and relativistic chaos that mark a culture which has lost its understanding of concepts like sin, redemption, forgiveness, and grace. So when a writer who is a Christian beautifully crafts words and stories that spring from a world-view informed by truth—he or she is salting modern culture.

C. S. Lewis did this brilliantly, his cogent, tough-minded logic riding on wings of lucid prose. But Lewis was not only the Oxford don who crafted the compelling didactic arguments in his superb *Mere Christianity* (a book instrumental in my conversion and thousands of others). He also consciously chose more whimsical forms, such as *The Screwtape Letters,* described as "the wittiest piece of writing the twentieth century has yet produced to stimulate the ordinary man to godliness."[8] Or his children's stories, The Chronicles of Narnia, which present the entire history of redemption and have been read and reread and enjoyed by millions.*

Several years ago a British film company produced the Narnia stories, and I was surprised and delighted when I discovered them on video here—and faithful to the original stories. I gave them to my grandchildren, who have watched them over and over. Charlie took them to his fifth grade class, where they were shown to all the students. This is part of the public school system, mind you, where the children can't pray publicly or, in some schools, say "Merry Christmas" to one another. That's infiltration!

Other Christian writers who have salted modern letters in compelling ways are as varied as Flannery O'Connor, Madeleine

---

*Lewis's science fiction trilogy—*Out of the Silent Planet, Perelandra,* and *That Hideous Strength*—tells the same story for adults.

L'Engle, Walter Wangerin, Dorothy Sayers, Frederick Buechner, Annie Dillard, and Katherine Paterson.

Paterson, the daughter of missionaries, whose books for young people have won wide critical acclaim, including two National Book Awards for Children's Books and the Newbery Medal, says about the salting potential of literature:

> Really good books . . . pull together for us a world that is falling apart. They are the words that integrate us, stretch us, judge us, comfort and heal us. They are the words that mirror the Word of creation, bringing order out of chaos. . . . I believe we must try . . . to give our children these words. . . . We must try as best we are able to give our children words that will shape their minds so they can make those miraculous leaps of imagination that no sinless computer will ever be able to rival— those connections in science, in art, in the living of this life that will reveal the little truths. For it is these little truths that point to the awesome . . . Truth, which holds us together and makes us members one of another.[9]

Another writer who points to the truth is the irrepressible Walker Percy, whose 1981 essay, "A View of Abortion, with Something to Offend Everybody," is typical of his vivid style. No platitudinous Christianese here, no indulging in push-button rhetoric. And in case the reader didn't get the point didactically, Percy portrayed it in his masterful novel, *The Thanatos Syndrome,* which sketches the horrors of abortion and euthanasia on a canvas of America in the late 1990s.

The twentieth-century novelist, Percy said, "should be a nag . . . a proclaimer of banal atrocities. People get desensitized. . . . True legalized abortion—a million and a half fetuses flushed down the Disposal every year in this country—is yet another banal atrocity in a century where atrocities have become commonplace."[10]

Whether in fiction or skewering prose, Percy has captured the imaginations of secular readers in a way that, for all of the good we may do, Christians who write for Christians have not. Because he was a master at surrounding his barbs with elegant prose and superb stories, reviewers applauded Percy enthusiastically even as he was assaulting their most cherished opinions.

Another Christian seeking to salt popular culture has received criticism, however—not from the secular audience, but from her fellow believers.

Amy Grant enjoyed more than a decade as contemporary Christian music's sweetheart; with three gold albums and five platinum, she had written and performed more than a hundred Christian songs, including praise and worship hymns. Then she decided to craft her lyrics more subtly and reach a wider audience.

Suddenly Christian critics charged that overt Christianity was lacking in her new album, *Heart in Motion*, which was nominated for Grammy awards and made it to number one on both the pop and Christian charts. *Where is the Christian message?* they asked.

"If somebody tells me, 'You're trying to go secular,'" responded Grant, "I answer, 'Of course I am. That's the whole point.' If I'm going to impact my culture, I need to come in on a different stage."[11]*

In Washington, D.C., there is one cause that draws together Republicans and Democrats, black and white, women and men: the Washington Redskins. The town's citizens—with a few cranky exceptions that no one takes seriously—are crazed for their team, whose impressive record over the last decade is enough to make even a skeptic realize that the Redskins have something going for them.

And they do. Great players, an excellent coaching staff, and, most notably, a humble, "aw shucks" kind of head coach named Joe Gibbs. In the National Football League, where vulgar language is often more predominant than "God bless you," Joe Gibbs is clearly a real salting influence.

Over the past ten years Gibbs has led the Redskins to six playoff berths, four division titles, five National Football Conference championship appearances, four Super Bowl trips, and three world titles. His standard, like that of any Christian worth his salt, is one of excellence. But whether the Redskins win or lose, it's clear that he has exerted an underlying influence on a team whose Christian contingent seems to grow every year. Coach Gibbs has been a key figure in the spiritual development of many of his players, as well as a quiet witness among others in the NFL.

During the height of the 1991-92 season, a *Washington Post* reporter joined the weekly Bible study held at the home of Redskins wide receiver Ricky Sanders, and the resultant story described the

---

*Grant's songs deal with the issues of everyday life—the common frustrations and joys of human experience to which all can relate. And the album's final song, "Hope Set High," explicitly points to Christ.

weekly study as "a spiritual lifeline," and quoted the beginning of defensive tackle Tim Johnson's opening prayer.[12] The *Post* is not exactly known for its interest in Christian issues. So any time it reports a story about "the grace and mercy of God" and the fact that people are "dead in their sins apart from God," it's safe to say that there is a salty influence at work.

One key to Joe Gibbs's quiet witness for Christ is his humility. I've seen that firsthand.

On January 26, 1992, the Redskins won their explosive Super Bowl victory over the Buffalo Bills. Seventy-five thousand celebrating Washingtonians rallied on the mall between the Capitol and the Washington Monument to cheer their team and Coach Gibbs.

Four days later I called Joe. I was taking a group of ministry volunteers into Lorton, the District of Columbia prison located in the Virginia suburbs. "Are any of the Christian players still in town?" I asked. "It would be great if one of them could join us at the prison rally the next day and deliver a message to the inmates."

"Gee, Chuck," Joe responded characteristically, "I think most of the players are gone. But will I do?"

*Would he do?* Five hundred inmates, many of whom would never have come to an ordinary chapel service, poured into the creaky old gymnasium to hear him.

Five days after the Super Bowl, Gibbs could have opened any door in Washington, beginning with the White House. But here he was locked behind the steel doors of Lorton.

Cheers, whistles, and applause rocked the building when Joe Gibbs stood up to speak.

"A lot of people in the world would probably look at me and say: 'Man, if I could just coach in the Super Bowl, I'd be happy and fulfilled. . . .' But I'm here to tell you, it takes something else in your life besides money, position, football, power, and fame," he told the inmates. "The vacuum in each of our lives can only be filled through a personal relationship with our Lord and Savior Jesus Christ. Otherwise, I'm telling you, we'll spend the rest of our lives in a meaningless existence. I've seen it in football players' eyes, and I've seen it in men who are on their deathbed. There's nothing else that will fill that vacuum."

*Is this really a Christian being salt?* you may be thinking. *Sounds like a serving of good, old-fashioned evangelism.* And it is. But believers must win the right to be heard—and that means infiltration.

Few of us can be a Joe Gibbs, a Walker Percy, or an Amy Grant. Few of us will ever be CEO of a multi-billion-dollar company like Raytheon. Not all of us are called to live in the inner city like Glen Kehrein. And not too many of us are Aaron Johnsons, placed in a position of authority where we can issue an order and fifteen thousand employees and twenty thousand prisoners will have to obey us. But all of us can be—*must* be—salt wherever we find ourselves.

*Each of us must see ourselves as ministers of the gospel.* We don't simply attend church, consuming a religious product. Rather, our whole understanding of ourselves as members of the Body is directed toward being equipped to serve effectively in our vocation and our community—wherever God places us.

Many Christians have a bifurcated view of life: Faith is over here in this compartment, and the rest of life—work, family, leisure time, and everything else—is over there.

Like the young woman who stopped me in an airport recently, "Mr. Colson, I so admire the work that Prison Fellowship is doing. I'm a believer; I wish that I could be in full-time Christian service like you."

"What is it you do?" I asked.

"Well, I'm still in school," she said. "I'm finishing up my doctoral work in molecular biology. I had planned to teach full time. I love it. But lately I've realized I should do more for the Lord. My parents were missionaries. I'm thinking of going to Brazil as a missionary."

"You are in a tremendous position to be a missionary right where you are!" I said adamantly. "How many Christians are there who are molecular biologists? The university needs people like you!"

She looked relieved, even excited, as it sank in: She was a missionary right where she was.

There are thousands of Christians who suffer from this same kind of false understanding of the glory of vocation, and a parallel misunderstanding of how God places particular people in particular places in every arena to be salt and accomplish His preserving, flavoring purposes.

*Also, we must be willing to be uncomfortable.* Living in a post-Christian culture means that our Christian faith will be ridiculed and that we will be regarded as strange. That can be costly. But obedience often is. If we love the approval of Christ more than the approval of our peers, we'll be willing to be perceived as odd now and then!

*Finally, we must learn how to support and encourage one another.* If we are to be the agents behind enemy lines, then it is critical that we establish a network whereby Christians can pass information back and forth to one another. We can learn a lot about the world from *Time* and *Newsweek,* but we must also equip one another with Christian perspectives on critical issues. And we need to exchange information. Recently, for example, I came across a great speech by historian Paul Johnson on the historicity of Scripture. Since it would never appear in the *New York Times,* I had reprints made and sent to friends. (In the same vein, Os Guinness's Trinity Forum has produced a number of excellent monographs.)

What Christians must do in a post-Christian age can be likened to the way the underground operated in Europe during the Nazi occupation in World War II. The underground had its own elaborate network of signals, method of communication, maps, charts, and its own command structure. The parallel is a bit extreme, perhaps, but useful as Christians determine how they will network with one another in a culture hostile to the open expression of Christian truth.

In seventeenth-century London, as Reformation thinking about the church's influence in society was making itself felt in the city, someone painted a billboard with a picture, among others, of a tailor, a cook, a porter, a blacksmith, and a saddle-maker. The inscription read: "These tradesmen are preachers in the city of London, 1647."

Who are the preachers of America in the late twentieth century?

Each of us, as we infiltrate the arena in which God has placed us.

And we begin, like Aaron Johnson, by falling on our knees in our workplace, our kitchen, our classroom, our neighborhood and praying those simple words, "Lord, here I am. Use me however You want to."

# 27

## *The Fear of the Lord Is the Beginning*

He who admits no fear of God is really a post-Christian man;
for at the heart of Judaism and Christianity lies a holy dread.

*Russell Kirk*

*J*UST AS THERE ARE NO PERFECT CHRISTIANS this side of heaven, so there are no perfect churches. Even the early church in Jerusalem had its problems: Ananias and Sapphira's perjury, the dissension between Paul and Barnabas that broke up the very first missionary team; young Eutychus falling asleep during Paul's sermon and dropping out of a third-story window. Just like us, those early Christians didn't have it all together.

But they did have something we don't.

Even as we have cited many wonderful things happening in congregations across the United States and around the world, we cannot escape a deepening sense of dismay over the church in the West. For all too often the twentieth-century church takes its cues and defines its role by the ways of the world. It accommodates a consumer-oriented culture that wants, above all else, to feel good. And it focuses on action at the expense of character, on doing rather than being.

There is nothing wrong with seeking to meet people's needs or creating programs to do so. The church setting should be an environment where non-Christians feel welcome. The church should grow. But when programs and growth become the central focus, the church is in danger of profaning her first Love . . . in danger of trivializing the holy.

How do we trivialize the holy? How do we profane the Lord?

To "profane" means to take the holy and make it common. To treat the sacred with irreverence. To take the Lord's name in vain—which comes from the Latin *vanus,* or "empty." How many times do believers do just that? Oh, perhaps we don't swear; swearing is too obvious. Instead, we profane the Name subtly.

We forsake our assemblies. Or when we do gather, we offer empty words of devotion. We sing hymns devoid of meaning. Our thoughts wander during corporate prayer. We expend loose God-talk on others: "I'll pray for you," we say readily, almost glibly, but do we really pray for that person? Our jargon sounds spiritual but too often hides an empty heart. We treat God as some distant, remote abstraction.

"You shall not take the name of the Lord your God in vain," the Lord thundered from Mount Sinai. Have we forgotten?

We do so at our peril. For the church is not His whim; it is His love for eternity. It is not a little business venture He founded two thousand years ago and now, in retirement, watches indulgently. Most of all, it is not our enterprise.

No, the church is the Lord's, bought with His blood on the rough wood of the cross. It is the holy city that will shine with light for all eternity. The Bride of the coming King. The assembly of believers redeemed by His grace, yet whose every deed will be scrutinized by His judgment. The Body that is His holy presence now, pointing the way to the coming kingdom.

If that is so, then today, as individuals and as the corporate body of Christ, we need to know what our predecessors in less sophisticated times knew.

*We need to know the fear of the Lord*—the overwhelming, compelling awe and reverence of a holy God. The fear of the Lord is the beginning of wisdom: It provides the right perspective on God's sovereign rule over all creation; the sense of God's power and perfection that dwarfs mere men and women, that causes them to bow and worship and glory in His amazing grace.

That's the same holy terror that mesmerized Martin Luther. His fear of the Lord compelled him to obey God rather than men, no matter what the cost.

Jonathan Edwards knew that same fear. He knew it was God's holy hand alone that held wretched men and women from tumbling into the furious flames of hell.

Maximilian Kolbe knew the fear of the Lord. It fueled his obedience—even to the point of pouring out his life for another. His fear of God was greater than his fear of the tyrants of Auschwitz.

The believers of Eastern Europe knew the fear of the Lord. They chose Christ over their communist oppressors. (Now they must choose Christ over materialism or whatever else follows.)

And fear of the Lord was the secret of the early church. The very first Christians were Jews steeped in the Law demanding that they be holy because a holy God dwelt in their midst. They knew what the actual presence of almighty God among them meant.

Early on, when Ananias and Sapphira fell to the floor and died because they lied to God—trivializing the holy—Luke describes the result:

> And great fear came upon the whole church, and upon all who heard of these things. . . . And at the hands of the apostles many signs and wonders were taking place among the people; and they were all with one accord. . . . But none of the rest dared associate with them; however, the people held them in high esteem. And all the more believers in the Lord, multitudes of men and women, were constantly added to their number.[1]

Odd. Fear of the Lord would not rank particularly high on the list of modern church growth strategies. But in the early church, it birthed multitudes of believers.

> So the church throughout all Judea and Galilee and Samaria enjoyed peace, being built up; and, going on in the fear of the Lord and in the comfort of the Holy Spirit, it continued to increase.[2]

We can feel that awe pulsating through the pages of Acts. The sense of worship and reverence, the conviction that Christ had risen and would return, the vibrant, absolute joy of their faith. It was a faith based on a series of heart-stopping paradoxes: God become man. Life out of death. And intimate glorious worship of the Lord they loved with holy fear.

So filled were they with this awe that they could face a hostile world with holy abandon. Nothing else mattered, not even their lives.

For the church in the West to come alive, it needs to resolve its identity crisis, to stand on truth, to renew its vision . . . and, more than anything else, it needs to recover the fear of the Lord. Only that will give us the holy abandon that will cause us to be the church no matter what the culture around us says or does. The fear of the Lord is the beginning . . .

We have seen this holy fear—in a way we'll never forget—in the lives of two men. One was Bob McAlister, chief of staff for the governor of South Carolina. The other was a young man named Rusty Woomer.

And it was Rusty—not a celebrated pastor of a megacongregation, not a great theologian, but an unknown country boy—who taught us the truth that has undergirded the whole of this book about what the church must be.

For if the church at large had what Rusty Woomer had, we might see a movement that would shake the very foundations of the world today.

# 28

## *Coram Deo*

$\mathcal{T}$HE CHAIR IS OAK, WITH WIDE ARMRESTS, a slightly scooped, polished seat, and a high back with four horizontal slats. It is eighty years old. By 1990, 243 people had sat in it, their arms and legs restrained by leather straps, their heads shaved and smeared with gel to better conduct the two thousand volts of electricity that killed them.

Rusty Woomer was the 244th person to sit in South Carolina's electric chair.

Bob McAlister's chair in the South Carolina State House swiveled behind his massive mahogany desk. By 1990, Bob had sat in it for four years as Governor Carroll Campbell's director of communications and deputy chief of staff. He could lean back, prop his feet on the desk, and survey the rose damask draperies extending nearly the height of the sixteen-foot ceilings, the plush wingback chairs, the photographs of himself with the governor.

Outside the granite walls of Bob's corner office, tourists would exclaim over the gash left by one of General Sherman's cannonballs during his Civil War bombardment of the State House. But when Bob sat in his chair in 1990, jabbing a chewed blue pen in the air as he gave statements to the press on this issue or that, he wasn't really thinking about the media, the tourists, or even the governor down the hall.

Rarely an hour went by that he didn't think of Rusty Woomer, the man who had become his best friend. Yet before their lives had converged five years earlier, Rusty Woomer and Bob McAlister could not have been more different.

Born in 1954, Ronald Raymond Woomer grew up in a hillbilly town in West Virginia. His parents divorced when he was a toddler, then met by chance on the street four years later and decided to re-marry. Later they divorced again.

The oldest of five children, Rusty loved the mountains and woods around his family's shack. The small, blond boy chased squir-rels, ate ripe tomatoes warmed by the summer sun in his mother's garden, and watched hawks wheel in soaring circles in the sky.

But if Rusty felt free in the woods, at home his life was fettered by fear, hunger, and poverty. In later years he would describe his shame and embarrassment at having only a couple of shirts and pairs of pants to wear to school.

Even worse, he said, was his father's drinking: Alcohol released all the anger and despair simmering inside the man, and he took it out on his wife and children. When Rusty ran away from home to escape, his dad would find him and bring him back, bruised and afraid.

Still, there were good things in Rusty's life. Fishing with his mother was one of his greatest pleasures. He knew she loved him. And there was the little country church a few miles from their house. In the winter Rusty would sit in a worn pew and look out the win-dow at long icicles hanging like fragile daggers from the eaves. In-side, an ancient potbellied stove warmed the small structure. The preacher's voice was so soft, so kind, so different from his father's screaming rages. Here Rusty felt welcome, insulated from the cold world of his everyday life.

James Robert McAlister was born in 1949, the only child of par-ents who inhabited a comfortable, modest home on a comfortable, modest block in a suburban Greenville, South Carolina, neighbor-hood called the "Welcome Community." Bob's father worked in the textile industry and coached Little League on weekends; his mother baked cookies and cakes for PTA bake sales. Bob's teachers, both at school and Sunday school, gave the quick, insightful, blue-eyed boy constant affirmation.

Early on special summer days, Bob, his father, and his grand-father would pack up their tackle boxes and Mom's thick sand-wiches and pile into the green family Ford. Then Bob's father would drive the three generations of McAlisters off for a day at Red's Fishing Lake. Bob's childhood passed in a happy haze of summer fishing, spring Little League, and church every Sunday.

As Rusty Woomer grew older, his few happy days grew even fewer. School bored and frustrated him, as did anything that confined him or took away his freedom. The fights with his dad grew more violent. Rusty would sometimes sleep in gas station rest rooms or under bridges to avoid going home.

Drugs provided an escape. He had little trouble getting marijuana. Before long, he was shooting liquefied amphetamines into his veins. He hung around with older boys who had already quit school, and when he was in the ninth grade, Rusty quit as well. He also left home.

By the time he was sixteen, Rusty had lost his childhood cuteness. A lank-haired, pale kid with habitually shifting eyes, he looked like a juvenile delinquent. Which he was. He was sent to the Boys Forestry Camp in Welch, West Virginia. By age nineteen, he had graduated to a state prison, Huttonsville Correctional Center, for stealing fourteen cases of beer.

Rusty Woomer had lost his name and become a number.

In addition to fishing and baseball, by the time he entered high school Bob McAlister had developed a third all-American passion: broadcasting. At sixteen he was already a disc jockey at a radio station outside of Greenville. A year or two later he became a DJ at WQOK, the Big Q, 1440 on the radio dial of every teenager in his town. Bob rode around in the green Ford, which by now his father had given him. Everywhere he went, people knew his name.

Bob's voice rolled smoothly over the airwaves. His words made people smile or laugh, and sometimes his ideas even made them think. He wasn't changing history, spinning records at WQOK, but he had found something else. Radio gave him a sense of fulfillment, power, and influence.

By his senior year in college, Bob had moved to a Greenville television station, WFBC, as a newscaster and a reporter. Then, while covering a group of high school seniors taking a class trip to Washington, D.C., he met Strom Thurmond, South Carolina's legend in the Senate. Senator Thurmond offered Bob a job as speechwriter and assistant press secretary.

So in the spring of 1972, with President Richard Nixon at the height of his power and Strom Thurmond one of the major architects of the Southern strategy that had gotten Nixon elected, twenty-three-year-old Bob McAlister arrived in Washington. As he accelerated his Dodge Charger up the incline of Capitol Hill, he thought with awe, *I am now a part of Washington. This is reality.*

Bob's job kept him in the office from early in the morning until late at night. Senator Thurmond was an affable, though demanding, boss who took Bob with him to the White House, onto the floor of the Senate, and on trips back to South Carolina.

Eventually Bob returned to South Carolina, where he steadily built his career in broadcasting—and his bank book—through the balance of the 1970s. He married. But since he was wedded to his job more than his wife, the marriage crumbled.

His ambition sharpened. He met every goal he set for himself, and then some. White House briefings, invitations to the governor's mansion, influencing hundreds of thousands of people.

While Bob McAlister was flying high, Rusty Woomer was spinning deeper and deeper into despair. After serving three years in prison for the beer burglary episode, he spent his newfound freedom in a constant cycle of drugs, drink, and stealing to get money for more drugs and drink. He married, but after a brief high, his marriage crashed.

Rusty was convicted of statutory rape after he picked up a fifteen-year-old girl in a bar. That gave him a year in a Kentucky prison. After his release, he returned to West Virginia, where his drug use escalated. He mainlined a homemade mix of amphetamines, twitching along without sleep for five days at a time. To come down, he chugged whiskey, vodka, and beer. In between he popped Quaaludes, Valium, and PCP.

Though dimly aware that he was breaking his mother's heart, he didn't care.

He hung around with men ten and fifteen years older than himself, realizing even in his druggy haze that he was looking for a father figure. One who filled that role was an ex-con named Eugene Skaar, who owned a grocery store where Rusty shopped. Neighbors said Skaar would come and go at odd hours of the night. Friends said he was infatuated with guns. Police said he was a sexual offender. He also had been convicted for possessing and selling altered U.S. coins.

Rusty sometimes said Skaar was his father when he introduced him to acquaintances. He bragged about how well Skaar could hold his drugs and alcohol and was flattered when the man let him in on a plan that could net them both a bundle of cash. All Rusty had to do was go with Skaar to South Carolina and help him steal a coin collection.

Armed with guns, Quaaludes, Valium, whiskey, and marijuana, the two men arrived in the rural South Carolina town of Cottageville on February 22, 1979. Skaar found the coins; Rusty shot the coin collector, John Turner.

Next Skaar picked out a house at random some miles northeast. There, Rusty shot and killed the occupants, Arnie Richardson and Earldean Wright, and wounded Richardson's daughter. They stole more guns and money before moving on.

Still drinking and popping pills, the two continued toward the coast. They stopped at Pawleys Island, where they robbed a convenience store and kidnapped the two clerks, Della Louise Sellers and Wanda Summers. Taking the women to a remote wooded area, the two men raped them; then Rusty shot them. Della Louise Sellers died; Wanda Summers lived, but lost the lower half of her face to a shotgun blast.

Rusty and Skaar finished their night at a Myrtle Beach motel as the police closed in. Just after midnight, Skaar shot himself rather than surrender; police took a drugged-out Rusty into custody. The next day, shaking and still high, he confessed to the murders.

*Disgusting!* thought Bob McAlister when the details of the violent spree filled the news wires. The awful suffering of the innocent victims certainly put one's own problems into perspective. *Well, at least they've caught the guy.* Bob himself got a bit caught in the early 1980s. News-talk radio was expensive, and budget crunching began to crunch on him. When the management changed in his company, new executives began tearing down what Bob had built over the previous five years—firing people, cutting budgets, changing formats and programming.

Bob had married again, and his wife, Carol, could see that he was slowly being pulverized by the pressure.

"Look," Carol finally said one morning. "When you come home tonight, I want you to come home without a job. I would rather have a live unemployed husband than a dead one with a job."

Bob knew she was right. He went to his office and gave notice, all the time thinking, *This is the worst day of my life.*

He had just resigned from his position as news director and assistant general manager for the most prestigious radio station in South Carolina. His entire identity was gone. He had no idea who he was apart from a title and a position—and soon he discovered that many of the people in his social and professional circles didn't care who he was apart from all that either. He was shocked when "friends" who once couldn't do enough for him now didn't even return his phone calls.

At the time Bob didn't understand his situation in theological terms; that would come later. But he knew enough to realize he was being broken.

"I came back to reality," he says. "The reality that no matter how meticulously you plan your life, no matter how diligently you pursue your goals, no matter how many hours you work, no matter how dedicated you are, the bottom line is you just don't have total control over your life."[1]

*When you do everything right and it turns out wrong, then what happens next?* Bob wondered. In desperation, he began to reach out to God.

Bob had no miraculous conversion, apart from the miracle of a proud man yielding himself to Jesus Christ. He began to read his Bible, began to pray, began to consciously seek to please God. Submitting his will to God's meant some big changes—the kingdom of heaven was a kingdom with very different values from the world of media and politics. His parents had "trained him up in the way he should go" during his happy childhood; now Bob was returning to those spiritual roots.

In January 1984, he and a friend started a public relations firm. It was a tough business. Yet Bob found that his old self-sufficiency had been replaced by a new dependence on God. He worked as hard as ever, striving for excellence, but his perspective had changed. Now he knew there was a lot more to life than public relations, political illusions, and personal advancement.

But if God took hold of Bob McAlister's heart in the marketplace, He broke it on a Columbia thoroughfare. Bull Street became Bob McAlister's Damascus Road.

It was a sweltering day in July 1984, and Bob was tooling along Bull Street's lanes at forty-five miles an hour in his gray Chrysler New Yorker when he noticed the traffic ahead diverting around some sort of obstacle.

It was a frail black man in a wheelchair, sweat running off him as he strained to roll his chair along the pavement at about half a mile an hour, right in the middle of traffic. Cars were passing him on the left and the right, drivers shouting at him to get out of the road.

*What's this guy doing?* Bob thought. *He's going to get killed. And he's going to make me late.*

Then Bob did something he had never done before. For the first time in his life, he stopped.

As Bob pulled over, the man wheeled toward his car. He was slight, glistening with perspiration, his clothes worn and reeking of sweat. His legs were thin, undeveloped, hanging uselessly like two bony sticks.

"Thank you for stoppin'," the man said with a grin. "I'm Odell."

"Odell, I'm Bob McAlister," Bob said, forcing himself to shake the dust-caked hand the man offered. "What are you doing in the middle of the highway? How can I help you?"

Odell explained that two friends of his, a mother and her thirty-year-old daughter, were ill. They lived in a shanty in one of the poorest parts of town; they had absolutely nothing and were too weak to get any food for themselves. So Odell was wheeling his way to a rescue mission he knew would wrap up some hot food for the women. Then he was going to take the meal back to his friends. Sort of a personal Meals on Wheels.

When Bob calculated Odell's proposed journey, he realized this man was talking about a seven-mile round trip.

"Odell, I'll take you to the mission," he said. "Let's get you in the car."

Bob helped the man into the passenger seat, pushing aside his briefcase as he lifted Odell's useless legs. Then, after wrestling the wheelchair into the trunk, Bob drove to the mission, got the food, then took it and Odell to the sick women's house.

Bob McAlister had written speeches about poverty, reported news stories about indigent families, given to charities. But he had never seen poverty up close. He had never smelled it.

*All of this is within a stone's throw of the luxury of the State House and historic downtown churches,* he thought. *How could I have been so near, yet so far away?*

And he had never met anyone like Odell. He had seen people give out of their excess; he had never seen anyone give like Odell. This frail old man was giving everything he had—two arms and a wheelchair—to help those whose need was greater.

Later, on his way home and for weeks to come, Bob couldn't get the question out of his mind: *When was the last time you gave everything you had to anybody?*

As he read his Bible, verses popped out at him in the apostle Paul's first letter to the Corinthians: "God has chosen the foolish things of the world to shame the wise, and the weak to shame the strong. God has chosen the base and the despised of the world. God has chosen the things that are not to shame the things that are, so that no man should boast before God."[2]

For days after meeting Odell, Bob felt paralyzed. Paralyzed with a burden for the man and his suffering, for the hungry, sick women, for the pain of poverty and need. Bob was seeing the heart of God's love for the unloved.

Soon after that, he signed on as a volunteer at Providence Home, a Christian shelter for the homeless. His advertising agency even did some free fund raising and publicity. Then one of the social workers at the mission called Bob with a request he never would have anticipated: could he go to visit a man on death row? The man, a Black Muslim named Wardell Patterson, needed a friend.

Bob had never set foot inside a prison, but he agreed to go.

As Bob entered death row the first time, he was terrified. It was located in the old Central Correctional Institution (CCI) near the river in downtown Columbia. Legend had it that General Sherman had quartered his horses there during the Civil War, and as Bob saw the long, dark row of stinking cells, he thought, *This is worse than a stable. You can't treat men worse than horses. Even if they are murderers, they're not monsters. They are still men.*

Bob visited Wardell for months, and their friendship grew. Soon other inmates began to ask if Bob could visit them, too.[3] Because he had known the corrections commissioner from his days as a reporter, Bob was able to make arrangements to get through the usual security barriers so he could regularly visit death row. Before long he was there every Friday night.

By now, Bob realized that he had found his peculiar calling. For it was on death row, among men convicted of the most heinous crimes, that for the first time in his life he felt wholly alive. God was using him, giving him the power to love these powerless, condemned men with the love of Christ.

In his new prison sphere, he soon met Ernie Pannal, Prison Fellowship's area director in South Carolina. And Ernie got both Bob and Carol involved in a weekly PF Bible study with some hundred inmates at nearby Kirkland Correctional Institution.

Through that Thursday evening group, Carol's Christianity caught fire. The faith of those imprisoned men seemed more real: an all-or-nothing choice rather than a social convention reserved for a proper Sunday morning pew.

"Without Odell," Bob says, "I don't know that we would have ever learned the heart of God for the suffering and the oppressed. I wonder if anything further would really have happened in our Christian lives."

One Friday night in October 1985 after Bob had visited a few of his "regulars" on the row, he was getting ready to leave the prison. It had been a long day, a long night, and Carol was waiting for him at home. Before he left, however, he stopped at one more cell.

By now Bob was accustomed to some horrible sights, but he had never seen anything like this. The inmate was sitting on the floor of his cell, looking like a pale, dirty shrimp. The concrete floor was strewn with papers, half-eaten sandwiches, toilet paper, old copies of *Playboy* and *Penthouse.* The cell stank. The man stank too, his long, dirty, blond hair and beard matted and greasy. His face was chalk-colored, like a rubber mask, like a dead person. And all over his cell, all over the man, crawled dozens of cockroaches. He didn't even move as they swarmed over his shoulders, his hair, his legs.

Bob had met this inmate and exchanged a few words with him. His name was Rusty Woomer.

Seeing the state he was in, Bob spoke to him—called his name. No response. It seemed like the man was trying to talk, but something wouldn't let him.

Bob was a Southern Baptist. He didn't often think in terms of demonic warfare or the physical presence of evil. But that night he knew he was facing it. Satan had a hold on this man.

So Bob called on the name of Jesus to cast out the evil and death in that cell. Then he said, "Rusty, just say the name, 'Jesus.' Call on Jesus."

Nothing happened for several minutes. Then the man's lips moved slowly. "Jesus," he whispered. "Jesus. Jesus!"

Bob gripped the bars of the cell so hard his hands hurt.

"Rusty," he called again. "Look around you, Son. Look at what you are living in!"

To his amazement the man slowly sat up straighter, his eyes actually focusing on the floor and walls of his cell. They widened as he saw the roaches.

"Your cell is filthy and so are you," Bob said gently. "The roaches have taken over, and you're spiritually a dead man, Son. Jesus can give you something better. Don't you want to pray to give your life to Him instead?"

Rusty nodded, his eyes glistening, then streaming with tears—the first tears he had wept in fifteen years—as his heart cracked open. He bowed his head like he remembered from his childhood.

"Jesus," Rusty prayed, "I've hurt a lot of people. Ain't no way that I deserve You to hear me. But I'm tired and I'm sick and I'm lonely. Please forgive me, Jesus, for everything I've done. I don't know much about You, but I'm willin' to learn, and I thank You for listenin' to me."[4]

As Bob left CCI that evening, he hurried through the night to his car, chased through the dark by a sense of terror he had never before experienced. Once again he prayed in the name of Jesus, and whatever the feeling was, it left him.

On Monday, Bob could wait no longer. Had Friday been a dream? Had he imagined Rusty Woomer's transformation, the sense of struggle not with flesh and blood, but with powers unseen? After work he drove to the prison and made his way to death row.

The guards let him in, good-naturedly joking, "We're gonna have to get you a cell of your own if you're going to spend so much time here."

Bob laughed with them, but once he was cleared to enter, he almost sprinted down the long row to Rusty's cell.

Once there he stopped short, breathing hard. He couldn't believe his eyes.

The walls were clean, bare, and glistening from the scrubbing they had received. The smell of disinfectant still hung in the air. The garbage was gone, the bed was made, and the roaches were history.

Rusty stood smiling and erect, enjoying his surprise.

"How do you like it?" he asked. "I spent all weekend cleaning out my cell 'cause I figured that's what Jesus wanted me to do."

"Rusty," said Bob, his heart swelling, "it may have taken you all weekend to clean your cell, but it took Jesus only an instant to clean your life."

And thus began a relationship that would last through Rusty Woomer's life on earth—and change Bob McAlister's life forever.

Rusty had no hesitation about accepting his own responsibility and accountability for his crimes. In fact, he was often tortured by the pain he had caused others. As he learned more about his faith, he knew that Christ's blood was sufficient to cleanse even the vilest sinner, but he could not undo the death and pain he had caused. He wrote letters to the families of his victims, asking their forgiveness—and was not surprised when he did not receive it.

Though he was only five years younger than Bob, Rusty called him "Paps." Carol was "Moms." Rusty loved to listen to Bob read the Scriptures out loud. In his concrete world, the fresh breezes of Psalm 104 sent his heart soaring.

> Bless the LORD, O my soul!
> O LORD my God, Thou art very great;
> Thou art clothed with splendor and majesty . . .
> He makes the clouds His chariot;
> He walks upon the wings of the wind;
> He makes the winds His messengers . . .
> He sends forth springs in the valleys . . .
> Beside them the birds of the heavens dwell;
> They lift up their voice among the branches. . . .
> O LORD, how many are Thy works!
> In wisdom Thou hast made them all;
> The earth is full of Thy possessions. . . .
> They all wait for Thee. . . .
> Let the glory of the LORD endure forever. . . .
> I will sing to the LORD as long as I live;
> I will sing praise to my God while I have my being.

He would lie on his narrow bed dreaming of the hawks circling in the skies of his childhood, thinking of the clouds, the wind, and the springs flowing through the West Virginia valleys. *If only I had known the Lord then,* he mused. *If only I could have lived to serve Him on the outside. If only I had not caused such hurt to innocent people.*

Seeing his agony, Bob could only take Rusty deeper and deeper into the Scriptures, assuring him of God's forgiveness and exhorting him to make peace the best he could with anyone he had not yet forgiven. Rusty thought about the man he had hated for so many years—and he asked God to enable him to forgive his father.

In 1986 Governor Carroll Campbell approached Bob about taking a position as one of his senior aides. Bob's company, Coulter-McAlister, Inc., was doing well, but Bob was ready again for the challenge of politics. He no longer had any illusions about how much the political world could really accomplish, but he wanted to help the governor. He took the job.

Governor Campbell knew about Bob's involvement on death row when he hired him. Still, with the political and public attention on crime, Bob was fearful that this aspect of his private life might someday hurt the governor politically.

When he brought it up one day, Governor Campbell assured him, "McAlister, if I couldn't understand that you're doing what you feel God wants you to do, then I don't deserve to be sitting in this chair." Not every politician would be so gracious, Bob knew.

Then in 1988, after George Bush's election, White House Chief of Staff John Sununu offered Bob a job. The president needed a top-notch speechwriter on his White House team. Was Bob interested?

Yes, he was. But when Bob and Carol prayed and talked about it, they couldn't imagine packing up and moving to Washington. The frenetic and costly lifestyle did not appeal to them at all, and their daughter Denise was in the midst of her senior year of high school. Also, it would mean leaving the men on death row.

Bob thought about Andy who had developed making birthday cards into an art form. Every year he sent Carol an elaborate birthday card, signed with Bob's name, because he was afraid Bob would forget. Or Elmo, who took rags and leftover material and made beautiful pillows, embroidering them with designs and names. The McAlisters had three of the pillows. Or Mad Dog Mullins, whose pet cockatiel rode contentedly on his shoulder—except when Bob came to death row. As soon as the guards cleared Bob onto the cellblock, the cockatiel would swoop for him and perch on his shoulder, cocking its head this way and that while Bob talked with the inmates. With his cotton pinstriped shirts, khaki pants, conservative striped ties, and the elaborately feathered bird draped next to his head, Bob looked like a cross between a deranged Republican and a Las Vegas showgirl.

Then there was Sly, who had made Carol a wonderful heart-shaped jewelry box out of cardboard and felt paper. Or Ron, a severely retarded man who had taught himself to draw beautiful pictures. Or Fred, the mature Christian to whom Bob himself would occasionally go for advice.

He thought about Christmas the previous year, when the death-row inmates had learned in a worship service about a family in a town nearby who would have no Christmas—there were three little children and the father was out of work. The men had taken up a collection from the canned goods and clothing they received from home—the only time during the year they were allowed this luxury. Then they had packed the food and clothing into three paper bags and asked Bob and the other volunteers to take the supplies to this family and wish them a Merry Christmas on behalf of death row! Rusty had led the way in giving.

Rusty. Going to Washington would mean leaving Rusty. George Bush could find plenty of others to help him, but Rusty Woomer could not.

So in the end, Bob and Carol stayed in Columbia.

By early 1989, Rusty's appeals had run out. He had been on death row for ten years. In March, the U.S. Supreme Court let stand his conviction and death sentence, and his execution date was set for June 16.

Three days before the scheduled execution he was taken from his cell at CCI and moved to South Carolina's new Capital Punishment Facility, what everyone called the Death House.

Rusty's few possessions were put into storage. He was photographed and fingerprinted in a final check to make sure officials were executing the right man. He settled his funeral arrangements, asking to be buried next to his mother.

While the execution team ran through daily training drills and the electricians tested and retested the new wiring, Rusty spent those final days with Bob McAlister.

Bob asked if he could interview him on videotape. The weight of a man's perspective days before he was to die would be riveting, Bob hoped. "Maybe I can make this into something to show to kids in school. A warning," he said.

"What would you say to kids about drugs, Rusty?" asked Bob.

"What about drugs? Well, 'just say no' isn't enough—because the human side of us isn't strong enough to do that. We need the power of God that comes through Jesus to say no to evil and to do what is right. That's the bottom line. And we don't get very long in our lives to make sure about where we're gonna spend eternity."

"Rusty," Bob asked, "what will your thoughts be when they strap you in that chair?"

"The human side of me is scared to sit down and be electrocuted," Rusty said slowly. "They tell me I won't feel nothin'. But I've stuck my finger in the socket and it hurt plenty. So even if it hurts for a millionth of a second, that's frightening. But I'm gonna be holdin' Jesus' hand. Long as He's my partner, what more can I say?

"After all, there's no way I'm gonna lose. If they execute me, I'll be in heaven. If they don't, I'll never be the same. He's made it impossible for me not to praise and love Him and tell people about what He's done."

Rusty also used the video to gently chide a friend. "You are out on the streets," he told her. "But I am the one that's free. I'm behind bars, but I can lay down at night and sleep. You can't."

*How many people are like that?* Bob thought. *Free on the outside, but tossing on their beds, unable to sleep, prisoners of a guilty conscience.*

Though Rusty appealed for clemency to the governor, Carroll Campbell's office issued a statement saying simply that the governor would "not intervene in the workings of the judicial process."

Bob McAlister was in an agonizing position. After all, as the governor's director of communications, he was usually the one who presided over such press statements. In this particular instance, however, he had removed himself from the process. He had worked shoulder to shoulder with Carroll Campbell for years; he loved and respected the man. Now his friend and boss was refusing to exercise his power to spare the life of Bob's friend and "son" in prison.

But to Bob's relief, the South Carolina press handled his situation with grace and sensitivity. He had already taken two weeks of vacation leave to be with Rusty during his final days and to spare the governor any potential embarrassment. The media seemed to respect the integrity with which Bob was handling his position—and they seemed to respect the governor for respecting Bob.

On the night before the scheduled execution, Rusty received an unexpected visitor: South Carolina's top prison official, Corrections Commissioner Parker Evatt, a United Methodist firmly opposed to capital punishment but required by his job to uphold and enforce it.

"If I'm going to kill somebody, I've got to know who I'm killing," Evatt once told reporters bluntly. "I couldn't do this if I didn't meet him first."[5]

So Parker Evatt met with Rusty. The two men shared a final Communion service together, along with Bob McAlister, Zeb Osbourne, head of a local Christian prison ministry who had become one of Bob's closest friends, J. Michael Brown, the prison chaplain, and Frankie San, a Christian man who had devoted his entire life to ministry in the prison. The circle of men prayed together, swallowing grape juice portioned out in small plastic cups.

After the others left, Bob stayed on with Rusty. About two in the morning Rusty asked Bob to read the Bible. Bob opened to John 14 and began reading, "Let not your heart be troubled . . ."

By that point, Bob was totally broken. His friend would be dead in twenty-three hours. Then, about halfway through the chapter, he heard a snore. Then another.

Rusty! That rascal was sleeping! His peace and tranquility were so certain that he was able to go right to sleep for the last time. Bob tucked a blanket around him and whispered good night. Then, at three in the morning, he walked to his car and drove to a Denny's to have breakfast. The first real meal he'd had in days. Rusty's peace had given him peace.

The next morning, Bob and Rusty worked on what Rusty would say as his final statement:

> So many things are on my heart tonight that I cannot find the words for. But I want to say some things the best way I know how to some people. I have written letters to the families of my victims asking them for forgiveness. I understand if they can't forgive me. I have lived with my actions all of these years. I would die a hundred times over if it would put one breath of life back into them. I have prayed for the families over and over again and my last prayer before my death tonight will be for them. . . .
>
> I want to tell Governor Campbell that I love him too. I appreciate him and I am sorry that I put such a load on him by asking him to spare my life. No man should have to bear that kind of load.
>
> I want to thank all the prison officials from Mr. Evatt on down for their kindness to me and my family. You have made it easier.
>
> I want to tell everybody that I am fine. I have never known peace like I have known it in my final days on earth. I know some

people say I got jailhouse religion and they are right. I turned to Jesus in prison when I had no place else to turn. Words cannot express what He did for me but He knows and that's all that counts. . . .

But Rusty never had to make that particular statement. As he and Bob sat in the death cell thirteen hours before the execution, the phone rang. It was Rusty's attorney, Gaston Fairey. The Supreme Court had granted a stay of execution.

Rusty asked a few questions, then hung up the phone. Bob stared at him as Rusty stared back. Reprieve! Bob glanced at his gold watch, then jotted the time on Rusty's laboriously typed final statement.

"12:17 P.M., 6/16/89," Bob wrote. "Praise be to God!"

Later when he got home and fell exhausted into his bed, he took his watch off and noticed it had stopped. At 12:17 P.M. The watch never worked again.

In spite of the reprieve, both men knew that Rusty's final journey was just a matter of time. But the stay gave Rusty a new urgency to share his faith, to seek to live for Jesus only.

"I want to live," he told Bob fervently. "And even if my sentence was somehow commuted to life in prison, Jesus is here just the same as He is on the outside. I can serve Him here."

But the reprieve also gave Rusty the final piece of freedom missing from his personal puzzle.

That summer of 1989 a letter made its way through the prison security checks to Rusty's cell. He eagerly picked up the plain envelope—then trembled when he saw the return address. It was from Lee Hewitt, the younger brother of Della Summers, the woman whose murder Rusty would die for.

> For years I hated you with all my heart. I could have blown your brains out for what you did to my sister. I only regretted you were in prison where I couldn't get to you.
>
> But I've spent time in jail myself—fifty-six different times over the years. I felt like a failure. But then I became a Christian. And the more I learned about being a Christian, the more I knew I had to forgive you. I didn't want to. But it got to where I couldn't even pray the Lord's prayer—"forgive us our trespasses as we forgive those who trespass against us."
>
> It made me so mad—now I had to forgive you. Now the ball was in my court. I've prayed about it, and God has done a

miracle in my heart. I forgive you. We are brothers in Christ. I love you.

Rusty looked up, blinded by his tears and the radiance of God's goodness to him. Forgiven! Not only by Christ, but now by the man he had offended most here on earth. It seemed the greatest blessing he could have ever hoped for.

Rusty wrote back to Lee, tears dotting the penciled pages of his letter. Watching, Bob was humbled by the enormity of Lee's obedience to Christ and overwhelmed by the absolute joy Lee's gift of forgiveness sealed in Rusty's heart.

Months passed. When he wasn't visiting death row, Bob traveled with the governor, wrote speeches, put in long days at work. He toured the state when Hurricane Hugo gutted South Carolina's coast late that summer. He sometimes went fishing on Saturdays, led a Wednesday morning Bible study at the State House and a Thursday evening group at his church. He and Carol looked at wallpaper samples and priced countertops, thinking about redecorating their kitchen.

The phone would ring often—sometimes an inner-city mom they had befriended, other times an inmate who had just been released from prison and needed some help finding a job. They watched with amazement the news of the fall of Communism in Eastern Europe, the Berlin Wall coming down, the tumultuous changes in the world as the 1980s drew to a close.

*At the beginning of this decade I didn't know Christ,* thought Bob. *I hadn't met Odell. I had never been to prison. I didn't know Rusty. Life was so different then.*

Meanwhile, Rusty finished out the year in his daily routine. By now all the condemned inmates had been moved to the new death row facility and away from the stinking cells of CCI, so their physical conditions were much improved.

Rusty's family never visited, but when other men's wives and families came, they almost always stopped to talk with him. One little girl, Patrice, was his favorite. In fact, her mother, Wanda, claimed that Rusty was the reason Patrice was even alive.[6]

Several years earlier, during a visit to the row, Wanda had tearfully confided to Rusty that she was pregnant, out of wedlock, and that the father of the child refused to acknowledge the baby was his. She had made an appointment to have an abortion.

"Don't do it," he pleaded. "Life is precious. I don't have no money, but I'll do whatever I can to support that child. If you need a name for the baby, it can have my name. I'll be its father. Just let it live."

Now Patrice was a beautiful little toddler with big, dark eyes and a special smile just for Rusty. *The man who took lives has saved a life,* Bob thought. *That's the difference Jesus makes.*

Rusty had no money, but he was rich in one thing: time. Until his time ran out, of course. So he spent hours reading the Scriptures, visualizing the glories of God in nature and the love of God for him.

> I will sing to the LORD as long as I live;
> I will sing praise to my God while I have my being.

After the new year, 1990, the Supreme Court came to Rusty's case again. And again they decided not to hear his appeal. Again the legal machinery of South Carolina ground, spitting out an execution date for Rusty Woomer: Friday, April 27, 1990, 1:00 A.M.

*Good Friday, April 13, 1990*
Rusty lay in his cell thinking about Jesus: He had been executed. He had gone through it all—arrest, trial, sentencing, death penalty. Except He was innocent.[7]

*Jesus went to His death for me already,* Rusty thought. *And He'll be with me when I go to mine.*

*Easter Sunday, April 15, 1990*
"I am the resurrection and the life; he who believes in Me shall live even if he dies."[8] *What an amazing thought,* Rusty mused. *A promise to me.*

Later that afternoon an unexpected gift arrived: a bright basket filled with chocolates, candies, and cookies. Rusty sat for fifteen minutes, picking each piece up, looking it over, putting it gently back in the basket.

"Paps," he said to Bob, who had brought in the gift, "I ain't never had an Easter basket before in my whole life."

The basket was from Lee and Barbara Hewitt. Lee had set Rusty free with his letter of forgiveness the previous summer. Now he wanted to visit, but he and his wife had not been able to get into the prison. So they had asked Bob to take their gift basket in to Rusty.

Before the week was over, Bob got special permission to bring the Hewitts and Rusty together in a prison conference room.

Initially there was an awkward moment as they sat down across from one another at the table. Bob sat in a corner, chewing a blue pen and taking notes so he could remember later what everyone had said. Lee slid a *Good News "God Loves You"* Bible across the table to Rusty.

"It's hard to know what to say," Lee began, "except I wish we could have met you long ago."

Rusty slid a small devotional book across the table to Lee and listened while he told about giving his life to Christ after years in and out of prisons.

Then Rusty told about his years on death row, how he had been spiritually dead even though his body was alive, and how Jesus had changed his life.

"You know," Rusty said slowly, "when I first accepted the Lord, I thought everything would change right then and that there would be no more hurt. Then when Mama died, I blamed God, and I asked Him why I done all these things. Then my brother died and my uncle died. But Bob here just kept me from giving up. . . . When I realized Mama was in heaven, I just said, 'When I get there, I'm goin' fishin' with Mama again.'"

Then Rusty turned to Lee, his voice thick with tears, but his blue eyes shining. "Your forgiving me has done more for me than anybody's ever done. I know I done these things. That day [of the murders] is like two minutes to me—just there and gone—but even with God's and people's forgiveness, I've never gotten the hurt out of my heart. I prayed and prayed. When I got that letter from you, I can't explain how I felt. Is my faith strong enough to do what you're doin'? I'd like to think I could, but I'm not sure."

"I can do nothing without Jesus," said Lee. "I have to draw from Him. I see Him hanging on the cross, saying, 'Father, forgive them.'"

"It's amazing, ain't it?" said Rusty, thinking of his Easter morning reflections. "I believe with all my heart in the Bible. Sometimes I'd like to see an ocean partin'. But God's already given me miracles I'd never dreamed of."

"What God can do, people can't comprehend," Lee nodded. "I don't have hurt or anger. I wouldn't want to walk around like that for nothin'. I have no anger because God took it and done away with it and threw it into the sea of forgetfulness. He loves you, and He don't want to remember.

"The only time He knows about it is when we bring it up. There's no words to describe hate. It's an ugly feeling. If you don't forgive, you don't deserve Jesus as your Lord. It took almost four years—now I hope the rest of my family can change. This is the way it's gonna be, no matter if my family talks to me or not." Lee's family had publicly castigated him and cut him off for forgiving Rusty, but he had chosen to obey God rather than please his family.

Rusty nodded. "Trust in God is the only way I've kept sane in this place," he told Lee. "If they took me over there to the chair right now, I could do it. What you have done has made God's Word complete to me."[9]

And Bob thought, *Both of these men have learned that God's will is the ultimate reality.*

By now their time was up and the guards motioned that Lee and Barbara and Bob had to leave. Before they did, however, Rusty and Lee held hands and prayed together in the name of the Lord Jesus who had saved them, forgiven them, and made them brothers in Him. They knew they would not see each other again this side of heaven.

*Tuesday, April 24, 1990*

At one o'clock that morning the officers came to get Rusty, giving him time to say good-bye to the other inmates on the row.

Once again he was taken to the cell in the Capital Punishment Facility. Once again he was fingerprinted and processed, his possessions packed away. And once again the death watch began.

South Carolina's Capital Punishment Facility is a small, clinical structure cordoned off into a maze of rooms, each with a strategic function in the execution process. The inmate is brought from death row and kept in one of four narrow, blue-barred cells, each about six by ten feet, with nothing but a cot and a stainless steel washbasin and toilet. Each cell has a narrow, vertical window, four inches wide by four feet high. More bars separate the cell area from a central hall and a guard center.

At the center of the small building sits the electric chair itself, which sits facing a small connected room with two rows of chairs. Here the witnesses view the condemned man's final moments.

As the sun rose on the dawn of Tuesday, April 24, Rusty found that even in this grim house of death God had not neglected to give him a reminder of His grace. In the triple spiral of razor wire coiled over the fence adjacent to Rusty's cell was a bird's nest.

If it had been inches to the right or to the left, Rusty would not have been able to see it. But there it was, dead center in the view from his narrow window. And as he watched throughout the morning, he saw a mother bird swooping in and out of that razor-nest, threading her way between the deadly wires with precision, tending her eggs.

When Bob arrived, Rusty took hold of his shoulders and pointed him toward the nest. Then the two men smiled at each other. No matter how horrible the next few days would be, God would provide for them. And in that simple bunch of twigs and grass He had sent a sign.*

"When Noah was riding out the floodwaters, God sent him a bird with an olive branch as a sign of hope," Bob told Rusty. "When Jesus was baptized, the Holy Spirit appeared in the form of a dove. And now here's this crazy bird with her eggs, right outside your death house window! God's sign of new life!"

Through the rest of that day and the next, Bob and Rusty read the Bible, prayed, and talked about the hills of West Virginia and the fishing holes of heaven. Also, a phone line had been installed, so Rusty was free to talk with anyone he could reach.

*Thursday, April 26, 1991*

His last sunrise.

Rusty watched the mother bird tend her nest. She was warm gray with a black mask, and the officers guarding Rusty were frustrated—they hadn't been able to figure out what she was. This morning one guard had come in with a bird book. Rusty could feel their urgency. *Got to find out what kind of bird this is before Rusty goes.*

His last lunch.

At this time a year ago the Supreme Court had come through for Rusty. No calls from the court today. The governor's office announced his refusal to intervene.

His last interview.

Rusty had a Christ-peppered talk with a reporter from the *Charlotte Observer*.

His last visit.

---

*Later, when the birds had flown, Warden George Martin got the bird's nest as a memento for Bob McAlister. Today it sits in the den in Bob's home.

At 4:00 P.M. Rusty's family came to say good-bye. Rusty demonstrated the forgiveness he had long ago given his father. His dad's face looked like mountain granite as they stood in a circle for a final farewell.

"I wish y'all would stop living so far apart," Rusty told his family. "And I wish y'all would fight less and hug more." Then he commanded them, "Bow your heads. We're gonna pray.

"Our precious Lord, I'm not cryin' 'cause I feel bad, but 'cause I'm happy. I'm gonna be with You, and You've done everything for me far beyond what I ever deserve. I ask You to watch over my family and take the hurt and sadness from their hearts. I pray that all this hurt and sufferin' will be gone, and I just praise You with all of my heart."

With that, Rusty lifted his head and broke the silence by gently patting his father's bulging stomach. "You need to lose some of that, Pappy!" he joked. And then they left.

His last meal.

Rusty could order anything he wanted—his first non-prison-prepared meal in more than a decade. A pizza with everything but anchovies. Rusty couldn't eat, but he had gotten it to make sure the guards would. But they weren't hungry either.

As the evening ticked by, Rusty drank several cups of coffee.

"Normally this would keep me up," Rusty quipped. "Tonight I guess it don't matter."

He returned a phone call from a girl who had called earlier—Patti, the friend of a friend.

"Oh, Patti's out tonight," her roommate told Rusty, obviously unaware of his situation. "She'll be back about one in the morning. Can you call back then?"

"No," Rusty drawled, grinning at Bob. "I'm afraid that'll be a little too late for me."

As the sun's rays angled lower and lower, the light on the bird nest fading, Rusty watched in silence. A golden sense of peace washed over Bob. Rusty felt it too.

"Ya know, Paps," he said finally. "I feel real happy. I just want to go on home now. I don't want to stay here; things are just too bad down here. I just feel real peaceful, and I know Mama's waitin' on me up there."

At 11:00 P.M. the execution team arrived, checking their equipment one final time. At 11:45 officers came to get Rusty and took him to the preparation room.

A final shower. Clean prison clothes.

Bob sat on the floor at Rusty's feet while a prison barber shaved his head and right leg in preparation for the application of the conducting gel that would help make a strong connection for the electric charge. The preparation room was filled with about a dozen officers and several corrections officials.

"Paps," Rusty said, "read me the Bible one last time."

As the electric razor buzzed, Bob turned to Revelation 21.

"And He shall wipe away every tear from their eyes; and there shall no longer be any death; there shall no longer be any mourning, or crying, or pain—" A shining clump of Rusty's blond hair felt onto Bob's open Bible.

Bob looked up. And when he saw Rusty's half-shaven head and his face filled with a heavenly expression—his eyes fixed not on the dark efficiency of the death house, but on the new heaven of Revelation—at that moment, Bob's emotions got away from him. It was the only time he lost his composure in front of Rusty. He handed his Bible to Chaplain Brown, who read the rest of the chapter. To Bob it was an awesome thing: in an hour his friend would experience the promises of Revelation 21.

At 12:40 A.M. George Martin arrived. Not in his official role as warden—that would come later. His stomach tense, George sat down beside Rusty on the cot, patting him on the shoulder.

"Are you doing all right?" he asked.

Rusty smiled at him. "Yep. Like I told you before, I have been taken care of, and I am gonna be all right. But what about you?"

George hadn't expected that a man who was to die in twenty minutes would have others on his mind. "I'm okay," he said.

Rusty's bald head, glistening as the light reflected off the conducting gel, made a surreal image as he talked with the warden. It was a hideous sight, and Bob thought about his own weaknesses during the past weeks, compared to Rusty's strength. How he would wake up in the middle of the night in a cold sweat, sobbing. And how Carol would just snuggle up close to him and hold him without saying a word. But somehow his fears and trembling vanished when he was with Rusty. God had so equipped him for his task that Bob and everyone else drew strength from him. The worst times were away from Rusty, not with him.

Rusty had never broken down during those last days. His sense of the imminent reality of seeing his Lord seemed to obliterate almost everything else. Bob couldn't help but think, *If only that reality were as vivid for all of us, the body of Christ would be transformed—and the world as well.*

The only thing that really hurt Rusty was seeing the pain and anguish of his friends. Now here he was, right up to the last, ministering to others. "I know this has been about as tough on you as it has on me," Rusty was telling Warden Martin earnestly. "But don't let it ruin you. These guys in this prison need you here too bad for you to leave them because of this."

George Martin smiled at Rusty. "All right, Son," he said and left the room.*

Fifteen minutes later he returned, this time with the death warrant in his hand, the paper that signified the will of the state in carrying out the sentence of death on one Ronald Raymond Woomer.

"Rusty, it is time to go," George Martin said.

"Let's go," Rusty replied.

The officers escorted him to the execution chamber, just thirty paces away, shuffling because they were so tightly bunched. Rusty was shackled with steel arm restraints. A line of officers stood stiffly as he passed out of the guard area. Bob, following, saw tears in some of their eyes.

Earlier, Bob and Rusty had agreed not to say good-bye. Though they had always ended their visits together with a brotherly hug, this time it would seem too final. So Bob put his hand on his friend's shoulder, looked into his eyes, and said, "Look to Jesus, Rusty."

Throughout their friendship, Bob had always felt Rusty needed him, and he had given everything he had. But now, he realized, there was nothing more *he* could give. Rusty had already moved beyond Bob's reach. Now it was all between Rusty and Jesus.

---

*Warden George Martin determined that carrying out the state's sentence would be done in the most professional and dignified way possible. He told Rusty that he would do everything in his power to try to help him get through it with as little difficulty as one could expect. "Don't worry 'bout me," Rusty told the warden. "I am not going to cause you any trouble."

But George Martin was deeply troubled. He had never hidden his distaste for the death penalty from the staff or the inmates or officials within the corrections administration, but at this point it was a matter of carrying out the official duty. The execution of another human being was an excruciating process for everyone involved, especially one as well liked by the staff as Rusty. George arranged for personal counseling to be available for any officers or staff members who felt they needed it. Quite a few did (George Martin, interview with Ellen Vaughn, Columbia, S.C. , August 1991).

The group of officers, Rusty, Warden Martin, Chaplain Mike Brown, and Bob entered the death chamber. The official witnesses sat in two short rows facing the electric chair. In the room adjacent to the death chamber, three executioners waited beside buttons recessed into the wall; the electrical current would alternate between the three buttons, so no one would know which had actually activated the current.

The warden took the microphone nestled in an alcove in the wall that also held three telephones: open lines to the deputy commissioner's office, the attorney general's office, the governor's office.

They strapped Rusty into the chair, buckling the thick leather restraining straps over his chest, legs, and arms.

"Do you have a final statement?" Warden Martin asked, walking toward him with the microphone.

Rusty had not prepared a formal statement this time. Since his first trip to the Death House, he had read about how Jesus told His followers not to worry about what they would say, for the Holy Spirit would give them the utterance they needed.[9]

He thought for a moment, then spoke simply. "I'm sorry," he said. "I claim Jesus Christ as my Savior. My only wish is that everyone in the world could feel the love I have felt from Him."

The electrician fitted Rusty's head into a leather beanie connected to the main, thick electrode, descending from the ceiling like an ugly stalactite. Another electrode was strapped to his leg. They placed a leather strap under Rusty's nose that pulled his head back into the cap. Then they fastened the copper headpiece over Rusty's head and dropped the leather death hood over his face.

*Darkness.*

Rusty could hear the warden's voice making the final phone check to the deputy commissioner to see if the governor or the Supreme Court had intervened. It sounded very far away. He could hear an officer escorting Bob out—a few footsteps, and a door closing. He could sense the executioners nervously waiting for the warden's order to hit the triggers that would activate the killing current.

The seconds ticked by. Darkness under the hood.

Then the jolt of two thousand volts.

*Light.*

# *Epilogue*

## *The Conclusion of the Matter*

A few days before he was electrocuted, Rusty Woomer talked about fear.

Not the fear of a man about to die, shaking in a desolate death row cell. No, in his final hours, Rusty knew more than the mere terror of imminent death. He knew the fear of the Lord—the immanence of his God.

I saw this in Rusty myself when I visited him on Easter Sunday, just eleven days before he died. But Bob McAlister, who knew Rusty best, was there to the very end, and he saw his friend's eyes fill with tears of joy when he thought about that quick step from the shadowed chair of death into the Light.

In his simple way, Rusty spoke to Bob of that holy awe: "I think of His radiance, His power, His love. It doesn't scare you that someone loves you enough that He can forgive you for anything that you do? It scares me sometimes. He is something that we have not got any idea what it is going to be like when we meet . . . His love is so strong that it might hurt us when we meet Him . . ."

Few people on the planet know the mystery that for Rusty was solved by the state of South Carolina: the time of their own death. He was not caught unaware, unrepentant, distracted by the things of this world and distant from his Lord. Yet Rusty's final journey is one we will all make.

For in reality, we are all on death row.

And Rusty's final perspective is one the church at large must have if we are to truly be the Body, the holy people of God, in these closing years of a darkening century.

Do we know the radiance of the Lord? His glory? His love that makes dead men and women sing His praises? Do we know that we are but a breath away from union with Him?

We live in a world that has lost the holy dread of the Creator—and exchanged the truth for a lie. How, then, should we live?

The writer of Ecclesiastes answered that question and closed his book, as we conclude ours, with these words:

> Now all has been heard;
> here is the conclusion of the matter:
> Fear God and keep his commandments,
> for this is the whole duty of man.
> For God will bring every deed into judgment,
> including every hidden thing,
> whether it is good or evil.

May His radiant goodness, and the grateful obedience of His people, compel His church to fear God and keep His commandments, to His glory, even to the end of the age. Amen.

# With Gratitude

$\mathcal{M}$OST WRITERS DO NOT RETREAT TO SOLITARY cloisters to ponder great thoughts and then, in a glorious moment of illumination, compose timeless prose. No, at least from our perspective, books are the product of a process.

They begin with what we read and study and think about; they are influenced by thinkers and mentors, as well as the trials and joys of personal experience. Gradually, ideas begin to emerge. Some ripen into convictions. And, at some point in the process, we even dare to think "This could be a book . . ."

But even at that point, writers don't have the luxury of retreating into solitude. Books get written in the midst of living. Even as you are writing about the church, you walk into a prison cell and meet a man who reflects the true fear of the Lord. *This is what the church needs,* you think. Then there are conversations with all sorts of people, more books read, ideas maturing, drafts written, consultation with theologians, and visits to churches, from South Central Los Angeles to Timisoara, Romania.

And then, most precious of all, are those moments when you sense the power and guidance of the Holy Spirit in forming convictions—and then articulating them.

We have spent almost three years in that process. And it has indeed been collaborative, not only between the two of us, who have worked together for twelve years and seven books now, but with Prison Fellowship colleagues, friends, pastors, and teachers.

There are so many to whom we are so much indebted.

The dedication expresses the first order of gratitude. We have sensed over and over God's anointing on this work, and so we can do no other than to first consecrate this work to Him for His glory.

Then we must thank the group of scholars who contributed to the first inspirations for this work. Foremost among them is Dr. Carl F. H. Henry, Chuck's friend and teacher since the earliest days of his Christian life. Carl has taught us through the wealth of his prodigious theological, historical, and sociological knowledge, as well as through the authentic model of his own personal life. His lectures on the church, given to the Prison Fellowship staff, formed a foundation of sorts for this work; his meticulous reading and editing of the manuscript were crucially important.

Next is the late Dr. Francis Schaeffer. Schaeffer's writings have profoundly affected so many evangelicals, and his writings on truth informed our theme here regarding the church as a pillar of truth in a lost culture.

Father Richard John Neuhaus has also been a tremendous inspiration. He has one of the keenest minds we've ever known. He writes with weight and gritty substance and profound insight. His book *Freedom for Ministry* was one of our richest sources.

Dr. R. C. Sproul, another remarkable intellect and one of Chuck's earliest teachers as a Christian, has contributed immeasurably to our world-view.

And Dr. J. I. Packer has been, through his writings and friendship, a powerful influence. We are especially grateful to him for his courageous stand in calling for unity of the Body.

In addition, we are indebted to Rev. T. M. Moore, president of Chesapeake Seminary, who helped formulate the earliest ideas at this book's conception and was of immense help throughout its gestation. We consider T.M. one of the bright lights in evangelical circles.

Father Tom Weinandy also reviewed and critiqued the entire manuscript, which was particularly gracious since he was teaching at Oxford University at the time. Weinandy is a classical scholar, a powerful thinker, and, as is apparent to all who are privileged to know him, a loving and holy man.

We owe a particular debt to Dr. J. Daryl Charles of Prison Fellowship's staff. He undergirded the whole of this book with vast amounts of painstaking research on everything from the "Donahue" show to the doctrine of the sacraments. Daryl's fact-finding missions and his theological critique of the whole were immensely helpful. He is a young theologian of the first rank.

As always, we would not have survived or produced this book without the matchless skill of Judith Markham. Judith's editorial and conceptual expertise make her not only the best editor in the business but the nicest as well.

In addition, we are grateful for the many pastors and laypeople in the United States who made their time available for interviews and who shared insights and experiences with us. It was a privilege to be part—even briefly—of so many tremendous and committed congregations across the country. And we will never forget the valiant brothers and sisters of Eastern Europe who so graciously opened their hearts and homes to us.

Particular thanks are in order for Rev. Bob Russell, whose taped sermons Chuck listens to faithfully each week, and Rev. John Aker, for reviewing and critiquing sections of the manuscript. Thanks also for their hospitality in opening their churches to us.

And special thanks to Mike Murray, whose witty perspective on life and the church made him the right person to research and draft chapter 8.

We give thanks as well to our wonderful colleagues at Prison Fellowship who patiently typed chapters and offered good insights throughout: first, Chuck's faithful and longtime assistants, Grace McCrane and Nancy Niemeyer; and to Bessie Cool, Evelyn Lauxstermann, Mary Lipka, and Carol Mills, Prison Fellowship's word processing department, who typed hours and hours of transcripts from recorded interviews. Thanks to Kim Robbins for her helpful NEXIS research. Thanks to Margaret Shannon for her special interest in Poland and World War II and for her help in accessing Library of Congress resources. And thanks to Cindy Wiggins and Donna Varnam for keeping the paper flow flowing!

We also thank Tom Pratt, PF president, the PF senior management team, and all of our colleagues and ministry volunteers who so graciously encouraged us and prayed for us and this project.

Thanks especially to Nelson Keener for his handling of the logistics of this book—as well as his ruthless guardianship of Chuck's schedule.

And, oh yes, thanks to the Reston, Virginia, Wendy's restaurant, whose grilled chicken sandwiches—hold the mayo—got us through some long evening sessions.

We owe a special debt to our home church pastors, who have given us a firsthand experience of what the local body should be: Neal Jones of Columbia Baptist in Northern Virginia, Chuck's loving friend and counselor over fifteen years, and Dr. Hayes Wicker of the First Baptist Church of Naples, Florida, which is where Chuck worships whenever he's fortunate enough to be in Florida, and to Steve Smallman, pastor of McLean Presbyterian Church in McLean, Virginia, a great friend to both of us and pastor to Ellen.

And finally, our thanks to the real heroes of every effort like this: our spouses, who put up with many a late night and more than a few sleepless ones.

Patty Colson has suffered through ten books now, and through each one has demonstrated the remarkable fortitude, generosity of spirit, and loving support that helps keep Chuck sane and continuously grateful to God for her.

And Lee Vaughn, who has seen Ellen through her work on seven books, starting with *Loving God.* Lee's enthusiasm and gracious, creative support is a great gift.

And we must also give special thanks to and for little Emily Miller Vaughn for waiting until the manuscript was completed—barely—before arriving in the Vaughn household!

As we have stressed throughout this book, the Christian life is a corporate undertaking. Even as we acknowledge and thank those who have contributed so kindly to the completion of this project, we see that fact made clear to us yet again. We thank God for His grace in bringing us to Himself—and then knitting us into the wonderful fellowship of His body.

Charles W. Colson
Ellen Santilli Vaughn
July 9, 1992

# Notes

## Chapter 2 • Identity Crisis

1. Robert Bellah, *Habits of the Heart* (New York: Harper & Row, 1985), 221.

2. George H. Gallup, Jr., *Religion in America 1990* (Princeton, N.J.: PRRC, 1990), 21, 45; idem and Timothy K. Jones, *The Saints Among Us* (Ridgefield, Conn.: Morehouse, 1992), 36.

3. *PRRC Emerging Trends* (December 1983): 3–5.

4. Roper poll cited in "Ethical Behavior Seen Declining," EP News Service, 21 September 1990. Also, a 1991 Barna poll found that 25 percent of regular church attenders claim they have not established a personal commitment to Christ that bears any significance in their life. "What kind of community of faith would allow such a circumstance to continue over time?" asks Barna. (*What Americans Believe: An Annual Survey of Values and Religious Views in the United States* [Ventura, Calif.: Regal, 1991]).

5. William D. Hendricks, "What's Wrong with This Picture?" *Wall Street Journal*, 6 August 1991.

6. Ibid. A Lilly Foundation survey, also cited in the Hendricks article, found that while disposable income increased 103 percent between 1968 and 1985, giving rose only 2 percent.

7. Robert Patterson, "In Search of the Visible Church," *Christianity Today*, 11 March 1991, 36, 38.

8. Acts 5:11, 9:31 NIV (emphasis added).

*Chapter 3 • Gimme That Hot Tub Religion!*

1. *USA Today* polls conducted by Gordon J. Black Corp., cited in *"Events and People," Christian Century*, 30 September 1987.

2. Ed Hindson, "Religion Is Alive and Well in America," *Religious Broadcasting* (November 1987).

3. Sandra D. Atchinson, "Christian Publishers Count Their Blessings," *Business Week*, 8 July 1991, 2–3.

4. Kenneth L. Woodward et al., "A Time to Seek," *Newsweek*, 17 December 1990, 17 (emphasis added).

5. Ibid., 11.

6. "Many Christians Accept New Age Beliefs," *PRRC Emerging Trends* (November 1991): 3.

7. Eli Lilly-funded study cited in Martha Sawyer, "Protestants Take Aim at Baby Boomers," *Naples Daily News*.

8. John Dart, "It's Not All in a Name for Some Churches," *Los Angeles Times*, 22 December 1990, S-1.

9. Woodward, "A Time to Seek," 17 (emphasis added).

10. Robert N. Bellah, *Habits of the Heart* (New York: Harper & Row, 1985), 229.

11. "Tai's Good Deeds," *Washington Times*, 26 November 1991, A-6.

12. Robert Coles, "New Forms of the Sin of Pride," *The New Review of Books and Religion* (December 1977): 3, cited in Richard Neuhaus, *Freedom for Ministry* (New York: Harper & Row, 1979), 75–76.

13. See *PRRC Emerging Trends* (November 1991): 2–4; see also "The Great Divide: Fantasies," *Atlanta Journal and Constitution*, 29 March 1991, 4.

14. Constance Casey, "Gimme That New Age Religion," review in "Book World," *Washington Post*, 2 February 1991, 2–4.

15. Woodward, "A Time to Seek," 13.

16. Rich Gilbert, "Corporate Worship," *Modern Reformation* (September–October 1991).

17. Acts 2:47.

18. Neuhaus, *Freedom for Ministry*, 89.


*Chapter 4 • The Story of the Church: Timisoara*

1. Chuck visited Ceausescu in Romania in 1973, and the two talked for more than an hour. He was a charming rogue. President Richard Nixon

and Ceausescu were fast friends because each could use the other—and did.

2. Hannah Pakula, "Elena Ceausescu: The Shaping of an Ogress," *Vanity Fair* (August 1990): 166.

3. Cited in *Programs of Compassionate Intervention for Romanian Orphans* (Monrovia, Calif.: World Vision, 1992).

4. Marius Miron, interview with Ellen Vaughn, Timisoara, Romania, 17 September 1990.

5. See Laszlo Tokes and David Porter, *The Fall of Tyrants* (Westchester, Ill.: Crossway, 1991).

6. Ibid., 95.

7. Ibid., 104.

8. Lajos Varga, interview with Ellen Vaughn, Budapest, Hungary, 19 September 1990; see also Robert Cullen, "Report from Romania," *The New Yorker*, 2 April 1990, 94–112.

9. Tokes and Porter, *The Fall of Tyrants*, 3–4.

10. Jack Friedman and Traudl Lessing, "Laszlo Tokes, the Pastor Who Helped to Free Romania, Is Home," *People*, 5 February 1990, 63ff.

11. Tokes and Porter, *The Fall of Tyrants*, 11.

12. Cullen, "Report from Romania," 96.

13. Peter Dugulescu, interview with Ellen Vaughn, Timisoara, Romania, 17 September 1990.

14. Adina Jinaru, interview with Ellen Vaughn, Timisoara, Romania, 16 September 1990.

15. Unfortunately, as Tokes makes clear in his account, the character of the crowd by this time was not entirely peaceful or Christian. Some became violent and headed downtown, where they tangled with the Securitate and started setting government-only shops on fire.

16. Peter Dugulescu, interview with Ellen Vaughn, Timisoara, Romania, 17 September 1990.

## Chapter 5 • On This Rock

1. Laszlo Tokes, interview with Ellen Vaughn, Budapest, Hungary, 19 September 1990.

2. Matt. 3:2 NIV.

3. Matt. 16:13–19 NIV.

4. Eph. 2:19–22.

5. Richard Avery and Donald Marsh, "We Are the Church" (Pasadena, Calif.: Hope Publishing House, 1972).

6. 1 Corinthians 12; 1 Pet. 2:9. Carl F. H. Henry, "Churches and Christian Fellowship," *Basic Biblical Beliefs: Six Foundational Christian Doctrines*, pt. 5, teaching sessions and internal study prepared for Prison Fellowship.

7. Acts 20:28.

8. Acts 20:28; Eph. 5:25.

9. Heb. 12:23; Rom. 16:5; Acts 15:22.

10. Acts 2:38 NIV.

11. Acts 2:42.

12. Acts 2.

13. Heb. 10:19–25.

14. J. Pelikan and H. Lehmann, eds., *Luther's Works*, 55 vols. (Philadelphia: Fortress; St. Louis: Concordia Publishing House, 1955), 21:127.

15. John Calvin, *Institutes of the Christian Religion*, ed. J. T. McNeill, 2 vols. (Philadelphia: Westminster Press, 1960), 2:1012.

16. Warren Wiersbe, *The Integrity Crisis* (Nashville: Thomas Nelson, 1988), 130.

17. Richard Neuhaus, *Freedom for Ministry* (New York: Harper & Row, 1979), 53.

18. Revelation 21; Ephesians 5.

19. Neuhaus, *Freedom for Ministry*, 11.

20. Ibid., 44; see also H. Richard Niebuhr, *The Purpose of the Church and Its Ministry* (New York: Harper & Row, 1956); also, references in Vatican Council II to the fact that many elements of sanctification of truth can be found outside of "her visible structure," as well as the powerful writings of eminent Catholic theologian Fr. Avery Dulles, S.J.

### Chapter 6 • I Will Build My Church

1. Irina Ratushinskaya, interviews with Ellen Vaughn, San Jose, Costa Rica, July 1989.

2. Irina Ratushinskaya, *In the Beginning*, trans. Alyona Kojevnikov (London: Hodder & Stoughton, 1990).

3. Ibid., 46.

4. Irina would not read the writings of British author C. S. Lewis until much later in her life, when as an adult she was exiled from her Russia into the West. But she had already found what Lewis called the Law of Right and

Wrong in his book *Mere Christianity:* "This Rule of Right and Wrong, or Law of Human Nature, or whatever you call it, must somehow or other be a real thing—a thing that is really there, not made up by ourselves. . . . It begins to look as if we shall have to admit that there is more than one kind of reality; that, in this particular case, there is something above and beyond the ordinary facts of men's behavior, and yet quite definitely real—a real law, which none of us made, but which we find pressing on us" (C. S. Lewis, *Mere Christianity* [New York: Macmillan, 1960], 30).

5. Ratushinskaya, *In the Beginning,* 46.

6. Ibid., 71.

7. Ibid., 106–7.

## Chapter 7 • *The Sin of Presumption*

1. Romans 1.

2. John 3:8.

3. For example, in cases of moral impropriety (1 Corinthians 5; Gal. 5:19–21; Jude 4); in cases of defiling the Lord's Supper (1 Cor. 11:17–34); in cases of profaning worship (1 Cor. 11:2–16); in cases of doctrinal deviance (Gal. 1:6–9; 3:1–14; 5:1–12; 1 Tim. 1:3–7; 5:1; 2 Tim. 4:2–3; 2 Pet. 2:1–3; 3:17; Jude 3; 1 John 4:1–2); miscellaneous (Gal. 2:11–14; 6:1; Eph. 4:25; 1 Thess. 5:21; 2 Thess. 3:11–12; 1 Tim. 5:19; 2 Tim. 2:14, 25; 4:2, 14; Titus 1:10-14; 2:15; 3:10; Jude 23; Revelation 2–3).

4. Matt. 7:15–23, 12:33–37; Luke 6:43–45.

## Chapter 8 • *Extending the Right Fist of Fellowship*

1. This chapter is based on interviews and research conducted by Mike Murray in Newton, Massachusetts—with special thanks to John DeBrine for originally sharing the story.

## Chapter 9 • *One Lord, One Faith, One Baptism*

1. Ari L. Goldman, "Religion Notes," *New York Times,* 27 January 1990, 2.

2. Francis Schaeffer, *The Great Evangelical Disaster* (Westchester, Ill.: Crossway, 1984), 82, 178.

3. Paul Tournier, *The Whole Person in a Broken World* (New York: Harper & Row, 1964), 34.

4. John 13:35.

5. Eph. 4:3–6 NIV.

6. Wolfhart Pannenberg, "The Present and Future Church," *First Things,* (November 1991), 51.

7. Richard Neuhaus, *Freedom for Ministry* (New York: Harper & Row, 1979), 9–10.

8. John 17:21 NIV (emphasis added).

9. Abraham Kuyper, *Lectures on Calvinism* (Reprint, Grand Rapids, Mich.: Eerdmans, 1981), 183.

10. Templeton address, given at Guildhall, London, England, 11 May 1983; excerpts printed in "Return to God; Solzhenitsyn Speaks Out," *Time,* 23 May 1983, 57.

11. C. S. Lewis, *Mere Christianity* (New York: Macmillan, 1952), 148.

12. Kuyper, *Lectures on Calvinism,* 184.

13. See Kefa Sempangi, *A Distant Grief* (Glendale, Calif.: Regal, 1979).

14. 1 Cor. 13:12; Neuhaus, *Freedom for Ministry,* 87. For a development of his thought, see 86–91.

15. John Calvin to William Farrell, from Strasbourg, 24 October 1538, in H. Beveridge and J. Bonnet, eds., *Selected Books of John Calvin: Tracts and Letters,* vol. 4, trans. D. Constable (Grand Rapids, Mich.: Baker, 1983), 101–2.

16. Helmut Thielicke, *Trouble with the Church* (Grand Rapids, Mich: Baker, 1965), 104–5; note particularly Thielicke's candid discussion of changing differences between Protestants and Catholics.

17. J. Stevenson, ed., *A New Eusebius* (London: SPCK, 1957, 1987), 111–13, 165–66.

18. Vatican Council II specifically repudiates this view, though many Catholics are unaware of the fact.

19. For a Roman Catholic perspective on this witness of healthy ecumenism, see Kenneth Craycraft, "Our Kind of Ecumenism: Why Catholics Need to Be More Evangelical and Vice Versa," *Crisis* (October 1991): 30–33.

20. Edward E. Plowman and J. L. Grady, eds., *National and International Religion Report,* 29 July 1991, 2.

21. EP News Service, 21 June 1991.

22. John Aker, *Lengthen Your Stride* (Old Tappan, N.J.: Fleming H. Revell, 1988), 190–92.

23. The community has undergone major changes and is involved in a major restructuring right now. Community building is not easy, but these

brothers and sisters have labored hard to make a point about unity to the church.

24. Steve Brown, *Key Life* (May-June 1990): 4.

25. George Cornell, Associated Press, *Washington Post*, 12 October 1991. Survey by periodicals for the American Baptists, *The Lutheran*, *The Church Herald* (RCA), *The Disciple*, *The Messenger* (Church of the Brethren), Presbyterian Survey, *United Church News*, and *U.S. Catholic*.

26. Schaeffer, *The Great Evangelical Disaster*, 160.

27. Acts 1:4; 2:44, 46.

## Chapter 10 • *The Flaming Word*

1. Iain H. Murray, *Jonathan Edwards: A New Biography* (Carlisle, Pa.: Banner of Truth, 1987).

2. Following Enfield, there arose an anti-revival movement that caused a number of Hampshire County pastors to band together to offer joint testimony in the year 1743 to the effect that "to the glory of God's grace . . . there has been a happy revival of religion in the congregations." The pastoral letter continues, saying that "abiding manifestations of a serious . . . and humble spirit, and a conscientious care and watchfulness in their behavior towards God and man [have] validated the sincerity of these professions" (C. C. Goen, ed., *The Works of Jonathan Edwards, Vol. 4: The Great Awakening* [New Haven: Yale University Press, 1972], 543). See also F. O. Allen, *The History of Enfield, Connecticut* (Hartford: n.p., 1900); Benjamin Trumbull, *A Complete History of Connecticut*, 2 vols. (New Haven: Maltby, Goldsmith and Co.; Samuel Wadsworth, 1818), vol. 2; E. H. Davidson, *Jonathan Edwards: The Narrative of a Puritan Mind* (Cambridge, Mass.: Harvard University Press, 1968); and Murray, *Jonathan Edwards*.

3. Matt. 28:19–20 NIV (emphasis added).

4. *Papal Encyclical on Evangelism*, January 1991; for the text, see John Paul II, "Redemptoris Missio," *Origins* 20/34 (January 1991).

5. Ephesians 4.

6. Acts 20:28.

7. Lectures on the church given by Dr. Carl F. H. Henry to Prison Fellowship staff, December 1990.

8. It is important for the pastor and congregation to have a clear understanding of their respective responsibilities and expectations. One of the best such covenants we've encountered was written by Dr. Hayes Wicker upon his call to the First Baptist Church of Naples, Florida. Note also the insightful way this defines the character of the church.

### Covenant Understanding Between Pastor and People

1. We must discover the activity of God and adjust to it. It will be unique to First Baptist Naples.

2. Undergird everything with prayer.

3. We must walk by faith. Think big not small. ("With God nothing is impossible.")

4. The bottom line is not "can we afford it?" but "is it God's will?" (Where He guides He provides.)

5. Everything should be done in the light of this mission statement, "To know Christ and to make Him known." (We glorify God by reaching people.)

6. All matters should be subjected to the Scriptures. (The issue is truth not tradition or convenience.)

7. The Church is a hospital for sinners not a country club for saints.

8. Problems will be dealt with, not ignored.

9. Hard work is necessary. (William Carey said, "Expect great things from God, attempt great things for God.")

10. Strive for week-long and year-long ministry (not just Sunday or the season).

11. There must be constant adjustment for growth. We cannot get overly comfortable. We must create new Bible study units, new ministries, and constantly improve the quality of education.

12. Recognizing that most people have limited time for church, then we must maximize time and do the most important.

13. Ministry is more important than meeting (committees, etc.).

14. Each Christian should discover his/her gift, passion and ministry.

15. We must seek to understand our cultural context and minster to it (baby-boomers, Florida leisure lifestyle, etc.).

16. We should strive for quality and excellence in every area (appearance, music, publication, etc.)

17. The Pastor and staff should be allowed to initiate and lead with trust, support and prayers of the church.

18. Criticism, murmuring and slander must not be allowed to disrupt the fellowship. The Deacons act as peacemakers.

19. We must recognize the need for additional staff to equip believers. (Rarely does a church have too many staff. They pay their way.) This involves more ministers and support personnel.

20. The family must be strengthened not undermined.

21. Outreach must be the priority.

22. We must be vitally concerned with meeting needs and healing hurts through ministries and developing relationships.

23. Biblical doctrine is nonnegotiable; methods are open to evaluation.

24. Since all sin and make mistakes, an attitude and atmosphere of grace must abound.

25. We must seek to develop a lighthouse ministry to all of Southwest Florida. (Drafted by Dr. Wicker and reprinted with his permission.)

9. Warren Wiersbe, *The Integrity Crisis* (Nashville: Thomas Nelson, 1988).

10. Martin Kahler, *Theologe und Christ,* cited in Helmut Thielicke, *The Trouble with the Church* (Grand Rapids, Mich.: Baker Book House, 1965.

11. Acts 20:28.

12. 1 Cor. 2:3.

13. Iain H. Murray, *The Forgotten Spurgeon* (Carlisle, Pa.: Banner of Truth Trust, 1966), 45.

14. Thielicke, *The Trouble with the Church,* 108–10. Whatever Thielicke's occasional theological deficiencies, it must be noted that after the Nazi era, university students crowded the Hamburg cathedral to hear Thielicke's sermons because of his bold resistance of Hitler; they were convinced that if a Word of God did exist, it might be found when this man spoke.

15. Ibid., 107–8.

16. Ibid.

17. Charles Finney, *Power from on High* (Fort Washington, Pa.: Christian Literature Crusade, n.d.), 108.

18. Richard Alderson, *No Holiness, No Heaven* (Carlisle, Pa.: Banner of Truth, 1986), 33.

19. *People,* 29 April 1991, last page.

20. Hos. 4:6.

## Chapter 11 • Communio Sanctorum

1. Louis Berkhof, *Systematic Theology* (Grand Rapids, Mich: Eerdmans, 1978), 357.

2. Rom. 14:17.

3. 1 John 1:3.

4. Cited in David Bercott, *Will the Real Heretics Please Stand Up?* (Henderson, Tex.: Scroll Publishing Co., 1989), 28.

5. "Abortion Rights Win Follows Bishop's Rebuke," *Washington Post*, 6 December 1989.

6. For a more complete account, see Charles W. Colson, *Kingdoms in Conflict* (Grand Rapids, Mich.: Zondervan, 1987), chap. 14.

7. Greg Bahnsen, "The Challenge and Duty of Church Discipline," *Antithesis* (May-June 1990): 28.

8. Rom. 12:1.

9. F. L. Cross and E. A. Livingstone, eds., *The Oxford Dictionary of the Christian Church* (New York and London: Oxford University Press, 1990), 1218.

10. Prison Fellowship Seminar Report, Luther Luckett Prison, La Grange, Kentucky, 26 May 1985.

11. Matt. 26:26, 28 NIV.

12. Lev. 10:1ff. NIV.

13. 2 Sam. 6:6.

14. 1 Cor. 11:17–18.

15. 1 Cor. 11:27, 29 NIV.

16. Acts 1:14.

17. Acts 1:14; 2:42–43; 4:21–31; 12:5; 16:25.

18. Acts 6:4; 13:34; 14:23.

19. William Temple, *Readings in St. John's Gospel* (New York: Macmillan, 1939), 68.

20. Charles G. Finney, *Power from on High* (Fort Washington, Pa.: Christian Literature Crusade, n.d.), 41–51. See also Ps. 66:18 NIV.

21. Richard Neuhaus, *Freedom for Ministry* (New York: Harper & Row, 1979), 126.

22. Edmund P. Clowney, *The Biblical Doctrine of the Church* (Philadelphia: Presbyterian and Reformed Publishing Co., 1979), 133–36. See also 1 Cor. 12:3.

23. Acts 4:31 NIV.

24. Acts 5:11 NIV.

25. Teddy Saunders and Hugh Sansom, *David Watson* (London: Hodder & Stoughton, 1992).

*Chapter 12 • What Is Truth?*

1. Philo, *De Legatione ad Gaium* 24.159–61.

### Chapter 13 • I Am the Truth

1. John 8:58 NKJV.

2. John 1:14.

3. Wolfhart Pannenberg, "The Present and Future Church," *First Things* (November 1991): 51.

4. Col. 1:15–17; Heb. 1:1–3.

5. Francis Schaeffer, *The Church at the End of the Twentieth Century* (Westchester, Ill.: Crossway, 1985), 21.

6. Loren Eiseley, *Darwin's Century* (New York: Doubleday, 1961), 62.

7. See Norman Podhoretz, *Breaking Ranks* (New York: Harper & Row, 1979); and Charles H. Malik, *A Christian Critique of the University* (Downers Grove, Ill.: InterVarsity Press, 1982).

8. Schaeffer, *Church at the End of the Twentieth Century*, 24.

9. Herbert Schlossberg, *Idols for Destruction: Christian Faith and Its Confrontation with American Society* (Nashville: Thomas Nelson, 1983), 222–27; and Donald Bloesch, *Crumbling Foundations* (Grand Rapids, Mich.: Zondervan, 1984).

10. John 17:17.

11. John 18:37.

### Chapter 14 • Lost in the Cosmos

1. Paula Span, "Where Do They Find These People?" *Washington Post*, 16 April 1992.

2. From a Barbara Walters special, as reported in *New York Guardian* (April 1992): 11.

3. Richard Neuhaus, *The Naked Public Square* (Grand Rapids, Mich.: Eerdmans, 1984), 75.

4. Statistics from Nielsen Media Research cited in A. Bunce, "Shock Talk," *Christian Science Monitor*, 5 October 1988, 7–8.

5. Charles P. Freund, "Save the Networks," *Washington Post*, 28 July 1991, 2–3.

6. Ellen Goodman, "Catholic Hierarchy, not Liberals, Created Problem for Thomas," *Chicago Tribune*, 14 July 1991, 3.

7. Ibid.

8. Ibid., 4.

9. Bill Moyers, *A World of Ideas* (New York: Doubleday, 1989), 63.

10. Allan Bloom, *The Closing of the American Mind* (New York: Simon & Schuster, 1987), 25.

11. From Arthur Schlesinger's speech at Brown University, in *Brown Alumni Monthly* (May 1989): 18, 22.

12. Dinesh D'Souza, *Illiberal Education: The Politics of Race and Sex on Campus* (New York: Free Press, 1991). For universities that are teaching a traditional view of truth and of the history of Western civilization, see Charles Sykes and Brad Miner, eds., *National Review College Guide* (New York: National Review, 1991). This publication lists schools according to the criteria of intellectual environment, faculty accessibility, and credentials and curricula offered.

13. Dinesh D'Souza, "Illiberal Education," *Atlantic Monthly* (March 1991): 58.

14. George Barna, *What Americans Believe: An Annual Survey of Values and Religious Views in the United States* (Ventura, Calif.: Regal, 1991).

15. "Few Believe in Moral Absolutes, But Most Want to Follow God's Teachings," *PRRC Emerging Trends* (February 1992): 3.

16. Cited in B. Asmus, "Building an Unlimited Future, *Imprimis* (January 1992).

17. "The 'Animal Rights' War on Medicine," *Reader's Digest* (June 1990): 70–76.

18. Asmus, "Building an Unlimited Future."

19. Paul Johnson, "Is Totalitarianism Dead? New Temptations for Today's Intellectuals" *Crisis* (February 1989): 9–16.

20. John Taylor, "Don't Blame Me," *New York Magazine,* 3 June 1991.

21. R. C. Sproul, *Lifeviews: Understanding the Ideas That Shape Society Today* (Old Tappan, N.J.: Fleming H. Revell, 1986), 89.

22. Walker Percy, *Lost in the Cosmos: The Last Self-Help Book* (New York: Washington Square Press, 1983), 48–59.

23. Ibid., 55.

## Chapter 15 • The Pillar of Truth

1. 1 Tim. 3:15.

2. *What Americans Believe: An Annual Survey of Values and Religious Views in the United States* (Ventura, Calif.: Regal, 1991), 85.

3. *PRRC Emerging Trends* (February 1992): 3.

4. For more on this, see Charles W. Colson, *Loving God* (Grand Rapids, Mich.: Zondervan, 1983), chap. 5.

5. For a more thorough discussion of *The Fundamentals* and the fundamentalist movement of the early twentieth century, see Ned B. Stonehouse, *J. Gresham Machen: A Biographical Memoir* (Carlisle, Pa.: Banner of Truth, 1987), 335–39; also, E. R. Sandeen, *The Roots of Fundamentalism: British and American Millenarianism, 1800-1930* (Chicago: University of Chicago Press, 1970).

6. Cal Thomas, "Guess Who's There for TV Dinner," *Washington Times*, 6 June 1991.

7. Mark 7:15, 23.

8. From transcript of "60 Minutes," vol. 15, no. 21, as broadcast over the CBS television network, 6 February 1983.

9. Francis Schaeffer, *The Great Evangelical Disaster* (Westchester, Ill.: Crossway, 1984), 81, 102.

10. Walker Percy, *The Second Coming* (New York: Farrar, Straus & Giroux, 1980).

11. Kenneth Hunter, "When Nice People Do Bad Theology," *First Things* (April 1991): 12–15.

12. *The New Book of Christian Quotations* (Westchester, Ill.: Crossway, 1984), 226.

13. Mal. 2:2–17; Amos 2:6–8, 5:10–13; Isa. 1:10–15, 21–23.

14. Ps. 78:1–8.

15. Mic. 4:1–5.

16. 2 Cor. 10:5b.

17. Matt. 13:33.

18. Matt. 25:14–30.

19. Rom. 12:2; Col. 2:8; 1 Pet. 1:16; 2 Cor. 10:5.

20. Harry Blamires, *The Christian Mind: How Should a Christian Think?* (Ann Arbor, Mich.: Servant, 1978), 3–4.

21. Abraham Kuyper, *Lectures on Calvinism* (Reprint, Grand Rapids, Mich.: Eerdmans, 1981), 52.

22. Charles Krauthammer, "Culture Has Consequences," *Washington Post*, 26 October 1990, A-27.

23. *A National Study of Protestant Congregations*, Search Institute, March 1990.

24. Geir Kjetsaa, *Dostoevsky: A Writer's Life* (New York: Viking Penguin, 1987), 376–77.

25. 1 Pet. 3:15.

26. Kuyper, *Lectures on Calvinism*, iii.

## Chapter 16 • Between Two Crosses

1. The material in this chapter is based on interviews conducted by Ellen Vaughn in Romania, Hungary, and Poland in September 1990, and by Chuck Colson in Russia, Hungary, and Czechoslovakia; we have also drawn on a wide variety of news reports, books, and articles.

2. Matt. 16:18 KJV.

3. Dr. Joseph Tson, interview with Ellen Vaughn, Oradea, Romania, 12 September 1990.

4. Paul Johnson, *Pope John Paul II and the Catholic Restoration* (Ann Arbor, Mich.: Servant Books, 1981), 19–20.

5. Bob Omstead, "People," *National Catholic Register*, 4 March 1990; see also Sister Nijole, *A Radiance in the Gulag* (Manassas, Va.: Trinity Communications, n.d.).

6. William Echikson, *Lighting the Night: Revolution in Eastern Europe* (New York: William Morrow and Co., 1990), 134.

7. Johnson, *John Paul II and the Catholic Restoration*, 47.

8. Father Jan Sikorski, interview with Ellen Vaughn, Warsaw, Poland, 27 September 1990.

9. These descriptions are based on extended interviews conducted by Ellen Vaughn with priests and citizens in Krakow, Poland, 25–26 September 1990.

10. John Fox, "Murder of a Polish Priest," *Reader's Digest* (December 1985): 65, 248.

11. Grazyna Sikorska, *Jerzy Popieluszko, A Martyr for the Truth* (Grand Rapids, Mich.: Eerdmans, n.d.), 56, 57, 58. Father Jerzy was preaching true "liberation theology." What we need to be liberated from is ego and fear, and that comes through submission to Christ. Whether under the Communist yoke in the East or materialistic bondage in the West, people need the message he delivered, made all the more poignant by his willingness to live out his commitment to the kingdom of God by refusing to knuckle under to the kingdom of man—and paying the price of death.

12. Father Antoni Lewek, *New Sanctuary of Poles* (Warsaw: n.p., 1986).

13. Peter Dugulescu, interview with Ellen Vaughn, Timisoara, Romania, 17 September 1990.

14. Echikson, *Lighting the Night*, 22.

15. Roddy Ray, "A Triumph of Spirit: Church Plays Role in Tearing Down

Communism," *Orange County Register*, 2 September 1990, Knight-Ridder Newspapers, from Leipzig, East Germany; see also Lance Dickie, "Keepers of the Faith: The Lutheran Church Played a Crucial, but Little-Known Role in East Germany's Peaceful Revolution," *Seattle Times*, 4 November 1990.

16. Ibid.

17. Ibid.

18. Mihai Gongola, interview with Ellen Vaughn, Arad, Romania, 14 September 1990.

19. Doru Popa, interview with Ellen Vaughn, Arad, Romania, 15 September 1990.

20. Ray, "A Triumph of Spirit."

21. Correspondents of the *New York Times*, *The Collapse of Communism*, ed. Bernard Gwertzman and Michael T. Kaufman (New York: New York Times Co., 1990), 237.

22. Ibid., 292.

23. Ibid., 291.

24. Ibid., 311.

25. Gelu Paul, interview with Ellen Vaughn, Timisoara, Romania, 18 September 1990.

26. Robert Cullen, "Report from Romania: Down with the Tyrant," *The New Yorker*, 2 April 1990, 101.

27. Marius Miron, interview with Ellen Vaughn, Timisoara, Romania, 17 September 1990.

28. Adina Jinaru, interview with Ellen Vaughn, Timisoara, Romania, 16 September 1990.

29. Nellie Iovin, interview with Ellen Vaughn, Arad, Romania, 15 September 1990.

30. Cullen, *Report from Romania*, 102.

31. Ibid.

32. Many Ellen Vaughn interviewed reported this. One Romanian journalist said that Milea killed himself out of guilt because he had given the order to fire on protestors in Timisoara. The truth may never be known, but today a street in Arad, once named for Lenin, now bears the name of General Milea.

33. Bruce W. Nelan, "The Year of the People," *Time*, 1 January 1990, 46.

34. The press was not alone. U.S. embassy officials in Moscow were oblivious to the spiritual forces at work, as Colson discovered during his visit in

1990. A consular officer asked him to quiet a protest of "Baptists" wanting to emigrate; they turned out to be Pentecostals. The embassy official didn't know the difference and seemed not to care or even recognize the persecution they had suffered. In Hungary, newly elected anti-Communist politicians told Colson that the Western officials they had met had had no inkling what was coming, let alone any information about the persecuted churches.

35. From Vaclav Havel's New Year's Address to the Nation (LD0101133190), Prague Television Service, 1 January 1990.

## Chapter 17 • The Church in Captivity

1. Hate Man information and observations regarding intolerance toward Christians come from Garrett Yamada, college pastor at First Presbyterian Church, Berkeley, interview with Ellen Vaughn, 10 October 1991.

2. Michael Novak, "Subverting the Churches," *Forbes,* 22 January 1990, 4–5.

3. "Clerical Illusion," *Crisis* (February 1990): 8.

4. Michael Rowe, "Spies in Cassocks," *Catholic World Report* (April 1992): 20–22.

5. Cal Thomas, syndicated column, *Miami Herald,* 4 August 1990.

6. See Colson, *Kingdoms in Conflict,* chaps. 10 and 11.

7. R. Gustav Niebuhr, "The Lord's Name: Image of God as 'He' Loses Its Sovereignty in America's Churches," *Wall Street Journal,* 27 April 1992, 2.

8. John D. Levinson, "Theological Liberalism Aborting Itself," *Christian Century,* 5–12 February 1992, 139.

9. "Keeping Body and Soul Together: Sexuality, Spirituality, and Social Justice," authored by a seventeen-member task force on sexuality, presented to the 203rd General Assembly of the Presbyterian Church (USA) meeting in Baltimore, Maryland (1991).

10. "Human Sexuality and the Christian Faith" (emphasis added), report released by the Evangelical Lutheran Church in America, issued by a seventeen-member task force of the Division for Church in Society (5 December 1991).

11. EP News Service, 10 January 1992, 5; see also George Cornell, "Lutheran Church's Sexuality Stops Short of Solutions," *Washington Post,* 7 December 1991.

12. *National and International Religious Report,* 29 June 1992, 4.

13. *Christianity Today,* 19 August 1991.

14. Francis X. Rocca, "God Is a Verb," *National Review*, 29 July 1991, 42.

15. Donald Bloesch, "Lost in the Mystical," *Christianity Today*, 19 August 1991.

16. James A. Sullivan, "Chill Out with Bill," *Fidelity* (September 1991): 16.

17. Ibid.

18. Peter Leithart, "The 'Mabelized' Church," *First Things* (May 1991): 9–11.

## Chapter 18 • *The Terror of the Holy*

1. This analogy is expanded from Roland Bainton's mention of what Karl Barth once said about his own unexpected reforming role. We are deeply indebted to Roland Bainton for his landmark 1950 biography of Martin Luther, *Here I Stand: A Life of Martin Luther*, which was of tremendous help in crafting this chapter. For readers who would like to further explore Luther's colorful life and thought, we recommend the following works: Roland Bainton, *Here I Stand: A Life of Martin Luther* (New York: Abingdon-Cokesbury, 1950); R. H. Fife, *The Revolt of Martin Luther* (New York: Columbia University Press, 1957), a more standard work; Eric W. Gritsch, *Martin—God's Court Jester: Luther in Retrospect* (Philadelphia: Fortress Press, 1985), a very readable work combining biography and some theological reflection; E. G. Schwiebert, *Luther and His Times: The Reformation from a New Perspective* (Saint Louis: Concordia Publishing House, 1950), a historical biography; P. Smith, *The Life and Letters of Martin Luther* (New York: Barnes and Noble, 1968); Martin Brecht, *Martin Luther: His Road to Reformation, 1483-1521*, trans. J. L. Schaff (Philadelphia: Fortress Press, 1985), the first in a threefold division of Luther's life; Heinrich Bornkamm, *Luther in Mid-Career, 1521–1530* (Philadelphia: Fortress Press, 1983), the second of a series of three (the third part of this trilogy, written in 1983, awaits translation into English). The Brecht and Bornkamm works, though written on a more scholarly level, constitute perhaps the most thorough biographical study yet attempted on Luther and would satisfy the needs of any Luther student. With regard to works written by Luther himself, we refer readers to Jaroslav Pelikan and H. T. Lehmann, eds., *Luther's Works*, 55 vols. (Philadelphia: Fortress Press; Saint Louis: Concordia Publishing House, 1955). Between 1516 and 1546 Luther published 93 forewords, 13 lectures, 64 open letters, 29 expositions of Scripture, 22 disputations, 178 sermons, and 130 treatises.

2. Bainton, *Here I Stand*, 21, 22.

3. Based on Luther's quote in ibid., 44.

4. Ibid.

5. Ibid., 50.

6. Ibid.

7. Ibid., 59–60.

8. Pelikan and Lehmann, "Introduction to the Theses," *Luther's Works*, 31.

9. Bainton, *Here I Stand*, 65.

10. Ibid., 77.

11. Ibid., 117.

12. Ibid.

13. Ibid., 140.

14. Ibid., 143.

### Chapter 19 • *Justice Unleashed: A World Transformed*

1. Roland H. Bainton, *Here I Stand: A Life of Martin Luther* (New York: Abingdon Press, 1977), 145.

2. Martin Luther, *The Babylonian Captivity*, in *Luther's Works*, ed H. T. Lehmann and A. R. Wentz, 55 vols. (Philadelphia: Fortress Press, 1959), 36:54.

3. Pope John Paul II, "Centesimus Annus ('The 100th Year')," *Origins* 21/1, 16 May 1991, 1–23.

4. J. Pelikan and H. T. Lehmann, eds., *Luther's Works*, 55 vols. (Philadelphia: Fortress Press; St. Louis: Concordia, 1955), 53:323.

5. Pope John Paul II, "Cristifideles Laici ('Apostolic Exhortation on the Vocation and Mission of the Lay Faithful in the Church and in the World')," *Origins*, 18/35, 9 February 1989.

6. *L'osservatore Romano*, weekly edition in English, 14 October 1991, 7–8.

7. Joseph Cardinal Ratzinger, *Introduction to Christianity* (San Francisco: Ignatius Press, 1990), 57.

### Chapter 20 • *The Body*

1. John 14:12 NIV.

2. John 14:16–17a NIV.

3. John 17:20 NIV.

### Chapter 21 • *Equipping the Saints*

1. Matt. 28:18–20.

2. Eph. 4:11–16.

3. See 2 Pet. 1:16 and 2 Cor. 10:5.

4. For reference to numerical growth, see Acts 2:46–47; for qualitative growth see also Heb. 5:11—6:3. The delineation and definition of these seven points taken from T. M. Moore, *Teaching in the Spirit: A Workbook and Training Program for Christian Education in the Church* (Ellicott City, Md.: Chesapeake Publications, 1989), 51–53.

5. Eph. 4:11–12.

6. Jacques Ellul, *Presence of the Kingdom* (New York: Seabury, 1948), 19.

7. Matt. 25:34–40.

8. John 21:25 NIV.

## Chapter 22 • Let This Mind Be in You . . .

1. Howard Fineman et al., "Filling the Political Void," *Newsweek,* 18 May 1992, 7.

2. 1 Sam. 8:4–22; 10:19; 12:19.

3. Ann Carnahan, "Pastor Lacks Time to Heal Thyself," *Denver Rocky Mountain News,* 19 April 1991.

4. Matt. 20:26; Mark 9:35; 10:41–45; Luke 22:24–27.

5. Heb. 2:9–11.

6. Phil. 2:5–8 KJV.

7. "Deliver Us from Evil," *Christianity Today,* 9 November 1984, 35.

8. Oswald Sanders, *Spiritual Leadership* (Chicago: Moody Press, 1967); see the twenty-two questions on page 39.

9. F. Booth Tucker, *Muktifanj, or Forty Years with the Salvation Army in India and Ceylon* (London: Marshall Brothers, n.d.).

10. William P. Showalter, "Zinzendorf, That Remarkable Man of God," *Crosspoint* (Summer 1991): 25.

11. Dietrich Bonhoeffer, *Letters and Papers from Prison,* ed. Eberhard Bethge (New York: Macmillan, 1967), 11–12.

## Chapter 23 • Who Are You?

1. Details in these descriptions come from James A Michener, *Poland* (New York: Random House, 1983), 514; and from William L. Shirer, *The Rise and Fall of the Third Reich: A History of Nazi Germany* (New York: Touchstone, 1959), 967–74. This chapter is based on interviews in Warsaw, Auschwitz, and Niepokalanow in Poland, conducted by Ellen Vaughn in September 1990.

2. Maria Winowska, *Our Lady's Fool* (Westminster, Md.: Newman Press, 1952), 138–39.

3. Sergius C. Lorit, *The Last Days of Maximilian Kolbe* (New York: New City Press, 1968), 142.

4. Shirer, *Rise and Fall of the Third Reich*, 937.

5. Ibid., 938.

6. Some biographers say Kolbe went to meet the Nazis. Father George at Niepokalanow told Ellen Vaughn that Kolbe was arrested in his room.

## Chapter 24 • *Being His Witnesses*

1. Acts 1:8 NIV (emphasis added).

2. Sheldon Vanauken, *A Severe Mercy* (New York: Bantam, 1977), 82.

3. 2 Tim. 4:5; Acts 8:29; 21:8.

4. Garth Rosell, "Charles Gradison Finney," in *Great Leaders of the Christian Church,* ed. John D. Woodbridge (Chicago: Moody Press, 1988), 318.

5. Romans 1.

6. From Ellen Vaughn interviews at Willow Creek, 24 August 1991.

7. For a detailed analysis of Billy Graham's discipleship-centered crusades, see Sterling W. Huston, *Crusade Evangelism and the Local Church* (Minneapolis: Worldwide Publications, 1984).

8. Waldron Scott, "Discipleship Evangelism," in *Evangelism: The Next Ten Years,* ed. Sherwood Eliot Wirt (Waco, Tex.: Word, 1978), 106.

## Chapter 25 • *Being the Light*

1. Lupe and Robert Alverado, interviews with Ellen Vaughn, Los Angeles, 7 October 1991.

2. John 8:12.

3. Gen. 1:3; Rev. 22:5 NIV.

4. Matt. 5:14–16 NIV.

5. Phil. 2:15b TEV.

6. G. R. Capp, ed., *The Great Society: A Sourcebook of Speeches* (Belmont, Calif.: Dickenson Publishing Co., 1967).

7. Beverly Barnwell and Jackie Russell, interviews with Ellen Vaughn, Los Angeles, 9 October 1991.

8. John Aker, interview with Ellen Vaughn, Rockford, Ill., August 1991.

## Chapter 26 • *Being the Salt*

1. Matt. 5:13.

2. Job 6:6. Salt was also used to season incense (Exod. 30:35); all offerings were to be salted (Lev. 2:13; Ezek. 43:24); salt was a symbol for the covenant (Lev. 2:13; 2 Kings 2:20; 2 Chron. 13:5).

3. Mark 9:50.

4. Glen Kehrein, interview with Ellen Vaughn, Chicago, August 1991.

5. Tom Phillips, phone interview with Chuck Colson, November 1991.

6. E. C. Baig, "Profiting with Help from Above," *Time*, 27 April 1987, 37.

7. Chris Thompson, interview with Ellen Vaughn, May 1992.

8. From jacket blurb of the 1968 Macmillan paperback edition.

9. Katherine Paterson, *Gates of Excellence* (New York: E. P. Dutton, 1981), 18.

10. Walker Percy, "A View of Abortion, With Something to Offend Everybody," in *Signposts in a Strange Land* (New York: Farrar, Straus and Giroux, 1991), 340.

11. T. Hafer, "Amy Grant: Why the Controversy?" *Christian Herald* (September/October 1991): 17.

12. "Weekly Bible Sessions Bring Redskins Together off the Field," *Washington Post*, 23 November 1991, C-6.

## Chapter 27 • *The Fear of the Lord Is the Beginning*

1. Acts 5:11–14.

2. Acts 9:31.

## Chapter 28 • *Coram Deo*

1. Bob McAlister, interviews with Ellen Vaughn, Columbia, S. C., August 1991.

2. 1 Cor. 1:27–29, Bob's paraphrase.

3. Wardell Patterson was eventually resentenced to life in prison.

4. Bob McAlister, "Countdown to Paradise," *Jubilee* (July 1990): 4.

5. Margaret N. O'Shea, "Death Issue Difficult," *The State*, 14 June 1989, 1-A.

6. Names changed.

7. Isa. 53:5.

8. John 11:25.

9. This conversation was reconstructed from detailed notes Bob made during the Easter Sunday meeting between Rusty and Lee.

10. Matt. 10:19.

# Recommended Reading

We could not presume to list the wealth of great books written through the centuries on the character and mission of the church. Nor have we cataloged here an exhaustive list of theological and doctrinal resources. But many of the following books and articles have been helpful in the preparation of this book. We recommend them for readers who would like to dig a bit deeper into the historical mandate of the church.

Aker, John D. *Lengthen Your Stride.* Old Tappan, N.J.: Revell, 1988.

Atkins, Stanley, and Theodore McConnell, eds. *Churches on the Wrong Road.* Chicago: Regnery Gateway, 1986.

Augustine. *City of God.* Translated by J. Healey. New York: E. P. Dutton and Co., 1956.

————. *On Christian Doctrine.* Translated by D. W. Robertson. New York: Bobbs-Merrill Co., 1958.

Bainton, Roland. *The Age of the Reformation.* Coronado, Calif.: D. Van Nostrand, 1956.

————. *Here I Stand: A Life of Martin Luther.* New York: Abingdon/ Cokesbury, 1950.

————. *The Horizon History of Christianity.* New York: Avon, 1966.

————. *The Reformation of the Sixteenth Century.* Boston: Beacon, 1952.

Bannerman, D. Douglas. *The Scriptural Doctrine of the Church.* Grand Rapids, Mich.: Eerdmans, 1955.

Barna, George. *The Frog in the Kettle.* Glendale, Calif.: Regal, 1990.

——. *User Friendly Churches.* Glendale, Calif.: Regal, 1991.

Barrett, C. K. *Church, Ministry, and Sacraments in the New Testament.* Grand Rapids, Mich.: Eerdmans, 1985.

Basden, Paul, and David S. Dockery, eds. *The People of God: Essays on the Believers' Church.* Nashville: Broadman, 1990.

Baxter, Ern. "What Makes God Angry?" *New Wine* (January 1978): 4-15.

Berger, Peter. *The Noise of Solemn Assemblies: Christian Commitment and the Religious Establishment in America.* New York: Doubleday, 1961.

——, and Richard John Neuhaus, eds. *Against the World for the World.* New York: Seabury, 1976.

Bettenson, H., ed. *Documents of the Christian Church.* New York: Oxford University, 1970.

——. *Early Christian Fathers.* New York: Oxford University, 1956.

Billingsley, K. L. *From Mainline to Sideline: The Social Witness of the National Council of Churches.* Washington, D.C.: Ethics and Public Policy Center, 1990.

Blamires, Harry. *The Christian Mind: How Should a Christian Think?* Reprint. Ann Arbor, Mich.: Servant, 1978.

——. *The Faith and Modern Error: An Essay on the Christian Message in the Twentieth Century.* New York: Macmillan, 1956.

——. *Where Do We Stand?: An Examination of the Christian's Position in the Modern World.* Ann Arbor, Mich.: Servant, 1980.

Blattner, John C. "One-to-One Pastoral Care." *Faith & Renewal,* 13 February 1988, 3–11.

——. *Leading Christians to Maturity.* Altamonte Springs, Fla.: Creation House, 1987.

—— et al., eds. Center for Pastoral Renewal Series. Ann Arbor, Mich.: Servant.

Bloesch, Donald G. *The Christian Witness in a Secular Age.* Minneapolis: Augsburg, 1968.

——. *Essentials of Evangelical Theology.* 2 vols. New York: Harper & Row, rep. 1982.

——. *The Evangelical Renaissance.* Grand Rapids, Mich.: Eerdmans, 1973.

——. "The Finality of Christ and Religious Pluralism." *Touchstone,* 3 April 1991, 4–9.

——. *The Future of Evangelical Christianity: A Call for Unity Amid Diversity.* New York: Doubleday, 1983.

——. *The Reform of the Church.* Grand Rapids, Mich.: Eerdmans, 1970.

——, and Robert Webber, eds. *The Orthodox Evangelicals.* Nashville: Thomas Nelson, 1978.

Boice, James M., ed. *Transforming Our World: A Call to Action.* Portland, Oreg.: Multnomah, 1988.

Calvin, John. *Institutes of the Christian Religion.* Edited by J. T. McNeill and F. L. Battles. 2 vols. Philadelphia: Westminster, 1960.

Campenhausen, Hans von. *Ecclesiastical Authority and Spiritual Power.* Palo Alto, Calif.: Stanford University, 1969.

Chadwick, Henry. *The Early Church.* New York: Penguin, 1967.

Chadwick, O. *The Reformation.* London: SCM, 1964.

Charles, J. Daryl. "Pomp, Circumstance and Capitulation." *Faith & Renewal* 17/3 (1992): 26–27.

Clowney, Edmund P. *The Biblical Doctrine of the Church.* Philadelphia: Westminster Theological Seminary, 1979.

Cochrane, Charles N. *Christianity and Classical Culture: A Study of Thought and Action from Augustus to Constantine.* New York and London: Clarendon, 1940.

Coleman, Richard J. *Issues of Theological Conflict.* Grand Rapids, Mich.: Eerdmans, 1972.

Cook, Harold. "Who Really Sent the First Missionaries?" *Evangelical Missions Quarterly* 12 (1975): 233–39.

Craycraft, Kenneth R. "Our Kind of Ecumenism: Why Catholics Need to Be More Evangelical and Vice Versa." *Crisis* (October 1991): 30–33.

Davis, John Jefferson. *Foundations of Evangelical Theology.* Grand Rapids, Mich.: Baker, 1984.

Dawson, Christopher. *Christianity and the New Age.* Manchester, N.H.: Sophia Institute, 1985.

Demarest, Bruce, and Gordon Lewis. *Integrative Theology.* Grand Rapids, Mich.: Zondervan, 1987, 1990.

Dulles, Avery. *Models of the Church.* New York: Doubleday, 1974.

Edge, Findley B. *A Quest for Vitality in Religion.* Nashville: Broadman, 1963.

Edwards, David L., and John Stott. *Evangelical Essentials: A Liberal-Evangelical Dialogue.* Downers Grove, Ill.: InterVarsity, 1988.

Edwards, Jonathan. *The Works of Jonathan Edwards.* 2 vols. Carlisle, Pa.: Banner of Truth, 1984.

Ellul, Jacques. *The Presence of the Kingdom.* New York: Seabury, 1948, 1967.

———. *The Subversion of Christianity.* Reprint. Grand Rapids, Mich.: Eerdmans, 1988.

Erickson, Millard J. *Christian Theology.* 3 vols. Grand Rapids, Mich.: Baker, 1983–85.

Eusebius. *The History of the Church from Christ to Constantine.* Translated by G. A. Williamson. Minneapolis: Augsburg, 1965.

*The Faith of the Early Fathers.* Translated by W. A. Jurgens. Collegeville, Minn.: Liturgical, 1970.

Finney, Charles G. *Power from on High.* Philadelphia: Christian Literature Crusade, n.d.

———. *Revivals of Religion.* London: Oliphant, 1928.

Fournier, Keith A. *Bringing Christ's Presence into Your Home: Your Family as a Domestic Church.* Nashville: Thomas Nelson, 1992.

———. *Evangelical Catholics.* Nashville: Thomas Nelson, 1990.

Frame, John M. *Evangelical Reunion: Denominations and the Body of Christ.* Grand Rapids, Mich.: Baker, 1991.

Gallup, George, Jr., and Jim Castelli. *The People's Religion.* New York: Macmillan, 1989.

———, and Timothy K. Jones. *The Saints Among Us.* Ridgefield, Conn.: Morehouse, 1992.

Green, Michael. *Called to Serve.* London: Hodder & Stoughton, 1978.

———. *Evangelism and the Early Church.* Grand Rapids, Mich.: Eerdmans, 1976.

———. *Evangelism Then and Now.* Downers Grove, Ill.: InterVarsity, 1979.

Greene, Colin. "Spirit-Led Evangelism." *Renewal* (June 1991): 37–39.

Gritsch, Eric W. *Martin—God's Court Jester: Luther in Retrospect.* Philadelphia: Fortress, 1983.

Guiness, Os. *The American Hour: A Time of Reckoning and the Once and Future Role of Faith.* New York: Free Press, 1992.

Harper, Michael. *Let My People Grow!* London: Hodder & Stoughton, 1977.

Hastings, Adrian. *A Concise Guide to the Documents of the Second Vatican.* Greenwood, S.C.: Darton, Longman and Todd, 1968.

Hauerwas, Stanley, and William Willimon. *Resident Aliens.* Nashville: Abingdon, 1989.

Henry, Carl F. H., ed. *Basic Christian Doctrines.* New York: Holt, Rinehart & Winston, 1962.

———. *Christian Countermoves in a Decadent Culture.* Portland, Oreg.: Multnomah, 1986.

———. *Evangelicals in Search of Identity.* Waco, Tex.: Word, 1976.

———. *God, Revelation and Authority.* 6 vols. Waco, Tex.: Word, 1976–83.

———, ed. *Revelation and the Bible: Contemporary Evangelical Thought.* Grand Rapids, Mich.: Baker, 1958.

———. *Toward a Recovery of Christian Belief.* Westchester, Ill.: Crossway, 1990.

Heppe, Heinrich. *Reformed Dogmatics.* Translated by G. T. Thomson. New York: George Allen and Unwin, 1950.

Hillerbrand, H. J. *Christendom Divided*. New York: Theological Resources, 1971.

———. *The World of the Reformation*. London: Hodder & Stoughton, 1975.

Horton, Michael S. *The Agony of Deceit*. Chicago: Moody, 1990.

———. "Members Only." *Modern Reformation* (July/August 1991): 1–3.

Hughes, Kent, and Barbara Hughes. *Liberating Ministry from the Success Syndrome*. Wheaton, Ill.: Tyndale, 1987.

Hunter, James Davison. *American Evangelicalism: Conservative Religion and the Quandary of Modernity*. New Brunswick, N.J.: Rutgers University Press, 1983.

———. "The Evangelical Worldview Since 1890." In *Piety and Politics: Evangelicals Confront the World*. Edited by Richard John Neuhaus and Michael Cromartie. Washington, D.C.: Ethics and Public Policy Center, 1987. Pp. 19–53.

———. *Evangelicals: The Coming Generation*. Chicago: University of Chicago, 1987.

Hunter, Kenneth E. "When Nice People Do Bad Theology." *First Things* (April 1991) 12–15.

Huston, Sterling. *Crusade Evangelism and the Local Church*. Minneapolis: Worldwide Publications, 1984.

John Paul II. "Cristifideles Laici." *Origins* 18/35 (February 1989).

———. *The Lay Members of Christ's Faithful People*. Boston: Daughters of St. Paul, n.d.

———. "Redemptoris Missio." *Origins* 20/34 (January 1991).

Kelly, George A. *The Battle for the American Church*. New York: Doubleday, 1979.

Kelly, J. N. D. *Early Christian Creeds*. London: Longmans, Green & Co., 1950.

Kimel, Alvin F., Jr. "The God Who Likes His Name." *Interpretation* 45 (1991): 147–58.

Kreeft, Peter. "The Good War." *Christianity Today*, 17 December 1990, 29–31.

Kuyper, Abraham. *Lectures on Calvinism*. Grand Rapids, Mich.: Eerdmans, rep. 1981.

Ladd, George E. *Jesus and the Kingdom*. New York: Harper & Row, 1964.

Latourette, Kenneth Scott. *A History of the Expansion of Christianity*. 7 vols. Grand Rapids, Mich.: Zondervan, 1970.

LeBlanc, Doug. "The Catholic Temptation: An Evangelical's Second Thoughts." *Crisis* (March 1991): 30–32.

Leith, John L., ed. *Creeds of the Churches*. Atlanta, Ga.: John Knox, 1979.

Little, Joyce A. "Naming Good and Evil." *First Things* (May 1992): 23–30.

Lovelace, Richard F. *Dynamics of Spiritual Life: An Evangelical Theology of Renewal.* Downers Grove, Ill.: InterVarsity, 1979.

Luther, Martin. *Selected Writings of Martin Luther.* Translated by T. G. Tappert. 4 vols. Philadelphia: Fortress, 1967.

Marsden, George. *Fundamentalism and American Culture.* New York: Oxford University, 1980.

Martin, Ralph. *A Crisis of Truth.* Ann Arbor, Mich.: Servant, 1982.

McGrath, Alister E. "Doctrine and Ethics." *Journal of the Evangelical Theological Society* 34/2 (1991): 145–56.

Mills, David. "The Creed of Our Salvation." *Mission and Ministry* (Spring 1992): 1–7.

Minear, Paul. *Images of the Church in the New Testament.* Philadelphia: Westminster, 1960.

Moore, T. M. *Teaching in the Spirit: A Workbook and Training Program for Christian Education in the Church.* Ellicott City, Md.: Chesapeake Publications, 1989.

Muggeridge, Malcolm. *The Third Testament.* Boston: Little, Brown and Co., 1976.

Murray, Iain H. *Jonathan Edwards: A New Biography.* Carlisle, Pa.: Banner of Truth, 1984.

Neuhaus, Richard John. *The Catholic Moment.* New York: Harper & Row, 1987.

———. *Freedom for Ministry.* New York: Harper & Row, 1979.

———. *The Naked Public Square: Religion and Democracy in America.* Grand Rapids, Mich.: Eerdmans, 1984.

———. "The Protestant Mainline." *Faith & Renewal* (July/August 1990): 4–6.

———, ed. *The Ratzinger Conference on Bible and Church.* Grand Rapids, Mich.: Eerdmans, 1988.

Niebuhr, H. Richard. *The Purpose of the Church and Its Ministry.* New York: Harper & Row, 1956.

Noll, Mark A., and David Wells, eds. *Christian Faith and Practice in the Modern World.* Grand Rapids, Mich.: Eerdmans, 1988.

Noll, Mark A., et al. *The Search for Christian America.* Colorado Springs: Helmers & Howard, 1989.

Oberman, Heiko. *Forerunners of the Reformation.* Reprint. Philadelphia: Fortress, 1981.

———. *The Harvest of Medieval Theology.* Grand Rapids, Mich.: Eerdmans, 1967.

Oden, Thomas C. *After Modernity . . . What? Agenda for Theology.* New York: Akademie, 1990.

———. "The Long Journey Home." *Journal of the Evangelical Theological Society* 34/1 (1991): 77–92.

———. "Then and Now: The Recovery of Patristic Wisdom." *Christian Century,* 12 December 1990, 1164–68.

Packer, J. I. *A Quest for Godliness: The Puritan Vision of the Christian Life.* Westchester, Ill.: Crossway, 1990.

———. *Evangelism and the Sovereignty of God.* Downers Grove, Ill.: Inter-Varsity, 1961.

———. *"Fundamentalism" and the Word of God.* Grand Rapids, Mich.: Eerdmans, rep. 1990.

———. *Hot Tub Religion.* Wheaton, Ill.: Tyndale, 1987.

———. "Shepherds after God's Own Heart." *Faith & Renewal* 15/3 (1990): 12–17.

Pannenberg, Wolfhart. "The Present and Future Church." *First Things* (November 1991): 47–51.

Patterson, Robert. "In Search of the Visible Church." *Christianity Today,* 11 March 1991, 36–40.

Pauck, W. *The Heritage of the Reformation.* New York: Oxford University, 1961.

Perotta, Kevin. "Who Pastors the Pastors?" *Faith & Renewal* 15/3 (1990): 3–11.

Petersen, Jim. *Church Without Walls.* Colorado Springs: NavPress, 1992.

———. *Living Proof.* Colorado Springs: NavPress, 1989.

Piercy, H. R. *The Meaning of the Church in the Thought of Calvin.* Chicago: University of Chicago, 1941.

Quebedeaux, Richard. *The Worldly Evangelicals.* New York: Harper & Row, 1978.

Quinn, John R. "Orthodoxy—as Opposed to Fundamentalism, Theological Liberalism, and Integralism." *New Oxford Review* (May 1991): 15–23.

Radmacher, Earl D. *The Nature of the Church.* Portland, Oreg.: Western Baptist Press, 1972.

Ratzinger, Joseph Cardinal. *Church, Ecumenism and Politics.* New York: Crossroad, 1988.

———. *Introduction to Christianity.* San Francisco: Ignatius, 1990.

Rayburn, Robert G. *O Come, Let us Worship: Corporate Worship in the Evangelical Church.* Grand Rapids, Mich.: Baker, 1980.

Reardon, Bernard M. G. *Religious Thought in the Reformation.* White Plains, N.Y.: Longman, 1981.

Riddlebarger, Kim. "Thy Kingdom Come." *Modern Reformation* (March/April 1992): 7–9.

Roberts, Richard Owen. *Revival.* Wheaton, Ill.: Tyndale, 1982.

Roof, Wade C., and William McKinney. *American Mainline Religion: Its Changing Shape and Future.* New Brunswick, N.J.: Rutgers University Press, 1987.

Ryken, Leland. *Worldly Saints: The Puritans as They Really Were.* Grand Rapids, Mich.: Zondervan, 1986.

Sanders, J. Oswald. *Spiritual Leadership.* Chicago: Moody, 1967, 1980.

Sayers, Dorothy. *Christian Letters to a Post-Christian World.* Grand Rapids, Mich.: Eerdmans, 1969.

———. *Creed or Chaos.* New York: Harcourt Brace, 1949.

Schaeffer, Francis A. *The Church at the End of the Twentieth Century.* Westchester, Ill.: Crossway, 1985.

———. *The Great Evangelical Disaster.* Westchester, Ill.: Crossway, 1984, 1987.

Schlossberg, Herbert. *Idols for Destruction: Christian Faith and Its Confrontation with American Society.* Nashville: Thomas Nelson, 1983.

———, and Marvin Olasky. "Piety and Pietism." In *Turning Point: A Christian Worldview Declaration.* Westchester, Ill.: Crossway, 1987. Pp. 25–41.

Simpson, Charles. *The Challenge to Care.* Ann Arbor, Mich.: Servant, 1986.

Smith, Glenn C. *Evangelizing Adults.* Wheaton, Ill.: Tyndale, 1985.

Smith, Timothy L. *Revivalism and Social Reform.* New York: Harper & Row, 1965.

Sproul, R. C. *Chosen by God.* Wheaton, Ill.: Tyndale, 1986.

———. *The Holiness of God.* Wheaton, Ill.: Tyndale, 1985.

———. *Lifeviews: Understanding the Ideas that Shape Society Today.* Old Tappan, N.J.: Revell, 1986.

Stephenson, J., ed. *Creeds, Councils and Controversies: Documents Illustrative of the History of the Church A.D. 337–461.* Nashville: Abingdon, 1988.

Thielicke, Helmut. *The Trouble with the Church.* Grand Rapids, Mich.: Baker, 1965.

Til, Cornelius Van. *Essays on Christian Education.* Nutley, N.J.: Presbyterian and Reformed, 1977.

Todd, J. M. *Luther: A Life.* Crossroad, 1982.

Walker, Andrew. "We Believe." *Christianity Today,* 29 April 1991, 25–27.

Walker, William, et al. *A History of the Christian Church.* Reprint. New York: Charles Scribner's Sons, 1985.

Watson, David. *I Believe in the Church.* Reprint. Grand Rapids, Mich.: Eerdmans, 1982.

Webber, Robert. *The Church in the World.* Grand Rapids, Mich.: Zondervan, 1986.

―――, and Rodney Clapp. *People of the Truth.* New York: Harper & Row, 1988.

Wells, David F. "Conversion: Our Work or God's?" *Action* (January/February 1991): 4–7.

Wesley, John. *The Works of John Wesley.* Edited by F. Baker. 9 vols. Nashville: Abingdon, 1975– .

White, Jerry. *The Church and the Parachurch: An Uneasy Marriage.* Portland, Oreg.: Multnomah, 1983.

Wiersbe, Warren. *The Integrity Crisis.* Nashville: Oliver Nelson, 1988.

―――. *Real Worship.* Nashville: Oliver Nelson, 1986.

Wilkes, Paul. "The Hands That Would Shape Our Souls." *Atlantic Monthly* (December 1990): 59–88.

Winter, Ralph D. "The Two Structures of God's Redemptive Mission." *Missiology* 2 (1974): 121–39.

―――. "Protestant Mission Societies: The American Experience." *Missiology* 7 (1979): 139–78.

# Index

PRINT

GHSMITH 45-102